HUMAN RESOURCE MANAGEMENT IN A POST-EPIDEMIC GLOBAL ENVIRONMENT

Roles, Strategies, and Implementation

HUMAN RESOURCE MANAGEMENT IN A POST-EPIDEMIC GLOBAL ENVIRONMENT

Roles, Strategies, and Implementation

Edited by
Tanusree Chakraborty, PhD
Nandita Mishra, PhD
Madhurima Ganguly, PhD
Bipasha Chatterjee

First edition published 2023

Apple Academic Press Inc.
1265 Goldenrod Circle, NE,
Palm Bay, FL 32905 USA

760 Laurentian Drive, Unit 19,
Burlington, ON L7N 0A4, CANADA

CRC Press
6000 Broken Sound Parkway NW,
Suite 300, Boca Raton, FL 33487-2742 USA

4 Park Square, Milton Park,
Abingdon, Oxon, OX14 4RN UK

© 2023 by Apple Academic Press, Inc.

Apple Academic Press exclusively co-publishes with CRC Press, an imprint of Taylor & Francis Group, LLC

Reasonable efforts have been made to publish reliable data and information, but the authors, editors, and publisher cannot assume responsibility for the validity of all materials or the consequences of their use. The authors, editors, and publishers have attempted to trace the copyright holders of all material reproduced in this publication and apologize to copyright holders if permission to publish in this form has not been obtained. If any copyright material has not been acknowledged, please write and let us know so we may rectify in any future reprint.

Except as permitted under U.S. Copyright Law, no part of this book may be reprinted, reproduced, transmitted, or utilized in any form by any electronic, mechanical, or other means, now known or hereafter invented, including photocopying, microfilming, and recording, or in any information storage or retrieval system, without written permission from the publishers.

For permission to photocopy or use material electronically from this work, access www.copyright.com or contact the Copyright Clearance Center, Inc. (CCC), 222 Rosewood Drive, Danvers, MA 01923, 978-750-8400. For works that are not available on CCC please contact mpkbookspermissions@tandf.co.uk

Trademark notice: Product or corporate names may be trademarks or registered trademarks and are used only for identification and explanation without intent to infringe.

Library and Archives Canada Cataloguing in Publication

Title: Human resource management in a post-epidemic global environment : roles, strategies, and implementation / edited by Tanusree Chakraborty, PhD, Nandita Mishra, PhD, Madhurima Ganguly, PhD, Bipasha Chatterjee.

Names: Chakraborty, Tanusree, editor. | Mishra, Nandita, editor. | Ganguly, Madhurima (Lecturer in business), editor. | Chatterjee, Bipasha, editor.

Description: First edition. | Includes bibliographical references and index.

Identifiers: Canadiana (print) 20220282382 | Canadiana (ebook) 20220282412 | ISBN 9781774911792 (hardcover) | ISBN 9781774911808 (softcover) | ISBN 9781003314844 (ebook)

Subjects: LCSH: Personnel management.

Classification: LCC HF5549 .H86 2023 | DDC 658.3—dc23

Library of Congress Cataloging-in-Publication Data

Names: Chakraborty, Tanusree, editor. | Mishra, Nandita, editor. | Ganguly, Madhurima (Lecturer in business), editor. | Chatterjee, Bipasha, editor.

Title: Human resource management in a post-epidemic global environment : roles, strategies, and implementations / edited by Tanusree Chakraborty, PhD, Nandita Mishra, PhD, Madhurima Ganguly, PhD, Bipasha Chatterjee.

Description: First edition. | Palm Bay, FL : Apple Academic Press, 2023. | Includes bibliographical references and index. | Summary: "This unique volume explores the various aspects of human resources management and challenges that leaders, managers, and employees are facing in dealing with the new normal that is the result of changing workplace conditions and priorities due to the COVID-19 pandemic. With the outbreak of the pandemic and the resulting nationwide lockdowns, business across the globe came to an unexpected halt. This volume looks at the paradigm shift in the workplace ecosystem and how the world has changed in a big way. It discusses HR's role in organizational growth strategies, employee well-being, and employee mental health during the economic downturn and offers coping strategies that aim to empower human resources through learning and resilience. This book explains strategies that will help in preserving healthy human resources, which are an important component of an organization's effectiveness and growth. Chapters explain current trends in business and technology, the need for constant upskilling and digital dexterity, managing tech detox, and the way employees should work in the new normal. Chapters in Human Resource Management in a Post-Epidemic Global Environment: Roles, Strategies, and Implementations cover how the role of HR has changed with the pandemic; workplace communication strategies; challenges and opportunities of technology use in work-from-home scenarios; flexible work practices; effective employee retention; preserving employees' well-being, mental health, and work-life balance; the effect on gender equity; HR challenges in the tourism sector; and much more. Organizations that adopt post-pandemic HR roles and strategies not only have the path to innovation but will also have a competitive landscape in the changing scenario. HR leadership and others at corporations and organizations-both large and small-will find this volume to be a useful resource for discussion, implementation, and innovation"-- Provided by publisher.

Identifiers: LCCN 2022031044 (print) | LCCN 2022031045 (ebook) | ISBN 9781774911792 (hardcover) | ISBN 9781774911808 (paperback) | ISBN 9781003314844 (ebook)

Subjects: LCSH: Personnel management. | COVID-19 Pandemic, 2020---Economic aspects.

Classification: LCC HF5549 .H787 2023 (print) | LCC HF5549 (ebook) | DDC 658.3--dc23/eng/20220811

LC record available at https://lccn.loc.gov/2022031044

LC ebook record available at https://lccn.loc.gov/2022031045

ISBN: 978-1-77491-179-2 (hbk)
ISBN: 978-1-77491-180-8 (pbk)
ISBN: 978-1-00331-484-4 (ebk)

About the Editors

Tanusree Chakraborty, PhD, is currently a faculty member at the Centre for Human Resource Development, Administrative Staff College of India, Hyderabad, in India, in organizational behavior/human resource management. With 17 years of overall work experience and 16 years of academic experience, Dr. Chakraborty has been associated with several reputable business schools and universities in India. She is a former research fellow of the Indian Council of Medical Research and has many publications to her credit in Scopus-indexed and ABDC-listed journals, as well as in University Grants Commission-approved journals. She has presented research papers at several conferences and is an impaneled corporate trainer with training consultancies and government productivity councils. She has conducted over 150 corporate training programs in the areas of behavioral science and HR and psychometrics. She has been an active member in clubs and committees of the institutes she has worked for. She has been editor of several journals and newsletters and a reviewer for many journals. She is currently working on multiple edited books with reputed publishers. Dr. Chakraborty holds a PhD in Applied Psychology from Calcutta University, India; an MA (Applied Psychology) with a specialization in Organizational Psychology; a Postgraduate Diploma in Human Resource Management; and MBA (Human Resources).

Nandita Mishra, PhD, Director and Professor, Chetana's Institute of Management and Research, Mumbai, INDIA, has more than 25 years of teaching experience in education and research. She has wide experience in teaching managerial economics and economic environment for business, business ethics and corporate governance, corporate grooming, and general management subjects to management students in India and abroad. She spearheads academic administration, industry institute collaboration, and management development programs. She has been the resource person and program director for more than 50 management development programs and has trained senior-level and middle-level managers and faculty in various programs in behavioral science, managerial effectiveness, corporate social responsibility, etc. She is a certified trainer in CSR from the Indian Institute of Corporate Affairs. She is an active researcher in management, with her main research interest areas being leadership, organizational behavior dynamics, consumer behavior, and economic environment of business. She is a nominated member of the Higher Education Council of the Women Indian Chamber of Commerce and Industry (WICCI), whose main goal is to engage and encourage higher education institutions in research, training, and entrepreneurship development. WICCI also aims to improve participation of women leaders in higher education and to evolve along the lines of the Indian National Education Policy. Dr. Mishra holds a PhD in Management (Jankidevi Bajaj Institute of Management Studies, Mumbai) and MA and MPhil in Economics. She is a gold medalist both at the undergraduate and postgraduate levels.

Madhurima Ganguly, PhD, has 16 years of work experience in teaching and research. She is currently Associate Professor at the Heritage Business School, Kolkata, India. Dr. Ganguly has numerous national and international publications in leading Scopus, ABDC, and UGC journals along with book chapters. She has presented papers at international conferences held at Indian Institutes of Management and Indian Institutes of Technology (IIT) as well as abroad. She has earned best paper awards at IIT Delhi and TISS (Tata Institute of Social Science) Mumbai, India. She has acted as a session chair for different international conferences. She is a reviewer with several journals. Dr. Ganguly is also the PhD supervisor of management students at Maulana Abdul Kalam Azad Technical University of West Bengal, India. Dr. Ganguly is the recipient of the "Excellence in Education (Management and Commerce) Award" conferred by the Global Research Forum, New Delhi, in 2020. She has successfully conducted training sessions and management development programs with government bodies and corporate houses. She holds an MBA with a specialization in Human Resource Management and a PhD from Bengal Engineering and Science University, Shibpur, West Bengal, India.

About the Editors

Bipasha Chatterjee, is an Assistant Professor in the Department of Psychology, Adamas University, Kolkata, India. Currently she is pursuing her PhD at the Department of Applied Psychology, University of Calcutta, India. She has teaching and research experience of seven years to date. Her areas of interest are work-life balance, stress at work, and communication in organizations. She is currently working as a co-editor for two books, has chaired scientific sessions at national conferences, and has also delivered invited lectures. She has published four research papers, out of which two are in Scopus indexed journals, and has presented five research papers in national and international conferences/seminars. She is also the author of three chapters in a book on industrial psychology and social psychology for undergraduate students. Her postgraduate dissertation was published as a book by Lambert Academic Publishing in 2014. She is a life member of the Indian School Psychology Association (InSPA). Prof. Chatterjee holds a First-Class Master of Science degree in Applied Psychology (specialization in Organizational & Environmental Psychology) from the University of Calcutta and qualified WBCSC SET in 2015.

Contents

Contributors .... *xi*
Abbreviations .... *xiii*
Acknowledgment .... *xv*
Introduction .... *xvii*
Preface .... *xxi*

1. **Changing Role of Human Resource Management in the New Normal: A Post-Pandemic Paradigm Change** 1
   Anupriyo Mallick, Sudin Bag, and Payel Aich

2. **Post-Pandemic HR Roles, Strategies, and Implementation: A Gen-Y Perspective** 17
   Shulagna Sarkar and R. K. Mishra

3. **Reimagining Post-Pandemic Communication Strategies at Workplace: A Mindful Shift** 35
   Trisha Barua and Angshuman Bhattacharya

4. **Tech Detox and Tech Savvy: Two New Post-Pandemic Verticals of HR** 53
   Ranita Basu and Indranil Bose

5. **Unveiling the Notion of "Knowledge Hoarding" in a Post-Epidemic Global Business Environment** 65
   Abhilash Acharya

6. **A Shift in Post-Pandemic Work Strategies: Challenges and Opportunities of Technology Use vis-à-vis Work-from-Home** 81
   Bhaswati Jana and Tanuja Kaushik

7. **The Shift from the New Normal to the Old Normal: Challenges and Solutions** 99
   V. Jayalakshmi

8. **Organizational Growth, Sustainability, and Flexible Work Practices in the Post-Pandemic Era: Overcoming Challenges through Green HRM** 111
   Malabika Tripathi, Manvi Sodhani, and Swaha Bhattacharya

9. **Effective Employee Retention: Are Post-Pandemic Strategies Going to Change?**..................133
Srijan Sengupta

10. **Preserving Employees' Well-Being: An Organization's Post-Pandemic Imperative**..................153
S. Sabesan and M. A. S. Vasanth

11. **Employee Well-Being under the Work-from-Home Culture: Toward an Alternative Framework**..................177
Suddhabrata Deb Roy

12. **Post-Pandemic Employee Wellness Focus: An Empirical Study on the Well-Being Aspects of Healthcare Sector Employees**..................197
Tahir Mumtaz Awan and Zakia Khurshid Kayani

13. **Work-Life Issues and Stress: Challenges and Coping in the Post-Pandemic Period**..................215
Nitesh Behare, Anup Shivanechari, and Shrikant Waghulkar

14. **Self-Development among College Teachers during a Pandemic: A Qualitative Study with Reference to West Bengal, India**..................233
Rituparna Basak and Senjuti Bandyopadhyay

15. **Mental Health and Economic Downturn: Are Post-Pandemic HR Roles and Responsibilities Changing?**..................253
Debraj Datta

16. **Covert Casualty in a Crisis: Gender Equity—Empowering Human Resources via Learning, Authenticity, and Resilience**..................281
Tusharika Mukherjee

17. **A Perspective on Green Human Resource Management (GHRM) During the Post-Pandemic Era**..................305
Upagya Rai, Anurag Upadhyay, and Richa Singh

18. **Post-Pandemic Vocational Compass: A Perspective on Career Navigation Dynamics**..................319
Malabika Tripathi, Sritama Mitra Ghosh, and Samrat Ray

19. **Post-Pandemic Business Scenario: Outlining HR Challenges in the Tourism Sector**..................331
Tahir Mumtaz Awan and Muhammad Awais

Index..................357

Contributors

Abhilash Acharya
Army Institute of Management, Action Area III, Newtown, Kolkata 700160, West Bengal, India;
E-mail: abhilash.acharya12fpm@iimranchi.ac.in

Payel Aich
EIILM, Vidyasagar University, Midnapore, India

Muhammad Awais
Department of Management Sciences, Comsats University Islamabad, Park Road, Islamabad, Pakistan

Tahir Mumtaz Awan
Department of Management Sciences, Comsats University Islamabad, Park Road, Islamabad, Pakistan;
E-mail: tahir_mumtaz@comsats.edu.pk

Sudin Bag
EIILM, Vidyasagar University, Midnapore, India; E-mail: sudinbag1@gmail.com

Senjuti Bandyopadhyay
Mrinalini Datta Mahavidyapith, Kolkata, India; E-mail: rtprnb@gmail.com

Trisha Barua
Talent Acquisition—CoE, Deloitte USI; E-mail: trisha.barua6@gmail.com.

Rituparna Basak
Muralidhar Girls' College, Kolkata, India

Ranita Basu
Globsyn Business School, Kolkata, India; E-mail: basu.ranita@gmail.com

Nitesh Behare
Balaji Institute of International Business, Sri Balaji University, Pune, India; E-mail: bcharcnb@gmail.com

Angshuman Bhattacharya
Paradip Refinery, Indian Oil Corporation Limited, Paradip, India; E-mail: hutomukhohangla@gmail.com

Swaha Bhattacharya
Department of Applied Psychology, Calcutta University, Kolkata, India

Indranil Bose
School of Business, University of Bolton, International Academic Campus, Ras Al Khaimah, UAE

Debraj Datta
Management Department, Sister Nivedita University, West Bengal, India; E-mail: debraj.datta@gmail.com

Sritama Mitra Ghosh
H. M. Education Centre (CBSE), Hoogly, India; E-mail: sritama.mitra@gmail.com

Bhaswati Jana
GD Goenka University, Sohna, Gurgaon, New Delhi, India; E-mail: bhaswati.chk09@gmail.com

V. Jayalakshmi
Trainer and Counselling Psychologist, Chennai, India; E-mail:jayamahi2004@gmail.com

Tanuja Kaushik
GD Goenka University, Sohna, Gurgaon, New Delhi, India

Zakia Khurshid Kayani
Tazeen Group of Companies, Islamabad, Pakistan

Anupriyo Mallick
EIILM, Vidyasagar University, Midnapore, India

R. K. Mishra
IPE Hyderabad, Hyderabad 500101, Telangana, India

Tusharika Mukherjee
Work and Organizational Psychologist, Lecturer, Trainer, Justus Liebig University Giessen, Germany; E-mail: tusharikamukherjee@gmail.com

Upagya Rai
IILM University, Gurugram, India

Samrat Ray
Peter the Great Saint Petersburg Polytechnic University, Russia

Suddhabrata Deb Roy
University of Otago, Aotearoa, New Zealand; E-mail: suddhabratadeb.debroy@otago.ac.nz

S. Sabesan
Bharathiar University, Coimbatore, India; E-mail: swaminathansabesan@gmail.com

Shulagna Sarkar
NLC India Limited (A Govt. of India Enterprise), Chennai, India; E-mail: shulagnasarkar@2gmail.com

Srijan Sengupta
Department of Psychology, Barrackpore Rastraguru Surendranath College, Kolkata, West Bengal, India; E-mail: srijansengupta24@gmail.com

Anup Shivanechari
Balaji Institute of International Business, Sri Balaji University, Pune, India

Richa Singh
Department of Psychology, Vasanta Collage for Women, Varanasi, India

Manvi Sodhani
Amity University, Kolkata, India

Malabika Tripathi
Amity University, Kolkata, India; E-mail:malabikatripathi@gmail.com

Anurag Upadhyay
Department of Psychology, Udai Pratap Autonomous College, Varanasi, India; E-mail: dr.anuragwits@gmail.com

M. A. S. Vasanth
Bharathiar University, Coimbatore, India; E-mail: swaminathansabesan@gmail.com

Shrikant Waghulkar
Balaji Institute of International Business, Sri Balaji University, Pune, India

Abbreviations

AI	artificial intelligence
AIH	anti-inflammatory hormones
AMO	ability, motivation, and opportunity
BCC	British Chamber of Commerce
BHP	behavioral health practitioner
BPO	business process outsourcing
CAD	coronary artery disease
CBR	case-based reasoning
CHRM	critical HRM
CMS	critical management studies
COPD	chronic obstructive pulmonary disease
COR	Conservation of Resources
CPSE	central public sector enterprises
EAP	employee assistance program
EI	emotional intelligence
EMI	equated monthly installments
EMS	Environmental Management System
ESS	employee self-service
EWB	employee well-being
EWC	employee well-being champion
FGD	focus group discussion
FOMO	fear of missing out
GAIL	Gas Authority of India Limited
GHRM	Green Human Resource Management
HR	human resource
HRD	human resource department
HRM	human resource management
IT	information technology
ITSW	information technology and software workers
MI	myocardial infarction
MIE	Monitoring Indian Economy
NAMH	National Association of Mental Health
PAT	profit after tax
PPP	positive psychology practitioner

PE	person-environment
PEOU	perceived ease of use
PPE	personal protection equipment
PU	perceived usefulness
PWB	psychological well-being
SARS	severe acute respiratory syndrome
SMAC	social, mobile, analytics, and cloud
SMEs	small and medium enterprises
SMS	sanitation, mask and social distance
SOP	standard operating procedures
SUD	substance user disorders
SWB	subjective well-being
TAM	Technology Acceptance Model
TCS	Tata Consultancy Service
TPB	Theory of Planned Behavior
VOIP	Voice Over Internet Protocol
WFHC	work from home culture
WFM	work from home
WFO	work-from-office
WHO	World Health Organization

Acknowledgment

At the outset, we express our gratitude and acknowledgment to all those individuals who were a part of this book editing process and have contributed to the successful compilation of the book.

We begin with our heartfelt thanks to the Almighty, without whose intention and enlightenment the journey of this job would not have been accomplished. There were several ups and downs, more particularly because of the pandemic, but we could continue our work with sustained efforts being blessed by him.

We thank our friends, family, colleagues, and various other people in our association who have played important roles in soliciting chapters, circulating the call for chapters, being with us with their tremendous support, and continuously motivating us to complete the project.

We should also recall today the contribution of the academicians who have helped us in reviewing the chapters and provided us with valuable suggestions from time to time.

Also, we thank all the chapter contributors of the book for their contributions, sustained quality work, and supporting us with timely revisions and corrections as and when required.

Thank you all for giving us this opportunity to reach our goal today by being able to complete the book successfully.

—**Editors**

Introduction

With the advent of the COVID-19 pandemic and in order to control the spread of infection, businesses across the globe have come to an unexpected halt and started witnessing a global recession. People have adopted flexible work-from-home modes in various roles that were earlier denied. They have seen a year of upended routines and makeshift policies in their daily schedules and work practices. People have had to work from home in addition to looking after their families, taking care of their households, and also accomplishing their everyday office work. There have been severe changes in the work hours, with work space reduced at home because of dual-career families, with crowding, and privacy disturbed, and employees had to practically be present at work virtually 24 × 7 in many kinds of jobs. All these led the management of businesses to be concerned about the sustainability of work, performance, and employee mental health. Organizations were required to look forward to the new normal to survive and flourish in the chaos.

Human resource management in organizations was not only required to reconfigure workspaces but had to redesign the work allocation to their resources and core HR functions. It became evident that after the pandemic, more and more employees will be working from home, and this would lead to challenges of changed ways of interpersonal communication, perceived isolation because of social distancing, and mental health issues. For the completion of work, companies resorted to a plethora of online platforms, like the Zoom, Google Meet, WebEx, and others, and these became the norm of the day. People also, more typically the knowledge workers, shifted from their work cities to their home towns. This led to a globalized workforce and especially HR teams encountering both challenges and opportunities at work. In order to handle this humongous responsibility, HR needed to adapt to the new normal, failing which could have tarnished the brand image of the companies. This was the time for the organizations and leaders to help their country and individuals to overcome obstacles and fears, and work on the development of the country with their sustained performance.

With increased digitization at every HR function, the HR also had to educate their workforce in adopting those changes. It was also a matter of fact that the different generations of employees responded to the changed roles of HR differently. Communication, which is an extremely important process in any organization, is crucial; there is an increased need for communication in a post-pandemic world that offers insight into important factors that engage the workforce productively and efficiently. Companies had to implement best communication plans during this crisis period. People are also suffering a dilemma of being tech-savvy and also accepting the need for digital detox for physical and mental well-being. An understanding leader and a well-focused HR team are utmost needed in this regard. Resorting to green human resource management (GHRM) is the most cost-effective method that can be deployed and practiced in organizations to avoid any future uncertainty. Environment-friendly approaches can help organizations to survive any catastrophe. Emphasis is also needed in terms of knowledge sharing, knowledge hiding, and resource management in post-pandemic workplaces.

Another major challenge of the post-pandemic HR responsibilities is the need to manage the physical and mental well-being of employees. HR has to actively engage in the enhancement of health-related behaviors, proactive prevention of diseases, and enduring promotion of holistic health of employees to embrace a culture of well-being within organizations. By maintaining a value-neutral approach, this study also focuses on the usage of human-machine networks and their role in making global capital function, along with their possible utilization to ensure higher job satisfaction and well-being of the employees. As the pandemic is also causing a great level of stress and anxiety because of a number of factors such as fear of infection, loss of livelihood, and prevailing uncertainty, an important goal of HR is also directed at stress management so that employees at this juncture can balance work and life with time relationships, and they can relax when stressed, and at the same time have fun. Resilience also has to be built up under pressure so that employees can meet challenges well. HR roles and responsibilities includes equipping and training the workforce, recognizing employee efforts, ensuring employee wellness, developing learning environment, employee upskilling, fostering culture of openness, and the like. It is also a matter of concern that whether the post-pandemic rhetoric vis-à-vis human resources strategies can evolve into a global and inclusive order that would rest on the authenticity of the equity measures, supportive leadership, and an inclusion fostering organizational climate.

The major focus of the changed roles of HR has been to explore and understand the roles of global and domestic leaders in order to maintain the sustainable development in the pandemic outbreak and also propose new and emerging role(s) of the human resource management in the new normal as a strategic measure.

Introduction

This book explores the different aspects of the HRM and HR challenges that managers are facing due to the COVID-19 outbreak, especially in the post-pandemic workplace; it is directed at exploring strategies that will help in preserving a healthy human resource and contribute to organizational effectiveness. It covers areas of interest for HR personnel and the policy-makers that would fit into the new normal. Academicians and researchers in this area will also have a bird's eye view of the various roles, strategies, and implementation of the HR function.

Preface

With the breaking of the pandemic and the nationwide lockdown, business across the globe came to an unexpected halt, resulting in a paradigm shift in the workplace ecosystem; the world has changed in a big way. The gravest concern every management is now facing is about its human resource. Organizations are now learning how to thrive and survive in the new normal with the workplaces opening up, albeit with constraints. Organizations and people have adapted to work from home, flexible working conditions, and online modes of working. Employees are grappling with the challenge of work from home and work for home. A great lesson learnt from the pandemic is that HR practices have changed, and leadership is all about restoring lives and livelihood.

The three main objectives of this book are the following: (1) It discusses the organizational growth strategies overpowering the HR challenges in this changed situation. (2) It focuses on employee well-being in the post-pandemic situation, discussing mental health in the economic downturn. (3) Finally, it suggests coping strategies and self-development, empowering human resources through learning and resilience.

This book explores the different aspects of HRM and HR challenges that leaders, managers, and employees are facing in dealing with this new normal. The book explains strategies that will help in preserving healthy human resources that will contribute toward organizations' effectiveness. There are chapters explaining current trends in business and technology; chapters explaining constant upskilling and digital dexterity, managing tech detox; and chapters discussing the way employees should work in the new normal.

Organizations adopting post-pandemic HR roles and strategies not only have to innovate but also have to adapt to a competitive landscape in the changing scenario. Areas in which organizations can implement changes are culture and human capital development, which will thrive in this uncertain business environment. Corporates and organizations can use the discussions in this book for working in the changed scenario and situation. The book is a blend of empirical and reviewed chapters based on real-time data in the current pandemic situation.

We thank our review board members for their valuable feedback and suggestions. We welcome diverse feedback and suggestions from all readers to help us improve our future book projects.

We hope that this book enriches its readers with contemporary areas of post-pandemic human resource management and understanding of the worldwide best practices.

We wish our readers a happy reading experience.

CHAPTER 1

Changing Role of Human Resource Management in the New Normal: A Post-Pandemic Paradigm Change

ANUPRIYO MALLICK, SUDIN BAG*, and PAYEL AICH

EIILM, Vidyasagar University, Midnapore, India

*Corresponding author. E-mail: sudinbag1@gmail.com

ABSTRACT

In the present external crisis, organizations have to maintain and adapt to the unforeseen threats that create unpredicted uncertainties and risk among their workflows and halt the productivity and viability from all aspects. However, with the current pandemic of COVID-19, organizations need to overcome challenges and therefore, find some sort of workable solution to overcome the unexpected challenges that arise in our daily operational activities. The aim of the present chapter is to explore and understand the roles of global and domestic leaders in order to maintain the sustainable development in the pandemic outbreak and also propose the new and emerging role(s) of the human resource management in the new normal as a strategic measure. In addition, the chapter proposed some new ways for further research studies in relation to tackle the unprecedented challenges of human resource management.

1.1 INTRODUCTION

The COVID-19 impact on health, finance, and markets is unabated, unprecedented, complex, and highly volatile in its ever-changing business

---

Human Resource Management in a Post-Epidemic Global Environment: Roles, Strategies, and Implementations.
Tanusree Chakraborty, Nandita Mishra, Madhurima Ganguly, & Bipasha Chatterjee (Eds.)
© 2023 Apple Academic Press, Inc. Co-published with CRC Press (Taylor & Francis)

environment. It has shown how dangerous it is in turning the history and transforming the social and economic systems where we will identify a new era of humanity. The rate and speed of falls in the various occupations that have been followed cannot be compared to anything that has befallen our lifetime (Gopinath, 2020). The strongest impact of the virus has been felt on employees, organizations, and workplaces. The employees spend almost the full day in their offices but now the scenario is fully different where all private sector employees are remotely working from their home with the work-fit environment (Carnevale and Hatak, 2020). Everyone wants to stay at home. But working all day at home and not able to hang out or relax during their work hours or even after work hours is becoming a stress for employees of all sectors (Chakraborty et al., 2021). With well-organized and work-fit environment, employees face challenges as life becomes monotonous due to the inability to look for places where they can go like cafes, libraries, or any other recreational centers. People find it difficult to extract the basic services of work (Chawla et al., 2020).

As the spread of coronavirus is not visible around the world, countries have announced closures, and organizations have struggled to comply with lockout restrictions while trying to continue operating. All kinds of job do not fit into work from home (WFH). WFH takes the only solution for the business community. People around the world are in crisis, various organizations are in a state of instability and they want to be led by teamwork. The traditional methodology of work is now a challenging fact for people. The reason is that people are unable to move out of their homes but again they have to earn money. The critical ideas to develop new technology are growing faster with the urgency in requirement. The new electronic devices, the meeting apps for organizations are demand for all to have a smooth running office work. So we all have to work hard as a team in order to achieve our goals successfully as a response to the crisis. The management of the organizations will have to definitely sort out the problems which the employees are facing and will be facing in future for the pandemic. This is the time for the organizations, the leaders to help the country, and the individuals to overcome obstacles and fears and work on the development of the country with their performance (Khalil, et. al., 2020).

1.2 PANDEMIC AND DIGITIZATION

New business jargons such as agility, art, flexibility guide HR professionals in a closed state. As staff began to log in remotely, HR operations turned brick and cement offices into real workplaces overnight. The guidelines for WFH for staff were outlined overnight and distributed among employees. Employees had to be supplemented with digital infrastructure—laptops, internet connections to ensure business continuity so that business operations could run smoothly.

As millennial join the workforce, organizational work and HR professionals focus on building a workplace for the future, which has led to a wide range of cultural issues—job security, job purpose, work integration, and a balanced lifestyle and similar other issues.. For the most part we would go on with these definitions and classifications; we had a mysterious virus from a lesser-known Chinese city that did not force us to rethink the way we humans have built the world and all its institutions. It is an exciting time because this diversion can persuade businesses to consider how they interact with consumers not only but also their larger assets, their employees.

Organizations have begun to focus on the planning and operational response needed to ensure business continuity with the rise of the deadly virus. Organizations for the benefit of the business, stakeholders, and the employees need to focus on how to create more stable communication system, trust, and openness in this epidemic to strengthen the employee management and products diversification.

Organizations are continuously making significant changes to their business plans and operating practices, most of it becoming digitized, when the business demanded the same after the spread of the virus. Everything was not possible in the preliminary stage but again with the help of the management, leaders, and employees the difficult times are changing in a fast pace. Employees were struggling with feelings of insecurity with their future; they are undergoing loneliness, ignorance, and more. The role of HR team who are considered as change agents in an organization has become the most crucial in this post-pandemic situation. To handle such a complicated and fast change, of course, HR in every organization has to work much harder, strategize their policies, and bring out the new work procedures that fit the situation the best. Managing the organization's "resources" in a "humane" manner is the way forward for HR, while WFH has ensured that organizations continued to operate during the lockdown against the spread of COVID, people are now pining for fresh air, the smell of the office, and the opportunity to meet coworkers and customers face-to-face. Virtual organizations to some extent have created a kind of cabin fever syndrome among employees (Chakraborty et al., 2021). In this time of crisis, personnel in health care and essential services have risen above and beyond the call of duty to care for others. The time has come for organizations to change. The welfare and well-being of all stakeholders has to be built into the culture of the organization. Can that happen while our prime focus remains performance and ensuring compliance by "Command and Control"? This a prime question that the HR is facing today. With this background, the present chapter attempts to discuss the overall changing role of HR professionals in the post-pandemic period, which emphasis on digitalization at workplace, paradigm shifts in HR role, and additional measures that are focused on by organizations as a response to the pandemic.

1.3 PARADIGM SHIFT IN HR ROLE

The current pandemic emerged as an imperative situation for human beings worldwide. While some have coped up with the situation and transformed themselves according to the needs of the situation and others are still struggling hard and soul to manage this new normal. The active participation of the managers along with employers, management, and employees helps to overcome the crisis and they are also relying on their insights which are again provided by HR professionals confirmed by the employers, to assure that their organization and employees feel supported. The media especially, social media have disclosed how the organizations are facing "n" number of problems and trying to solve the critical brainstorming processes but failing in their endeavors to save organizations, employees, and jobs. According to the report of Miller and Berk (2020) in the United States, it is observed that in the first quarter of 2020, more than 560 organizations have filed for bankruptcy, out of which 10% organizations are in retail sector (Danziger, 2020). These numbers are probable to keep on increasing all round the year, and what is missing is to the lack of interest and preparedness among the leaders to tackle this crisis, might be because of the suddenness of the situation and lack of a robust preparation to handle the crisis.

Over the past few years, the department of HR has been trusted more with employee engagement issues and easy work processes. This profession has undergone radical changes, keeping in mind how the employees will be benefited, specially, in the ways employees work, learn, grow, and communicate. The opportunity for change has been huge, and the digital transformation in the businesses made the work of the employees much easier. The virus has again started the revolution majorly for labor revolution, accelerating the behavior of the labor or the employees which is unimaginable. Price stabilization is important always, since when the industrial revolution started, as it has helped companies and the business man to empower their internal operations in partnership with productivity tools and improve strategic performance for agile business continuity.

Remotely working employees need to be supported immensely to make the business successful. As businesses strive to stay afloat, it is important to know the key changes that this global epidemic will bring. The current epidemic, however, focuses on the risks, uncertainties, and unequal conditions and risk areas that exist in leadership processes (McNulty et al., 2019). Employee performance, employee physical and psychological health related to working environment, workload, and employee income create significant problems in employees' work performance in this epidemic (Bader et al., 2019).

Therefore, new contributions from the HR department could include the following few activities; however, it can be changed whenever needed and could go a long way in looking at the impact of global pandemic.

1.4 NEW ROLES OF HR

1.4.1 COUNSELLING AND COLLABORATION

The communication process is essential for effective engagement of the employees. The HR team with the HR managers must have a two-way process for communication with the employees. Providing appropriate counselling sessions with the employees helps in reducing their stress and to overcome their anxiety and helps them to relax. During this pandemic, all organizations from public to private sectors are facing communication challenges due to changing circumstances or situations and working style. The survey conducted by Orangefiery (2020a) established the idea that the employees' views on the need for communication is something interesting which included: (1) clarity and transparency, (2) knowledge about employees' emotional and mental health in dealing with stress, fear, and anxiety, and (3) and a strong acknowledgment when there is difficulty of the situation.

The similar manner was approached by Bogusky-Halper (2020) while conducting the study on the communication of leaders during the pandemic and they noticed that these are the top six responses present. Those are announced during the current epidemic includes (1) mangers need honest communication, (2) clarity with much more transparency with the work details and the policies, (3) to remain calm and encouraging when the employees work remotely, (4) managers need to put effort in assisting employees to stay safe and healthy in every way may it be physically or physically or mentally, (5) there should be trust and honesty among all the employees which should be nurtured with care, (6) any problems the organizations and the employees face must be understood clearly and should be straight forward whenever necessary. All these roles of the HR are extremely relevant in the post-pandemic situation. When considering the needs of employees during the COVID-19 period, organizations analyze how employees can be cared for and maintained in every way possible. Psychological, emotional, and physical safety is assessed and organizations use the necessary resources for employees to be happy. Brower (2020) said health facilities are set up and meditation times are provided at work and overtime.

Management in every organization meets and engages more closely with employees for clarifying what factors can motivate the employees. Brower (2020) predicts that during any form of risk and crisis, the support system should be strong, which can easily build strong and dedicated workforce, and that is possible when the management can manage the employees properly; or when the managers can lead the team with wide range of motivation. The corporate culture of the organization if required to be changed should be done at the very early stage. The new norm to WFH can be recognized as a quality treatment for a great balance of work life with the family. Frequent group involvement, greater flexibility, and significant use of technology can reduce any fears and stress from employees. Companies will increase their speed in improving the standard of work and enhance profitability, balance each employee's performance, and reduce unnecessary programs that have led to increased turnover of employees and increased job insecurity (Brower, 2020). Moreover, from an organizational perspective, Brower (2020) suggested that the effect of COVID-19 would be that organizations would start working more closely instead of competing, by eliminating inefficiency. Employees look forward to being accepted for their unique value propositions that leads to organizational development. HR professionals need to recognize different characteristics of employees' needs and wants, so as to improve the coordination among each levels of hierarchy with proper communication and counselling. To foster social support in the organizations is the need of the hour. To facilitate regular discussions between the management and employees, HR should establish guidelines and explain its need to the management properly. This will help the management with the necessary systematic guidance on how to deal with critical issues arising from the post-COVID-19 epidemic, including occupational safety alternatives, and confidence in the environmental performance.

1.4.2 REINFORCING ORGANIZATIONAL VALUES

Effective reinforcement and job awareness are very important in any critical situation. McGuinness (2020) associated with business leaders in various industries and conducted a study and posited how and when the four skills are needed at workplace and they asserted that those are very essential. First, leaders need to have a positive outlook about the responsibilities, and see how the work approach can be dealt when there is huge amount of pressure. The work and circumstances are the important part of managing the employees during a disaster. In the next stage, leaders need foresight, they need to develop the ability to disseminate false information, discipline and intent, and they need to have knowledge of the environment and conditions that can affect any employee. Recognition helps leaders anticipate barriers to business. In the third stage, leaders need to put people in first priority. In times of risk and crisis, leaders must ensure gratitude while crossing any challenges during the work. This helps to build trust and improve commitment between the employees on behalf of the organization. In the last stage, leaders need to have decisive actions. The leaders are different because of their thinking and the ideas with the decisions they take while facing challenging situations, especially during epidemics. Therefore, leaders should capture emotions, process information quickly, understand and prioritize needs, and respond peacefully without any haste. Decisions should be made with certainty, values, actions, and positive reinforcement. Efficacy has a profound effect on feelings of mental security. Thus, HR should make every attempt to align values of employees with the values of the organization.

1.4.3 INNOVATION AND UPSKILLING

The current era of alteration and disruption demands innovation and improvement as there are risks which are crucial to employee support and organizational growth. When an organization has problems with new investments, HR managers should emphasize the opportunities for process development and also review the technology development, including switching to remote workplaces and also implementing the new policies for better and effective human communication. The dramatic changes in how employees perform and where they work have a significant impact on employees' perceptions and experience of human fit with the work-fit environment (Kristof, 1996). It is rightly identified by the person-environment (PE) fit theory that employees will be attracted toward those organizations and will be selected only with a work environment that replicates the equality, cultures, and job characteristics such as their own core beliefs and attitude, needs and desires (Kristof and Guay, 2011). In light of these mechanisms, employees who get into organizations where PE fit is developed tend to grow and experience superior levels of satisfaction, commitment, general well-being, and work-life balance (Kristof et al., 2005). One way employers can show their appreciation through various workshops and development programs. This not only helps employees feel valued but also helps to fill information or communication gaps within the company. In this situation, HR professionals need to have programs that would strengthen employees' values and principles. They need to be communicated well how the organizations care for them and their families.

1.4.4 UNDISRUPTED WORKFLOW

Educating and equipping the employees with relevant information about the pandemic is the responsibilities of the management, which can be undertaken by the HR department. The safety tips, healthy eating information various other modified rules and regulations are required to be updated regularly by the HR team. HR needs to communicate the steps taken by the company during this situation in an open manner so that they reach every employee. There can be many possible ways to do so, like, HR can create interesting posts about growing events and topics around this issue in the job feed or can start with the dashboards creation. As COVID-19 creates significant disruption, and detects employee involvement in various fields, HR managers need to multiply their efforts for recognition. Active recognition and appreciation during times of insecurity motivates the recipient. This serves as a strong indicator for other employees who should emulate it. Recognition can take place in many forms other than financial rewards such as public consent, thank you tokens, career progressions, appreciative leadership and building positivity in the work environment (Chakraborty and Mishra, 2019; Chakraborty and Ganguly, 2019). This strengthens the organization's commitment to long-term work force with work success. With new and reorganized employees, companies also want to digitalize the work environment and streamline procedures, techniques, and workflows to enhance efficiency. Therefore, modern human resource solutions for mechanical ride, automatic desk, and production tools, as well as developed HR tools which provide better collaboration and communication equipments, are gaining grip in the society. Green human resource management is also gaining momentum in this period and HR should emphasize on that more.

1.4.5 EMPLOYEE WELLNESS

As organizations are continuously changing HR policies, practices, and procedures during the severe pandemic COVID-19, knowing how these miraculous and unequal changes affect employees' experiences and how these policies can be addressed, becomes increasingly important. For example, nowadays business houses have to switch to hybrid forms of employees training and development programs and recruitment and selection methods instead of one to one contact (Maurer, 2020a). Thus, it is very important to predict how these hybrid practices will affect the future of structure and practices of organizations. It has to be done to stay safe; and these new habits can attract and keep people differently than conventional face-to-face interactions. In this regard, researchers must focus on the impact of COVID-19 on workers' capability to navigate the process of job search, how all changes from traditional selection to availability of candidates affect their capacity to develop and evaluate appropriate employment perceptions, and the performance of visual testing centers and training programs. After realizing the concerns and pressures of the severe COVID-19 pandemic, HR will need to focus more on physical and psychological health and well-being of employees. Complete benefits are a common way to bring health to a company. These facilities cover all aspects of well-being, including financial security and employees' mental stress. While these programs will vary in their natures, the idea is to provide employees with utmost financial and nonfinancial benefits that uplift the employees' well-being beyond normal health care facilities.

1.4.6 NEW AGE POLICIES

With the severity of the coronavirus blocking everyone in their homes, business houses around the globe have authorized or encouraged employees to WFH. Even after the epidemic is over, when the workers have returned to workplaces, still the remote work will play an important role in business as it improves the profits and supports business continuity. To ensure its success, companies have to implement policies and teach flexible policies—establish long-term operating guidelines, manage employee performance in digital workplaces, and build up leadership employees working virtually. In addition, the application of digital personnel and bots will increase, which will also create an urgent need to formulate policies regarding cyber security, auditing, and redefining human intervention situations. The entire method in the value chain acquisition will be documented to create it more efficiently—from the use of machine learning (ML) and artificial intelligence (AI) algorithms to identify and test applicants in the use of visual chatting tools to enable remote presence, and bots ensure a high-end employee experience and engagement. During the COVID-19 lockdown, the job market will also undergo major changes; while the requirement for certain jobs will rise but the overall labor market will surely decline. Businesses should try to make a strong staff planning in order to ensure their access to the right talent, and strategize on existing talents to ensure maximum involvement and productivity. Therefore, talent identification and human resource management are important.

1.4.7 VIRTUAL LEARNING

Organizations that rely heavily on conventional learning will need to improve evidence of the concept of hybrid learning using the updated digital technologies. The long-distance performance model and the increasing power of digital technology will also uplift the need for capacity building for staff. Thanks to COVID-19, businesses have become more aware of their spending and are looking for less expensive solutions for their employees, which add to the attraction of distance education. In order to maximize profits, organizations will need to consider not only necessary skills and competencies but also specific interpersonal skills that can help identify and evaluate potential ideas among potential employees, and how they can best be used (Sacco and Ismail, 2014). Following on a previous example in relation to the need for social relations, the current solution for measuring social interactions adopted by many organizations includes real means of communication such as lunch times, happy hours, etc. (Maurer, 2020b). While these practices may reduce feelings of inadequacy due to the rapid change in the social workplace environment, it can also leave employees feeling overwhelmed as they seek the social cohesion they had in their pre-epidemic lives (Fetters, 2020). HR professionals need to engage their employees virtually so that they do not feel the challenges of social distancing; on the other hand the opportunity to learn and develop should also continue in the process.

1.4.8 WORK-LIFE BALANCE

The COVID-19 pandemic has brought the importance of employee well-being, including physical, emotional as well as psychological health, to the forefront. The future HR health agenda may have two aspects: First, the workforce, which includes tools and policies that help employees plan their regular activities, especially if they work remotely and have to deal with additional stress and worries about changing benefits from health and leave risks; and, second, the workforce, which includes tools that monitor employee feelings and help improve employee support, thereby ensuring better employee engagement. But as the current epidemic continues to emerge, the potential for conflict between work and family groups may be greater due to boredom or job insecurity. Indeed, in addition to managing the increased difficulties that can result from switching to remote operations especially for those unfamiliar and complex workplaces. HR should address increased childcare concerns through widespread schooling and childcare services, and address ongoing concerns for the health and safety of family and friends with work responsibilities. These newly developed needs also distorted the roles of work and family, making it so difficult than ever to maintain adequate boundaries for family activities (Giurge and Bohns, 2020). HR should support employees in adopting the changes in their roles in the workplace, and help them to understand how they can perform tasks or methods used for sustained performance (Langfred, 2000).

1.4.9 WORKFORCE ANALYSIS

As employees become more and more (literally) scattered, and as new work situation is emerging, HR leaders have to maintain the good track records for their organizations. Effective collection of data and excavation tools will be a great instrument to predicting the nature of changes. The HR managers should increasingly embrace tools that track how employees are performing their work, interact, and feel like accessing information to improve performance and engagement. These modern equipments, along with highly demanded AI capabilities, will also convey the potential for more accurate and effective decision-making in a short period of time. To make the work your own, personalization processes can be a factor. Thus, HR has to reorganize unique and effective process that leads to make employees more efficient. It is quite important to keep the employee at the center of these processes. This critical situation is an opportunity to rebuild the role-playing people—the worker.

1.4.10 KEEP EMPLOYEES MOTIVATED

With increasing levels of wage deduction and uncertainty in the present situation, businesses should focus on the effective strategies in order to keep their employees motivated. Organizations should adapt the robust Recognize and Reward (R&R) strategy to motivate their potential employees that can help to reduce the mental stress of the employees during this ongoing epidemic and as a result, ethical and moral values of the employees will increase. With an emphasis on financial well-being, rising unemployment rates, wage conditions, and market downturns, financial security is a major concern for many workers. To alleviate this kind of stress within employees, companies can offer the options for financial well-being. Features such as budget management tools, financial training, and financial pressure management tools, as well as paid leave, much-needed breaks, and prepaid cards, can help with these unpredictable and trying times. These strategies will be effective tools for the businesses live in a normal life while employees get engaged with their own cup of tea and also satisfied, whether they grow internally or work with service providers to deliver them.

1.4.11 LOOKING FORWARD

While these programs have become the new roles of HR professionals, all of these may not work for all companies. However, in the post-pandemic period, where employees have to accustom with their work, all HR should move to a more human-centric approach. What emerges depending on how the HR professionals react or respond when faced with difficulties and uncertainties?

1.5 CONCLUSION

Until the COVID-19 vaccine is available in the next 12–18 months, companies should look forward to periodic enforcement of public disposal and plan accordingly. Important considerations include job descriptions, office/conference spaces, and whether the work can be done remotely. HR leaders have played a key role in building a strong organizational culture that will retain top players and attract new talents that will help their companies grow the backlash. At the time, many small and medium enterprises (SMEs) were struggling to compete in skill battles but were determined to achieve their employment plans. Research data in the current context also shows that WFH is "normal" for many businesses and, if necessary, should be continued in the future. As they became accustomed to this new reality, many leaders with the help of HR staff began to think about how to better treat their employees when they came across another epidemic. Some key factors that help business leaders and HR teams prepare for the next step, which may be to set up for workplace, frequent and everyday communication with employees, product, and decision-making that eliminates toxic workers. Concurrently, the great challenge of severe pandemic provides an ideal time for managers and HR managers to conduct research works and turn it into possible information to stabilize organizations in dealing with one of the greatest challenges in modern history. It also provides employees with an exciting opportunity to look at all sectors to gain leadership and inspiration. Because there may be possible solutions, this global problem requires systematic and integrated research results. Although the long-term effects of COVID-19 are not yet known, there is little reason to believe that its impact on the health of the organization will be temporary. So, it is evident that the role of HR has changed and will keep changing in times to come as a result of the pandemic and there should be support from the top management to actualize the changed role of the HR at this crucial time.

KEYWORDS

- **leader**
- **unforeseen threats**
- **uncertainties**
- **sustainable**
- **pandemic**
- **new normal**

REFERENCES

Bader, A. K.; Reade, C.; Froese, F. J. Terrorism and Expatriate Withdrawal Cognitions: The Differential Role of Perceived Work and Non-work Constraints. *Int. J. Human Res. Manag.* **2019**, *30*(11), 1769–1793.

Bogusky-Halper, K. Study: Organizations Rising to the Challenge of COVID-19 Communication, but Needs Persist; Leaders Must Address Concerns and Demonstrate Transparency, Clarity and Openness. Business Wire, 2020. https://www.businesswire.com/news/home/20200403005278/en/STUDY-Organizations- Rising-Challenge-COVID-19- Communications-Persist (accessed May 10, 2020).

Brower, T. 5 Predictions About How Coronavirus Will Change the Future of Work. Forbes. https://www.forbes.com/sites/tracybrower/2020/04/06/how-the-post-covid-future-will -be- different-5-positive-predictions-about-the-future-of-work-to-help-your-mood-and-yoursanity/#92e6193e227f (accessed May 10, 2020).

Carnevale, J. B.; Hatak, I. Employee Adjustment and Well-Being in the Era of COVID-19: Implications for Human Resource Management. *J. Bus. Res.* **2020**, *116*, 183–187.

Chakraborty, T.; Ganguly, M. Crafting Engaged Employees Through Positive Work Environment: Perspectives of Employee Engagement. In *Management Techniques for Employee Engagement in Contemporary Organizations*; IGI Global, 2019; pp 180–198.

Chakraborty, T.; Mishra, N. Appreciative Inquiry: Unleashing a Positive Revolution of Organizational Change and Development. *Int. J. Econ. Commer. Bus. Manag.* **2019**, *6*(2), 32–37.

Chakraborty, T.; Kumar, A.; Upadhyay, P.; Dwivedi, Y. K. Link Between Social Distancing, Cognitive Dissonance, and Social Networking Site Usage Intensity: A Country-Level Study During the COVID-19 Outbreak. *Internet Res.* **2021**, *31*(2), 419–456. DOI: 10.1108/intr-05-2020-0281

Chawla, N.; MacGowan, R. L.; Gabriel, A. S.; Podsakoff, N. P. Unplugging or Staying Connected? Examining the Nature, Antecedents, and Consequences of Profiles of Daily Recovery Experiences. *J. Appl. Psychol.* **2020**, *105*(1), 19–39.

Danziger, P. List of Retail Companies on Bankruptcy Watch is Growing Fast Amid Coronavirus Crisis. Forbes, 2020. https://www.forbes.com/sites/pamdanziger/2020/04/03/retail-companies-on-death-watch-is- growing-fast-as-covid-19-puts-non-essential-retailers-onlife- support/#355b43a325ea (accessed May 16, 2020).

Fetters, A. We Need to Stop Trying to Replicate the Life We Had. The Atlantic, April 10, 2020.

Giurge, L. M.; Bohns, V. K. 3 Tips to Avoid WFH Burnout, 2020. https://hbr.org/2020/04/3-tips-to-avoid-wfh-burnout (accessed May 25, 2020).

Gopinath, G. The Great Lockdown: Worst Economic Downturn Since the Great Depression. IMF Blog, 2020. https://blogs.imf.org/2020/04/14/the- great-lockdown-worst-economic-downturn-since-the-great-depression/ (accessed May 6, 2020).

Khalil M. D.; Mehrangiz, A.; Amin, A.; Barhate, B.; Garza, R. C.; Gunasekara, N.; Ibrahim, G.; Majzun, Z. Leadership Competencies and the Essential Role of Human Resource Development in Times of Crisis: A Response to Covid-19 Pandemic. *Hum. Res. Dev. Int.* **2020**, *23*(4), 380–394.

Kristof, A. L. Person-Organization Fit: An Integrative Review of its Conceptualizations, Measurement, and Implications. *Pers. Psychol.* **1996**, *49*(1), 1–49.

Kristof-Brown, A.; Guay, R. P. Person-Environment Fit. In *APA Handbook of Industrial and Organizational Psychology, Maintaining, Expanding, and Contracting the Organization*. American Psychological Association, 2011; Vol. 3, pp 3–50.

Kristof-Brown, A. L.; Zimmerman, R. D.; Johnson, E. C. Consequences of Individuals & Fit at Work: A Meta-Analysis of Person–Job, Person–Organization, Person–Group, and Person–Supervisor Fit. *Pers. Psychol.* **2005**, *58*(2), 281–342.

Langfred, C. W. The Paradox of Self-Management: Individual and Group Autonomy in Work Groups. *J. Org. Behav.* **2000,** *21*(5), 563–585.

Maurer, R. Job Interviews go Virtual in Response to COVID-19. Society for Human Resources Management, March 17, 2020, 2020a.

Maurer, R. Virtual Happy Hours Help Co-Workers, Industry Peers Stay Connected, 2020b. https://www.shrm.org/hr-today/news/hr-news/pages/virtual- happy-hours-help-coworkers-stay-connected.aspx (accessed May 10, 2020).

McGuinness, J. 4 COVID-19 Leadership Lessons. Chief Executive, 2020. https://chief executive.net/4-covid-19-leadership-lessons/ (accessed May 12, 2020).

McNulty, Y.; Lauring, J.; Jonasson, C.; Selmer, J. Highway to Hell? Managing Expatriates in Crisis. *J. Global Mob.* **2019,** *7*(2), 157–180.

Miller, H.; Berk, C. C. JC Penney Could Join a Growing List of Bankruptcies During the Coronavirus Pandemic. CNBC, 2020. https://www.cnbc.com/2020/05/15/these-companieshave-filed-for-bankruptcy-since-the- coronavirus-pandemic.html (accessed May 12, 2020).

Orangefiery. Leadership Communications during COVID-19: A Survey of US Organizations, 2020. https://orangefiery.com/uploads/Orangefiery_COVID19_Leadership_Communications_Resear ch_040320.pdf (accessed May 11, 2020).

Sacco, D. F.; Ismail, M. M. Social Belongingness Satisfaction as a Function of Interaction Medium: Face-to-Face Interactions Facilitate Greater Social Belonging and Interaction Enjoyment Compared to Instant Messaging. *Comput. Human Behav.* **2014,** *36*, 359–364.

CHAPTER 2

Post-Pandemic HR Roles, Strategies, and Implementation: A Gen-Y Perspective

SHULAGNA SARKAR[1*] and R. K. MISHRA[2]

[1]NLC India Limited (A Govt. of India Enterprise), Chennai, India

[2]IPE Hyderabad, Hyderabad, Telangana 500101, India

*Corresponding author. E-mail: shulagnasarkar@2gmail.com

ABSTRACT

It is an established fact that becoming a leading organization is easier than continuing to be the leader. Past records state that number of the organizations that reached the top of the Fortune rankings just a few decades ago, do not feature there any longer. The magic mantra of success that took them to the very top was not enough to keep them there. Changes in market are inevitable and "changing with the changes" has become mandatory for survival. COVID-19 outbreak has changed the way business operates and this has led to changes in the way the various departments have to operate.

COVID-19 has impacted people and has encouraged both the organizations and HR departments to look for new mechanism to attend to the people-related challenges at workplace. The chapter is an attempt to understand the Gen-Y perspective of post-pandemic HR and mainly focuses on understanding the youth anxiety of business operations and expectations from HR. Various students who are in the final year of the courses and the ones who have recently been placed will be considered for the study. A structured questionnaire will be administered to achieve the objectives.

Changes being a constant, differentiation have evolved as a relief to the organizations. Differentiate or perish is a fact that none can disagree especially in the post-pandemic scenario. The role of HR in post-pandemic scenario is an interest to all as HR is equally responsible for creating a responsive workforce with a business survival focus. The future is for organizations which can strategize for "survive the survival."

2.1 INTRODUCTION

The novel coronavirus pandemic has unprecedentedly resulted in an unimaginable loss of human lives and also to the global economy in an era of global peace. Not only are the numbers upsetting, but the speed at which the challenges have emerged across the world is intimidating. Governments, health professionals as well as businesses are constantly calibrating the response to the pandemic yielding to frequent strategic adjustments. The companies have been attempting to balance the business sustainability with humanity. This has become an issue for businesses across nations.

Though vaccination has been initiated, yet the effective medication is highly uncertain and is affecting the future of the industries and economy. Researchers and analysts around the world have formed a consensus that coronavirus is unlikely to be eradicated and despite costly lockdowns that have brought much of the global economy to a halt would be phased revival with restart for many industries. Already, there have been discussions on the possibilities of having worse impact of Phase III spread of COVID-19. The pandemic is one of those changes which have made remarkable difference to the ways companies have been operating. It was never imagined until the pandemic made us think that our living rooms could be turned into offices and work can continue irrespective of where and how we are. The human resource management practices were witnessed to be completely different by the end of 2019. The more visionary business leaders were deep in the throes of shaping their own company cultures while the advent of pandemic has transformed the workplace itself. Best of companies worldwide including TCS has now come up with a policy to continue Working from Home (WfH) for 75% of its employees till 2025 (BS, 2020).

The workplace of the future is now more forced to adopt frequent changes pertaining to technology, culture, and economies as these factors impact the existing people processes across the globe. Companies are attempting to find ways to leverage new technology to supplement and complement the existing skilled jobs. Technological and cultural changes have always incessantly driven workplace forward, and now companies are forced to adopt the fast-paced global transformation which is witnessed by almost all major business sectors.

With this background, present chapter focuses on discussing the role of HR in post-pandemic scenario. The chapter is an interest to all HRs as they are equally responsible in creating a responsive workforce with a business survival focus in these difficult times of pandemic. This chapter shares the impact of pandemic on Gen-Y and shares HR strategies that can be undertaken to cater to the situation and enabling a suitable workplace.

The COVID-19 has spread across the world miserably and affected organizations, departments, and individual employees. The spread of the pandemic clearly indicates that it differentiates none and so is true in the case of businesses too. Businesses have been affected in some or the other way like marked by market demand, supply chain, vendor operations, accessibility to unskilled workers. Even pharmaceutical companies did find it difficult to operate irrespective of increased demand in market. WEF (2020) data clearly indicate that 93% of the world's workers resided in countries which are practicing "workplace closure" as a strategy to prevent the spread of coronavirus. The report clearly indicates that only 30% of the businesses are focusing on reskilling and upskilling programs. An attempt has been made to identify the status of COVID-19 in top affected countries of the World as given in Table 2.1.

TABLE 2.1 COVID-19 Scenario—A World View.

S. No.	Country Other	Total Cases	Total Deaths	Total Recovered	Deaths 1 m pop	Population
	World	5,59,34,708	13,42,942	3,89,54,566	172.3	
1	USA	1,16,95,711	2,54,255	70,87,796	766	33,17,43,344
2	India	89,12,704	1,31,031	83,33,013	95	1,38,51,60,148
3	Brazil	59,11,758	1,66,743	53,61,592	782	21,31,35,258
4	France	20,36,755	46,273	1,43,152	708	6,53,28,835
5	Russia	19,71,013	33,931	14,75,904	232	14,59,58,474

Source: Worldometer Statistics (2020), accessed on November 20, 2020.

The report of challenges in pandemic scenario is not confined to businesses but has been impacting human beings across all generations. The ways different generations have become inclined on social network usage are also varying, but on the whole, the social network usage has also increased

(Chakraborty et al., 2021). The population in India is relatively divided on which segment of India will emerge stronger or weaker from the COVID-19 crisis. The report of Duffy (2020) clearly indicates that the pandemic has been worse for older people than younger generation. There is a relatively very low change in opinion when the respondents were asked to consider the longer term impacts irrespective of the imminent economic scenario predicted for the younger generations. It is in this connect, this chapter attempts to understand the perspective of the Generation-Y in India on the post-pandemic HR and mainly focuses on understanding the youth anxiety of business operations and expectations from HR.

2.2 POST-PANDEMIC IMPACT

Various studies including WWF (2020), The Guardian (2020) have concluded that the spread of pandemic has a strong relation to the unsustainable way the human race has affected the natural ecosystem. The impact of COVID-19 is not unknown or unexplored in short term. There are studies on the current impact, yet not much explored in measuring the impact of COVID-19 in long term. The impact of the pandemic that is an experience of life time for individuals has already impacted us in many ways including physically, socially, mentally, and behaviorally. Studies have confirmed that COVID-19 has impacted generations differently. There have been numerous studies on older population, yet the demographic dividend lies with the youth and studies on the impact of COVID-19 on youth is of importance.

Umachandran (2020) has explained that COVID-19 has turned millennia's as the India's worried generation. Karasek and Theorell (1990) has shared that workplace mental health issues have increased over a period of time irrespective of workplace being slowly opening. There have been several studies including understanding the continuous communication approach in the pandemic scenario (Greer and Payne, 2014) while studies have also been focused on quarantine and confinement (Parmet and Sinha, 2020). Brooks et al. (2020) and Galea et al. (2020) in the Lancet reviewed substantial studies and explained the effect of quarantine on the mental health of patients. The major mental health issues that have been identified to have been accompanied with the spread of COVID-19 pandemic are stress, anxiety, depressive symptoms, insomnia, denial, anger, and fear globally (Torales et al., 2020).

It is not wrong to express that there is strong relation to individual organizational fit within a given environment, to individual and organizations' success. While studies of Takeuchi et al. (2009) explained that organizational support can positively affect adjustment in a newer situations and practices. The organizations operating in the pandemic scenario has been working on practices to define better engagement for its employees, while hiring scenario during the pandemic times has been a concern for the youth those who are in the final year of their studies and were set to enter the corporate world.

In such state, a concern worth discussing is the agenda of workplace transformations that are making a difference to employees as well as business as a whole. Businesses have changed the means and mechanism in handling people and the anxiety during the pandemic while making numerous digital efforts as well as automation efforts to ensure workflow. Pandemic has affected businesses across sectors differently and so has the employment in the respective sector. COVID-19 has affected companies both negatively and positively. The negative effects are prominent, discussed worldwide while the positive effects are there where companies which did not attempt to earlier think on options like work from home (WfH) are encouraging online learning, virtual interactions, enabling larger digitalization of HR efforts, and enabling access to needed information, ensuring work-life balance, etc. In fact, the Government of India too has undertaken larger mission of digitalizing India, enabling a Fit India and many others. The Government of India has introduced Apps, such as Cowin, Umang, Aarogya Setu, and many other apps truly believing that the life of every individual is precious and is taken care off. While at the individual level, the benefits include increased concern toward health and better and improved cooking at homes. COVID-19 has transformed the way individuals desired work and how the organizations delegated work. Table 2.2 elaborates the different approaches to HR practices in pre- and post-COVID-19 scenario.

Organizations are now more flexible in hiring and encouraging candidates with desired qualities to be approached from anywhere using technology. No barrier of location to hire. COVID-19 has ensured that location is no more important to be explaining ones' candidature. Baker (2020) explains that 32% of organizations are replacing full-time employees with contingent workers as a cost-saving measure while in a post-COVID-19 environment employees are expected to adjust how they work while the HR would shift toward a more human-focused approach (Mishra, 2020).

On one hand where the HR is making considerable effort to encourage, retain, and ensure performance for all its employees, the ready young generation to enter corporate world is worried and anxious and impacted in several ways. Generation-Y has been discussed in several studies and the impact that they may have in the business world, yet the thoughts and experiences of this generation as they have entered the work force are scarce (Meier et al., 2010). Gen-Y suggests different ideals in the workplace (Nagle, 1999).

TABLE 2.2 Differentiating Approach to HR Practices.

	Traditional HR approach	Post-COVID HR approach
Overall	People process oriented	Human-focused approach
Recruitment and selection	Formal	Dynamic
	Tenured—annual/Biannual/Quarterly	Staggered
Learning and development	Knowledge, skills, and behavioral program	More skill-based program
		e-Learning courses
	Development program both regular and virtual	Virtual programs
		Learning anywhere and anyhow
Onboarding	In person	Virtual onboarding with induction and orientation also virtual
		Companies are sharing videos and contents about work operations prior to onboarding
Work from home policy	Selective option	Policy encouraging WfH depending on business sector
		Clarifications to performance evaluations, team bonding, work time, differential pay, etc.
Performance management	Formal	Work/assignment-based, team-based
	Tenured—annual/Biannual/Quarterly, variables	

Generation-Y is defined as the ones born between 1982–2001 (Shimp, 2007). They are the ones who have grown up with technology and high-tech gadgets (Hunter, 2012). Characteristics of Gen-Y have been explained by various authors including multitasking having entrepreneurial initiative (Cennamo and Gardner, 2008), work quickly but with defined objectives (Bristow et al., 2011) (Table 2.3).

The labor force participation was witnessed to be increased from 37.2% to 36.8% in the trailing quarter while the worker population ratio increased to 34.2% from 33.7% in the September quarter. The reports of the MIE (Center for Monitoring Indian Economy) indicate that of 18.9 million salaried jobs lost in April–July, yet to be sought state-wise details. The data available clearly indicates that there are not many data available while it comes to

TABLE 2.3 Impact of COVID-19 on Youth.

	World	Source	India	Source
Education	COVID-19 disrupts education of more than 70% of youth	ILO (2020)	320 million learners in India have been adversely affected and transitioned to the e-learning industry, which comprises a network of 1.5 million schools	UNESCO (2020)
Mental health	One in two youths subject to depression anxiety says ILO survey on the effects of COVID-19	ILO (2020)	Common overreactive behavior among the general public	Das (2020)
	45% of youths of the USA reported a negative impact on mental health	Panchal et al. (2020)	Suicide cases in the state of Kerala increased	Yadav (2020)
	Study revealed that 40.4% of the sampled youth were suffering from psychological problems	Liang et al. (2020) Singh (2020)		
Employment	38% of young people are uncertain of their future career prospects	ILO (2020)	Over 1.3 crore youngsters lost their jobs in the lockdown. Another 1.4 crore jobs were lost in the age group of 25–29 years	Pettiwala (2020)
	Recently, it was announced that the UK unemployment rate has risen to its highest level for 2 years, with over 695,000 people being made redundant as a result of the pandemic		Labor force participation rate rose to 37.2% from 36.8% in the trailing quarter while the worker population ratio increased to 34.2% from 33.7% in the September quarter	McInnes and Rankin (2020)

category of jobs lost and the major sector and location of job lost. It is also clear that India lacks with systemic nationwide study (*Nathiya et al., 2020*). *Banerjee (2020) shares that there are a* scarce narrative discussions and cases on psychological impact of COVID-19 outbreak on youth. Thus, it is important to understand the perspective of Gen-Y on COVID-19 and its effect on their day-to-day routine life.

Gigauri (2020) shared that HRs lacked experience in managing stress due to unanticipated change due to spread of COVID-19 while simultaneously ensuring safe operations. Thus, there were opportunities to look into management practices which could make a difference to these drastic changes that were witnessed. Golden Pryor (1998) earlier explained the concept of 5P'S being purpose, principles, process, people, and performance as a strategic quality management effort. Discussing its relevance Shil et al. (2020) emphasized that the HR functions during the pandemic can attempt the 5Ps as explained by Pryor (1998) and can transform workplace by driving e-management.

Parry and Battista (2019) demonstrated that human resource management should help employees to use the advanced technologies in organizations. HRs over a period of time realized the importance of technology not just making an ease to HR operations but started exploring aligning all HR functions to the mainstream operations using technology. It is this which made a difference to cater to the business needs of transforming the overall viewpoint of looking at businesses and people perspective of operations. This compelled HRs to drive workplaces not limited to spaces and infrastructure and increase conveniences of people as a solution to operations.

2.3 METHODOLOGY

A survey was conducted among management students ranging between an age group of 20–35 years. 1000 students were sent an e-mail with a structured questionnaire using Google form, yet only 135 students responded back. Considering the online mode of response and disengagement of students in the pandemic scenario, the response rate of the questionnaire was calculated being 13.5%. The data collected reflects perspectives of the students on describing the role and challenges of the HR in post-COVID-19 scenario. 53% of the respondents did not have any experience. 30% of the respondents have experience up to 2 years. 15 respondents had experience of more than 2 and up to 5 years. 7 respondents had more than 5 years of experience.

Fifty students were also asked to send a written response to two open-ended questions as given below:

- *How has life changed as a student in the pandemic scenario?*
- *What do you see as the role of HR in post-pandemic scenario?*

Forty-six students responded and the subjective data was analyzed using qualitative methods. Word cloud was generated with and attempt to understand the popularity of terms used in response to the questions answered (Figure 2.1).

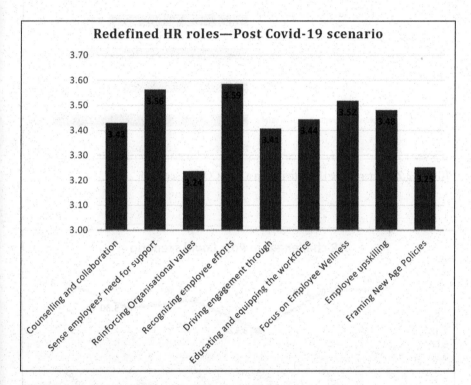

FIGURE 2.1   Redefined HR roles—Post Covid-19 scenario

Response analysis clearly indicates that recognizing employee efforts is the new role of the HR function in the post-COVID-19 circumstances. The respondents also feel that HR is now expected to be more concerned of the employees need for support and employee wellness (Figure 2.2).

The respondents were also of an opinion that the HR activities in a post-COVID scenario would majorly include employee social safety and engaging officials online on task basis. HRs are also expected to be encouraging learning for multitasking among its employees (Figure 2.3).

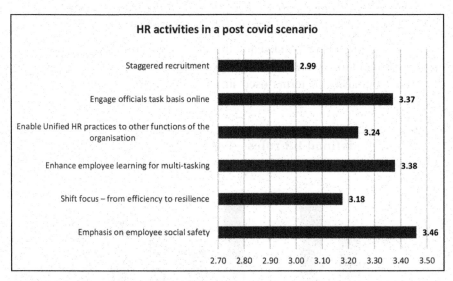

FIGURE 2.2 Perspective HR activities in a post-COVID scenario

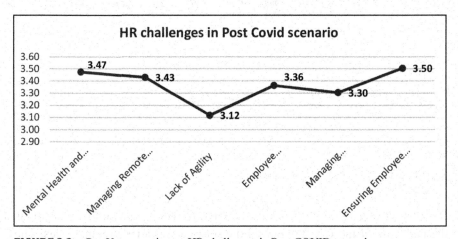

FIGURE 2.3 Gen Y perspective on HR challenges in Post COVID scenario

The Gen-Y respondents were of a clear opinion that ensuring employee engagement, mental health and well-being are some of major challenges that HR officials may face. Managing remote work and work allocation considering time, work-life balance of employees is equally challenging for officials.

The qualitative details of the data generated through the written response to the two questions asked have been as given in Table 2.4. On analyzing the qualitative data, it was very obvious that Gen-Y spend more time with family while they also extensively spend time on social media. A few respondents indicated that they have increased food intake with reduced physical movement. They also indicated that they understand the need for a healthy life, yet considering an average house in cities limited to two rooms was extremely difficult for them to think of health-conscious exercising. The routine of the respondents changed from focusing on studies to logins, online classes, etc. There were several students who mentioned that they found themselves to be lost during pandemic initial days. Many faced low interest in studies including concentration issues in spite of attending online classes (Table 2.5).

TABLE 2.4 Changes in Life Witnessed by Gen-Y.

Questions	Words	Types	Ratio	Words/Sentence
How has life changed as a student in the pandemic scenario?	2604	757	29%	21.5
What do you see as the role of HR in post-pandemic scenario?	2163	659	30%	23.0

An attempt has been made to create a word cloud based on the responses received as well as word linkage diagram. It is evident that the Gen-Y feels that most of their time was spent in classes or in social media. The Gen-Y opines that there are disadvantages as well as advantages associated with the pandemic. Many students were of the opinion that they played video games from morning to night or spent their time in front of blue screens. Many reflected their thoughts on it being a holiday yet with learning opportunities while others were worried of their examinations and career. A few of them also highlighted their increased efforts in ensuring a placement and considered it as a situation with opportunity.

While most of the Gen-Y respondents shared varied thoughts, yet, they responded with similarity in foreseeing the role of HR in post-pandemic scenario. It is very clear that HRs are likely to face numerous challenges. Yet, they are expected to be balanced in their approach in ensuring communication, motivation, engagement. Few respondents were reflective in sharing that the opportunities for the people are likely to continue while skill sets required to be grabbed, the opportunities need to be significantly developed.

TABLE 2.5 Qualitative Data Analysis.

2.4 ENSURING RIGHT HR POLICIES TO MANAGE COVID-19

NTPC has set a high benchmark with its polices for COVID-19-affected deceased employees. The organization has undertaken numerous efforts to ensure financially sustained and dignified life for affected family members. NTPC policies have supported continuing of medical facilities to all dependent family, facility of retention of company accommodation, extension of educational facilities to the school going children of deceased employees. The company also strategizes to enable economic rehabilitation scheme to ensure monthly income, group insurance to death (Millenium Post, 2021). Several companies made it simple for its employees to avail health facilities through Telemedicine like NLC India Limited.

Another company which has made up to media for their outstanding effort is Shriram Bioseed Genetics, A division of DCM Shriram Ltd. The company has focused on 21 days leave policy with immediate financial assistance of Rs. 10 k for employees with CTC below 7 lacs. The company also provides medical policy, financial loans for employees, ICU, nonrecoverable funeral benefits, etc. (LinkedIn, 2021).

Mellam (2021) in TCS context, explained the need for integration of work from home data with attendance, payroll system, performance, etc. The companies are also required to maintain and process working from office employee's data as per the redefined organization policies and business rules (Mellam, 2021). The HRs has now become enablers to health and safety of employees. Many organizations are working on anxiety, mindfulness, awareness on vaccination and overall well-being of employees.

There is a need for corporates to make a mind-set shift enabling organizational transformation during the difficult times. Companies need to make a focus on purpose than profit by enabling networks than traditional existing hierarchies. Leaders need to be more empowering and building trust than focusing on controlling. HRs are now required to be experimenting than working on plans. Finally, transparency matters the most. Sharing the reality with employees, setting right expectation and encouraging innovations and new ideas at workplace is the future to the post-pandemic scenario. A number of companies are organizing vaccination drives for the employees and their families by collaborating with nearby hospitals. A very important statement by UNICEF points out that "No one is Safe until everyone is safe" and the role of HR is vital while it focuses on ensuring everyone's safety at workplace by encouraging vaccination, only then the workplace is safe for all.

2.5 CONCLUSION

Human Resource is a multifaceted function that mainly manages people-related issues at workplace. HR managers are facing additional responsibility of ensuring employee well-being as well as addressing all people-related challenges that the organization or the employees may face during the pandemic. Organizations in association with HR teams have been able to tackle people-related concerns during and after lockdown with options, such as multiple shifts, alternate workdays, and rearranged workspaces, etc. Smaller companies have radically reformed their HR plans from hiring to letting employees go off. Driving strategic efforts to remote positions was essentially ensured to every employee who works on computer systems and is not required physically to be present in their job role.

The Gen-Y definitely has numerous anxieties associated with opportunities, work profile, and satisfaction, yet, they are optimistic toward business leaders and HR managers that focused efforts will enable performance-driven workforce. It is evident that remote communication will have to be more intensified in case the companies are looking forward to reinforce positive messages, rewards good behavior and initiative, and set firm expectations for the future.

Over a time, Work from Home has been accepted as a new normal even of COVID-19. It has become an acceptable fact that remote working situation are now continued indefinitely in specific sectoral companies. There are various behaviors associated with the HR policies. Identifying and differentiating between positive and negative employee behavior will need to be addressed differently. Strategies and tactics are likely to be modified to suit remote working that the physical workplace scenario.

The post-pandemic human resource official will have to go through an alteration where the new job role will not majorly differ yet the specifications and procedures they practice and enforce in the workplace will change drastically to suit the new reality. In most sectors, remote working conditions will definitely enable higher performance and lower cost-driven workplace changes.

2.6 KEY TAKEAWAYS OF THE CHAPTER

The chapter shares the perspective of Gen-Y on HR challenges and activities in post-COVID-19 scenario. The chapter is a unique attempt of sharing the HR practices pre- and post-COVID-19 scenario. The chapter provides an insight on the impact of COVID-19 on Youth in relevance to majorly education, mental health, and employment scenario. There is an insight of policies which have made a difference in pandemic scenario.

KEYWORDS

- post-pandemic HR
- Gen-Y
- best practices
- employee expectations

REFERENCES

Baker, M. 9 Future of Work Trends Post-COVID-19. June, 2020. https://www.gartner.com/smarterwithgartner/9-future-of-work-trends-post-covid-19/ (accessed Sep 15, 2020).

Banerjee, D. The COVID-19 Outbreak: Crucial Role the Psychiatrists Can Play. *Asian J. Psychiatr.* **2020,** *50,* 102014.

Bristow, D.; Amyx, D.; Castleberry, S. B.; Cochran, J. J. A Cross-generational Comparison of Motivational Factors in a Sales Career among Gen-X and Gen-Y College Students. *J. Pers. Sell. Sales Manage.* **2011,** *31* (1), 77–85.

Brooks, S. K.; Webster, R. K.; Smith, L. E.; Wesseley, S.; Greenberg, N.; Rubin, G. K. The Psychological Impact of Quarantine and How to Reduce It: Rapid Review of the Evidence. *Lancet* **2020,** *395* (1), 912–920.

Business Standard (BS). Post-COVID, 75% of 4.5 Lakh TCS Employees to Permanently Work from Home by '25; from 20%. 2020. https://www.businesstoday.in/current/corporate/post-coronavirus-75-percent-of-3-5-lakh-tcs-employees-permanently-work-from-home-up-from-20-percent/story/401981.html.

Cennamo, L.; Gardner, D. Generational Differences in Work Values, Outcomes and Person-organization Values Fit. *J. Manage. Psychol.* **2008,** *23* (8), 891–906.

Chakraborty, T.; Kumar, A.; Upadhyay, P.; Dwivedi, Y. K. Link between Social Distancing, Cognitive Dissonance, and Social Networking Site Usage Intensity: A Country-level Study During the COVID-19 Outbreak. *Internet Res.* **2021,** *31* (2), 419–456. doi:10.1108/intr-05-2020-0281.

Das, S. Mental Health and Psychosocial Aspects of COVID-19 in India: The Challenges and Responses. *J. Health Manage.* **2020,** *22* (2), 197–205.

Duffy, B. The Coronavirus Crisis: Who Has Been and Who Will Be Most Affected? Health Protection Research Unit in Emergency Preparedness and Response at Kings College London. IPSOS, August 23, 2020.

Galea, S.; Merchant, R. M.; Lurie, N. The Mental Health Consequences of COVID-19 and Physical Distancing: The Need for Prevention and Early Intervention. *JAMA Intern. Med.* **2020,** *180* (6), 817–818.

Gigauri, I. Effects of COVID-19 on Human Resource Management from the Perspective of Digitalization and Work-life-balance. *Int. J. Innov. Technol. Econ.* **2020,** *4* (31). doi:10.31435/rsglobal_ijite/30092020/7148.

Greer, T. W.; Payne, S. C. Overcoming Telework Challenges: Outcomes of Successful Telework Strategies. *The Psychol. Manage. J.* **2014,** *17* (2), 87.

Hunter, M. Generational Attitudes and Behaviour—The Nordic Page, 2012. https://www.tnp.no/norway/global/2859-generational-attitudes-and-behaviour.

ILO. ILO Youth and COVID-19, August 11, 2020. https://www.ilo.org/global/about-the-ilo/newsroom/news/WCMS_753060/lang--en/index.htm.

Karasek, R.; Theorell, T. *Healthy Work: Stress, Productivity, and the Reconstruction of Working Life.* Basic Books: New York; Vol. 66, No. 4, 1990, pp 525–526.

Liang, L.; Ren, H.; Cao, R.; Hu, Y.; Qin, Z.; Li, C.; et al. The Effect of COVID-19 on Youth Mental Health. *Psychiatr. Q.* **2020,** *17* (1), 15–54.

LinkedIn. 2021. https://www.linkedin.com/company/shriram-bioseed-genetics-a-division-of-dcm-shriram-ltd/?originalSubdomain=in.

McInnes, K.; Rankin, L. The Generational Impact of COVID-19. 2020. https://www.lexology.com/library/detail.aspx?g=5c1c1410-1bd1-4501-9a99-1e37fcb099db.

Meier, J.; Stephen, F.; Crocker, M. Generation Y in the Workforce: Managerial Challenges. *J. Human Res. Adult Learn.* **2010,** *6* (1), 1–11.

Mellam, S. Redefine the Office and Work Life after COVID-19. 2021. https://www.tcs.com/blogs/employees-remote-work-from-home-hrms-application.

Mishra, A. K. Role of Human Resource in the Post-COVID Environment. June 2020. http://bwpeople.businessworld.in/article/Role-of-Human-Resource-in-the-Post-COVID-Environment/19-06-2020-289219/ (accessed September 23, 2020).

Millenium Post. NTPC Sets Benchmark with Its Employee Friendly Policies. 2021. http://www.millenniumpost.in/business/ntpc-sets-benchmark-with-its-employee-friendly-policies-441599?infinitescroll=1.

Nagle, T. Coaching Generation X. Center for Coaching and Mentoring, 1999. http://www.coachingandmentoring.com/Articles/x's.html.

Nathiya, D.; Singh, P.; Suman, S.; Raj, P.; Tomar, B. S. Mental Health Problems and Impact on Youth Minds during the COVID-19 Outbreak: Cross-sectional (RED-COVID) Survey. *Soc. Health Behav.* **2020,** *3* (1), 83–88.

Panchal, N.; Kamal, O.; Cox; et al. The Implications of COVID-19 for Mental Health and Substance Use. KFF, 2020, https://www.kff.org/coronavirus-covid-19/issue-brief/the-implications-of-covid-19-for-mental-health-and-substance-use.

Parry, E.; Battista, V. The Impact of Emerging Technologies on Work: A Review of the Evidence and Implications for the Human Resource. *Emerald Open Res.* **2019,** *1* (5), doi:10.12688/emeraldopenres.12907.1.

Parmet, W. E.; Sinha, M. S. COVID-19: The Law and Limits of Quarantine. *N. Engl. J. Med.* **2020,** *382* (15), 28.

Pettiwala. Indian Youth can Revitalise COVID-battered Economy. June 29, 2020. https://economictimes.indiatimes.com/jobs/view-indian-youth-can-revitalisecovid-battered-economy/articleshow/76691975.cms?from=mdr.

Shimp, T. A. *Advertising, Promotion, and Other Aspects of Integrated Marketing Communications.* 7 (e) Thomson Corporation: Mason, USA, 2007.

Shil, M.; Barman, R.; Zayed, N.; Shahi, S.; Neloy, A. Global Transition of HR Practices in Covid-19 Pandemic Situation: A Systematic Review through 5P's Model of HRM. *Manage. Hum. Resour. Res. J.* **2020,** *9* (6), 50–56.

Singh, *The Week*, August 12, 2020. 10:29 IST. https://www.theweek.in/wire-updates/international/2020/08/12/fgn13-ilo-youth-depression.html.

Takeuchi, R.; Wang, M.; Marinova, S. V.; Yao, X. Role of Domain-specific Facets of Perceived Organizational Support during Expatriation and Implications for Performance. *Organ. Sci.* **2009,** *20* (3), 621–634.

Torales, J.; O'Higgins, M.; Castaldelli-Maia, J. M.; Ventriglio, A. The Outbreak of COVID-19 Coronavirus and Its Impact on Global Mental Health. *Int. J. Soc. Psychiatr.* **2020,** *66*, 3–6.

Umachandran. India COVID Tally, Gen Y & Democracy, Warming Africa and Others. 2020. https://www.livemint.com/news/business-of-life/mint-lite-india-covid-tally-gen-y-democracy-warming-africa-and-others-11603986915128.html.

UNESCO. Promoting Digital Education with Equity. 2020. https://en.unesco.org/news/promoting-digital-education-equity, (accessed Oct 21, 2020).

WEF. Resetting the Future of Work Agenda: Disruption and Renewal in a Post-COVID World. http://www3.weforum.org/docs/WEF_NES_Resetting_FOW_Agenda_2020.pdf (accessed October 25, 2020).

Worldometer Statistics. Reported Cases and Deaths by Country, Territory, or Conveyance. 2020. https://www.worldometers.info/coronavirus/ (accessed Oct 25, 2020).

WWF. To Prevent the Next Pandemic, We Must Transform Our Relationship with Nature. https://medium.com/@WWF/toprevent-the-next-pandemic-we-must-transform-our-relationshipwith-nature-c42ce9dffc62 (accessed Sep 15, 2020).

Yadav, P. N. COVID-19 Lockdown May Have Debilitating Effect on Alcoholics, Drug Addicts, Those in Rehab: Psychiatrists. Outlook, April 1, 2020, https://www.outlookindia.com/website/story/india-news-covid-19-lockdown-may-have-debilitating-effect-on-alcoholics-drug-addicts-those-in-rehab-psychiatrists/349820 (accessed Sep 15, 2020).

CHAPTER 3

Reimagining Post-Pandemic Communication Strategies at Workplace: A Mindful Shift

TRISHA BARUA[1*] and ANGSHUMAN BHATTACHARYA[2]

[1]*Associate, Talent Acquisition—CoE, Deloitte USI*

[2]*Deputy General Manager, Paradip Refinery, Indian Oil Corporation Limited*

*Corresponding author. E-mail: trisha.barua6@gmail.com

ABSTRACT

Unprecedented advent of events is a major challenge because it hits hard when the world is least ready to retaliate. The year 2020 will be etched in the pages of history for being a harbinger of chaos and uncertainty owing to the COVID-19 outbreak worldwide. The pandemic has been a real testing time for not only the world economy facing real challenges to grapple for existence, it wreaked havoc on human emotions too and raised real questions on existentialism.

To elucidate some of the salient problems that the outbreak of the virus has had on employee communication in the workplace, this chapter sought to critically identify, diagnose, and offer a solution to the unexplored topic in the field of importance of communication of employees. To address the gap, the following chapter introduces the need for communication in a post-pandemic world and offers insight into factors of the importance of the same in the present time to engage the workforce into productivity.

Human Resource Management in a Post-Epidemic Global Environment: Roles, Strategies, and Implementations.
Tanusree Chakraborty, Nandita Mishra, Madhurima Ganguly, & Bipasha Chatterjee (Eds.)
© 2023 Apple Academic Press, Inc. Co-published with CRC Press (Taylor & Francis)

To keep the communication going, especially during trying times like these, compassion, touch, and comprehension are required more than ever. It cannot be expected that since we may out of nowhere be working forever from home, the whole family unit will curve to suit our necessities. Consequently, how to speak with individuals dispersed in diverse locations and assorted conditions is the issue that should be tended to both from employers and employees' point of view.

Dominated primarily by secondary data, the study shows how internal communication, employee–supervisor communication, management–employee communication and the colossal importance of communication has undergone a paradigm shift since the outbreak of the grave pandemic and is susceptible to more structural change in days to come. The world will open to new normal communication and the latter will be given its due recognition as people look for community well-being and solidarity.

3.1 EMPLOYEE RELATIONS IN ORGANIZATIONS POST-PANDEMIC: AN OVERVIEW

There was a time when organizational communication was predominantly a top-down approach with very little scope for feedback to play any role of amendment. Management generally used to create policies and procedures in a way which used to be circulated among the employees more as a diktat than as a participatory activity. Communication now is a more flexible approach to building a strong relationship between the management, the employees and the customers. With a plethora of options available in the modern time, employee communication has changed over the years. From face-to-face interaction to communication on social media platforms, employee communication has undergone a veritable metamorphosis.

Effective communication leads to efficient employee relations in the workplace. An organization must be focused on maintaining a cordial and positive relationship with its employees so that it has full professional commitment and workplace loyalty of the latter. The typical touch points in an efficacious employee relation include liaison between the management and the employees which demands creation of policies surrounding issues such as fair compensation, useful benefits, reasonable working hours, proper work-life balance, equal pay for equal work, etc.

The year 2020 will be etched forever in the pages of history as a "notified disaster" owing all due credit to the pandemic. From losing jobs to waking up in the novel set up of work from home, human emotions, integrity, and perseverance all these months have been tried and tested. The age-old employer–employee relationship status has undergone a stupendous change and remodeling the same is now been considered a herculean task in several organizations big and small. The uncertainties and unprecedented nature of COVID-19 will compel employees to maintain a harmonious and diplomatic relationship with both their managers and the HR departments of the organization. The status of the employer–employee relationship has hence experienced a huge paradigm shift with the onset of the pandemic. The true effect of it will be reflected in how positive both the employer and employee remain with each other in days to come.

"Catastrophes like the COVID-19 pandemic normally occur in a cyclical pattern. Every bad economic cycle characterized by economic slowdown, job cuts, and supply chain disruption will be followed by a good economic cycle characterized by robust economic growth, boost in demand, and enhanced employment opportunities," says Mahesh Singhi, MD, Singhi Advisors (Singhi, 2020). With India officially entering into recession in November 2020, the leadership and HR departments of the organizations have a major role to play in keeping their teams motivated and maintaining a positive ambience within the organization. The HR departments need to be more watchful than ever of any negative influence that the current situation may brew and have to ascertain if the employees have been successful in remaining positive and adjusted to the ongoing adverse condition by force or by choice. The advent of an unprecedented change in the market can effectively act as an acid test for employer–employee relationship that can help differentiate between the employee who is truly committed to organizational objectives and the one who is working under unavoidable obligation. Singhi also adds that when the economic uncertainties show some improvements in days to come, post the pandemic, and the periphery of the job market gets broadened, employees who stuck to a particular company forcefully due to lack of opportunities or the poor condition of the job market would largely remain unhappy and unproductive due to their failure to strike the right balance with the organizations.

3.2 CHANGES IN EMPLOYEE COMMUNICATION AFTER COVID-19

Experts believe that only companionship, a helping attitude and an effective communication stance can help the community to overcome this crisis by helping each other and holding each other up. Internal communication professionals ensure a smooth sailing of the business with the help of effective cross-departmental collaboration, flawless communication, employee empowerment, and engagement to help build a positive employee experience. Internal communication expedites timely information that helps keep employees engaged so they can remain focused on achieving corporate goals. The role of internal communication team is all the more vital now as organizations are still adapting to the changes introduced in the COVID-19 stricken market.

The pandemic has played a major role to identify the benefits of internal communication and has highlighted notable shifts in the process of employer–employee communication which are given below:

3.2.1 DIGITAL TRANSFORMATION OF INTERNAL COMMUNICATION

The phrase "work from home" is not new in the professional domain, but it is the cult word of 2020 as remote work is both a change and challenge for many. There are constraints, such as poor internet connection and lack of proper workspace at home. Parents have to divide their time between their work and looking after their children.

While most of the companies have shifted to remote working, companies, especially dealing with essential services like insurance, banking, petroleum products, healthcare, traveling (goods and freight), etc. have staff working in combination pattern, that is, both remotely and from the usual workplace. Therefore, the companies are in dire need of an upgraded communication tool so that they can reach the employees devoid of time and location constraints.

While staying at home has been a blessing in disguise for many, for many others, it is still a curse because they usually end up feeling lonely at home, especially those who are stuck in some other cities away from their families. People are even finding it difficult to maintain a proper work-life balance, because they are mostly unable to differentiate between working hours, weekends and day offs. Earlier which was a 9-to-7 job is now occasionally extended to 9-to-11 with barely any time left for the self or the family.

3.2.2 PARADIGM SHIFT FROM TRADITIONAL COMMUNICATION METHODS

Many companies are finding that remote working is rather facilitating the medium of communication with the aid of digital platform, with more speed, timeliness, and effectiveness. Digital platforms, such as video conferencing, instant messengers, corporate social media have had unimaginably positive impact over the few months to strengthen organizational communication like never before.

Printed newsletters, townhall conferences and meetings in persons, lengthy e-mail correspondences will soon be obsolete. These traditional communication channels were anyway turning redundant even before the pandemic. It was however very difficult to get the organizations ditch these outdated mediums because the former was highly resistant to change. Now that the organizations have experienced the benefits of fast and instant communications, this newly adapted change is here to stay for a good amount of time even after the pandemic fares us a final adieu.

3.2.3 IMPORTANCE OF TIMELY AND FACTUAL INFORMATION

Since the global crisis is an unexpected guest with no prior notice, news and events revolving around it is as ambiguous and uncertain. The situation with COVID-19 has been in constant change with all directives, policies, rules, regulations, and news related to it has been constantly changing.

With the slightest occurrence of anything important and crucial must be immediately communicated to the employees to safeguard their safety and health. Time-lags jeopardize the immediate need of the hour. They are voids which are usually filled with speculation, rumor, and misinformation. This pandemic has witnessed several fake news, conspiracy theories and hoaxes circulating on the internet and social media. Organizations must keep abreast of the ongoing news circulation and continue timely communication with their employees, lest it exploits the latter's weaknesses during trying times.

3.2.4 GREATER FOCUS ON EMPLOYEE WELL-BEING

It was always of utmost importance to the internal communication team to keep a keen eye on employee health and well-being, owing to the pandemic, it is more in demand than ever. Employees working remotely are isolated, stressed, and worried most of the time. For them struggling with mental health issues, wellness programs, and activities can help with coping mechanism. Employees working remotely need to ensure that they are working from safe workplaces. If they meet with an accident or are injured during remote working, appropriate guidelines for the same must be issued by the organization. Organizations too are cooperating hand in hand with their employees because it is trying time for both the parties. To cope with employee burnout and exhaustion, organizations are conducting online activities like weekend lunch sessions, workout at home sessions and regular water cooler conversations to break the monotony of indoor working.

3.3 ONLINE COMMUNICATION: UTILIZATION OF TECHNOLOGY IS A POST-PANDEMIC AGENDA

Even before the pandemic made its unannounced official appearance, the traditional internal communication strategy was already experiencing a paradigm shift with workplace communication landscape changing with the latest virtual communication trends and use of intelligent bots to answer commonly asked employee questions. Recruiters are now relying more on texting to stay connected with their employees. Employees too are more dependent on instant messaging and have gladly given up the lengthy and formal e-mail communication. However, communication with the use of latest technology is not an easy ball game. Informal methods of communications may be the latest trend, but people also need to know how to use this platform more accurately and not let communication go haywire.

The most common strategies for putting technology to an effective use for communication are:

3.3.1 AVAILABILITY OF VARIOUS COMMUNICATION CHANNELS

While some employees feel more comfortable communicating through phone or messaging tools, some employees still prefer face-to-face communication to address any query or an issue. An open-door policy works best for these kinds of employees. Organizations must be inclusive in adapting strategies that will benefit both the kinds of employees. Organizations must assure their employees that digital communication is an easy and more convenient way to reach out to their employers at any time and that their issues will be dealt with without fail.

3.3.2 CLARIFY WAYS IN WHICH ORGANIZATIONS WILL COMMUNICATE DURING A CRISIS

Internal communication of an organization needs to assure the employees that during any emergency situation, all sorts of communication will be conveyed to the latter with utmost accuracy and on time. Besides office, WhatsApp groups and common mail groups, organizations can use their official social media pages to stay connected with the employees. For example, organizations can announce the name of the monthly star performers on social media. Similarly, during the cyclone "Amphan" several areas in Kolkata and around West Bengal were worst affected. Many areas went without electricity and drinking water for more than a week. For employees who have to work remotely after a storm or any other disaster, regular updated workplace communication and empathy for the challenges they are facing will be held in high regard and will bring the workforce together.

This is another situation where mobile communication will be beneficial for the employers and employees. Employers can provide with time-sensitive updates in a jiffy and employees too can seek help for any ongoing project without having to wait for a formal face-to-face appointment. Deloitte, for instance, has also suggested after a study that organizations if can set up internal channels for their communication platform can give employees an opportunity to provide feedback on how far the organization has been successful in handling the crisis.

3.3.3 ENGAGING THE GROUPS WORKING REMOTELY

Remote working has taken a toll on employees' personal life as well as mental health. Managers in these cases need to wear capes of superheroes as well as be proactive and come to their rescue with utmost humility, cooperation, and empathy. Managers can provide the employees with information on what level of quality is expected and what measurable goals are to be achieved for the overall success of the organization. Direct and frequent communication can help a lot in these cases and a clear channel of conversation must be maintained.

Training and development are the keys to competitive advantage. Blended learning tools like e-learning platforms or virtual classrooms besides the traditional in-person teaching sessions allow employees to maintain a flexible schedule. Managers can use for one's own ends, these learning tools and enthusiasm of the employees to increase employee engagement.

Social engagement within the workplace is another way to strengthen the employer–employee relationship. Employees can take part in promotion of company thoughts, ideas, and upcoming projects on the official website or social media pages to feel a sense of belongingness in the entire activity. Introducing employees to the latest technology will also help whip up ideas, ameliorate innovation, and fortify company performance.

3.4 LEADERS' ROLE IN LEADING TEAM COMMUNICATION IN THE POST-PANDEMIC PERIOD

It requires no elaboration to mention that motivation of employees toward performing their job has hit rock bottom during the crisis that has shaken the entire world. Organizations are trying really hard to keep their workforces' spirit high so that the ultimate goal of doing business does not get derailed. The companies need to take care of not only the safety of the employees but they also must cater to the higher level needs. Along with that it must also help them to distinguish the different phases of the crisis based on their nature and length, which are the shelter-in-place, the re-opening and the post-COVID-19 phases (Joly, 2020).

According to an article in McKinsey and Company, the fundamental tools of effective communication will act as a catalyst in bettering employee communication during crisis. To achieve the target, leaders need to focus on four primary organizational behavior to navigate the pandemic and recovery.

3.4.1 BUILDING A DYNAMIC AND COLLABORATIVE TEAM STRUCTURE

The teams need to have a flexible built so that it can be remodeled according to future needs and changes. Each team should be small units comprising of mixed individuals with cross-functional skills and must be assigned a leader to have unity of command. The chosen leader needs to have creative problem-solving skills along with critical thinking abilities, needs to be resilient, and battle tested. The leaders will then empower the teams by staying connected by not participating directly in the decision-making process but by letting the teams to take decisions with a clear goal.

Collaboration and transparency between the teams and the leaders will lead to a successful communication. Leaders should be cognizant of the employees who are taking smart risks and be empathetic toward those who are anxious.

3.4.2 DEMONSTRATION OF CALM AND OPTIMISM DURING A CRISIS

For staying calm and remaining optimistic under pressure, leaders must adapt themselves to the practice of integrative awareness, that is, being aware of the changing reality in the outside and their emotional and physical response to the same. A personal operating model can help leaders perform their best.

A leader can be proactive only when he is aware of the myriad of situations that can unfold during testing times. Therefore, it is essential for the leader to be interactive with both the internal and external world so that he is able to communicate the best options and alternatives to their teams.

Regulation of emotions is another important criterion for effective communication. While in a stressful situation, it is important to take a pause to ruminate and scrutinize the situation and engage the rational mind before choosing to respond. For example, during a videoconference the leader is not able to answer particular questions related to the day's agenda (due to some prior stress he or she is undergoing) and the most common way to evade the situation is to avoid. But if the leader takes a long pause, engages in some casual chats and then decides to response, the result will be much more effective than just being ignorant.

Contemplating on how it could have been better or how was it better than the last time and what are the blind spots that need to be addressed next. Only a true leader can inculcate this practice in a team and it can henceforth contribute toward a healthy feedback session where there will be lot more opportunities for collaborative learning than judgemental criticism.

What may seem like a difficult thing to do during the times of crisis is to balance work commitments with the physical well-being. Remote working has taken a heavy toll on both employee personal and mental health. To cope with this, meditation, breathing exercises, indoor cardio activities and even power naps can help rejuvenate both the mind and the body. Leaders need to be more observant of employee well-being and burnout during a crisis situation. Group activities on a weekly basis can be encouraged to help keep the performance level high and mental health stable (Brassey and Kruyt, 2020).

3.4.3 MAKING DECISIONS AMID UNCERTAINTY

Pausing and taking a break can facilitate far better a decision-making process rather than one taken in haste or under stress. It is extremely important for a decision maker to step back and anticipate. Taking a break also allows for the perspective to broaden and helps clear the fog in the head. The ability to probe and evaluate how things might in future unfold, and to proactively commence working accordingly can help avoid knee-jerk reactions that might lead to poor outcomes. However, as a result, to have maximum cooperation, leaders must involve as many stakeholders as possible because crisis is the team where teamwork comes to the rescue. The "fishbowl" method of decision-making can be a useful way to plan things in advance in which decision makers and key experts mutually consult and come to a consensual conclusion. A majority of team members can observe the meeting which builds understanding without having to make an extra communication step forward.

3.4.4 COMPASSIONATE LEADERSHIP DURING CRISIS

Awareness, empathy, and compassion are the key qualities of a true business leader that can help him lead during a crisis. Leaders must pivot from their traditional management style and must demonstrate compassion in order to be effective.

There are five major ways in which compassionate leadership can be initiated in group communication:

Initiate talks of compassion: It is never an easy task to show compassion and empathy to others, more so in a crisis situation when people are most likely to misunderstand empathy as sympathy. A leader must know how to initiate a conversation on empathy. He or she must be a patient and empathetic listener and must clarify their intention about the conversation.

Treat oneself with compassion: While meting out empathy to others, a leader must not forget to treat oneself with compassion. Only a sound mind can provide sound solutions to pressing problems. It is always better to remember the example of airplanes in this context, when it says "put your oxygen mask first before helping the person sitting next to you."

Schedule time to practice compassion: As leaders, a person has to know the organization like the palm of his hands. He or she has to be fluent with the group dynamics that works best for the teams. Practicing compassion is as important as daily exercise. Human emotions are dynamic and so to keep up with the dynamism of the members of the team, a leader must be proactive in his or her thought process.

Foster a strong connection with different work groups: Building a strong connection with all the employees is essential in the work space. For example, a marketing manager can think of allowing an employee to take a day off if the weather is too stringent like heavy rain. If there is a fresher in the team, and if he or she is driven toward pursuing higher studies through online programs, a leader must encourage by having a long conversation and also suggesting best-suited programs for the employee that will be aligned with the organizational needs. If there is a woman who had just had a baby, a leader must be empathetic toward her and can relax her time schedule by allowing her to work at her pace rather than pressing her with deadlines.

Use one's leadership position to alleviate challenges: Weekly team meets are usually potboilers for conversations mostly related to organizational policies. As a leader starts hearing inputs from the team, he or she must consider what he or she can do to provide the best solutions. The crisis situation has given rise to issues like extended paid leave, additional sick days, expanded healthcare coverage, flexible schedules to accommodate the needs of the self and the family and remote work policy as location agnostic.

3.5 THE NEW HR COMMUNICATION TOOLKIT FOR A POST-COVID WORLD

The HR toolkit has ample assets to adapt successfully to support a remote workforce that can help in effective leading, managing, and engaging employees remotely.

3.5.1 ENSURING CONTINUITY IN COMMUNICATION

What organizations have learned from the pandemic is that proactive and consistent communication is an indispensable part of employee engagement. Effective corporate communication is a kickstart to a great way of promoting stability and employee cohesion during uncertain times. For example, weekly feedbacks or communication sessions on best practices, employee needs and expected future needs will help in cohesive decision-making and help leaders develop the necessary skills to guide a remote workforce and foster productivity. Moreover, not all employees are tech savvy or are game for a remote working set up. It is extremely vital for these kinds of employees to develop the ability to communicate effectively with the team members, leaders, managers, and stakeholders. For coping with such issues, encouragement toward regular use of online video communication platforms, such as Skype, Google Hangouts, Zoom, Google Meet, Microsoft Teams, and others can facilitate collaboration, group cohesion, foster belongingness, reinforce relationships, and trust and help build culture (Mishra et al., 2020).

3.5.2 PRESERVING ORGANIZATIONAL CULTURE IN CHALLENGING TIMES

No matter what exigent circumstances the organization is going through, it is important to make an effort to maintain and uphold the company culture and keep staff motivation high to promote teamwork. HR department's role here can be elaborated as a facilitator to newly set up remote workers by helping them identify the most ergonomic set up in the house to work remotely. Other ways that HR can help the remotely placed employees are to make available necessary supplies at subsidized rates, nudging staff to take breaks to allow for both physical and mental rejuvenation and also providing an internal platform to the employees to informally engage digitally to foster camaraderie and culture when assembling around the coffee machine or at the office canteen is no longer an option (Shelton, 2020).

3.5.3 ESTABLISHING SUSTAINABLE LEADERSHIP

Now it is the best time for both the managers and the staff to contemplate on what best practices can they implement in their daily routine to succeed remotely. Proactive and self-motivated besides, both the managers and the employees need to be abreast with the changing policies and occurrence of events. Remote working is the new normal but is here to stay for quite some time more even after the crisis evades. Since all hard work expects as well as desires recognition, HR managers can enable remote reward programs to recognize the talents to boost employee engagement and motivate them toward better performance. It is of paramount importance of both the HR fraternity and the HR staff to play a primal role in how the remote work experience is aligned, shaped, and delivered to the employees.

COVID-19 has been a transformational experience for the entire world. One of the most important lessons learned is how to help each other and be each other's companion in such horrid times. Even after the crisis passes, few shifts in work-life pattern will be a long-term change in the organizational policies. For instance, a sustainable remote work environment is attainable only if few modifications are made to the existing programs and strategy, with the help of which, the HR can ameliorate employee experience, engagement, and productivity.

3.6 UPDATING EMPLOYEE COMMUNICATIONS PLAN FREQUENTLY: NEED OF THE HOUR

The current state of affairs regulating the organizations is temporary. With further unprecedented events awaiting reveal, companies must be proactive and visionary in facing any challenging situation at any time. As the crisis is not static, the aftermaths are going to be dynamic as well and to stay upfront and at par with it, organizations need to constantly update its policies ahead of time so that they are future ready.

Till now, we have sufficiently discussed in our study that internal communication is the bedrock of any organization and without an effective employee communications strategy, it becomes highly challenging for organizations, big and small to strengthen collaboration, contribute to employees' health and well-being, and help them stay productive. Organizations need to be more committed toward keeping their employees constantly updated about any recent changes in the market and for this, the communication need to be timely, factual, and refurbished.

With all the complexities of the modern world worsened further by the effects of the pandemic, employees face constant clutter and overloaded with information. In a time of information galore, the competitive edge of the companies would lie in their competency to affect the behaviors, attitudes, and actions of the employees through timely, relevant, genuine, and contextual information and dialogue. With proper platform to connect and communicate, the end result will be a workforce that will be able to make decisions on time, with accuracy and with consistence with the business strategy that will uphold the purpose, mission, and vision of the organization.

A management model with the right cauldron mixes of leadership, teambuilding, and communications to hold them all together will help foster organizational effectiveness. Gary F. Gates in his article published in the Institute for Public Relations, talked about few relevant points that can be considered as the need of the hour for reinforcing the internal communications strategy that can be adapted by the companies into their existing ones. He begins by mentioning how internal communications must be so planned that it helps aid the actions and decisions of the C-Suite in clear understanding, engagement, discussion, and debate. Just like any other expense borne by the organization, internal communication and its accoutrements must be funded because it is an essential part of the holistic development of the organization. Communication within the organization should be regularly updated on the basis of facts and has to have a touch of empathy so that the organization is able to sense the workforce's state of mind and respects the need for information and context and satiates the demand for prudence and sensitivity. Since global business has moved to virtual medium now, the need for clarity and honesty is all the more relevant now. Only with the help of mutual conscientiousness and commitment toward each other, both the employers and the employees will be able to build a sustainable communication channel that will withstand the test of time.

3.7 BEST PRACTICES IN MAINTAINING POST-PANDEMIC CRISIS COMMUNICATION STRATEGY

Pandemics and epidemics have occurred before and it can strike again in future. To combat similar situations in future, organizations need strategies that leverages a number of components. Proactive planning helps in ensuring that the right information reaches the employees on time. Developing a communication plan to sail through crisis should form a critical part of the internal communications strategy. The following steps can be considered as effective ways to ensure the plan to mitigate any future occurrence of similar crisis.

Anticipate crises: A regular enactment of faux situations of crises can help organizations simulate their actions and decisions based on the same. For this, a crisis management team must be allotted in organizations who will engage in brainstorming sessions with representative employees and the management.

Create a crisis team and assign responsibilities: Whenever a crisis hits, it is always the top management that delivers the public statements. But a lot goes internally when it comes to effectively managing a crisis. Therefore, having a backup team comprising representatives from HR, legal, communications, and subject experts will be able to provide the organizations the much-needed resort during the crisis period.

Map out internal audience for better reach: The organization must be flexible enough to accommodate the requirements of each and every employee undergoing the situational crisis. For example, an employee working remotely will have connectivity problems at home. Whereas another employee involved in sales will have problem with smooth transportation and might not be able to make it on time at the client meeting. Offline workers like delivery drivers might face problem with lack of logistics. Warehouse operatives might have to tackle a fire that has broken out. Therefore, with a huge inclusive workforce comes a plethora of hindrances. Grouping these individuals according to their unique needs will help the organization identify any communication gaps that could cause issues during a crisis.

Audit communication channels according to the chosen audience: Identifying the appropriate communication channel for the appropriate audience will provide a better accessibility to the organization. A multichannel communication approach, such as e-mail, social media, manager cascades, and printed posters are appropriate for communal areas. The organization needs to be aware of whether the information stored in these channels are updated on a regular basis and when was the last time their feasibility was tested.

Install two-way crisis alert system: Crisis communication can never be one-sided. As one arrives with potential threats to safety, the employees must be able to instantly connect with the managers as well as the crisis management team must have an instant visibility and identify a beneficiary at risk. For example, intranet broadcast messages on WhatsApp or through SMS can send instant alert to all the employees and they too are prompted to confirm receipt.

Safety and emergency protocols must be well versed: Ensuring that the staff are well informed and take cognizance of their responsibilities both during a crisis and in their day-to-day roles can help manage situations way more effectively. The protocols must be accessible, visible, and easy to locate. A regular update of the protocols must be initiated by the organization and they must ensure that the staff has read them. Many companies include the safety protocols right during the onboarding but regular training or monthly awareness days with quizzes and polls can help the staff reminisce the protocols and their applicability by heart.

3.8 CONCLUSION

The COVID-19 pandemic has proved yet again that change is the only constant. It took another 100 years and another pandemic since the Spanish Flu for the mankind to realize that impermanence is the only permanent thing. And to overcome such situations people must hold each other closer and must thrust trust on one another to build a sustainable future with a reliable network based on strong teamwork. The study helped us to a conclusion that internal communications managers and employees in any situation of crises are two overlapping worlds that can exist only in coexistence. The organizational policies must cater more to the needs of the employees in critical situations as they are the fuel for the businesses to run. The paradigm shift is from the organization as a whole to the individuals who make up the organization as often the makers are left ignored while celebrating the achievements of the organization as a whole.

The 3 Ps that will help the management to proactively design and implement cope up mechanisms in future similar situations are predicting a crisis, planning the defence and practicing the protocols (Lombardi, 2016). Joly in his book states that business is all about putting employees and human relationships at the heart of how a business operates. This is a time when organization's performance is not defined by the profits earned in share but a time when it will be judged on the basis of company's leadership prowess during a crisis and its abilities in upholding its stakeholders. In an article by McKinsey and Company, communications are set to become more personal post-pandemic as organizations gear up for the re-opening phase. Leaders during this re-entry phase need to be more sensitive than before to employees' needs. They need to gauge the mental readiness of the employees before initiating the re-entry. While some workers will be enthusiastic about returning to office, there still will be many others who will not be ready to venture out yet. Even if people are ready or are forced to enter back into the workspace, they will be constantly worried about their own health and that of their families (Alexander et al., 2020).

COVID-19 has not only been a sad experience but a powerful experience for all of us. It has not only brought the world closer together spatially, but emotionally we have been able to take cognizance of the fact that human camaraderie and not share market reports will lead an organization to its ultimate success.

KEYWORDS

- **employee communication**
- **post-pandemic communication**
- **new normal**
- **leadership roles**
- **role of technology**

REFERENCES

Alberti, S. COVID-19: How Can HR Ensure Communication is Effective Post-pandemic? *HRD Connect.* 2020. https://student.unsw.edu.au/how-do-i-cite-electronic-sources.html (accessed September, 2020).

Baker, M. Nine Future of Work Trends Post-COVID-19. *Gartner.* 2020. https://www.gartner.com/smarterwithgartner/9-future-of-work-trends-post-covid-19/.html (accessed October, 2020).

Burjek, A. Employee Communication How-to's During a Crisis. *Workforce.com.* 2020. https://www.workforce.com/news/employee-communication-how-tos-during-a-crisis.html (accessed October, 2020).

Burjek, A. How to Use Technology in Your Internal Communications Strategy. *Workforce.com.* 2020. https://www.workforce.com/news/how-to-use-technology-in-your-internal-communications-strategy.html (accessed November, 2020).

Caroline, D. How COVID-19 Has Changed Employee Communication. *Deskalerts.* August 13, 2020. https://www.alert-software.com/blog/covid-employee-communications.

Fallon, N. *Managing from Home? Here's How to Keep Your Team Engaged during Coronavirus,* CO. 2020. https://www.uschamber.com/co/run/human-resources/keeping-remote-employees-engaged.html (accessed November, 2020).

Grates, G. How COVID-19 Is Forcing CEOs to Rethink the Importance of Internal Communications. Institute for Public Relations, 2020. https://instituteforpr.org/how-covid-19-is-forcing-ceos-to-rethink-the-importance-of-internal-communications/.html (accessed October, 2020).

Gupta, S. Employer-Employee Relations: Challenges during and Post-COVID-19. *HR World from The Economic Times.* July 8, 2020. https://hr.economictimes.indiatimes.com/news/workplace-4-0/employer-employee-relations-challenges-during-and-post-covid-19/76858266.html (accessed October, 2020).

Harter, J. COVID-19: What Employees Need from Leadership Right Now. *Gallup.* 2020. https://www.gallup.com/workplace/297497/covid-employees-need-leaders-right.aspx.html (accessed October, 2020).

How Will Employee Communications change after COVID-19?. Reward Gateway: The Employee Engagement People., n.d. Retrieved December 2nd from https://www.rewardgateway.com/employee-engagement-guide/employee-communication-changes.

Irani, R. Personal Communication [Personal Interview published in HR World from *The Economic Times*]. June 22, 2020. https://hr.economictimes.indiatimes.com/news/workplace-4-0/managing-employee-emotions-will-be-a-major-challenge-for-hr-heads-in-a-post-covid-environment-ruzbeh-irani-mm/76508405.html (accessed November, 2020).

Joly, H. Lead Your Team into a Post-pandemic World. *Harvard Business Review.* May 08, 2020. https://hbr.org/2020/05/lead-your-team-into-a-post-pandemic-world.html (accessed October, 2020).

Jouany, V.; Martic, K. Remote Work: Twenty Ways Engage and Connect with Your Remote Employees. *Smarp.* April 08, 2020. https://blog.smarp.com/remote-work-20-ways-to-engage-and-connect-with-your-remote-employees.

Jouany, V. Six Experts Explain How COVID-19 Is Changing Internal Communications. *Smarp.* May 7, 2020. https://blog.smarp.com/experts-explain-how-covid-19-is-changing-internal-communications.

Leroy, C. Employee Engagement and Communications in a Post-Coronavirus World. *Switch by Payfit.* September 17, 2020. https://switch.payfit.com/en/employee-engagement-and-communication-in-a-post-coronavirus-world/.

Lombardi, G. Personal Communication [Personal Interview]. February 14, 2016.

Mazzei, A.; Ravazzani, S. Manager-employee Communication during a Crisis: The Missing Link. *Corp. Commun.* **2011,** *3,* 243–254.

Mendy, A.; Stewart, M.; VanAkin, K. *A Leader's Guide: Communicating with Teams, Stakeholders and Communities during COVID-19,* McKinsey and Company, 2020. https://www.mckinsey.com/business-functions/organization/our-insights/a-leaders-guide-communicating-with-teams-stakeholders-and-communities-during-covid-19.html (accessed December, 2020).

Mishra, A. K.; Kar, A. K. Role of Human Resource in the Post-COVID Environment. *People.* June 19, 2020. http://bwpeople.businessworld.in/article/Role-of-Human-Resource-in-the-Post-COVID-Environment/19-06-2020-289219/.html (accessed November, 2020).

Rowinski, T. Five Steps to Practicing Compassionate Leadership during a Crisis. *People Matters*. September 13, 2020. https://www.peoplemattersglobal.com/blog/leadership/5-steps-to-practicing-compassionate-leadership-during-a-crisis-26960.

Segal, C. Five Ways to Boost Employee Engagement rhrough Technology. CoxBLUE, n.d. https://www.coxblue.com/5-ways-to-boost-employee-engagement-throughtechnology/#:~:text=Technology%20within%20the%20workplace%20continues, portals%20make%20employee%20engagement%20limitless.html (accessed November, 2020).

Shelton, J. Adapting the HR Communications Toolkit for a Post-COVID World. 2020. https://www.tlnt.com/adapting-the-hr-communications-toolkit-for-a-post-covid-world/.html (accessed November, 2020).

Singh, P. Abraham Maslow's 'Hierarchy of Needs' Becomes Even More Relevant in the Era of COVID-19. *Psychreg*. April 08, 2020. https://www.psychreg.org/hierarchy-of-needs-covid-19/.html (accessed October, 2020).

Singhi, M. Examining Employer-Employee Relationship in the Context of COVID-19. *HR World from the Economic Times*. August 10, 2020. https://hr.economictimes.indiatimes.com/news/trends/employee-experience/examining-employer-employee-relationship-in-the-context-of-covid-19/77456361.html (accessed September, 2020).

Theologi, R. How to Effectively Communicate with Your Employees during Crisis. *Speakap*. 2020. https://www.speakap.com/en/blog/how-to-communicate-with-employees-during-crisis.

Thurtle, C. How to Communicate Effectively to Employees During a Crisis. *Qualtrics*. April 9, 2020. https://www.qualtrics.com/blog/employee-communication-during-crisis/.

Vaughan, T. Employee Communications and the Coronavirus: What You Need to Know. *Poppulo*. March 21, 2020. https://www.poppulo.com/blog/employee-communications-and-the-coronavirus-what-you-need-to-know/.

Waytz, A.; Gray, K. Does Online Technology Make Us More or Less Sociable? A Preliminary Review and Call for Research. *Perspect. Psychol. Sci.* **2018**, *13*, 473–491. https://pubmed.ncbi.nlm.nih.gov/29758166/.

Zurich. The Future of Employee Benefits and Insurance in a Post-COVID World. 2020. https://www.zurich.com/en/knowledge/topics/workforce-protection/the-future-of-employee-benefits-and-insurance-in-a-post-covid-world.html (accessed November, 2020).

CHAPTER 4

Tech Detox and Tech Savvy: Two New Post-Pandemic Verticals of HR

RANITA BASU[1*] and INDRANIL BOSE[2]

[1]*Globsyn Business School, Kolkata, India*

[2]*School of Business, University of Bolton, International Academic Campus, Ras Al Khaimah, UAE*

*Corresponding author. E-mail: basu.ranita@gmail.com

ABSTRACT

Pandemic has played a very vital role in almost everyone's life all over the world. Along with the bane, people have also witnessed the boons of pandemic. In this chapter, we have discussed two self-contradictory concepts which have some significant impacts on people's lives. Digital detox and tech savvy—two important factors evolving so strongly, and after the pandemic it is evolving even stronger with a whole new connotation. Purpose of this chapter was to find out the importance of these two factors and how to implement them to have a hazard free life. In this chapter, it was explained that when and how technology should be used before it causes any detrimental effect on human body and mind. It was also explained that, in today's era, why it is so important to become tech savvy. Various other factors like, benefits of digital detox, importance of tech savvy, emergence of digital HR, damaging effect of excessive use of technology, etc were also discussed here. This chapter has a strong connection with how pandemic is ruling and impacting the industry and the human lives, and how we are still managing to be agile while shredding some negative impact of digitalization with the help of digital detox.

Human Resource Management in a Post-Epidemic Global Environment: Roles, Strategies, and Implementations.
Tanusree Chakraborty, Nandita Mishra, Madhurima Ganguly, & Bipasha Chatterjee (Eds.)
© 2023 Apple Academic Press, Inc. Co-published with CRC Press (Taylor & Francis)

4.1 INTRODUCTION: OVERVIEW OF TECH DETOX

HR is considered as a perennially an emerging and developing field. It includes all human behavioral, organizational, and technical aspects which help the organization to run smoothly and make it hassle-free. One such concept of HR that has emerged a few years back is known as tech detox, or more specifically, digital detox. In this world of growing technologies, digital detox has become an utmost important factor, through which people can feel and realize the actual importance of being connected to humans or more specifically the damaging effect of overusing technology. It is a well-known fact, that technology is the key factor behind all industrial revolutions. It is also considered as the backbone for all the industrial development. But, as every coin has two sides, needless to mention, technology has also some negative impacts. As it is said that, anything in extreme is bad; in the same way when technology is used for a prolonged period of time without any proper purpose, for example, excessive access to digital device, social media, apps, digital games etc., becomes harmful for us. In this new era of HR, digital detox helps people to recover from this issue.

Digital detox is basically a concept where people are advised and instructed not to use the technology unless it is required; and how not to use it, that is also explained. We have seen the development of the era of industrial revolution, where it is now transformed from Industry 4.0 to Industry 5.0 and it is still growing. We learned many things from these revolutions, and among those things one is definitely, how to adapt the technology. If we consider the brighter side then it is a boon for the entire world where we learned and applied many versions of technology and digital activities. Amidst the world embracing this technology and digitalization, one important contradictory concept was also evolved, and that was digital detox (Newport Institute, 2020). It disallows people to get unnecessarily stuck to any digital platform, specifically when someone is actually not working or doing anything but just can't keep their digital device aside.

Following the same context, the significant role of digital detox should be mentioned. It is usually a process, where all the digital connections are cut off, and people are encouraged to get engaged in practicing their hobbies, spending some quality time with their friends, families or loved ones, or any productive activity which are stress relieving in nature. In recent times, many organizations took the initiative and offered their employees an opportunity to be a part of their digital detox program, as a part of the HR activities. Many organizations took their employees for a vacation, and the technological connection is cut off, phone calls are limited, and they can enjoy time in the lap of nature, play outdoor/indoor games, sing, dance, basically rejuvenate themselves.

Out of many, a few positive impacts can be listed as follows:

1. Reduces stress
2. Reduces fear of missing out (FOMO)
3. Improves sleep habits
4. Allows for a stressless and positive life situations
5. Helps maintain work-life balance.

From a study conducted by Basu (2019) on digital detox, it was found that: widespread impact of the overuse of technology and the internet is on the rise. People are getting badly affected by the overuse of technology. Eventually, many behavioral issues and disorders are also rising. Many cases on obsessive-compulsive behavior, anxiety, social isolation, frustration, dysfunctional social relationships, insomnia, anger, and depression, etc were reported because of this. Usually, the affected people display many behavioral and abnormal psychological symptoms that severely impact their healthy lives. As a result many serious issues can occur, more than expected. This phenomenon, with internet addiction disorder was identified in 1995. The threatening part of it is that more and more people are having the access to digital devices which helps them to connect to people in the virtual world. Most importantly, the misuse might lead to social issues.

Now, let us highlight some negative impacts also. As mentioned by Ellen Wermter of Charlottesville Neurology and Sleep Medicine, explained how blue lights' wave, specifically in mobile devices, can disrupt our sleep patterns. All the factors like, communication, endurance, creativity, reaction time, productivity, memory, concentration, mood, etc can be improved only through one biological phenomenon and that is proper sleep. It is well known that one of the main influences of our sleep patterns is light. When we use phones, tablets, and laptops excessively, which are often close to our face and the lights are coming through that, many of us use late into the evening and even in our bedrooms can actually affect our sleep patterns which can again trigger many problems as mentioned earlier.

4.2 DIGITAL DETOX: EXPLORING THE NECESSITY

Detox is a widely used phenomena in our lives. It is a process through which we reduce the toxic substances from our body and mind. The digital detox is used exactly in the same way. We know that tech savvy is the new fad in the corporate world. People look for digitally trained employees, especially while working on a hybrid mode after the pandemic. But they fail to control the unnecessary use of the digital device and that causes many damage to their eyes, brain, etc (Thomée, 2012). There digital detox works as the rescue program. It helps people to get disconnected from the device through proper means.

4.3 DIGITALIZATION AND HR FUNCTIONS: AN UPSURGING TREND

In this paradigm shift of HR, many transactional and strategic HR activities are evolving with the full support of digitalization. Many software solutions and apps like PeopleSoft, Ask Dexter, and many others are already developed to minimize the transactional human effort and utilize the human resources in some transformational HR activities (Ulrich et. al., 2012). After this pandemic, almost the entire world got acquainted with the concepts like, remote working, hybrid, and blended mode of working, etc and the organizations are trying to develop more tools on HRM which can be used remotely or in the time of crisis without any interruptions. There are several benefits of these digital HR functions. The details are discussed below.

4.4 THE BENEFITS OF DIGITAL HR

This era of industrial revolution, and more specifically after this pandemic, brings on many dynamic and vastly used technologies like automation, robotics process automation, artificial intelligence, and digitalization. All of these have taken a new place in business, which has reduced the expenses and have made processes more efficient and data-driven. We know the importance of the strategic HR functions and its impact on any business. Post pandemic, the relation of digital transformation and the strategic HR has made it more important and significant to the HR leaders. It is discussed that the HR leaders should prepare to embrace digital HR through the data literacy (WillNeverGrowUp, 2020), so that they can adapt and apply complex problem solving and project execution skills and methodologies. For example, design-thinking can be used as the new face of HR to accelerate the activities of strategic HR. In one of Deloitte's study on HR tech disruptions, it was observed that the use of cognitive bots, AI, and other intelligent predictive software within HR have all increased (Newport Institute, 2020). As a result of this, today many organizations are quickly bringing new technologies, apps, digital platforms into HR domain to manage the workforce (Newport Institute, 2020). The other benefit can be, time/leave management: Starting from managing information, the shifting focus is on the core activities, using data and analytics, developing employees, improving employee experiences, etc (Munisamy, 2013).

4.5 DIGITAL HR JOURNEY

Digital HR journey denotes the entire development and implementation of digitalization in the field of HR. Basically, it indicates one of the important paradigms of HR, where HR emerges digitally with all its transactional, analytical, strategical, and transformational roles. According to Chakraborty et al. (2021), social network usage intensity has also risen up because of the pandemic. So, on an average people are engaging more into digital platforms for work and beyond work. Probing into the phases, as mentioned by Ulrich (2019), any company has four phases of their digital HR journey:

1. **HR efficiency:** This is the 1st phase of the digital journey. In this phase, usually there is an existing HR technology provider. The companies build technology platforms through investment which efficiently manage HR processes.
2. **HR effectiveness:** This is the next phase. In this phase, technology is used in such a way that upgrades the transactional HR practices which is linked with people, for example, recruitment, training, performance management, communication, and individual development, etc.
3. **Information:** This is the 3rd phase. In this phase, information is used and shared to bring various impacts on business. One can access data; both the internal and external data can be combined, and HR analytics is used to create business-relevant insights.
4. **Connection/experience:** This is the final phase. Here, digital HR is utilized to create a connection between people. Various other factors like social networks, people experiences, and technology help to build a strong HR system.

4.6 COMPONENTS OF DIGITAL HR

After the pandemic, digital HR has become the need for the hour. Starting from managing and mapping the performances of the employees while working remotely or through blended mode, providing training sessions or workshops digitally, and then mapping the skill gap again digitally— the world has seen the importance of digital HR. It is also important to mention here that any kind of positive learning in the field of digital HR will eventually increase the knowledge and the skill of the employees and make them savvier. Now, let us have a look on the domains which are considered as the fundamental components of digital HR (Verlinden, n.d.), growing phenomenally and also indicating a positive relation with tech savviness:

4.6.1 DATA AND ANALYTICS

This is one of the fastest growing areas of HR, that is, data analytics. In fact, in recent times, HR analytics is said to be an expertise of its own, and probably have the most significant relation with digital HR. Various tools are developed and still emerging to use in this field. Even if we look at the education sphere, HR analytics is emerging as one of the majors that students are encouraged to take up these days.

4.6.2 DIGITAL RECRUITMENT

A video interviewing platform called Spark Hire is a good example of how different social, mobile, analytics, and cloud (SMAC) technologies are combined into one digital solution. The benefits of this platform are that the candidates are interviewed in real-time platforms; also, they can schedule their interviews. Finally, their interviews are shared easily with the hiring board or panel or other managers for immediate feedback.

4.6.3 A BETTER EMPLOYEE EXPERIENCES

Performance management is quite a traditional aspect of HR but recently, even after the pandemic, gained a lot of importance. Employees prefer to be evaluated on the basis of their performances and like to receive their feedback, which they do not hesitate to share also in real time or on any kind of device. In this century, another performance management tool IMPRAISE provides a digital feedback experience to the managers and employees.

4.6.4 EMPLOYEE SELF-SERVICE

Various other HR strategical and transactional activities can be managed by the employees themselves by using Employee self-service (ESS). Activities like, accessing and managing their payroll information, leave requests and other HR information are allowed through this platform. This is one of the digital self-service solutions of HR.

4.7 EXCESSIVE DIGITALIZATION: THE HAZARDS

During this pandemic, we have seen people arguing on topics like whether digitalization was a boon or bane to the world. Now, while having a discussion on the topic like digital detox and digital dependence, it might be a boon for the business but a bane for health, surely. Burnout which is known as a mental health illness, that is also distressing the corporate world as the pandemic grows. Many employees, while working remotely, are suffering from this. The fear of being laid off is prompting professionals to work strictly round the clock, through the week, and with very limited breaks (WillNeverGrowUp, 2020).

In the post pandemic situations, mostly for the remote work, people are relying entirely on technology and the digital platforms. All the skill development programs, trainings, and meetings are being conducted digitally. People are embracing the boon aspects of the technological growth, and somehow, unknowingly many other negative aspects are unknowingly being faced by them. Many studies (Hrdconnect, 2020) have shown that the working hours are increased because of this remote working system. Employees are investing more time on their regular work and eventually the engagement with the digital platform and using the gadgets are increased as found by Hrdconnect (2020). They are plugged in more into this virtual world than before, and practically they can't escape this. This over engagement of people, with their digital device can also lead to many physical and mental health hazards. Blurred vision and dry eyes, eyestrain, sleep problems, reduced physical activities are among the physical hazards and isolation, depression and anxiety are among some common prominent psychological hazards, as reported by Johnson (2020). He also mentioned that while taking the rapid advancement of the technology, people actually forgot where to trigger the stop button.

4.8 DIGITALIZATION AND IMPACT ON SOCIAL-INTERPERSONAL SKILLS

The best positive impact of digitalization is connection. We were never connected this much, with each other and also, gaining knowledge has become much easier than before. But the negative effects are also many. From a study conducted by Lengacher (2015), it was found that digital technologies, mainly too much usage of mobile technology, reduce the interaction and face-to-face communication. It seems that excessive internet usage can cause loneliness, withdrawal tendency from interpersonal relationships and negate relationship satisfaction (Lengacher, 2015). In modern civilization, texting has replaced the face-to-face interactions; accessing social media has reduced spending quality time with family; though there is always a chance to misinterpret the digital message. Chakraborty et al. (2021) have suggested how interpersonal skill at workplace gets affected by too much media infiltration. Many important social skills like, verbal communication, building relations with others, empathy, are getting severely affected by the overuse of digital device (Baker, 2020).

4.9 PANDEMIC COVID-19 AND DIGITAL DETOX: ARE THEY NOT CONTRADICTORY?

Now getting into the other side of the reality. Pandemic COVID-19 has shown the entire world the need for learning and using technology to the most. It has shown why technology is so important to mankind. About 90% of sectors started operating from home during this time (Hrdconnect, 2020). People learned technology and became tech savvy. Most of the organizations allowed their employees to work from home and trained them how to use technologies while working from home. Artificial intelligence and machine learning have made it possible for all of us. Many online platforms like Zoom, Google Meet, Microsoft Team started emerging to maintain smooth online activities while people have been working from home or remotely. Eventually, this technology dependence made human beings more occupied with the use of technology, though the suggestion was to get rid of it. Most of the organizations, while recruiting, started prioritizing the incumbents who are more conversant on online platforms. Employees started receiving training from their organizations to acquire more skills on technology, even the little children who were prohibited once to use mobile phones, are now depending entirely on their gadgets for attending their online classes. So, we can say that the digital HR is developing and growing to the fullest in this era, specifically after this pandemic. Just we have landed up in an era, where we cannot really detox digitally though we should. Digitalization has become the need of the hour (Papadopoulo, 2020). To be specific, besides other sectors, healthcare sector has seen a steep rise in digitalization (Golinelli, 2020). Though the word tech savvy and digital detox are little contradictory in nature, but the coexistence can be observed. If we look at the target group of who actually needs detox, then the answer would be the adults, mostly the young adults (Hrdconnect, 2020). According to Nielsen research conducted by Newport Institute (2020), it was found that per day, most of the American adults spend over 11 h in various digital activities like watching, reading, listening to, or generally interacting with media. Again, it was predicted by some experts (Donohoe, 2016) that this number might be increased to an average of 13 h per day in 2020 as a result of the pandemic. However, it was observed that the people are becoming inundated by the regular influx of attractive apps on their mobiles and other devices. In addition to this, it was proved from several studies (Thomée, 2012; May, 2018) that our nervous systems are always negatively affected by the amount of time spent accessing and staring at screens. Hence, people have realized the importance of taking a break and getting disconnected from the digital device. Digital detox has become more popular as people have identified its benefits on mental and physical health (Newport Institute, 2020).

4.10 DIGITAL DETOX PROGRAMS: ARE WE HEADING RIGHT?

As we are getting gradually more attached to digital platforms, and as we have just discussed the hazards of digital engagement, it has become imperative now to discuss how to manage this controversial situation. Are we heading right in managing our hazards? It is always not easy to arrange digital detox programs or sometimes just 2/3 days of rejuvenating events do not work. To have or to plan any kind of detox, it is the most important thing for the person to decide it first. It is with the person who will decide whether he wants to detox or it is still ok with the quantity of digital engagement in his day-to-day life. Detox is mostly required when it is interfering with other activities of life and sometimes become hazardous too. There are many usual ways to detox, which are easy to implement but should be followed strictly by the person who is opting for it. As proposed by Moore (2016) and May (2018) the general ways are:

1. Be realistic with the limits,
2. Fix the time of using social media or unnecessary access of gadgets and limit the use of it,
3. Try to take breaks in between, while working,
4. Turn off notifications,
5. Delete apps or keep the minimum apps required for living,
6. While not working, keep the phone in other rooms and leave it behind,
7. Plan tech free activities as much as possible, maintaining all the new normal and safety protocols, for example, driving a car or bike, walking with a friend maintaining the social distance, weekend camping, or any real-life activities with others that actually don't include any use of technology,
8. Reading book is always a good option,
9. Spending more time with family and discussing things which are productive and stress releasing in nature,
10. Reconnecting with nature.

These are the usual recommended ways to have the digital detox.

Several studies have shown the benefits of digital detox and how it is linked with employee performance (Basu, 2019; May, 2018; Moore, 2016). It helps to calm down and feel contented. Several social experiments found (WillNeverGrowUp, 2020; and TollFreeForwarding, 2018) that taking a scheduled break away from the smartphone or digital device can actually lower the stress levels, it makes people more productive and of course people feel better about themselves.

4.11 CONCLUSION

In the workplace, interpersonal relationships and productivity can be affected by digital disorder. In the post pandemic era, to minimize the negative impact on employee health, the HR leaders should have a vision to introduce new policy and take preventative measures. There are a number of ways to do this through virtual platforms. Solutions are manyfold, depending on the situations. Encouraging face-to-face communication, role-playing sessions, fun activities, and driving engagement and collaboration through face-to-face meetings are the examples to deal with the side effects of digital work structure. Many measures can be initiated by the organizations, for example, digital detox packages can be introduced as a type of perks to motivate the employees and to help them overcome the side effects of prolonged use of digital device. We shouldn't forget about the side effects of this, while continue to benefit from digital technology, and make our digital journey smoother.

KEYWORDS

- tech detox
- digital detox
- tech savvy
- HR efficiency
- HR effectiveness
- digital HR
- digitalization

REFERENCES

Baker, L. *The Impact of Technology on Social Skills*. Junior Learning. https://juniorlearning.com/blogs/news/the-impact-of-technology-on-social-skills (accessed Jan 2020, 15).

Basu, R. Impact of Digital Detox on Individual Performance of the Employees. *Int. J. Res. Anal. Rev.* (IJRAR) **2019,** *6*(2), 378–381.

Chakraborty, T.; Kumar, A.; Upadhyay, P.; Dwivedi, Y. K. Link Between Social Distancing, Cognitive Dissonance, and Social Networking Site Usage Intensity: A Country-Level Study During the COVID-19 Outbreak. *Internet Res.* **2021,** *31*(2), 419–456. DOI: 10.1108/intr-05-2020-0281

Chakraborty, T.; Tripathi, M.; Saha, S. The Dynamics of Employee Relationships in a Digitalized Workplace: The Role of Media Richness on Workplace Culture. In *Critical Issues on Changing Dynamics in Employee Relations and Workforce Diversity*; IGI Global, 2021; pp 175–205.

Donohoe, A. *Employee Performance Definition*. BizFluent. https://bizfluent.com/facts-7218608-employee-performance-definition.html (accessed June 7, 2019).

Golinelli, D.; Boetto, E.; Carullo, G.; Nuzzolese, A. G.; Landini, M. P.; Fantini, M. P. How the COVID-19 Pandemic is Favoring the Adoption of Digital Technologies in Healthcare: A Literature Review. *Med. Rxiv.* **2020.**

Hrdconnect. *What are the Benefits of Digital HR? HRD Connect*. https://www.hrdconnect.com/2020/01/17/what-are-the-benefits-of-digital-hr/ (accessed Jan 17, 2020).

Johnson, J. *Negative Effects of Technology: What to Know*. Medical News Today. https://www.medicalnewstoday.com/articles/negative-effects-of-technology (accessed Feb 25, 2020).

Lengacher, L. *Mobile Technology: Its Effect on Communication and Interpersonal Interaction*. Digital Commons @Butler University. https://digitalcommons.butler.edu/urc/2015/psychology/14/ (accessed April 10, 2015).

May, T. *6 Ways to Introduce a Digital Detox to Your Employees (and Why it Could Boost Productivity)*. https://hrdailyadvisor.blr.com/2018/07/24/6-ways-introduce-digital-detox-employees-boost-productivity/ (accessed July 24, 2018).

Moore, S. *Is it Time for a Digital Detox?* https://www.gartner.com/smarterwithgartner/is-it-time-for-a-digital-detox/ (accessed March 30, 2016).

Munisamy, S. *Identifying Factors that Influences Job Performance Amongst Employees in Oil Palm Plantation,* 2013. http://library.oum.edu.my/repository/979/1/library-document-979.pdf.

Newport Institute. *What is a Digital Detox and Why Should You Do One? Newport Institute.* https://www.newportinstitute.com/resources/mental-health/digital-detox/ (accessed Oct, 2020).

Papadopoulos, T.; Baltas, K. N.; Balta, M. E. The Use of Digital Technologies by Small and Medium Enterprises During COVID-19: Implications for Theory and Practice. *Int. J. Inform. Manag.* **2020**, *55*, 102192.

Thomée, S. *ICT Use and Mental Health in Young Adults. Effects of Computer and Mobile Phone Use on Stress, Sleep Disturbances, and Symptoms Of Depression;* University of Gothenburg, Sahlgrenska Academy, 2012. https://gupea.ub.gu.se/handle/2077/28245

TollFreeForwarding. *Could Employees and Companies Benefit from a Digital Detox? TollFreeForwarding.com.* https://tollfreeforwarding.com/blog/could-employees-and-companies-benefit-from-a-digital-detox/ (accessed June 6, 2018).

Ulrich, D. *The Four Phases of Digital HR.* HRM-The News Site of the Australian HR Institute. https://www.hrmonline.com.au/technology/dave-ulrich-four-phases-digital-hr/ (accessed March 28, 2019).

Ulrich, D; Younger, J; Brockbank, W; Ulrich, M. *HR from the Outside in: The Next Era of Human Resources Transformation;* McGraw-Hill: New York, 2012. ISBN 9780071802666.

Verlinden, N. *Back to Basics: What is Digital HR?* https://www.digitalhrtech.com/back-to-basics-what-is-digital-hr/

WillNeverGrowUp. *Digital Detox: Pulling the Plug on Technology.* https://blog.willnevergrowup.com/digital-detox-pulling-the-plug-on-technology/ (accessed Sep 25, 2020).

Winter, C.; Wermter, E. Charlottesville Neurology and Sleep Medicine. http://www.cvilleneuroandsleep.com/about-us.html.

CHAPTER 5

Unveiling the Notion of "Knowledge Hoarding" in a Post-Epidemic Global Business Environment

ABHILASH ACHARYA[*]

Army Institute of Management, Action Area III, Newtown, 700160 Kolkata, West Bengal, India

[*]E-mail: abhilash.acharya12fpm@iimranchi.ac.in

ABSTRACT

As our readers ponder deeply over the context of organizations in the post-pandemic scenario, workplaces are tending to change through a little more than a year until now. This has definitely affected every individual employee (or any organizational member), almost daily during the period mentioned, primarily with regards to how knowledge can be created, sustained, and transferred. Expectedly, an understandable impact on organizational performance by and large has been reported quite extensively. And professionals are simply hopeful that the "menace of knowledge hoarding" can be mitigated with time.

As such, it would be imperative to state here that "knowledge hoarding" is a comparatively less intentional or discriminatory form of concealment in the workplace because in this case: (1) knowledge or information is not subjected to a professional request (unlike "knowledge hiding") and (2) the behavioral scope offered by "knowledge hoarding" is lower.

As time passes, "knowledge hoarding" becomes extensively deliberate, and strategic efforts are put in to resist sharing of relevant knowledge. Here, factors like "modified" organizational culture and level of commitment toward work and peers (in the wake of workplaces surviving "online" and work-groups remaining virtual) will allow any employee (or organizational member) a "free pass" for indulging in "knowledge hoarding" practices. Intentional actions pertaining to "knowledge hoarding" cans harm the organization and its members in many ways and shall be detrimental to both organizational and individual performances in the long run.

In order to prevent "knowledge hoarding" efficaciously, enhanced open participation of employees (or organizational members), and their empowerment must be ensured alongside taking into account the "correctness" of the implementation processes within an "online" workplace. Going forward, a hybrid workplace shall dictate newer terms with respect to "knowledge hoarding." Dependence on extended social capital inside such a workplace can offer multiple challenges too!

5.1 INTRODUCTION

Workplaces tend to affect every individual employee (or any organizational member), almost daily. This phenomenon became much more conspicuous in the postepidemic global business environment—which is still our current situation in the professional realm. We can observe significant changes there, especially with regards to how knowledge can be created, sustained, and transferred when it comes to the context of professional knowledge sharing during and after the Covid-19 outbreak. Expectedly, an understandable impact on organizational performance by and large has been reported quite extensively. Professionals are simply hoping that it can be mitigated with time.

However, for the time being, our focus remains on "organizational behaviors" that obstruct sharing of any kind of professional knowledge or related information, more so in the postpandemic space of business transactions. Such motivated obstructions have been categorized into two popular constructs: "knowledge hiding" and "knowledge hoarding." Connelly and Zweig (2015) have defined "knowledge hiding" as a dyadic workplace relationship between one employee (or organizational member) who makes a professional request to acquire specific knowledge from another employee (or organizational member) while the latter actually withholds that knowledge in response to the former. On the other hand, Webster et al. (2008) made a reference to knowledge hoarding as preemptive or anticipatory withholding of knowledge even prior to any professional request coming in from another employee (or organizational member).

Our readers can gauge that these two constructs are both related to an act of withholding professional knowledge and thus, there exists a possibility of conceptual overlap and/or synonymous usage. This notion though has already been dispelled by Connelly et al. (2012) who claimed that these two ideas have been clearly distinguished, theoretically as well as empirically. Theoretically, they can be differentiated from each other on the basis of three key factors: scope, request, and intentionality. Empirically, too, they appear to be very weakly correlated and bear no appreciable commonality.

As such, it would be safe to assert that "knowledge hoarding" is a comparatively less intentional or discriminatory form of concealment in the workplace because in this case: (1) knowledge or information is not subjected to a professional request (unlike "knowledge hiding"), and (2) the behavioral scope offered by "knowledge hoarding" is lower. Having said that, it shall be important to note what Evans et al. (2014) opined about "knowledge hoarding": that the process has the potential to capture all those knowledge elements that are neither explicit nor are directly understood by another employee (or organizational member). Therefore, it may become relatively impossible and equally confusing to make a professional request for such knowledge and/or information, although it may be highly essential in particular for overall organizational success. An organizational crisis like this one has already been amplified by the Covid-19 outbreak, as workplaces had to shut down dramatically and physical one-on-one interactions amongst employees were practically eroded!

In the extant academic literature pertaining to knowledge management research, "knowledge hoarding" is definitely an under researched and new topic under consideration. Evans et al. (2014) believed that "knowledge hoarding" has the potential to cause negative organizational outcomes, which could range from deteriorated workplace relationships, diminished professional interactions amongst employees (or organizational members), counterproductive unit, or departmental performance and till the risk of compromising one's professional position in the organization. In essence, "knowledge hoarding" can lead to indirect workplace bullying and other work-related negative acts.

Stenmark (2002) has identified knowledge and information as two distinct entities, where information is just a form of knowledge and knowledge itself is a complex and valuable organizational asset. Here, arguments related to classifying the aforementioned two would not be offered; on the contrary, the core of the emphasis in this discourse will be on how and why "knowledge hoarding" by employees (or organizational members) continue to influence any organization negatively in the postepidemic global business environment. There the highlights of the present chapter that are as follows:

1. The core notion of "knowledge hoarding" at workplaces (and how distinct it is from "knowledge hiding."
2. The underlying reasons for hoarding knowledge and whether it is suitable or detrimental to an organization's success and/or survival.
3. The postpandemic global business environment posing as a challenging context to normalize as well as neutralize the effects of hoarding relevant knowledge.
4. The "online" workplace that made way for various newer forms of the interactive impact of "knowledge hoarding."

5.2 KNOWLEDGE HOARDING—"THE ART OF NEGATING"

"The art of negating" relates to negative acts or actions at the workplace that can lead to a variety of unwanted behaviors getting combined and creating a bubble of bullying. Nielsen et al. (2011) have observed that bullying is experienced over time and engulfs harassment, professional offences, social exclusion, and concerted negative influence on an employee's (or organizational member's work). Bullying can also be looked upon as professional mobbing or heckling in relation to a particular workplace activity, organizational process, or professional interaction. Einarsen et al. (2009) have stated that if repeated occurrences of the same kind of negative behavior happen at regular intervals (daily/weekly), then that becomes synonymous with bullying over a period of time (in 1–3 months).

Right from the time a nationwide lockdown was announced, professional activities via the internet had started taking a toll on an individual's mental health and overall well being. During and after the Covid-19 outbreak, they continued to experience negativities in the professional space, albeit in the virtual mode. Such experiences in terms of negative acts "at work" (that would be carried out online) can have permanent individual and organizational consequences. Opinions were sought from 12 medical experts (including psychiatrists and neuroscience consultants) and five organizational psychologists regarding similar issues. They provided insightful examples of consequential impact both at the individual and organizational levels. Factors such as high degree of anxiety, common and uncommon cardiovascular diseases, bouts of depressed mood, and general long-term depression were predominantly observed in employees (or organizational members).

Organizations were facing an unexpected turnover rate (even when the job market was shrinking and the number of attractive opportunities had dwindled), reduced productivity, and professional disconnect (which is rather a digital equivalent of conventional unmindfulness or absenteeism). Evans et al. (2014) had suggested that "knowledge hoarding" tends to increase under similar circumstances, whether at the physical workplace or even virtually nowadays, since the quality of work-related interactions keep dipping beyond negotiation. A counterproductive "workplace," online or offline, will catalyze behaviors that promote "knowledge hoarding" amongst employees (or organizational members). Without a doubt, it is warranted that a deep link exists between negative acts in the workplace and knowledge hoarding tendencies; what becomes of significance is that "knowledge hoarding" becomes prominent and gets augmented as online professional interactions through virtual teams, social media groups and other similar formats run the show everywhere!

Taking the help of Homan's (1961) social exchange theory and its theoretical framing for academic applications, it can be posited that "the history and the quality of interpersonal interactions" decide the course of future professional interactions (offline then and online now). We can unarguably rely on Bouty's (2000) two expressions that convey the quality of interpersonal interactions for work—a sense of organizational justice and the psychological state of trust. These can serve as potential mediators to explain the efficiency and the effectiveness of both individual and collective organizational performance in the changed scenario of the postepidemic global business environment. Such modified professional interactions will give shape to a "new history" for further reference at different "online workplaces."

Certain other factors that influence "knowledge hoarding" in an "online workplace" can be borrowed from Wang and Noe (2010), Jabeen et al. (2020), Albana and Yeşiltaş (2021) and those include perceived sense of organizational fairness, manager's or immediate supervisor's support, and climate for knowledge sharing. Chances are that owing to "knowledge hoarding," an employee's (or organizational member's) individual performance may improve; however, these acts will definitely have negative outcomes like hampered work-related interactions (more so when the interactions are happening online), a unit or department's inability to respond quickly to critical problems (more so when the groups are over social media), and decreased unit performance (more so when the work teams are virtual). Hence, ideally, the "neo-workplace" disturbances have to be nipped in the bud to regain positive control.

5.3 "KNOWLEDGE HOARDING" VS. DISTURBANCES IN THE "ONLINE" WORKPLACE

As time passes, "knowledge hoarding" becomes extensively deliberate, and strategic efforts are put in to resist sharing of relevant knowledge. Here, factors like "modified" organizational culture and level of commitment towards work and peers (in the wake of workplaces surviving "online" and work-groups remaining virtual) will allow any employee (or organizational member) a "free-pass" for indulging in "knowledge hoarding" practices. Intentional actions pertaining to "knowledge hoarding" can harm the organization and its members in many ways and shall be detrimental to both organizational and individual performances in the long run, especially by giving way to ostracism in the "online" workplace.

Workplace ostracism in general can be defined as the extent to which an employee (or organizational member) perceives that he or she is "rejected, ignored, or excluded by others in the workplace" (Williams, 2007; Al-Abbadi et al., 2020). Although workplace ostracism can appear to be a one-dimensional construct, side lining of an employee (or organizational member) can stem for more than a single source in the "online" workplace. Ignoring the roles of supervisors/managers and coworkers can put a smokescreen on the realities of ostracism in "online" workplaces. It has already been acknowledged by research scholars and practicing managers that transfer of knowledge in an efficient manner can facilitate organizational development—which means that in case there are hindrances to this in the form of "knowledge hoarding" then it can push the organization into an irrevocable phase of disaster. As far as workplace ostracism is concerned, then anti-social and counterproductive work behaviors are bound to seep into the workplace system; since the organizational processes have shifted online, this disturbance can easily spread across the organization (through its employees' virtual work teams).

It has not been proven if workplace ostracism is a core interpersonal antecedent of "knowledge hoarding"; still, the influence of ostracism (whether conscious or otherwise) in an "online" workplace scenario may cause an organization to break down in the postepidemic global business environment. Our readers will understand that the multilayered relationship between workplace ostracism and "knowledge hoarding" (when the organizational processes are getting conducted online) is not explicit and rather very complex.

Interestingly, professional capabilities of employees (or organizational members) when combined can present a situational context for "online" workplaces in terms of individual reactions to ostracism. A specific capability in this regard would be the professional skill to deal with organizational politics. Terming the same as "political skill," it shall explain the professional ability of an employee (or organizational member) to comprehend the influence of others in the "online" workplace, thereby engaging in pro-social or anti-social organizational behavior as a reaction to effected ostracism.

> **Situation 1:** An Indian start-up, currently having business interests in skill up-gradation of frontline workers (from the logistics and mining sectors) through remote training using advanced simulators, does not own any regular office space at the moment. They primarily engage in online, cloud-based work interactions and submissions. As such, many of the high performers have subconsciously resorted to "knowledge hoarding" (involving all that knowledge, which gives them an edge). Consequently, they were subjected to repeated bullying and workplace ostracism, albeit online.

5.4 "KNOWLEDGE HOARDING" AND THE UNDERCURRENT CALLED "POLITICAL SKILL"

Pfeffer (1981) was a pioneer in organizational change research who had argued that there will exist a political perspective vis-à-vis conventional organizational behaviors. Ferris et al. (2005) went on to define "political skill" in the following manner:

> "It is an individual's ability to effectively understand others at work and to use such knowledge to influence others to act in ways that enhance one's personal and/or organizational objectives."

Thus, technically, "political skill" will contain distinct yet related factors like:
a. social astuteness (which refers to one's innate ability to realize about all the socially-induced situations as accurately as possible, along with "interpersonal" interactions that are taking place in the "online" workplace),
b. interpersonal influence (which represents any employee's or organizational member's capability to adapt oneself to professional triggers

and consequently calibrate one's own "behaviors" under each situation, in order to elicit precise responses from others in the given virtual team),

c. networking ability (which talks of an individual's ability to intermingle professionally with key resources or assets that are valuable and absolutely essential for successful personal and organizational growth, currently via social media-driven work groups), and

d. apparent sincerity (which means a person's competence to appear to his or her manager, peers, and other coworkers as possessing high levels of integrity, authenticity, sincerity, and genuineness, albeit during "online meetings" over video calls).

In the aforementioned context, "knowledge hoarding" will censoriously act as a defense mechanism to save oneself from getting cornered or even removed from the existing and new-age "online" professional space. Next, we will explore further on "knowledge hoarding" as a concept for the post-epidemic global business environment.

5.5 DEPENDENCE OF "KNOWLEDGE HOARDING" ON COR THEORY

Hobfoll (2001) elaborates on the Conservation of Resources (COR) theory to explain how and why employees (or organizational members) develop a natural proclivity to protect and retain all current "resources" and make attempts to acquire new "resources." He continues to classify these "resources" as "objects/assets, personal characteristics, conditions, or energies that are valued in their own right or that are valued because they act as conduits to the achievement or protection of valued resources."

Drawing from the above, Halbesleben et al. (2014) mentioned that "social relationship, social support, and the chance for better development in workplace can be perceived as valued resources." Going by the two core tenets of the COR theory, namely, primacy of resource losses and resource investment (Hobfoll, 2001; Ayub et al., 2021), "knowledge hoarding" earns another academic lens of analytical evaluation where "knowledge" is treated as a necessary and irreplaceable organizational asset (Acharya and Mishra, 2017; Acharya et al., 2018). According to the primacy of resource losses, an employee (or organizational member) will initiate actions to inhibit and/or control extra loss of relevant knowledge (resource) that gives him or her an edge over others in the "online" workplace. This happens because an employee's (or organizational member's) awareness of conserving one's existing resources (knowledge hoarding activity) is stronger than that of acquiring newer resources (requesting for relevant knowledge). In addition, resource investment ensures that employees (or organizational members) actually invest resources (time and effort) to deter themselves from pertinent resource losses (by opting for "knowledge hoarding" as opposed to "knowledge sharing"). An "online" workplace in the postepidemic global business environment will end up boosting organizational behaviors that categorically support "knowledge hoarding."

Injustice, mistrust, ostracism in "online" workplaces can severely affect service performance. Following the Covid-19 outbreak, the same negative factors can cause psychological distress (in the form of job-related tension, unwanted irritation, emotional exhaustion, and a consistently depressed mood at work) and fuel the issues like supervisor ostracism and coworker ostracism. Organizations will need to start deploying professional "combat-resources" to streamline "online" workplace functions and rebuild their systems and processes in the postepidemic global business environment.

5.6 DISCUSSION—PRACTICING MANAGERS' WAYS TO NEUTRALIZE "KNOWLEDGE HOARDING"

The problem of "knowledge hoarding" at workplaces that were running virtually and managed carefully by online work groups was discussed with 16 senior professionals across the organizational hierarchy and belonging a mix of five industrial sectors (IT and ITES, BIFS, Consulting, Logistics and Transportation, and Chemicals and Petroleum). They not only acknowledged the notion of "knowledge hoarding" in the modified workplaces but also deliberated upon the intricacies around the very idea in the postepidemic global business environment.

All were in agreement with the fact that "knowledge hoarding" is and will be unavoidable within "online" workplace settings. At best, the "political skills" of employees (or organizational members) can be tempered to neutralize the effect of "knowledge hoarding." Pursuing intensive efforts to build a neo-congenial environment for distributed "online" workplaces may yield better results on performance and productivity.

Even now, it is inevitable for employees (or organizational members) to make professional contact with others for work-based requirements. This online mode of "contact" establishment provides the employees (or organizational members) with fresh and/or unseen interpersonal interaction cues; and these cues could be utilized in a number of favorable (or unfavorable) approaches to either influence or adapt or even react to the virtual workplace processes and systems. Perceived levels of injustice, mistrust (including intolerance), and workplace ostracism must be reduced by communicating more and via online channels of informal nature. Else, rendering professional help to complete an organizational task may be compromised when the physical space of interpersonal interactions has been dissolved for the time being—it is practically easier to "disconnect" and not reply or revert back even when the situation demands.

It is also possible that all employees (or organizational members) are not result oriented or do not bother much about their professional future. Chances of inflicting unjust actions, inducing mistrust amongst virtual team members and ostracizing fellow peers are higher in their cases. These can wreck any "online" workplace and thus, it is imperative to conduct passive digital monitoring of organizational interactions to generate feedback concerning negative/counterproductive behaviors. This will be needed to keep the main motive behind knowledge management research alive and intact—i.e., creation, sharing, upgradation and retention of knowledge for organizational success, and critical improvements in vulnerable areas.

Behaviors that promote resistance to knowledge sharing have to be continuously identified, measured, and evaluated after monitoring of organizational events as mentioned above, as their occurrences were already known to be quite regular across virtual teams. There are specific processes by which "knowledge hoarding" behaviors transpire, and being apprised of the how, why, and when is essential for all practicing managers. Understanding the ways to prevent such behaviors from making an "online" workplace compromised, repairing, and eventually eliminating such behaviors would be the manager's or supervisor's lookout.

There always exists a vicious circle of "negative acts and behaviors" amongst work groups that contribute toward organizational development via the online mode. If "knowledge hoarding" is observed at the individual employee's (or organizational member's) level, then those "negative acts and behaviors" could be reflected in an organization-induced reciprocation mechanism based on perceived sense of trust and justice. Hence, managers or supervisors shall look upon "knowledge hoarding" as some kind of opportunistic, self serving conduct against the organization, while certain social sanctions by managers or supervisors at the "online" workplace may sow a few seeds of doubt in the minds of employees (or organizational members) and coax them to believe that the importance of their presence will be diminished once their tacit knowledge gets extracted. A duality of this kind is detrimental for organizational growth and needs to be arrested immediately so that progress keeps on happening even online.

Overall, the construct of "knowledge hoarding" is not dyadic in nature and primarily relates to nonsharing behaviors without targeting any individual employee (or organizational member) in either direction. The relation between "knowledge hoarding" and "negative acts and behaviors" at the work unit or departmental level can be interpreted by managers and supervisors as "potential self-interest" (which have been revealed or are yet to be revealed) among employees (or organizational members) that generally results in "unequal access to workplace resources" (Zhang, 2009; Khalid, 2020). This actually causes the degree of justice to reduce and offers an indirect mechanism to get involved in "knowledge hoarding." Any "online" workplace adds more trouble to this existing problem because of physical/geographical distances and increased aloofness through the work-from-home situation that permits "one-click" disconnection at will. A manager's or supervisor's personality, added with a history of calmness, composure, and patience, will be key in addressing such "voluntarily-done involuntary action" linked issues.

At this point, it will be easier to gauge that noncooperative, hostile "online" work environments will produce more reasons of "knowledge hoarding." An environment like this will be the outcome of a collective mental state of organizational professionals that is under the influence of the current covid19 outbreak. There is every possibility of withdrawal for individual protection or collective retaliation leading to an organizational breakdown. Thus, the social norms at "online" workplaces have to be compulsorily redefined by practicing managers or supervisors.

It will be expected that a psychological breach mechanism (categorized by reduced trust) in an "online" workplace is neutralized. The same can go on to neutralize further negatively affected basic world assumptions in that "online workplace (characterized by reduced justice). A breach in the informal organizational contract will be engulfed by "negative acts and behaviors" that can have severe implications. The employees (or organizational members) may respond to such a breach by not complying with the rules and regulations as mandated for an "online" workplace and make persistent efforts in order to de-establish equitable work relationships within the virtual teams. Destruction of a cooperative and/or friendly "online" work environment shall increase the intent of "knowledge hoarding," owing to self-beliefs surrounding manipulations in organizational justice.

> ***Situation 2:*** A collective of smaller organizations engaged in the domain of e-sports (organizing virtual tournaments, playrooms and training-pods) has been facing issues related to "knowledge hoarding" by various specialist collaborators. They have expressed a need to migrate from the "purely online mode" to a "reasonably phygital mode" of operations in order to curtail "knowledge hoarding" and its impact. Essentially, it is reiterated that "knowledge hoarding" is a negative act, which can hinder the progress of any organization.

5.7 THE FUTURE OF "KNOWLEDGE HOARDING"

A number of effects, as discussed earlier, have been identified by senior professionals in the realm of management and organizational administration. For scholarly substantiation of the same, a study (or a combination of multiple studies) must be conducted over a period of 2–3 years. Academic reinforcement will require this minimum number of years to establish fundamental and applied theories on the reciprocal impact of "knowledge hoarding" on "online" workplaces. Immediate negative outcomes can be dealt with as suggested earlier; however, the practicing managers and/or supervisors need to make themselves aware of the phenomena called "knowledge hoarding" and keep decoding the interrelated negative acts and behaviors, which signal dire consequences for an "online" workplace.

"Knowledge hoarding" has gone beyond dyadic interpersonal interactions at an "online" workplace (Silva de Garcia et al., 2020; Aljawarneh et al., 2020). It occurs at the virtual work-unit or team level, and spreads across a department (with no confirmed source or recipient of knowledge-based asset). As "online" workplaces have slightly distorted the physical organizational hierarchy and reporting relationships, employees (or organizational members) are experiencing vertical and horizontal shifts in the levels of perceived trust and organizational justice. Both of these factors significantly control "knowledge hoarding" behavior and related negative acts in an "online" workplace. It is not a necessary condition that only personal motives can induce withholding of knowledge in an individual; on the contrary, it could be a prolonged degenerative behavior demonstrated by a work-unit online and push the organization toward a long-standing worry. If the quality of social exchange deteriorates within an "online" workplace, then collective "knowledge hoarding" shall become like an activated Marshal-shield, which the organization would not be able to penetrate. It can even start building a normative culture of "knowledge hoarding" inside the virtually placed organization.

Typically, a modern "online" workplace tries to counter "negative acts and behaviors" through amended policies that have been written down, traditional surveys that are conducted "online" to know about the employees' (or organizational members' changed professional mindset and other sentiments), interactive "online" training programmes for personal development and "online" information exchange sessions. Though such actions reduce "knowledge hoarding" to an extent, these are not supposed to be the most effective or efficient methods.

A recent review published by McKellar et al. (2020) on OD interventions for the "online" workplace did mention that knowledge management strategies of the past were getting rejected autonomously in the "new normal" era. Subtle "digital" forms of incivility were replacing conspicuous "negative acts and behaviors" at the "online" workplace. The assumption that a manager's/supervisor's clear notion of the "knowledge hoarding" phenomenon can solve all related organizational problems will not be enough for the organization to succeed, rather survive, in today's unusually dynamic global business environment. In the upcoming hybrid organizations (which operate concurrently as a combination of "online" and "offline" workplaces), the expansive pool of managers and supervisors must become more indomitable, decisive as well as assertive while responding to "knowledge hoarding" activities and other negative forms of organizational behavior.

In addition, in order to prevent "knowledge hoarding" efficaciously, enhanced open-participation of employees (or organizational members), their empowerment and being embedded in the prevailing context must be ensured alongside taking into account the "correctness" of the implementation processes within an "online" workplace. Moving forward from here, a hybrid workplace shall encounter new-fangled difficulties to come to terms with "knowledge hoarding." Dependence on social capital inside such a workplace can pose concealed challenges too!

5.8 KEY TAKEAWAYS

1. "Knowledge hoarding" is a reality at workplaces and that continues in the "online" space as on date.
2. "Knowledge hoarding," in effect, is distinct from "knowledge hiding."

3. The conscious intent behind hoarding knowledge is substantially lower; as such, the act of hoarding inadvertently puts more serious impetus on a workplace than hiding behavior.
4. "Knowledge hoarding" can drastically impact organizational performance and vice-versa.
5. By and large, "knowledge hoarding" has deep and negative influence on organizations.
6. Evidence-based decision may be compromised in an organizational setting owing to "knowledge hoarding."
7. It is highly possible that operational difficulties for even "phygital" workplaces are increasing by the day because of "knowledge hoarding."
8. "Knowledge hoarding" will continue to play a pivotal role in organizational politics.
9. Optimized deployment of resources in "online" workplaces takes multiple turns via all issues related to "knowledge hoarding."
10. Dealing with "knowledge hoarding," as part of the greater corporate strategy and governance, shall make "new normal" workplaces better prepared in terms of executing big-ticket projects.

KEYWORDS

- **knowledge hoarding**
- **knowledge hiding**
- **organizational success**
- **negating**
- **efficiency**
- **effectiveness**
- **organizational development**

REFERENCES

Acharya, A.; Mishra, B. Exploring the Relationship between Organizational Structure and Knowledge Retention: A Study of the Indian Infrastructure Consulting Sector. *J. Knowl. Manage.* **2017**, *21* (4), 961–985.

Acharya, A.; Singh, S. K.; Pereira, V.; Singh, P. Big Data, Knowledge Co-creation and Decision Making in Fashion Industry. *Int. J. Inf. Manage.* **2018**, *42*, 90–101.

Al-Abbadi, L.; Alshawabkeh, R.; Rumman, A. Knowledge Management Processes and Innovation Performance: The Moderating Effect of Employees Knowledge Hoarding. *Manage. Sci. Lett.* **2020**, *10* (7), 1463–1472.

Albana, M. J.; Yeşiltaş, M. Impact of Linguistic Ostracism on Knowledge Sharing, Hiding and Hoarding and the Moderating Role of Cultural Intelligence. *Kybernetes* **2021**, *51* (13). doi:10.1108/JWL-07-2019-0088.

Aljawarneh, N. M.; Abd Kader Alomari, K.; Alomari, Z. S.; Taha, O. Cyber Incivility and Knowledge Hoarding: Does Interactional Justice Matter? *VINE J. Inf. Knowl. Manage. Syst.* **2020**. doi:10.1108/VJIKMS-12-2019-0193.

Ayub, A.; Ajmal, T.; Iqbal, S.; Ghazanfar, S.; Anwaar, M.; Ishaq, M. Abusive Supervision and Knowledge Hiding in Service Organizations: Exploring the Boundary Conditions. *Int. J. Confl. Manage.* **2021**. doi:10.1108/IJCMA-02-2021-0029.

Bouty, I. Interpersonal and Interaction Influences on Informal Resource Exchanges between R&D Researchers across Organizational Boundaries. *Acad. Manage. J.* **2000**, *43* (1), 50–65.

Connelly, C. E.; Zweig, D. How Perpetrators and Targets Construe Knowledge Hiding in Organizations. *Eur. J. Work Organ. Psychol.* **2015**, *24* (3), 479–489.

Connelly, C. E.; Zweig, D.; Webster, J.; Trougakos, J. P. Knowledge Hiding in Organizations. *J. Organ. Behav.* **2012**, *33* (1), 64–88.

Einarsen, S.; Hoel, H.; Notelaers, G. Measuring Exposure to Bullying and Harassment at Work: Validity, Factor Structure and Psychometric Properties of the Negative Acts Questionnaire-Revised. *Work Stress* **2009**, *23* (1), 24–44.

Evans, J. M.; Hendron, M. G.; Oldroyd, J. B. Withholding the Ace: The Individual- and Unit-level Performance Effects of Self-reported and Perceived Knowledge Hoarding. *Organ. Sci.* **2014**, *26* (2), 494–510.

Ferris, G. R.; Treadway, D. C.; Kolodinsky, R. W.; Hochwarter, W. A.; Kacmar, C. J.; Douglas, C.; Frink, D. D. Development and Validation of the Political Skill Inventory. *J. Manage.* **2005**, *31* (1), 126–152.

Halbesleben, J. R.; Neveu, J. P.; Paustian-Underdahl, S. C.; Westman, M. Getting to the "COR" Understanding the Role of Resources in Conservation of Resources Theory. *J. Manage.* **2014**, *40* (5), 1334–1364.

Hobfoll, S. E. The Influence of Culture, Community, and the Nested-self in the Stress Process: Advancing Conservation of Resources Theory. *Appl. Psychol.* **2001**, *50* (3), 337–421.

Homan, G. C. *Social Behavior: Its Elementary Forms*; Harcourt, Brace and World Inc.: New York, 1961.

Jabeen, S.; Danish, R. Q.; Sheikh, L.; Ramzan, M.; Hasnain, M. Influence of Workplace Mistreatment and Structural Empowerment on Employee Engagement through Knowledge Hoarding. *Pak. J. Prof. Psychol.: Res. Pract.* **2020**, *11* (2), 1–18.

Khalid, B.; Iqbal, R.; Hashmi, S. D. Impact of Workplace Ostracism on Knowledge Hoarding: Mediating Role of Defensive Silence and Moderating Role of Experiential Avoidance. *Fut. Bus. J.* **2020**, *6* (1), 1–10.

McKellar, K.; Sillence, E.; Neave, N.; Briggs, P. There Is More Than One Type of Hoarder: Collecting, Managing and Hoarding Digital Data in the Workplace. *Interact. Comput.* **2020**, *32* (1), 209–220.

Nielsen, M. B.; Notelaers, G.; Einarsen, S. Measuring Exposure to Workplace Bullying. In Einarsen, S., Hoel, H., Zapf, D., Cooper, C. L. (Eds.); *Bullying and Harassment in the Workplace: Developments in Theory, Research, and Practice*. CRC Press: Boca Raton, FL; pp 149–174.

Pfeffer, J. *Power in Organizations*, Pitman: Marshfield, MA, 1981; p 33.

Silva de Garcia, P.; Oliveira, M.; Brohman, K. Knowledge Sharing, Hiding and Hoarding: How Are They Related? *Knowl. Manage. Res. Pract.* **2020,** 1–13. doi:10.1080/14778238.2020.1774434.

Stenmark, D. Information vs. Knowledge: The Role of Intranets in Knowledge Management. In *Proceedings of the 35th Annual Hawaii International Conference on System Sciences*, IEEE, January, 2002; pp 928–937.

Wang, S.; Noe, R. A. Knowledge Sharing: A Review and Directions for Future Research. *Hum. Res. Manage. Rev.* **2010,** *20* (2), 115–131.

Webster, J.; Brown, G.; Zweig, D.; Connelly, C. E.; Brodt, S.; Sitkin, S. Beyond Knowledge Sharing: Withholding Knowledge at Work. *Res. Pers. Hum. Resour. Manage.* **2008,** *27* (1), 1–37.

Williams, K. D. Ostracism. *Ann. Rev. Psychol.* **2007,** *58*, 425–452.

Zhang, M. J. IS Support for Knowledge Management and Firm Performance: An Empirical Study. In *Knowledge Management, Organizational Memory and Transfer Behavior: Global Approaches and Advancements*, IGI Global, 2009; pp 234–254.

CHAPTER 6

A Shift in Post-Pandemic Work Strategies: Challenges and Opportunities of Technology Use vis-à-vis Work-from-Home

BHASWATI JANA[*] and TANUJA KAUSHIK

[1]GD Goenka University, Sohna, Gurgaon, New Delhi, India

[*]Corresponding author. E-mail: bhaswati.chk09@gmail.com

ABSTRACT

The global pandemic created due to Novel Coronavirus Covid-19 forced many companies to close down their offices and workplaces, and give the employees the option to work-from-home (WFH). In the WFH environment, the key driver was the use of tools and technology like Skype, Zoom, Google Meet, WebEx, and Microsoft Team. These tools and technologies helped the workforce to communicate and collaborate among themselves and also offer services to their clients. However, this was also a new experience for many employees who were also not well trained or mentally equipped for a sudden change in work orientation. This chapter will explore the various challenges faced by employees in different organizations, the strategies they employed to take care of the bottlenecks, and the feasibility of the different tools that were used for continuing the work in WFH mode.

6.1 INTRODUCTION: THE OUTLINE

The sudden impact of the Covid-19 pandemic has compelled many companies to adopt work-from-home (WFH) mode of operations to sustain their business and continue the operations in a seamless manner. This chapter examines the issues and challenges faced by companies while adopting the WFH mode of operations and the ways in which they are overcoming that. We have started by giving a detailed history of how businesses across the World got affected due to Covid-19 pandemic.

We have described different models of technology adoption that have been propagated to top researchers and experts. There is a description of different technology tools like Zoom, Google Meet, WebEx, and Microsoft Teams that has been extensively used for communication while doing WFH during the pandemic period. It is also a matter of fact, as stated by Chakraborty et al. (2021) that people have become much more depended on social networks subjected to the social distancing imposed. We have shared the findings of a primary research conducted with 100 respondents from all over India to find out the various challenges faced by employees in different organizations, the strategies they employed to take care of the bottlenecks, and the feasibility of the different tools that were used for continuing the work in WFH mode. The chapter ends with a conclusion on what shape the WFH mode of work will take after all employees are vaccinated and normalcy sets in

6.2 SNAPSHOT OF COVID-19 CHALLENGES

In mid-November, the Chinese healthcare authorities in the city of Wuhan detected patients getting afflicted with a virus that was similar to SARS but had characteristics, which were more deadly as it was contagious in nature (Jeanna, 2020). After more in-depth research, it was named as Novel Sars Coronavirus Covid-19 or Novel Sars-Cov-2. Initially, it was thought that the virus spread from bats to human beings. But subsequent research showed that it was contagious and was spreading rapidly from humans to humans. The virus was quite complicated as it was showing external manifestations in some patients, while it was asymptomatic in others. This virus also proved quite deadly in patients with preexisting lungs, heart, or kidney afflictions leading to comorbidity.

Starting from Wuhan, China, this deadly virus spread to neighboring areas like Huanggang and Ezhou in the Hubei Province of China. The coronavirus affected 84,165 people in China and lead to the death of 4634 people (Sukumar, 2020).

The Chinese authorities were quick to clamp down and prevent the menace of coronavirus from spreading. They stopped all kinds of movement of people and transport from Wuhan and Hubei Province. Around 760 million citizens of China were confined to their homes. The Chinese authorities identified coronavirus-infected patients using big data analytics and ensured that they remained quarantined in home if the condition was not serious and at hospital if the condition was serious. They created two 1000-bed makeshift hospitals in Wuhan in 10 days at Wuhan to treat the patients who got infected with coronavirus.

The coronavirus spread peaked in China on 26th January, and gradually started coming down with pre-emptive measures in place. But meanwhile, this highly infectious virus had spread to Italy, Spain, and Iran causing major havoc out there. Till today, Italy recorded 4.3 million cases and 127,949 deaths. Spain recorded 4.2 million cases and 81,221 death. Iran recorded 3.7 million cases and 89,122 death (Worldometers, July 26, 2021).

By the time the Italian, Spanish, and Iranian authorities could control the spreading of coronavirus using containment and quarantine measures, there were people in Germany, France, UK, and Russia who got infected. Germany recorded 3.7 million cases and 92,037 deaths, France recorded 5.9 million cases and 111,622 cases, UK recorded 5.6 million cases and 129,158 deaths, and Russia recorded 6.1 million cases and 129,158 deaths (Worldometers, July 26, 2021).

But the worst affected countries have been Brazil, India, and USA. Brazil recorded 19.6 million cases and 549,999 deaths. India recorded 31.4 million cases and 421,117 deaths. USA recorded 35.2 million cases and 626,769 cases (Worldometers, July 26, 2021).

Because of the severity of the spread, WHO had to declare a situation of pandemic on 11th March 2020 (WHO, 11 March 2020).

After reaching the pandemic stage, several governments took pre-emptive and corrective measures to control the further spread of the virus and deaths due the ill-effects of the same. The American Government declared national emergency on March 13th and imposed travel restrictions within the country and between USA and other countries. The Canada Government followed suit and imposed similar restrictions on travel and started a support system to help the affected patients and also the economically hit citizens. The UK Government started a test and trace scheme and also announced a lockdown. The German, French, and other European countries also followed suit with similar measures. The Australian Government gave support to the business people and citizens through a stimulus package. The New Zealand

Government, led by Prime Minister Ms. Jacinda Arden, won a lot of praise for imposing a quick lockdown, tracking the infected patients, and monitoring the lockdown in a strategic manner to keep the spread of coronavirus to a bare minimum. The African countries were facing a bigger problem because of the lack of testing kits and the WHO and developed nations stepped in to help them with the same.

In India, the coronavirus spread was initially contained and then spread like wildfire. It was first detected in Kerala in the end of January, 2020. By 3rd February, it was three cases in Kerala. By 20th March, there were 500 cases of Corona all across India, barring North East States and Goa. The Indian Government tried to contain the spread by announcing a 1 day Janta Curfew. As things did not work out, 21 days lockdown was announced from 2nd March to 14th April, 2020. There were three consecutive lockdowns announced one after another from 15th April to 31st May. After that, the Indian Government went for an unlocking process with reopening of bus, trains, domestic airlines, shops, places of worship, offices, and other establishments (Amarnath, 2020).

Now, let us look at the statistical figures. After 21 days lockdown, we had 10,300 cases and 342 deaths (Kunal and Asim, 14 April 2020). After the second lockdown ended on 17th May (54 days), we had 31,094 cases and 1306 deaths. 10,886 patients had also meanwhile recovered. After the third lockdown ended on 3rd May (40 days), we had 90,000 cases and 2800 deaths. Maharashtra became the epicenter of coronavirus spread. The coronavirus pandemic has spread rapidly all over India with the states of Maharashtra crossed 1 million cases, Karnataka, Tamil Nadu, and Delhi accounting for maximum cases (BS Web Team, September 11, 2020) The different measures taken by Governments across the World, besides testing, detection containment, and quarantine, are lockdown, travel restrictions, stopping of all forms of transport, and WFH. Exemptions were given only to suppliers of essential commodities and medicines. Overnight, many companies had to shift their workforce from the regular office mode to WFH.

While service-based industries could do the transition with ease, many production-oriented units had to down the shutters and go for a complete shutdown. The Indian Economy reduced by 23.9% in the quarter April to June 2020 (Pallavi, August 31, 2020).

6.3 WFH: THE NEW NORMAL

As per research done by Global State of Remote Work, around 40% of companies across the World are now adopting a hybrid model wherein they give their employees the option to choose between WFO (work-from-office) and WFH. Many multinational companies give women employees the option to WFH as they need to manage their family and children to achieve a work-life balance. Many companies in metro cities prefer to give their employees the choice to WFH because of commuting problems and traffic jams, and also because of high cost of overheads like electricity, air-conditioner and security options in maintaining an office. Many organizations are also creating a virtual office, where employees from all over the World can connect on a technology platform and collaborate to perform tasks in a synchronized manner.

There are many difficulties faced by employees doing WFH. There could be interruptions from family members like children. There could be a feeling of loneliness as the employee is not meeting the coworkers. There could be a communication gap because of network problems, slow internet, or call drops. The biggest problem is a distrust brewing up between employees and their bosses as the feeling of employees is being overloaded with job task and the employer feels he is not getting the best output within the determined time frame.

The execution of tasks in WFH situations is flawless, just because of the use of Technology. Often, the employer needs to deploy technologies like Slack, GoToMeeting, WebEx, Zoom, Google Hangout, TeamViewer, and Microsoft Meetings. The employee needs to learn how to use these technologies in an effective manner in order to make the execution of tasks in work from environment more effective. The important question is: Will the employee be motivated to learn new skills? What are the factors that will motivate the employee to learn new skills to make the execution of tasks more effective in WFH scenario?

Icek Ajzen (1985) has given the Theory of Planned Behavior (TPB), which links beliefs with behaviors. Ajzen's TPB states that: *"intention toward attitude, subject norms, and perceived behavioral control, together shape an individual's behavioral intentions and behaviors"* This theory helps to explain the beliefs and behavioral intentions that shape the acceptance of new technology. We have described the constraints and challenges of adopting the WFH mode of operations by dividing them under three categories: *"Communication, Collaboration, and Conflict Resolution"*.

Fred Davis (1989) has given a model called Technology Acceptance Model (TAM) that uses two constructs Perceived Usefulness (PU) and Perceived Ease of Use (PEOU) to explain whether an employee will be motivated to adopt a new technology. Davis has explained *"PU as the degree to which a person believes that using a particular system would enhance his or her job performance"*. He has explained PEOU as "the degree to which a person believes that using a particular system would be free from effort"

(Davis, 1989). *"If the technology is easy to use, then the barriers conquered. If it's not easy to use and the interface is complicated, no one has a positive attitude towards it".*

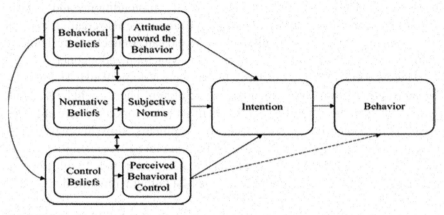

FIGURE 6.1 Theory of planned behavior
Source: Adapted from Ajzen, 1985.

Another model that has been given by Rogers (2003) is Diffusion of Innovations. Through this model, Rogers explained how a new technology goes through several phases of adoption. Different people adopt technology in different manner and they can be stratified as *"innovators, early adopters, early majority, late majority and laggards."*

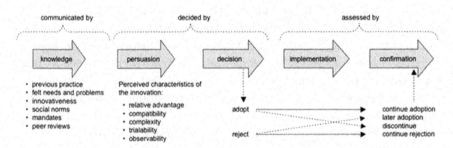

FIGURE 6.2 Diffusion of innovations.
Source: Adapted from Rogers, 2003.

Rogers specified that the adoption or rejection of a new technology or process is dependent on knowledge as well as persuasion. For an employee to adopt new technology to be able to WFH, he or she needs to be adequately trained and also persuaded with incentives or future growth prospects in order to adopt the new technology.

Our research work seeks to analyze the degree of technology adoption by employees doing WFH. We have conducted the study among employees of different organizations whose residence was in Mohali, Punjab, using a structured questionnaire to understand the challenges faced by them while doing WFH.

6.4   REVIEW OF LITERATURE

In their research paper, Kreiner et al. (2009) have investigated how people balance their priorities between work and home life. They have classified four parameters, namely, behavioral, temporal, physical, and communicative that are crucial for successful execution of work in WFH environment. They have developed a model based on boundary violations that help to reduce the negative effect created due to imbalance between professional life and personal life.

In their research paper titled, Peeters et al. (2005) have analyzed three factors, namely, mental demands, emotional demands, and quantitative demands that play a major role to determine the quality of work executed in WFH environment. It was found that employees were facing difficulty in balancing between family pressure and job pressure and that was having a burnout effect on employees who were doing WFH.

In their research paper titled, Working at home with computers: Work and nonwork issues, the authors Olson and Primps (1984) describes issues pertaining to telecommuting. Telecommuting refers to working in home using computers, phones and technological gadgets, software, and interfaces. The authors have taken two extreme cases to illustrate the challenges faced in WFH scenario. In the first case, the employee enjoys a higher degree of autonomy and self-control because the employee has expertise in her job and proper skills. In the second case, the employee will have reduced autonomy and less salary because of low expertise in the job and her skills also are not much in demand. The authors conclude that WFH will not become a widespread trend.

6.5   THE CHALLENGES WITH WORK-FROM-HOME (WFH)

The current pandemic has compelled the companies to adopt the WFH model, both in India and across the world. Still there is a success story in

WFH in the service-oriented companies like Information Technology, Business Process Outsourcing, Call Centers, Banking, Telecommunication, and Education sector. Some hospitals have adopted WFH for their doctors. But, the constraints and challenges are always there to WFH. There are mainly three categories of constraints and challenges observed: Communication, Collaboration, and Conflict Resolution.

6.5.1 COMMUNICATION

In a normal workplace, communication happens through meetings between employees or meetings between employees and clients. There are chances of discussion giving suggestion asking question and all. But in case of a WFH, the scenario is different as conversation is done through Telephonic conversations, mails, messages, and WhatsApp.

The challenges are here: because of poor telephone and internet connections, there are misunderstandings. Because of low internet facility sometimes sending big files, videos through emails has became another problem. A flood of WhatsApp messages also creates a multitude of issues. Using MS Office on mobile phones was extremely tough.

6.5.2 COLLABORATION

In physical office setup, it is easier to collaborate with colleagues and interact with clients. In online mode, the communication happens through telephones and internet.

Interpersonal relations at work got disturbed as Chakraborty et al. (2021) asserted that too media rich environment is harmful of interpersonal relations.

6.5.3 CONFLICT RESOLUTION

Conflict between the bosses and employees is one of the main problems in WFH. Bosses feel employees are not putting up enough efforts and employees feel they are being overworked. The feeling of employee is they have to work more hours and the employer thinks employees are not enough loyal towards their work and working hour.

Working from home also creates difficulties in performance Appraisal and task evaluation. Using surveillance on an employee might be irrational as per the employee's view, which can be the cause of low job satisfaction for the employees. An equitable balance should be found out to create a harmonious work environment.

6.6 OPPORTUNITIES WITH WFH

Benefits of WFH is uncountable. Many of the variable and overhead costs get reduced. In bigger cities, commuting challenges are not there with WFH. For women, WFH is most preferred to maintain the work-life balance. WFH in a proper professional way can give higher level of job satisfaction for employees and can bring down the cost of business transactions.

6.7 USE OF TECHNOLOGY FOR WFH: THE GAMECHANGER

Technology plays a key role in facilitating the execution of tasks in WFH situations. Often, the employer needs to deploy technologies like Slack, GoToMeeting, WebEx, Zoom, Google Hangout, Google Meet, TeamViewer, and Microsoft Teams. The employee needs to learn how to use these technologies in an effective manner in order to make the execution of tasks in work from environment more effective.

6.7.1 SKYPE

Skype was initially a Peer-to-Peer service, but became famous as VOIP (Voice Over Internet Protocol) that allowed users to make calls using internet services. eBay acquired Skype and created Skype casts with Skype that allowed video-conferencing with upto 100 participants. Later, they sold Skype to Microsoft. Microsoft replaced it's proprietary messaging system with Skype and installed a Bing search bar. Since then, the popularity of Skype has skyrocketed.

6.7.2 WEBEX

WebEx is a video conferencing and web conferencing application developed by Subrah Iyar and Min Zhu. The global telecom equipment giant

Cisco acquired WebEx in 2007 for $3.2 billion. For companies who were already comfortable with using Cisco's equipment, technology tools, and software solutions, WebEx was an added advantage. During the lockdown, many top corporate bodies preferred using WebEx instead of Zoom for it's robust security firewall. WebEx also has a free version that can accommodate hundred users and can be used for forty minutes for free.

6.7.3 ZOOM

The company Zoom was setup in 2011 in San Jose, California by Eric Juan. Erin Juan is a former employee of Cisco WebEx and he started the company with forty ex-employees of WebEx. He, along with his team, created a video conferencing tool that was relatively easier to use than WebEx. Like Cisco WebEx and Zoom does not need a preinstallation of Cisco environment that is required in the case of Zoom.

During the lockdown period, the popularity of Zoom zoomed to the extent that saw many companies use the software for meetings and collaborative work. The Zoom software gained wide acceptance among educational institutions and later was being used for conducting training sessions by Corporate. Zoom offered a 45 min session with 100 people for free, beyond which the users needed to subscribe to a paid version.

However, a major drawback of Zoom has been the issue of security and the concern that Eric Juan was born in China and later took the citizenship of America. Though he now shares American antecedents, big blue-chip companies were always apprehensive of his Chinese roots and preferred not to use Zoom.

6.7.4 GOOGLE MEET

For users who wanted a longer duration online meeting for free, Google Meet was the viable option. Google Meet was initially launched as a free tool as a part of G-Suite, but now has been converted into a freemium model. This tool allows 100 participants and a time limit of one hour for free. However, Google has not restricted the time limit as of now because of the coronavirus pandemic. While Google Hangout has a limitation of 150 users, Google Meet can accommodate up to 250 participants.

6.7.5 MICROSOFT TEAM

Microsoft Team was released by Microsoft in the year 2017. This was promoted as a tool for communication and collaboration. Microsoft announced that Team was a superior product to Skype. The Team software scores higher over Skype because of superior audio and video calls, better chat and messaging services, better integration with telephony app and systems, file transfer facilities, and guest access. Microsoft Team also has got a free model that can have up to 300 users and 10 GB of Cloud Storage.

6.8 RESEARCH AND FINDINGS

We conducted a research with 100 respondents from all over India to find out the various challenges faced by employees in different organizations, the strategies they employed to take care of the bottlenecks, and the feasibility of the different tools that were used for continuing the work in WFH mode.

The respondents were selected using the snowball sampling method, and the data were collected using a structured questionnaire, which comprised of open ended, close ended, and questions with a five-point Likert scale to measure the attitudes and preferences. The respondents were mostly employees of various organizations in India who were doing WFH during the pandemic.

When asked which tool they preferred for communication and collaboration while doing WFH during the lockdown period, a large majority (45%) of the respondents said that they preferred Zoom. The second most preferred choice was Google Meet (14%) followed by Skype (11%).

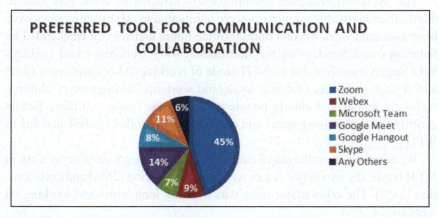

FIGURE 6.3 Preferred tool for communication and collaboration.

The inclination towards Zoom (45%) is understandable considering the fact that it is much easier to install and much easier to use. Zoom can be easily used even in low internet bandwidth that gives comfort to people who do not have strong telecom towers nearby or do not have access to high end smartphones.

When asked if the Work-Life Balance was affected by WFH, an overwhelming majority (67%) replied in the affirmative, while smaller number of people (33%) replied in the negative.

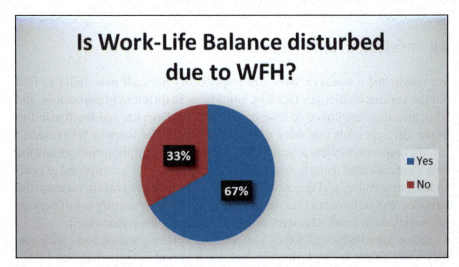

FIGURE 6.4   Effect on work-life balance due to WFH.

The Work-Life-Balance got immensely affected as there was now to fixed office hours that employees were habituated to. Many employees have been allocated work beyond normal office hours and also on weekends like Saturdays and Sundays as the line demarcating work days and holidays have largely vanished due to WFH mode of working. Also, employees faced added responsibilities of doing household work and taking care of children and their studies and elderly people present in the house. All these factors contributed to the rising stress and disturbance in Work-Life-Balance due to WFH.

When asked about the major challenges faced during execution of work in WFH mode, the two major issues were communication (26%) and collaboration (21%). The other major issue was working long hours and working on weekends (27%).

A Shift in Post-Pandemic Work Strategies 93

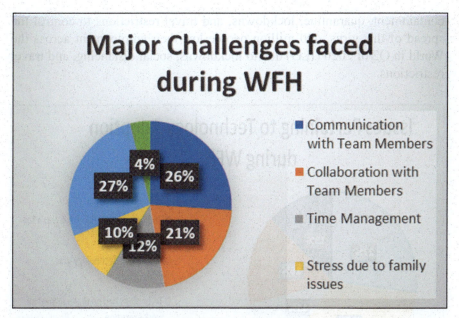

FIGURE 6.5 Major challenges facing WFH.

The employees, who have been habituated in the process of physical interactions for conversations and meetings, definitely feel at odds while communicating through video conferencing tools or messaging platforms like WhatsApp. With most of the telecom companies having bandwidth constraints, proper communication was a big challenge.

A majority of respondents (33%) have said that adapting to technology was easy for them. This was primarily because they received proper and adequate training (27%).

It was the process of effective training that facilitated the process of technology adoption by employees to work in the WFH Mode.

6.9 ADAPTING TO THE NEW NORMAL

The coronavirus outbreak started in the city of Wuhan in China and by the time the global leaders understood that it was a major threat to lives and livelihood, it had spread across the World causing major devastation. The reaction to this pandemic was knee-jerk in the beginning with USA and developing nations blaming China and WHO, and then going for containment, quarantine, lockdowns, and travel restrictions to control the spread of this virus. 400 million people lost their employment across the World in Q2 of 2020 (ILO) due to lockdowns, social distancing, and travel restrictions.

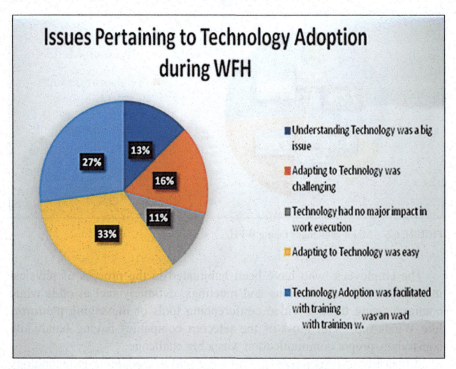

FIGURE 6.6   Issues pertaining to technology adoption during WFH.

Some companies were quick and agile to react to the situation and shifted their workforce to the WFH mode to ensure that there was no loss in employment or fall in productivity. However, this WFH Mode had posed its own set of challenges. Due to the lack of face-to-face interactions that usually happens in office or workplace, communication and collaboration became a big challenge. For employees, distraction from work and creating the ambience of a workplace in home settings was an additional challenge. As children were also attending school or college in online mode, attending to them and giving them adequate space and quietude were also important along with executing the task. The discipline of working the eight-hour shift with lunch break in between also got hampered as employers felt that employees could take up added responsibility and workload as they were doing WFH. The trust between employer and employees also got strained as the employer felt the employees were in a state of perpetual relaxation at home and employees felt they were being overburdened with work.

It was in this situation that companies looked up to technology and tools to facilitate proper work execution in the WFH environment. Employees were given laptops, desktops, and smartphones with high-speed internet connections so that they could communicate and collaborate more effectively in WFH environment. The companies also used collaboration tools like *"Zoom, Google Meet, Microsoft Team, and Webex"* for meetings and collaborations. The team members were also given training on how to use gadgets, apps, tools, technologies, and devices to create virtual workplaces and operate in a remote mode while maintaining the same level of efficiency and efficacy. Some of them were early adopters and incorporated the tolls quite smoothly in their execution of the tasks while others had to be given rigorous training to get up-to-date with the usage of technology.

Our research showed that Perceived Utility (PU) and PEOU plays a major role in the adoption of technology for executing tasks in the WFH Mode. The constructs PU and PEOU were given by Fred Davis (1989) in the TAM. Employees doing WFH felt comfortable, if they found it easy to use and they got benefits in terms of better communication and collaboration. That explains why both companies and employees felt comfortable in using Zoom for communication and collaboration although there were perceived risks in the form of data breach.

Companies have also benefitted from WFH mode of executing work. Absenteeism and late coming to work have drastically reduced. The problem of commuting and providing vehicles to employees for transportation is also no more there. The lease and rental charges have come down. Electricity costs, housekeeping costs, and security costs have come down. Conflicts between employees are also down due to less physical interaction.

Many companies have now expressed the intention to prolong or continue work done in WFH mode even if the vaccine comes into place and the threat from coronavirus is largely diminished. Tata Consultancy Service (TCS) has announced a 25 × 25 model where 25% of its employees will work from designated office complexes and 75% of its employees will do WFH. This strategy will come into force by 2025 and that is why this is called 25 × 25 Model. Many other companies like Infosys and Wipro have also announced that 99% of employees will do WFH.

However, not everything is hunky-dory in executing tasks in WFH mode. Many companies have reduced the pay of employees doing WFH as their business earnings have been impacted due to social distancing, lockdowns, and economic downturns. This has caused difficulty for employees who have high Equated Monthly Installments to pay for the loans they had taken prior to coronavirus pandemic and lockdown, then there is the added challenge of managing children and attending to household work as maids are also on leave and the employee is there all the time in the house. There are cases of psychological breakdowns, domestic violence and prevalence of psycho-somatic illness creeping in due to being confined in home for longer periods.

If the current news is to be believed, the vaccine for coronavirus is just around the corner. So, the next important dilemma for companies would be whether to continue with the WFH mode or call the employees to do full-time work from office premises. A detailed study might be required in this context to understand whether WFH is really beneficial in the long run and companies should attach much importance to it or should it be discarded to give way to full-time work from office.

6.10 RECKONER OF THE POSTPANDEMIC WORK LIFE

The Virus Covid-19 Pandemic forced many companies to close down their offices and workplaces and give the employees the option to WFH.

As per research done by Global State of Remote Work, around 40% of companies across the World are now adopting a hybrid model wherein they give their employees the option to do WFH or WFO.

WFH has several challenges like interruptions at home, feeling of isolation, communication problems, slow internet or call drops, and distrust brewing up between the Employee and the Employer as the employee's feeling of overburdened with workload and the employer feeling of not getting the best output within the determined time frame.

The constraints and challenges in adopting WFH mode of work can be classified as: *"Communication, Collaboration, and Conflict Resolution"*.

In the WFH environment, the key driver was the use of tools and technology like Skype, Zoom, Google Meet, WebEx, and Microsoft Team.

PU and PEOU plays a major role in the adoption of technology for executing tasks in the WFH Mode.

Once the vaccination drive is completed, the next important dilemma for companies would be whether to continue with the WFH mode or call the employees to do full-time work from office premises.

6.11 CONCLUSION

The coronavirus pandemic literally came out of the blue and shook up the entire economic system across the World. This was similar to the 1918 Flu Pandemic when the H1N1 Virus spread rapidly, infecting, and killing millions of people. Repeating the past history, the Novel Coronavirus Covid-19 has infected 63 million people across the World till now and killed 1.47 million.

KEYWORDS

- work-from-home (WFH)
- technology
- communication
- human resource

REFERENCES

Ajzen, I. The Theory of Planned Behaviour. *Organ. Behav. Hum. Decis. Process.* **1991,** *50* (2), 179–211. doi:10.1016/0749-5978(91)90020-T.

Amarnath, T. Coronavirus India Lockdown Day 67 Updates. May 30, 2020. https://www.thehindu.com/news/national/india-coronavirus-lockdown-may-30-2020-live-updates/article31708100.ece.

BBC News India. India Coronavirus: Delhi to Gradually Come Out of COVID Lockdown. May 28, 2020. https://www.bbc.com/news/world-asia-india-57280968.

BS Web Team. Coronavirus LIVE: Maharashtra Cases Cross 1 Million-mark, toll at 28,724. September 11, 2020. https://www.business-standard.com/article/current-affairs/coronavirus-india-live-updates-cases-mohfw-global-death-toll-vaccine-status-on-11-september-120091100133_1.html.

Chakraborty, T.; Kumar, A.; Upadhyay, P.; Dwivedi, Y. K. Link between Social Distancing, Cognitive Dissonance, and Social Networking Site Usage Intensity: A Country-Level Study During the COVID-19 Outbreak. *Internet Res.* **2021a,** *31* (2), 419–456. doi:10.1108/intr-05-2020-0281.

Chakraborty, T.; Tripathi, M.; Saha, S. The Dynamics of Employee Relationships in a Digitalized Workplace: The Role of Media Richness on Workplace Culture. *Critical Issues on Changing Dynamics in Employee Relations and Workforce Diversity*; IGI Global, 2021b; pp 175–205.

Davis, F. D. Perceived Usefulness, Perceived Ease of Use, and User Acceptance of Information Technology. *MIS Q.* **1989,** *13* (3), 319–340. doi:10.2307/249008.

Jeanna, B. 1st Known Case of Coronavirus Traced Back to November in China. March 14, 2020. https://www.livescience.com/first-case-coronavirus-found.html.

Khetarpal, S. Post-COVID, 75% of 4.5 Lakh TCS Employees to Permanently Work from Home by '25; from 20%. April 25, 2020. https://www.businesstoday.in/latest/corporate/story/post-coronavirus-75-percent-of-3-5-lakh-tcs-employees-permanently-work-from-home-up-from-20-percent-256494-2020-04-25.

Kreiner, G. E.; Hollensbe, E. C.; Sheep, M. L. Balancing Borders and Bridges: Negotiating the Work-home Interface via Boundary Work Tactics. *Acad. Manage. J.* **2009,** *52* (4), 704–730.

Kunal, D.; Asim, K. COVID-19: About 10,300 Cases, 342 Deaths in 21 Days of Lockdown; Experts Say It Would Have Been Worse Without Shutdown. April 14, 2020. https://www.outlookindia.com/newsscroll/.

Olson, M. H. Work at Home for Computer Professionals: Current Attitudes and Future Prospects. *ACM Trans. Inf. Syst.* (*TOIS*) **1989,** *7* (4), 317–338.

Olson, M. H.; Primps, S. B. Working at Home with Computers: Work and Non-work Issues. *J. Soc. Issues* **1984,** *40* (3), 97–112.

Pallavi, N. India GDP Contracts a Record 23.9% in April–June Quarter. August 31, 2020. https://www.bloombergquint.com/business/india-gdp-contracts-a-record-239-in-april-june-quarter.

Peeters, M. C.; Montgomery, A. J.; Bakker, A. B.; Schaufeli, W. B. Balancing Work and Home: How Job and Home Demands Are Related to Burnout. *Int. J. Stress Manage.* **2005,** *12* (1), 43. doi:10.1037/1072-5245.12.1.43.

PTI, Economic Times. 41 Lakh Youth Lose Jobs in India Due to COVID-19 Pandemic: ILO-ADB Report. August 18, 2020. https://economictimes.indiatimes.com/news/economy/indicators/41-lakh-youth-lose-jobs-in-india-due-to-covid-19-pandemic-ilo-adb-report/articleshow/77613218.cms.

Rogers, E. M. Diffusion Networks. *Networks in the Knowledge Economy*; 2003; pp 130–179.

Sukumar, R. What Can Explain the Mystery of China's Covid-19 Numbers? July 31, 2020. https://www.hindustantimes.com/india-news/what-can-explain-the-mystery-of-china-s-covid-19-numbers/story-HuG99971H6xng1O4LCNrGP.html.

WHO. Coronavirus Confirmed as Pandemic by World Health Organization. March 11, 2020. https://www.bbc.com/news/world-51839944.

Worldometers. July 26, 2021. https://www.worldometers.info/coronavirus/.

CHAPTER 7

The Shift from the New Normal to the Old Normal: Challenges and Solutions

V. JAYALAKSHMI[*]

Trainer and Counselling Psychologist, Chennai, India

[*]*E-mail: jayamahi2004@gmail.com*

ABSTRACT

The Business Process Outsourcing (BPO) industry in India has helped the country see its economic boom, and has made the country turn into a high-demand destination by several countries all over the globe. Unfortunately, the country is facing huge economic downfall due to the onset of the Covid-19 pandemic. While several businesses have come to a standstill due to the lockdowns being imposed, the BPO industry made a big shift to working-from-home. Working-from-home for the BPO industry was a never-thought-of option during any scenario in the past. Hence, this study aimed to understand the experiences of the BPO employees while working-from-home, which has become the new normal, the benefits as well as the challenges. While the need may arise any time, to shift back to the old normal of working-from-office, it is highly crucial to understand the challenges that the BPO employees foresee. An understanding of these challenges would help the companies with the ability to take the necessary measures to deal with the challenges in effective ways. Twenty women and sixteen men employees working in BPOs in Chennai city were chosen for the study, through convenient sampling technique. A semistructured interview schedule was prepared for the collection of data. Qualitative as well as quantitative measures were used to analyze the data collected. Results revealed the

---

Human Resource Management in a Post-Epidemic Global Environment: Roles, Strategies, and Implementations.
Tanusree Chakraborty, Nandita Mishra, Madhurima Ganguly, & Bipasha Chatterjee (Eds.)
© 2023 Apple Academic Press, Inc. Co-published with CRC Press (Taylor & Francis)

benefits and challenges experienced by the BPO employees while working from home. Based on the challenges that they foresee while having to shift back to working from office, strategies have been suggested to deal with the challenges.

7.1 INTRODUCTION

The term "pandemic" was unknown to many from the recent generations, until the world was hit by the Covid-19 disease, caused by the coronavirus, and then learnt that it is an epidemic that occurs worldwide, or over a wide area, across international boundaries, and usually affecting large masses of people. On further learning that the virus is majorly transmitted through droplets generated when an infected person coughs, sneezes, or exhales, the governments of all countries had to impose lockdowns, and India was no exception to it. With several businesses going standstill, the country's economy faced a major disruption. Business Processing Outsourcing (BPO) industry looked for the feasibility of having work done from the employees' homes. Not in the history of the BPO industry, had there been a situation, where the possibility of working from home could have been imagined; as the BPOs deal with customers all over the globe, for various purposes, using highly complicated technological aspects (Jayalakshmi and Sujaritha, 2019). That was "easier said than done." Huge changes had to be made to the network and other work requirements, to be made suitable for employees to work from home (WFH), in the quickest time possible, to ensure all was in place by the time the lockdowns were announced. This helped serve the millions of customers during one of the toughest times of their lives, the pandemic.

This being said, the BPO employees had to face a completely new and sudden scenario of working from home. The virtual work thus brought in a big moment to remote working. But as the employees settled down, it became quite apparent that the employees could be more focused and productive while WFH, than while work-from-office (WFO) (Birkinshaw et al., 2020). Thus, it became evident for the employers that remote work really works. This has posed a big question to companies with respect to the nature of work in the postpandemic world. Companies would have to decide whether they would go back to "business as usual" and have employees WFO or if they would be convinced that flexible work is the way that would help in the long run!

However, having got adjusted to the new normal of WFH, again shifting back to the WFO pattern could post a lot of challenges, to the employees, which in turn might impact the employers. Thus, in this regard, it is highly imperative to understand the benefits experienced by the BPO employees while WFH, which in turn would help in understanding the challenges that they might face, while having to shift back to WFO, basis which employers could take necessary measures to provide the required support to the employees.

7.2 METHODOLOGY

7.2.1 OBJECTIVES OF THE STUDY

1. To identify the benefits experienced due to WFH among the BPO employees.
2. To identify the possible challenges while shifting back to WFO.
3. To provide appropriate suggestions to effectively deal with the challenges.

7.2.2 METHOD

Descriptive survey method has been used in the present study.

7.2.3 PARTICIPANTS

Thirty-six employees (women = 20 and men = 16) from six BPO companies in Chennai city, were chosen as participants for the present study, through convenience sampling technique. The age range of the participants ranged from 25 to 43 years.

7.2.4 INCLUSION CRITERIA OF PARTICIPANTS

- Employees working in private BPOs
- Married employees
- Employees with full-time working spouses
- Employees with at least one child

7.2.5 TOOLS

A researcher developed semistructured interview was used for gathering information from the BPO employees, through telephone calls, as face-to-face interviews could not be held due to the Covid-19 lockdowns. The semistructured interview was used to understand in depth the benefits experienced due to WFH, the possible challenges while shifting back to the WFO pattern, and to provide appropriate suggestions to effectively deal with the challenges.

7.2.6 DATA ANALYSIS AND INTERPRETATION

Quantitative and qualitative analyses and interpretation of data have been made use of in this study, on the basis of the nature of the data, which have been furnished in the tabular form.

From Table 7.1 of the response made by the BPO employees, it is observed that majority of the employees experienced benefits in working from home, in aspects like: flexible working hours (81%), safety from epidemics/pandemics (91%), reduced exposure to external pollution (85%), healthy sleep patterns (92%), spousal support in sharing of household responsibilities (83%), child care (92%), elder care (86%), personal time (88%), family time (98%), healthy food patterns (94%), better work-life balance (84%), time for exercises and health management activities(80%), time for hobbies (87%), location independence (100%), comfortable work environment (84%), money savings (96%), active/nonsedentary lifestyle (82%), convenience of not being physically monitored by supervisors (94%), no conflict with colleagues (70%), flexibility of breaks (90%), possibility to rest during breaks (89%), time and energy saved on commuting to office (97%) and leaves saved to meet personal commitments/vacations (93%).

Table 7.2 shows that location independence was scored as the topmost benefit of WFH among all other benefits, by the women BPO employees. Ninety-eight percent of them had experienced the possibility to rest during breaks, and provide enough time for family. Child care and healthy food patterns were scored by 97% of the women employees, time and energy saved on commuting to office was scored by 96% of them, 95% of them had scored money savings as the benefit of WFH. Flexibility of breaks and saving leaves to meet personal commitments and vacations were experienced by 94% of them, and 93% of them experienced comfortable work environment while WFH.

Table 7.3 shows that location independence was scored as the topmost benefit of WFH among all other benefits, by the men BPO employees. Time and energy saved on commuting to office was rated as the second topmost benefit, by 98% of them. Money savings and family time were rated by 97% of the employees; and 96% of them experienced the convenience of not being physically monitored by supervisors while working from home. Leaves saved to meet personal commitments/vacations and healthy food patterns were found to be beneficial by 91% of the men BPO employees. Ninety percent of the men employees felt WFH gave the benefit of time for hobbies, precaution from spreadable diseases and healthy sleep patterns.

TABLE 7.1 Responses by BPO Employees Regarding the Benefits Experienced While Working from Home.

No.	Responses by BPO employees regarding the benefits experienced while WFH	% Of positive responses Total ($N = 36$)	Women ($n = 20$)	Men ($n = 16$)
1	Flexible working hours	81%	85%	76%
2	Precaution from spreadable diseases	91%	91%	90%
3	Reduced exposure to external pollution	85%	86%	83%
4	Healthy sleep patterns	92%	93%	90%
5	Spousal support in sharing of household responsibilities	83%	84%	82%
6	Child care	92%	97%	86%
7	Elder care	86%	85%	87%
8	Personal time	88%	90%	86%
9	Family time	98%	98%	97%
10	Healthy food patterns	94%	97%	91%
11	Better work-life balance	84%	92%	75%
12	Time for exercises and health management activities	80%	72%	88%
13	Time for hobbies	87%	83%	90%
14	Location independence	100%	100%	100%
15	Comfortable work environment	84%	93%	74%
16	Money savings	96%	95%	97%
17	Active/nonsedentary lifestyle	82%	86%	77%
18	Convenience of not being physically monitored by supervisors	94%	92%	96%
19	No conflict with colleagues	70%	88%	52%
20	Flexibility of breaks	90%	94%	86%
21	Possibility to rest during breaks	89%	98%	80%
22	Time and energy saved on commuting to office	97%	96%	98%
23	Leaves saved to meet personal commitments/vacations	93%	94%	91%

TABLE 7.2 Responses by Women BPO Employees Regarding the Top 10 Benefits Experienced While Working from Home (WFH).

No.	Responses by BPO employees regarding the top 10 benefits experienced while WFH	Women ($n = 20$)
1	Location independence	100%
2	Possibility to rest during breaks	98%
3	Family time	98%
4	Child care	97%
5	Healthy food patterns	97%
6	Time and energy saved on commuting to office	96%
7	Money savings	95%
8	Flexibility of breaks	94%
9	Leaves saved to meet personal commitments/vacations	94%
10	Comfortable work environment	93%

TABLE 7.3 Responses by Men BPO Employees Regarding the Top 10 Benefits Experienced While Working from Home (WFH).

No.	Responses by BPO employees regarding the top 10 benefits experienced while WFH	Men ($n = 16$)
1	Location independence	100%
2	Time and energy saved on commuting to office	98%
3	Money savings	97%
4	Family time	97%
5	Convenience of not being physically monitored by supervisors	96%
6	Leaves saved to meet personal commitments/vacations	91%
7	Healthy food patterns	91%
8	Time for hobbies	90%
9	Precaution from spreadable diseases	90%
10	Healthy sleep patterns	90%

7.3 MAJOR FINDINGS OF THE STUDY

- Among the total sample, location independence, family time, time and energy saved on commuting to office and money savings, each with

a score beyond 95%, were the top benefits of working from home by the BPO employees.
- While location independence was scored 100% by both men and women BPO employees, possibility to rest during breaks, family time, child care, healthy food patterns, and time and energy saved on commuting to office seemed to be the most beneficial aspects by women BPO employees, while working from home. The time and energy saved on commuting to office, money savings, family time, and convenience of not being physically monitored by supervisors were the top benefits experienced by the men BPO employees, while working from home. These top benefits experienced while WFH could be the top challenges faced while having to WFO.

7.4 DISCUSSION

Working from home aids in better work-life balance, as it gives the flexibility of schedules, wherein employees can start and end their day as they choose, as long as their work is complete and leads to strong results. Such control over work schedule is invaluable when it helps the employees in attending to the needs and commitments of their personal lives, such as attending a fitness class in the mornings, balancing school schedules, household chores, medical appointments, child and elderly care, being home for a contractor, etc.

BPO employees spend 2 hours on an average in commuting to office, as most of the BPO companies are away from the main city; several commuters face a much longer commute time of even 5 hours per day (Schaefer, 2005). Studies have shown that 30 min of daily one-way commuting is associated with increased levels of anxiety and stress (Jayalakshmi, 2019), and other health-related issues like higher cholesterol, elevated blood sugar, increased risk of depression, etc., and also that long-distance commuters suffer from much higher rates of psychosomatic disorders (Schaefer, 2005). Working from home has thus helped employees in avoiding the commute, which aids in supporting their mental and physical health. The time savings not only allow the employees to focus more on work, thus increasing productivity (Caramela, 2020; Aithal, 2015), but also allows them to focus on priorities outside of work, like getting some additional sleep in the morning, eating a healthy breakfast, getting into workouts, and spending more time with family.

Working from home gives the benefit of location independence. It serves as a boon for people with disabilities or caregivers who would need flexible schedules, and allowing them the flexibility to get to doctors and other healthcare appointments when required. Remote working helps employees to work from the comfort of their own homes, in their own hometowns and cities, thus paving the way for more people living in small towns and rural communities find meaningful careers, which may not be available locally. Alongside, remote working is a great option which would help in avoiding high rents and high mortgages when having to work in cities or major metropolitan areas with high cost of living.

Working from home provides the benefit of money savings not only for the employees, but also for the employers. Companies can benefit on long-term cost saving aspects like overhead costs, transit subsidies, real-estate costs, continuity of operations, etc. (Stieg, 2020). Employees can benefit from having to spend on transportation, gas, car maintenance, parking fees, lunches bought out, a professional wardrobe, etc.

Majority of the BPO companies have central air conditioners. Working in air-conditioned environments for longer durations causes severe health issues. Working from home can solve this problem; thus enhancing well-being of employees. Further, employees can have a seating and working arrangement comfortable of their own. At office, employees may have to sit for several continuous hours and work. This sedentary lifestyle could be changed while WFH, as employees can take breaks as and when required, and stretch-out and shift tasks and have an active lifestyle. Several employees also develop back pain due to sitting for several hours, and might require to lie down or stretch-out now and then to avoid pain, which might be a challenge while WFO. Many employees also feel it uncomfortable, when having to work under constant monitoring.

Working from home helps employees develop healthy eating and sleeping patterns, allows more family and personal time, provides opportunities for hobbies and recreation, and to do exercises and other health care activities. Further, it paves ways for child care and elderly care, and provides opportunity to share the household responsibilities with their spouse and other family members.

While the benefits of working from home have been discussed, it is quite evident that these benefits that the employees enjoy could seem challenging while having to go back to the old normal of working from office. It is important for employees to develop a positive mind-set, learn effective coping mechanisms to cope with the challenges, while they take care of their well-being.

7.5 SUGGESTIONS TO COPE WITH SHIFTING BACK TO THE OLD NORMAL

Employees need to learn effective time management techniques, which would help in completing their work on time, avoiding unnecessary shift extensions, thus leaving home on time, and being able to take care of personal responsibilities.

Employees need to equip themselves with effective coping mechanisms to deal with the daily stressors of life, and ensure their physical, mental and emotional well-being is taken care of (Jayalakshmi and Sujaritha, 2020). Employers also need to remind employees to take physical and mental breaks, exercise, and participate in other non-work-related activities to reduce anxiety and enhance productivity.

Employees need to understand that change is inevitable and accept the changes. Further, as technology keeps advancing every moment, employees need to enhance their skills and acquire the required knowledge to cope with the technological advancements.

As employees would have got comfortable with the new normal, it would take time to adapt to the old normal again. Companies need to allow time for the employees to get adjusted to the change. The transition from WFH to WFO could happen gradually. Rather than a complete shift, a mix of WFH and WFO could be initiated, which would allow employees to learn ways of adapting to the changes.

Employers could provide the facility of flexible working hours, which would allow the employees still take care of their personal responsibilities; thus aiding in better work-life balance. Companies need to leverage on breaks and leave approvals (Jayalakshmi, 2018, 2019, 2020a).

Companies need to have in-house counsellors, who could provide psychological counselling to employees, for all their career and personal problems. Further, trainings to employees could be provided on topics like emotional resilience, resilience, stress management, coping, financial planning, yoga, and other wellness sessions, etc. (Jayalakshmi, 2020a).

It is highly imperative for employers to invest in the well-being of their employees, as it would help in increasing employee satisfaction and morale, improve employee retention, increase productivity and reduce absenteeism (Jayalakshmi, 2020b). It aids in better relationships between the employees and the management, lowers costs and increases open communications, thus creating a more sustainable workforce (Jayalakshmi and Aravindakshan, 2020).

7.6 CONCLUSIONS

From the present study, the benefits experienced by the BPO employees while WFH could be understood. The same also helps in understanding the challenges they could experience, while having to shift back to the old normal of WFO. When done in the right manner, remote working allows employees and companies to focus on what really matters—performance (Caramela, 2020; Aithal, 2015). Alongside, WFH would help companies save on rentals, improving productivity by helping employees save time spent for commuting and enhance employees' well-being. However, if planning to shift back to WFO, it becomes highly imperative for the employers to provide abundant support to the employees, to be able to transition from WFH to WFO, and to sustain WFO.

7.7 IMPLICATIONS OF THE STUDY

The factors identified as the benefits of working from home among the BPO employees would help in developing appropriate questionnaires for future researches, as there are not many relevant questionnaires currently for this population.

- The findings would help organizations take appropriate decisions, which would help the employees as well as the organizations, in the long run.
- The suggestions would help employees and organizations cope with the transition from the new normal to the old normal.

KEYWORDS

- **BPO industry**
- **pandemic**
- **COVID-19**
- **work-from-home**
- **work-from-office**
- **stress management**
- **resilience**

REFERENCES

Aithal, S. An Empirical Study on Working from Home: A Popular E-business Model. *Int. J. Adv. Innov. Res.* **2015**, *2*, 12–18.

Birkinshaw, J.; Cohen, J.; Stach, P. Research: Knowledge Workers Are More Productive from Home. *Harvard Business Review*. August 31, 2020. https://hbr.org/2020/08/research-knowledge-workers-are-more-productive-from-home.

Caramela, S. Working from Home Increases Productivity. *Business News Daily*, March 31, 2020. https://www.businessnewsdaily.com/15259-working-from-home-more-productive.html.

The Economic Times. Indians Spend 7% of Their Day Getting to their Office. *The Economic Times*, Sep 3, 2019. https://economictimes.indiatimes.com/jobs/indians-spend-7-of-their-day-getting-to-their-office/articleshow/70954228.cms

Jayalakshmi, V. Work-life Balance and Well-being among IT Professionals. *Contemporary Technologies: Prospects and Challenges for Psychological Well-being*, 2018; pp 132–142.

Jayalakshmi, V. Occupational Stress and Coping Strategies in Information Technology Professionals. *Traumashastra* **2019**, 218–226.

Jayalakshmi, V. Job stress and stress management: The healing power of nature. Ecological Well-Being: A psycho-social perspective, 2020a; pp 21–28.

Jayalakshmi, V. Promoting Ecological Well-being through Environmental Consciousness. Ecological Well-being: A Psycho-social Perspective, 2020b; pp 47–55.

Jayalakshmi, V.; Aravindakshan, M. Does Emotional Intelligence Contribute to One's Satisfaction in Life and Work: An Empirical Study on School Teachers. *Health Care Challenges in India: Psycho-social Perspectives*, 2020; pp 53–70.

Jayalakshmi, V.; Sujaritha, M. The Work-family Conflict, Well-being, Job Satisfaction and Organizational Commitment Among BPO Employees. *Future of Mental Health—Importance of Integrated Approach*, 2019; pp 128–141.

Jayalakshmi, V.; Sujaritha, M. Emotional Intelligence for Better Coping—A Pilot Study to Assess the Effectiveness of an Emotional Intelligence Intervention Programme. In *National Seminar on "Innovation and Integration in Education of Modern School Sciences and Mathematics,"* January 29, 2020.

Schaefer, A. Workers Are Traveling Ever Longer to Attain the Job or Home Life they Want, But the Daily Stress may Outweigh the Gains. *Scientific American*, October 1, 2005. https://www.scientificamerican.com/article/commuting-takes-its-toll/#:~:text=Several%20 studies%20have%20shown%20that,problems%20and%20high%20blood%20pressure.

Stieg, C. Working from Home Actually Makes You Better at Some Tasks and Worse at Others—Here's What you Need to Know. *Health and Wellness*, March 12, 2020. https://www.cnbc.com/2020/03/12/study-how-working-from-home-boosts-and-hurts-productivity-creativity.html

CHAPTER 8

Organizational Growth, Sustainability, and Flexible Work Practices in the Post-Pandemic Era: Overcoming Challenges through Green HRM

MALABIKA TRIPATHI[1*], MANVI SODHANI[1], and SWAHA BHATTACHARYA[2]

[1]*Amity University, Kolkata, India*

[2]*Department of Applied Psychology, Calcutta University, Kolkata, India*

*Corresponding author. E-mail: malabikatripathi@gmail.com

ABSTRACT

The present Covid-19 pandemic has forced all organizations to adopt to different novel techniques and strategies to increase its sustainability across the world. In this unprecedented situation, organizations are finding solutions to existing challenges through different HR operations. Green Human Resource Management (GHRM) practices have the potentiality to become the most effective answers to all prevailing questions ensuring the maximum sustainability. It encourages optimum level of environmental friendliness in operations within an organization and its employees, which leave minimum carbon footprint. The present scenario of Covid-19 has already taught the human race to use resources more wisely and effectively to promote growth and development. Researchers in the entire world are busy investigating the multidimensional impact of Covid-19 on human race, but there exists dearth of research in this area of environmental sustainability practices in human resource management. Hence, it is important to understand the

---

Human Resource Management in a Post-Epidemic Global Environment: Roles, Strategies, and Implementations.
Tanusree Chakraborty, Nandita Mishra, Madhurima Ganguly, & Bipasha Chatterjee (Eds.)
© 2023 Apple Academic Press, Inc. Co-published with CRC Press (Taylor & Francis)

different aspects of environmental awareness strategies, which can enable any organization to achieve its progressive goals. This article will discuss, how extensive use of GHRM can endorse advancement in organizations. The method section of the article will incorporate widespread review of existing academic researches along with available online articles from reliable sources. This article intends to put forward research questions like, how GHRM practices can (1) promote organizational growth, (2) help organizations to become more sustainable under any given crisis condition, and (3) how it can facilitate flexible working operations in postpandemic era. Analysis of literature establishes that GHRM is the most cost-effective method, which can be deployed and practiced in organizations to avoid any future uncertainty. Environment-friendly approach can help them to survive any catastrophe. This review-based research article also provides scope for further researches in this field.

8.1 INTRODUCTION

Green Human Resource Management, more commonly known as GHRM, involves a set of policies and behaviors that induce or promote environment-friendly practices or "Green Behavior" (Dutta, 2012). It helps the company's employees to create a workplace that is sensitive and sustainable to the environment, makes resource utilization more efficient and the overall organization socially and ecologically responsible (Nath, 2012). This has been conceptualized to influence employee workplace green behavior (Dumont et al., 2016). The development of modern cutting edge and competitive companies leads to the simple question of including environmentally sensitive practices into the field of Human Resources, referring to GHRM (Margaretha and Saragih, 2013).

In the globalized 21st century, the need for sustainability is growing worldwide with the challenging climatic changes and catastrophes, such as Covid-19. Along with the senior management of any company, the functioning of HR leaders is equally important to strategically incorporate GHRM to help them to do their part as socially responsible citizens and employees (Hart, 1997; Lee and Ball, 2003). The major policies that need to be practiced for GHRM include recruitment and job design, selection methods, HR operations and onboarding process, performance and development, compensation and reward, employment relations, and ways of going green (Bebbington, 2001).

According to Deshwal (2015), GHRM is an asset to the future of the corporate world. It is not just limited to corporate social responsibility, rather it includes the broader aspects of generic company goals such as being advantageous over its competition, saving major costs and most importantly, acquiring and managing talent (Cherian and Jacob 2012). In addition, GHRM also aids in the reduction of labor turnover, employee retention, company relations, boost in employee morale, and extensive company branding including marketing strategy and overall company cost. Further, with the innovation of Green technology the improvement of technology facilitates growth, procedural enhancements, and quality improvement (Florida and Davidson, 2001; Ichniowski et al., 1997). Ultimately, all these benefits collate into efficiency in employee behavior and breeding of employment opportunities (Daily and Huang, 2001).

That said, there are also multiple challenges that come with GHRM. The most important being the psychological and behavioral barriers—mostly it takes a long period of time to cultivate new policies into practices and not every employee is willing to collaborate in the propagation of GHRM (Collier and Esteban, 2007). Moreover, the initial cost of development of GHRM is comparatively higher in terms of the Rate of Return (Deshwal, 2015). When it comes to Human Resources, HR professionals have already faced a multitude of problems that are expected with "Green Structures" such as environmentally sensitive thinking, tools, and processes, which should ultimately lead to a network of problem solvers (Sathyapriya et al., 2014).

There have been multiple researches, which argue that the Environmental Management System (EMS) can only be efficient with the accurate Talent Management and Acquisition (Daily and Huang, 2001). In this manner, HR Practices should be useful toward EMS initiatives, which will provide organizations with the expertise they need to discover and utilize this knowledge (Scarbrough, 2003). Along with the company's access to accurate knowledge, they should have human capitalism tools and effective application in the knowledge of management (Sudin, 2011).

In the postpandemic era, organizations and especially the HR department will have to find novel ways to create and impart knowledge and training for green practices and policies. The traditional ways cannot be as productive in the online culture that is prevalent in the current time. GHRM will be the most beneficial aspect that will help organizations gain a competitive advantage over other businesses. This is a major need of the hour, because of the prevalent awareness regarding the environment and corporate social responsibility.

Thus, this extensive review-based study argues that GHRM with its effective and accurate implementation will promote organizational growth. In addition, it will aid in organizations to become more equipped and sustainable not only in the monotonous life, but also in challenging crisis situations. Finally, GHRM will be conducive in facilitating flexible working operations in the postpandemic era. Thus with this background, the present chapter endeavors to focus (a) on how extensive use of GHRM has been adapted to endorse advancement in organizations, (b) organizational sustainability through the availability of apt resources, conservation of paper, and energy and the Work-from-Home culture (GHRM), and (c) how GHRM promotes flexible work culture and enhances cost-effectiveness.

A proposed model for successful GHRM practice for future research in the field.

TABLE 8.1 Definitions of GHRM.

Author	Definition
Mandip (2012, p. 244)	"Green human resources refer to using every employee interface to promote sustainable practices and increase employee awareness and commitments on the issue of sustainability."
Jackson et al. (2011, p. 101)	"Links between HRM and environmental management."
Shen et al. (2018, p. 1)	"GHRM refers to a specific set of practices that organizations adopt to improve employee performance in the workplace as green performance."
Zoogah (2010, p. 118)	"Utilization of HR policies and practices that promote the sustainable resource utilization to prevent environmental harm from the point of view of businesses and organizations."

8.2 PROCESSES INVOLVED IN GHRM

GHRM is essentially a novel concept that is becoming popular in recent times. This is not just because of the Covid-19 Pandemic, but also because of people's comprehension of the environment and the need for sustainability (Pham et al., 2019). In an organization, there are major aspects that HRs need to consider during the process of going green (Grolleau et al., 2012; Jabbour et al., 2013; Unnikrishnan and Hegde, 2007).

8.2.1 GREEN HR OPERATIONS AND ONBOARDING PROCESS

Major industries are going paperless, and the Human Resources department is no different (Ahmad, 2015). From receiving online employee applications to working from home in the current pandemic situation, the concept of traditional offices will reduce in the postpandemic era. The advanced technologies available have not only reduced the need for papers in major processes such as providing job descriptions, selection, recruitment, offer letters, testimonials, and credentials (Deshwal, 2015). Essentially, it will not just benefit the environment, but will also make the accessibility of important documents extremely handy, yet safe.

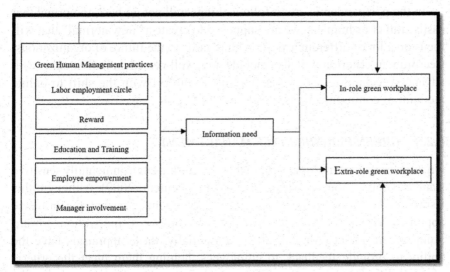

FIGURE 8.1 Process involved in GHRM.
Source: Reprinted from Zhang et al. (2019). https://creativecommons.org/licenses/by/4.0/

Amongst the widespread uncertainty that the pandemic has spread, a lot of new businesses are rising and failing. The need for valuing a safer ecosystem is increasing immensely, and so is the need to value employees mental and physical health. According to McKinsey and Company (2020) a multinational organization, the postpandemic era will shape organizations according to its purposes, cultures, and values. The on-boarding process will face a drastic shift for new hires, making the process completely digital—conserving paper and unnecessary expenses.

8.2.2 GREEN RECRUITMENT

GHRM can begin much before the stage of actual recruitments. Candidates can be screened through their CV/resumes regarding their inclination toward environmental progress (Deshwal, 2015; Dutta, 2012; Opatha and Arulrajah, 2014). Furthermore, formal information can be provided specifying environmental aspects in the job descriptions including green tasks and future goals of the organization (Ahmad, 2015; Dutta, 2012). "Green Aware" as a concept should be understood by prospective employees (Liu, 2010). This specific form of screening will benefit the organization to continue "Going green" by assuring that future employees are familiar with the culture of the specific organization (Wehrmeyer, 1996).

In the postpandemic era to follow, things will not go back to normal that easily; rather as humans, we are supposed to create a "new normal" that will focus on a lot of different aspects with regards to the future of organizations. Recruitment criterion will also include how well versed an individual is with advanced technological gadgets and their comfort with the shift to online medium of communications.

8.2.3 GREEN PERFORMANCE MANAGEMENT

Organizations face multiple issues when instituting environmentally sensitive standards throughout the firm (Marcus and Fremeth, 2009). Although, this issue can be reduced by using green recruitment, constant performance appraisals should be awarded to keep the employees' motivation, toward going green, intact (Ahmad, 2015). Essentially, these appraisals have the ability to provide feedback to employees, helping them meet the criteria of reliability, fairness, and validity, which in turn results in improving the organization's corporate social responsibility (Jackson et al., 2011). In addition, providing appraisals throughout the year will equip employees with better skills, ability, and knowledge (Ahmad, 2014).

Green performance management will become an extremely difficult task in the postpandemic era. Following the regulations of "Work-From-Home (WFH)", the HR department will have to work in a completely different way to understand if the employees believe in the green culture of the organization. In addition, providing any form of appraisal in this scenario is not ideal, because of the uncertainty present. The only solution that is foreseeable is that the employees need to be honest about their actual green practices. In addition, the HR Department can provide more strict guidelines and higher performance appraisals as incentives for employees to achieve them.

8.2.4 GREEN DEVELOPMENT

Green development is an essential aspect that should be practiced by organizations to educate the employees in the specific culture of the organization going green (Zoogah, 2010). Activities involved in green development will train employees in conserving energy, reducing waste, and proper waste management, providing employees with the opportunity of environmental problem-solving issues to become equipped to deal effectively with different environmental issues (Ahmad, 2015; Zoogah, 2010). HR has an extremely important role in helping managers establish proper environmental training to facilitate the integrated future goals of the company on the environmental forefront (Ramus, 2002).

In the postpandemic era, innovation is the key to success—be it in any field. Converting all communications from face to face to the digital set-up, HRs need to come up with novel ways to develop green behavior in employees. Educating employees in green practices thus becomes more important and extremely difficult in this scenario. The employees, additionally, need to be educated in the correct measures of safety during Covid-19, making the role of HRs crucial in the organizational field.

8.2.5 GREEN COMPENSATION AND REWARD

Substantially, reward and compensation in terms of GHRM can behave like an instrument as the footing for environmentally sensitive activities in the organization (Ahmad, 2015). According to a survey conducted by Phillips (2007) in the UK by CIP/KPMG, green behaviors were rewarded in 8% of organizations with different types of awards, including both financial and nonfinancial incentives. Along with monetary and nonmonetary rewards, awards based on recognition are also fairly rewarding to the employees, which in turn can promote employee initiatives toward going green (Deshwal, 2015; Ramus, 2002). Creating a positive work environment (Chakraborty and Ganguly, 2019), creating interpersonal relationship in a media-rich environment (Chakraborty et al., 2021) are crucial predictors of employee satisfaction. Green rewards and compensation can include both lifestyle benefits as well as benefits in the workplace, providing an extremely broad range to include both self and other in the practice GHRM (Pillai and Sivathanu, 2014).

In the postpandemic era, green compensation and reward are taking a new face. With a sudden lack of funds, companies barely have enough to stay afloat with current number of employees. In this sense, rewarding individual is a dream, when the reality is that organizations do not have enough to pay the monthly salary of all employees.

8.2.6 GREEN EMPLOYMENT RELATIONS

Green initiatives including employees and managers promote the chance of green management because it coordinates the green management system with the specific employee's abilities, approach and inclinations (Ahmad,

2015). According to different studies, the involvement of employees in the ecological initiatives itself can improve the chances, exponentially, of utilization of resources efficiently (Florida and Davidson, 2001), reduction of wastes (May and Flannery, 1995), and the reduction of pollution from organizations (Kitazawa and Sarkis, 2000). Multiple studies have concluded that the empowerment of employees individually can have an affirmative impact on self-control, effective problem-solving, productivity, and the performance as a whole (Renwick, 2008; Wee and Quazi, 2005).

Communicating with employees in the new normal will become essentially important for organizations, not just to help increase the productivity of each employee making the organization grow; but also, to aid employees with mental and physical help if needed. GHRM mandates the need for employment relations to make resource utilization efficient, but steps should also be taken to make the human capital more resourceful for the organization.

8.3 ADVANTAGES OF GHRM

There are various benefits of practicing GHRM. Predominantly, the chief objectives include a healthier environment, corporate social responsibility, retaining costs, employee management, and being advantageous over all competitors in the market (Deshwal, 2015). Other benefits include (Brio et al., 2007; Dolan, 1997; Hart, 1997; Siegel, 2009):

- Promote or boost the morale of employees.
- Attracting better employees that experience healthy competition amongst themselves, which increases productivity.
- Facilitate the rate of retention of employees and reduce the turnover of laborers.
- Generation of additional employment opportunities.
- Serves as a behavioral refinement of employees in developing ecologically sensitive habits.
- Creates a culture wherein employees achieve job satisfaction, consequently influencing the productivity of the organization.
- Facilitate in cost reduction without hampering talent acquisition.
- Boost the brand image, attract good human resource, and facilitate in positive marketing.
- Increasing the scope of the business providing a competitive advantage, by tapping into opportunities that deal with only environmentally sensitive companies.

- Quality improvement of the organization as an integrated whole (internal and external).
- Going green is comparatively easier, with the support of central government and local authorities through rebates and tax benefits.
- Creates a need for innovation and novelty toward promoting organizational growth, sustainability, and procedural enhancements.
- Facilitates in the realization for the need of self-actualization in employees and a positive environmental impact of the organization.

8.4 CHALLENGES OF GHRM

No field of study is without milestones, and GHRM has quite a few challenges to overcome (Ahmad, 2015; Brio et al., 2007; Deshwal, 2015; Fernandez et al., 2003). They are

- Developing a completely novel process in an ongoing organization is a challenging task, which is often prolonged.
- The initial costs required to set up GHRM is very expensive.
- All employees might not equally be sensitive toward the environment, impacting the GHRM in organizations negatively.
- It is not possible to constantly alter the behavior of adults to suit the needs to the organization. It becomes a very tedious task, which results in demotivation.
- Acquiring employees with a motivation toward corporate social responsibility is also very tenacious.
- Judging the efficiency of environmental behaviors by employees fairly for monetary benefits and performance.
- As a whole, HR department has faced multiple issues to facilitate organizations with structures, tools, and processes that are valid for going green.

The main objective of this paper is to understand and comprehend the practices and policies of GHRM. Furthermore, we aim to analyze how GHRM has promoted organizational growth, benefitted organizations during the global pandemic of Covid-19, and the importance of sustainability and flexible working hours in the postpandemic era. By critically evaluating these points, we proposed a new model and provided scope for future research.

8.5 RATIONALE OF THE STUDY

The world has seen an unimaginable global pandemic over the past year. Where organizations like Zoom and Microsoft Teams were soaring, others were trying hard to stay afloat because of their traditional practices. There was a dire need for the practices and policies of GHRM to not only sustain their livelihoods, but also ensure environmental sustainability. A thorough review of literature was conducted to evaluate the established practices of GHRM that can promote organizational growth bridge the gap to assure sustainability of organizations moving forward. Another aspect of this study focused on the postpandemic era and the new normal where aspects like social distancing and Covid-19 safety measures needed to be installed by the organizations. In this context, the study was also conducted to answer how flexible working hours were the new.

8.6 METHODOLOGY

The current research is based on the extensive structured review of literature, which facilitates the readers to gain an in-depth understanding by answering specific research questions. In addition, this study also provides an analytical rumination and assists in the scope for future research. A literature review is the analysis of sources including articles, books, journals, and more, which are pertinent to the area of study in this article providing a critical assessment (Fink, 2014). We conducted a search on Google Scholar, SSRN, and other online journals for the terms "GHRM," "Organizational Growth," "Flexible working hours," "Covid-19," "Postpandemic Era," and other such terms related to the study at hand. The data were critically evaluated to establish and construct the paper.

The current study directs toward the following research questions:

- How can GHRM practices promote organizational growth?
- How does GHRM help organizations to become more sustainable under any given crisis condition?
- How GHRM can facilitate flexible working operations in postpandemic era?

8.7 FINDINGS

RQ 1. How does GHRM promote organizational growth?

Organizational growth is essentially a quantitative process, measuring the increase in the roles and different links within the organization by the numbers. Outcomes of the organizational progress or lack thereof in perfectly understood by the Ability–Motivation–Opportunity (AMO)

Framework (Bailey, 1993). Organizational outcomes are positively corelated with the AMO Framework. This means that an employee in an organization who has learnt novel abilities, is highly motivated, and is provided with the opportunity to utilize his resources will equip themselves to commit to the organization's need for environmental sustainability, showcasing green behaviors (Benevene and Buonomo, 2020). This will increase the likelihood of appropriate Green Performance in the Organization (Singh et al., 2020; Anwar et al., 2020).

There are two important aspects while a connection is made between organizational performance and the practices of HRM, including the commitment of the employees of the organization and behaviors that are discretionary in nature (Appelbaum et al., 2000; Bailey, 1993; Purcell et al., 2003). Speaking of the first, it is already mentioned that higher motivation of employees will result in organizational growth. This is because of the deep-rooted inclinations of the individual. The more the employee is in a position to cherish his responsibilities and see first-hand the results of his commitment toward corporate social responsibility, the higher his productivity would be. Furthermore, these practices would also grow exponentially. Fundamentally, this aspect will be true not just for Green Performance or employee behavior, but on all the integrated aspects of GHRM practices and policies (Purcell et al., 2003).

Older organizations have been evolving into new cutting-edge green businesses nearly 5% every year, over the past 3 years (Mandip, 2012). It is because of the multiple benefits, not just for the environment, but also for competitive advantage a marketing strategy that organizations are thinking of going green. According to Kassaye (2001), organizations need to practice either one of the 4Rs, which are Reusing, Reducing, Recycling, and Recovery. Each of these Rs include a set of responsibilities ranging from green buildings to green financing. Essentially, all organizations strive for growth, and in the postpandemic era of the world—the most fully functional businesses will be the firms that practice GHRM.

Hence it can be said that, after Covid-19, the processes of GHRM including recruitment, performance management, training and development, employment relations and reward, and compensation will see a drastic shift. Going paperless is not just the only green practice that will be largely enforced. But with the strict rule of social distancing, there will also be minimal percentage of employees working in offices. This would instate the "WFH" culture, which will help in the conservation of energy. Essentially, all these practices will promote organizational growth because the traditional working hours have disappeared, making employees work at any time they feel they are prepared to complete the task and are productive. There is no limit to innovation, rather a need for creative solutions at this stage, which means employees can voice their opinions making the sky their limit to achieve company goals. Essentially being more productive with lesser resources available is the path to success in the postpandemic era.

RQ 2. How does GHRM help organizations to become more sustainable under any given crisis condition?

The postpandemic world will be the era of competition for businesses to stand tall again. Not all businesses have followed the same strategy, so there will come a need for competitive advantage (Mohammad et al., 2019). According to the CIPD (2012), we are stepping into the age of sustainability.

Sustainability, in extremely simple terms, refers to the need for "future proofing" (Colbert and Kurucz, 2007). Organizational sustainability is no different, it is a long-term organizational operation, which focuses on the aspect improving societal, environmental, and economic systems within which the operations of any business occurs (CIPD, 2012). With the advent of technology, there are products for every aspect of life we can think of, so the innovation from creativity needs to shift temporarily toward sustainability, without which the world will observe the downfall of the economy, and with that life as we know it will disappear.

A research by Govindarajulu and Daily (2004) depicts that sustainability in organizations can only be established by implementing the environmental policies accurately by the HR department. Accordingly, GHRM will include similar managerial objectives to the HRM Practices, focusing more on environmental sensitivity and sustainability (Renwick, 2008).

Under any crisis, the key aspect of a sustainable organization is that it keeps on functioning. During the Covid-19 worldwide pandemic, this is exactly what was experienced by civilians. There are four major aspects of green initiatives for HR for organizations to function effectively, including green building, paperless office, conservation of energy, and recycling and waste disposal (Ahmad, 2015). Majority of organizations were not equipped with GHRM to function at all. However, it did not take them much time to adapt to the crisis. Multinational and local companies soon shifted toward paperless offices—not just working from remote locations, but also accessing major documents using the cutting-edge technology available. Soon after we realized the need for GHRM, came newer cultures, such as the "WFH" culture and the most important, the culture of "Flexible working hours."

RQ 3. How GHRM can facilitate flexible working operations in postpandemic era?

One of the key concepts that are arising in the corporate world is the need for flexible working hours. This is because of the simple fact that not all departments have the same pressure of work all round the year. According to a Harvard Business Review Article (McCord, 2014), Netflix as an organization tapped right into this strategy to utilize optimum human capital along with efficient use of minimum resources available. This was done long before anyone had foreseen the world of Covid-19.

Postpandemic, major organizations would have to shift to this working style because of one important aspect—"social distancing." A concept that we have come to understand completely in 2020, personal space is the need for the hour. GHRM with its initiatives can also promote the need for flexible working hours. With the advent of the pandemic, GHRM is the only aspect that can facilitate flexible working hours—which will inadvertently reduce waste disposal and management and also facilitate the need for conservation of energy because in an office only specific computers will be working, simultaneously saving other sources of energy as well.

Essentially, what we can notice is that competition among organizations did not stop because of a global pandemic. The ones that were successful to adapt to the new normal are soaring to new heights, but the ones who failed to do so are now out of business. The key aspect involved in this adaptation was offices shifting to the digital mode—making them paperless offices. With the use of video conferences, emails, and cloud computing employees were taught the need for less paper utilization and energy consumption, simultaneously taking a more environment-friendly approach.

8.8 DIRECTION OF FUTURE RESEARCH

Based on the research findings, it can also be said that the core aspects of the AMO framework (Purcell et al., 2003) and the Technical Acceptance Model (TAM) (Davis, 1986) would be beneficial for successful GHRM practices in organizations during postpandemic era. It has already been established by the current research findings that the HR department will have to work in novel ways to bridge the gap in the "new normal" era. The postpandemic era has seen an increase in two major aspects—namely, the WFH culture and the culture of flexible working hours.

The AMO framework focuses on three vital aspects in organizations—the AMO (Appelbaum et al., 2000; Boxall and Purcell, 2003). This model was renowned for its link between employee's performance and the need for human resource management (Marin-Garcia and Martinez Tomaz, 2016). Initially brought into light by Bailey (1993), the AMO Framework suggested that employees needed the required skills for the job, had to be properly motivated, and must be given different opportunities by the employers to show their skills (Appelbaum et al., 2000). This model includes the basic concepts of Psychology (Kroon et al., 2013) that shape the personal attitudes of individuals. In the context of organizations, providing them with the three elements of this model will empower employees to be more productive and increases organizational outcomes (Boselie, 2010; Boxall and Purcell, 2003; Choi, 2014; Marín-García et al., 2011; Marín-García, 2013; Raidén et al., 2006; Chakraborty and Mishra, 2019).

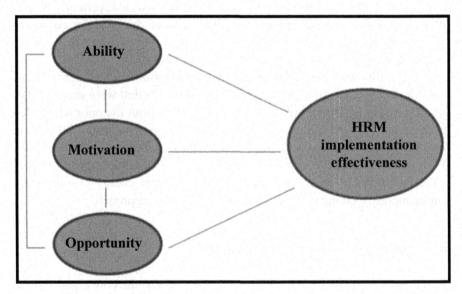

FIGURE 8.2 The AMO framework.
Source: Smelt (2017).

Initially proposed by Davis (1986), the TAM was essentially an explanation of accepting computers as a part of the general organizational culture (Zhang et al., 2019). Davis focused on two main areas with respect to computers—perceived usefulness (PU) and ease of use (EU) (Legris et al., 2003). PU was considered to be the main determining factor, referring to the limit to which employees consider a particular system to be productive and beneficial (Hajiha, 2015; Hajiden, 2003). EU, being the second determinant was understood as the extent to which the particular system was easy or effortless (Rauniar, 2014). There cannot be a system that can be considered efficient if it is difficult to use, thus easier systems are more easily accepted in organizations. In organizations, employees always strive to be more productive to achieve compensations and rewards (Davis, 1989).

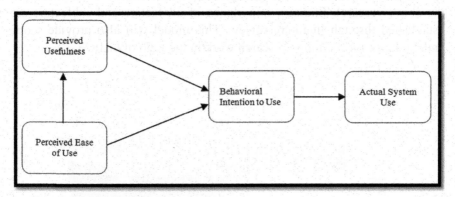

FIGURE 8.3 Technical acceptance model.
Source: Naeini and Krishnam (2012).

In the present scenario, combining these two models will help the HR department to utilize human capital more efficiently. Green recruitment will become considerably simpler by taking these models into consideration. With the help of the AMO Framework, an employee's abilities can be assessed with regards to the acceptance of the online work culture in the postpandemic era, taking into account the fact that employees will find it more productive to work with novel technologies, continuously. Employees who believe in the concept of corporate social responsibility and help the organization in its mission to go green will work in an effective manner and will remain more engaged (Chakraborty et al., 2020), trying to conserve paper and minimize energy utilization wherever possible will find innovative opportunities to make their work more effortless. This will provide new opportunities for employees to become more productive with their work. Lastly, the motivation factor can be addressed by the green compensation and reward offered to the employees at the workplace by creating novel policies and practices that adapt with the situational demands (Ren et al., 2018; Saeed et al., 2019; Zibarras and Coan, 2014; Renwick et al., 2013).

8.9 PROPOSED MODEL FOR SUCCESSFUL GHRM PRACTICE IN POSTPANDEMIC ERA FROM THE PERSPECTIVE OF ORGANIZATION AND INDIVIDUAL EMPLOYEE

In the challenging postpandemic era "sustainability" is questionable for every organization. Organizations can win the race if they are motivated enough to spread the concern for GHRM practices at both organizational and employees, level, managing the subfactors mentioned in the model. In the above research findings, importance of all factors and subfactors are established through literature review. This model will also provide scope and guidance for the future research work in the field of GHRM.

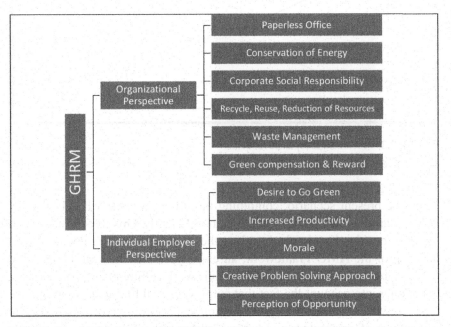

FIGURE 8.4 Model of successful GHRM practice. Source: Developed by authors.

8.10 CONCLUSION

The present theoretical paper aims to analyze and understand the importance of GHRM ensuring organizational growth, sustainability, and flexibility; it also aspires to establish the relationship between the constructs. It further explains different aspects of GHRM and why it is essential in postpandemic era for successful HR Management.

8.11 KEY TAKEAWAYS

- GHRM promotes environmentally sound and "green behavior" among the working force.
- Covid-19 has forced organizations to look at novel ways to increase productivity and maintain sustainability across the world.
- GHRM will be considered as an asset in the postpandemic world, with regards to its efficiency and growth in the industry.
- GHRM can be substituted for all general human resource practices and functions in various cost-effective ways.
- Although GHRM has many advantages, it does not come without a multitude of challenges for organizations and their employees.
- GHRM will give its practicing organizations a competitive advantage in the postpandemic world, as the human beings becomes more environmentally sound.
- GHRM simultaneously makes an organization a sustainable structure, as well as promote the growth and development of its employees as well as the company itself.
- Flexible working hours, paperless offices, conservation of energy, and recycling and waste disposal are the drastic change that will be seen in organizations post pandemic.
- The proposed model for successful GHRM practice will not only help the organization as well as the individual employees, at the same time providing a scope for future research.
- GHRM will inevitably become an integral part of the corporate world as human beings slowly move into the postpandemic era.

KEYWORDS

- **organizational sustainability**
- **flexible work**
- **GHRM**
- **COVID-19**
- **post pandemic era**

REFERENCES

Ahmad, S. Green Human Resource Management: Policies and Practices. *Cogent Bus. Manage.* **2015,** *2* (1). doi:10.1080/23311975.2015.1030817.

Anwar, N.; Nik Mahmood, N. H.; Yusliza, M. Y.; Ramayah, T.; Noor Faezah, J.; Khalid, W. Green Human Resource Management for Organizational Citizenship Behavior towards the Environment and Environmental Performance on a University Campus. *J. Clean. Prod.* **2020,** *256,* 120401.

Bangwal, D.; Tiwari, P. Green HRM—A Way to Greening the Environment. *J. Bus. Manage.* **2015,** *17,* 45–53.

Bebbington, J. Sustainable Development: A Review of the International Development, Business and Accounting Literature. *Account. Forum* **2001,** *25* (2), 128–157.

Bhowal, M.; Saini, D. Environment: Perspectives of Employee Engagement. In *Management Techniques for Employee Engagement in Contemporary Organizations: A Volume in the Advances in Human Resources Management and Organizational Development (AHRMOD).* IGI Global, 2020; pp 180–198.

Brio, J. A. D.; Fernandez, E.; Junquera, B. Management and Employee Involvement in Achieving an Environmental Action-based Competitive Advantage: An Empirical Study. *Int. J. HRM* **2007,** *18* (4), 13.

Chakraborty, T.; Ganguly, M. *Crafting Engaged Employees through Positive Work,* IGI Global, 2019; p 19.

Chakraborty, T.; Mishra, N. Appreciative Inquiry: Unleashing a Positive Revolution of Organizational Change and Development. *Int. J. Econ.: Com. Bus. Manage.* **2019,** *6* (2), 32–37.

Chakraborty, T.; Gohain, D.; Saha, R. What Comes in the Way of Engagement? Moderation Analysis of Stress on Women Marketing Executives' Work Life Balance. *Int. J. Hum. Resour. Dev. Manage.* **2020,** *20* (3-4), 349–368.

Chakraborty, T.; Tripathi, M.; Saha, S. The Dynamics of Employee Relationships in a Digitalized Workplace: The Role of Media Richness on Workplace Culture. In *Critical Issues on Changing Dynamics in Employee Relations and Workforce Diversity*; IGI Global, 2021; pp 175–205.

Cherian, J.; Jacob, J. A Study of Green HR Practices and Its Effective Implementation in the Organization: A Review. *Int. J. Bus. Manage.* **2012,** *7,* 25–33.

CIPD. *A Collection of Thought Pieces—Responsible and Sustainable Business: HR Leading the Way*; CIPD: London: UK, 2012.

Colbert, B. A.; Kurucz, E. C. Three Conceptions of Triple Bottom Line Business Sustainability and the Role for HRM. *Hum. Resour. Plan.* **2007,** *30* (1), 21–30.

Daily, B. F.; Huang, S. C. Achieving Sustainability through Attention to Human Resource Factors in Environmental Management. *Int. J. Oper. Prod. Manage.* **2001,** *21,* 1539–1552.

Davis, F.D. (1986) "Technology Acceptance Model for Empirically Testing New End-user Information Systems Theory and Results" Unpublished Doctoral Dissertation, MIT.

Davis, F.D. (1989) "Perceived Usefulness, Perceived Ease of Use, and User Acceptance of Information Technology" *MIS Quarterly 13*(3), pp. 319–340.

Dutta, S. Greening People: A Strategic Dimension. *ZENITH: Int. J. Bus. Econ. Manage. Res.* **2012,** *2,* 143–148.

Fernández, E.; Junquera, B.; Ordiz, M. Organizational Culture and Human Resources in the Environmental Issue: A Review of the Literature. *Int. J. Hum. Resour. Manage.* **2003,** *14,* 634–656. doi:10.1080/0958519032000057628.

Fink, A. *Conducting Research Literature Reviews: From the Internet to Paper*, 4th ed. SAGE: Thousand Oaks, CA, 2014.

Florida, R.; Davison, D. Gaining from Green Management: Environmental Management Systems Inside and Outside the Factory. *Cal. Manage. Rev.* **2001**, *43*, 64–84. doi:10.2307/41166089.

Govindarajulu, N.; Daily, B. F. Motivating Employees for Environmental Improvement. *Ind. Manage. Data Syst.* **2004**, *104*, 364–372. doi:10.1108/02635570410530775.

Grolleau, G.; Mzoughi, N.; Pekovic, S. Green Not (Only) for Profit: An Empirical Examination of the Effect of Environmental-related Standards on Employees Recruitment. *Resour. Energy Econ.* **2012**, *34*, 74–92. doi:10.1016/j.reseneeco.2011.10.002.

Hart, S. Beyond Greening: Strategies for a Sustainable World. *Harv. Bus. Rev.* **1997**, *75*, 66–76.

Ichniowski, C.; Shaw, K.; Prennushi, G. The Effects of Human Resource Management Practices on Productivity: a Study of Steel Finishing Lines. *Am. Econ. Rev.* **1997**, *87* (3), 291–313.

Jabbour, C. J.; Jabbour, L. S.; Govindan, K.; Teixeira, A. A.; Freitas, W. R. Environmental Management and Operational Performance in Automotive Companies in Brazil: The Role of Human Resource Management and Lean Manufacturing. *J. Clean. Prod.* **2013**, *47*, 129–140. doi:10.1016/j.jclepro.2012.07.010.

Jackson, S.; Renwick, D.; Jabbour, C. J. C.; Muller-Camen, M. State-of-the-art and Future Directions for Green Human Resource Management. *Zeitschr. Pers.: Ger. J. Res. Hum. Resour. Manage.* **2011**, *25*, 99–116.

Kassaye, W. W. Green Dilemma. *Mark. Intell. Plan.* **2001**, *19* (6), 444–455. doi:10.1108/EUM0000000006112.

Kitazawa, S.; Sarkis, J. The Relationship between ISO 14001 and Continuous Source Reduction Programs. *Int. J. Oper. Prod. Manage.* **2000**, *20*, 225–248. doi:10.1108/01443570010304279.

Koshish, J. Green HRM–People Management Commitment to Environmental Sustainability. In *Proceedings of 10th International Conference on Digital Strategies for Organizational Success*, Gwalior, India, 2019; pp 1332–1346. doi:10.2139/ssrn.3323800.

Lado, A. A.; Wilson, M. C. Human Resource Systems and Sustained Competitive Advantage: A Competency Based Perspective. *Acad. Manage. Rev.* **1994**, *19*, 699–727.

Lee, K. Opportunities for Green Marketing: Young Consumers. *Mark. Intell. Plan.* **2008**, *26* (6), 573–586. doi:10.1108/02634500810902839.

Lee, K. H.; Ball, R. Achieving Sustainable Corporate Competitiveness: Strategic Link between Top Management's (Green) Commitment and Corporate Environmental Strategy. *Greener Manage. Int.* **2003**, *44*, 89–104.

Liebowitz, J. The Role of HR in Achieving a Sustainability Culture. *J. Sustain. Dev.* **2010**, *3*, 50–57.

Liu, W. The Environmental Responsibility of Multinational Corporation. *J. Am. Acad. Bus. Cam.* **2010**, *15* (2), 81–88.

Mandip, G. Green HRM: People Management Commitment to Environmental Sustainability. In *Proceedings of 10th International Conference on Digital Strategies for Organizational Success*. Available at SSRN: https://ssrn.com/abstract=3323800 or http://dx.doi.org/10.2139/ssrn.3323800.

Marcus, A.; Fremeth, A. Green Management Matters Regardless. *Acad. Manage. Perspect.* **2009**, *23*, 17–26.

Marin-Garcia, J.; Tomás, J. M. Deconstructing AMO Framework: A Systematic Review. *Intang. Cap.* **2016**, *12*, 1040–1087.

Naeini, F. H., Krishnam, B. Usage Pattern, Perceived Usefulness and Ease of Use of Computer Games among Malaysian Elementary School Students. *Research Journal of Applied Sciences, Engineering and Technology, 2012, 4*(23), 5285–5297.

Opatha, H. H.; Arulrajah, A. A. Green Human Resource Management: Simplified General Reflections. *Int. Bus. Res.* **2014**, *7*, 101–112.

Pham, N. T.; Hoang, H. T.; Phan, Q. P. T. Green Human Resource Management: A Comprehensive Review and Future Research Agenda. *Int. J. Manpow.* **2019**, *41* (7), 845–878. doi:10.1108/IJM-07-2019-0350.

Phillips, L. Go Green to Gain the Edge Over Rivals. *People Manage.* **2007**, *13*, 9.

Pillai, R.; Sivathanu, B. Green Human Resource Management. *Zenith Int. J. Multidiscip. Res.* **2014**, *4*, 72–82. www.zenithresearch.org.in.

Purcell, J.; Kinnie, N.; Hutchinson, S.; Rayton, B.; Swart, J. *Understanding the People and Performance Link: Unlocking the Black Box*, CIPD Publishing: London, UK, 2003.

Ramus, C. A. Organizational Support for Employees: Encouraging Creative Ideas for Environmental Sustainability. *Cal. Manage. Rev.* **2001**, *43*, 85–105.

Ramus, C. A. Encouraging Innovative Environmental Actions: What Companies and Managers Must do. *J. World Bus.* **2002**, *37*, 151–164. doi:10.1016/S1090-9516(02)00074-3.

Renwick, D. *Green HRM: A Review, Process Model, and Research Agenda (Discussion Paper Series).* The University of Sheffield, 2008. http://www.shef.ac.uk/content/1/c6/08/70/89/2008-01.pdf.

Renwick, D. W. S.; Redman, T.; Maguire, S. Green Human Resource Management: A Review and Research Agenda. *Int. J. Manage. Rev.* **2013**, *15* (1), 1–14. doi:10.1111/ijmr.2013.15.issue-1.

Saifulina, N. Sustainable HRM and Green HRM: The Role of Green HRM in Influencing Employee Pro-environmental Behavior at Work. *Corp. Sustain.* **2020**, *2* (3). doi:10.20900/jsr20200026.

Scarbrough, H. Knowledge Management, HRM and the Innovation Process. *Int. J. Manpow.* **2003**, *24* (5), 501–516.

Shoeb, A. Green Human Resource Management: Policies and Practices. *Cogent Bus. Manage.* **2015**, *2* (1). DOI:10.1080/23311975.2015.1030817.

Siegel, D. Green Management Matters Only If It Yields More Green: An Economic/Strategic Perspective. *Acad. Manage. Perspect.* **2009**, *23* (3), 5.

Singh, S. K.; Del Giudice, M.; Chierici, R.; Graziano, D. Green Innovation and Environmental Performance: The Role of Green Transformational Leadership and Green Human Resource Management. *Technol. Forecast. Soc. Chang.* **2020**, *150*, 119762.

Smelt, K. (2017). Resolving the AMO Confusion: Results of a qualitative study into HRM implementation (Master's thesis, University of Twente).

Sudin, S. Strategic Green HRM: A Proposed Model that Supports Corporate Environmental Citizenship. In *International Conference on Sociality and Economics Development IPEDR*, 2011, 10.

Uddin, M.; Islam, R. Green HRM: Goal Attainment through Environmental Sustainability. *J. Nepal. Bus. Stud.* **2016**, *9* (1), 14–19. doi:10.3126/jnbs.v9i1.14590.

Unnikrishnan, S.; Hegde, D. S. Environmental Training and Cleaner Production in Indian Industry—A Micro-level Study. *Resour. Conserv. Recycl.* **2007**, *50*, 427–441. doi:10.1016/j.resconrec.2006.07.003.

Wehrmeyer, W. *Greening People: Human Resources and Environmental Management*; Greenleaf: Sheffield, 1996.

www.ETHRWorld.com. *Impact of Covid-19 on HR Practices and Future Workforce—ETHRWorld*, 2020. *ETHRWorld.com*.hr.economictimes.indiatimes.com/news/industry/impact-of-covid-19-on-hr-practices-and-future-workforce/75653859.

Zhang, Y.; Lua, Y.; Zhang, X.; Zhao, J. How Green Human Resource Management Can Promote Green Employee Behavior in China: A Technology Acceptance Model Perspective. *Sustainability* **2019**, *11* (19), 5408. doi:10.3390/su11195408.

Zoogah, D. The Dynamics of Green HRM Behaviors: A Cognitive Social Information Processing Approach. Working Paper, Morgan State University: Baltimore, MD, 2010.

CHAPTER 9

Effective Employee Retention: Are Post-Pandemic Strategies Going to Change?

SRIJAN SENGUPTA[*]

Department of Psychology, Barrackpore Rastraguru Surendranath College, Kolkata, West Bengal, India

*E-mail: srijansengupta24@gmail.com

ABSTRACT

What are the main resources to run an organization? The answer is easy and quite obvious, organization's employees. Money is not the only thing required to run an organization. So an employee leaving the organization makes some sort of imbalance likes pelting a stone in a static pond. Now in this pandemic situation, the major thrust area is employee turnover, but steadily another factor that also creates issues within the organization is effective retention of the skilled and knowledgeable employees. It became the major challenge an organization is facing postpandemic and there is a need to restructure their different policies in the new normal. As predicted by ASSOCHAM in a webinar that the biggest difficulty an organization faced is to retain their skilled employees. In this regard, one needs to focus on the new factors of employee retention, though classically, the major factors of retention remain the same but in new normal different new factors must influence employee retention. As well as one also needs to consider the job market of India. In some sectors, as predicted by different governance and monitoring bodies, the requirement of skilled employees became a major concern for the organization. So a sector-wise, analysis also needs to be considered, in which sector attrition hit the most. Postpandemic situations not only changed the dynamics of our lives but also modified the dynamics of different organizations. The present chapter endeavors to understand the effective strategies of retaining an employee after the pandemic and what are its main challenges in doing so; it also focuses on the role of HR managers to restructure the policies for retention of employees.

9.1 INTRODUCTION

An organization runs smoothly when it has all the resources at an optimum level and the most important resource for any organization is its human resources. No machinery operates without the human capital in any organization. So in this era of organizational development, the prime focus of any organization is on the retention of employees. Recently, the world economy faced a global challenge like COVID, which detrimentally affected all the organizations in different ways. In the precorona virus era ASSOCHAM reported that many sectors like MSME, IT, healthcare, education, etc., suffered a huge loss in every financial year both in fiscal and nonfiscal terms due to high attrition rate. On the contrary, in postcorona era growth as well as job opportunities though have shrunk a bit, but the scenario might not be the same at a later stage. A recent report published by the British Chamber of Commerce in 2020 showed a crunch will arise for skilled and experienced employees in the postcorona era and a surplus of skilled manpower might be on the card. Even in the current scenario, some organizational sectors like healthcare, pharmaceuticals, etc., showed a crunch in manpower. So the importance to retain an employee would be a great challenge for the HR professionals as well as the organization. Because recruiting new employees would cost more as they required orientation, training, as well as time, also it needs to enhance employee job skills. Now the organizational development is determined by the intellectual capital of an organization. An organization gets a competitive edge in the market because of its intellectual capital. Now in the knowledge era, it provides an upper hand to the organizations.

Now considering the current sociocultural as well as economic scenario, it will be an organizational constraint to create a new workforce instead of retaining the existing skilled and experienced workforce. Organizations are, in the post-COVID era, not in a position to bear the cost of employee replacement. So here the HR professionals need to play a crucial role on behalf of the organization in order to select and implement the pull as well as a push factor to retaining employees for better organizational growth. In

Effective Employee Retention 135

this context, here the focus now is on understanding the factors to employee retention.

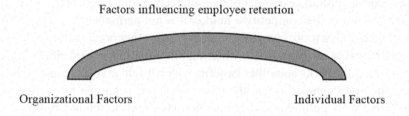

9.1.1 EMPLOYEE RETENTION DEFINED

Though there is no predominant single definition of employee retention found in literature, but still employee retention is defined as how long an employee stayed with the employer. In the workforce development literature, the word retention typically refers to the amount of time an employee is attached to the workforce. Though it is evident from the introduction that employee replacement creates a burden on the organization, it is also true that employee retention is solely not dependent on the organization. There are many factors that influence employee retention. Those factors mainly fall under the paradigm of either organizational level or individual-level factors. So this chapter will discuss the two contexts of employee retention, first organizational and then individual-level factors. With this approach, the chapter attempts:

➢ Contextualizing the different factors, both organizational and personal, of employee retention.
➢ Exploring the impact of pandemic on employee retention.
➢ Challenges and opportunities of employee retention in the diverse workforce.

9.2 ORGANIZATIONAL LEVEL FACTORS OF EMPLOYEE RETENTION

9.2.1 SALARY AND OTHER PERKS

Now in this competitive market, the first and the foremost important factor influencing employee retention is the salary as well as perks that an employee gets from the organization. Considering the current reports from different sources, it is quite evident that this is the testing time for both the organization and employees in terms of the economic resources due to the pandemic (Federation of Indian Chamber of Commerce in India, 2020). This is a critical situation, but in the competitive market it is not permanent, so whenever an employee finds a more competitive salary from other organizations, he or she might be swept away soon. Considering this situation, organizations need to focus upon the perks and other benefits which might give a competitive edge over the other competitors in the labor market. It is known for instance that a positive work culture in an organization also helps to retain employees and boost their morale (Chakraborty and Ganguly, 2019). So, not only financial perks are important, organizations need to focus on positive work culture as well. However, perks can be divided into two types, traditional like retirement plans, insurance, etc., or nontraditional like providing benefits in child care providers, etc. When it comes to women employees in an organization, such provisions that appear to be women friendly must be taken care of, as women take a hard toll balancing family and work (Desai et al., 2011). So, organizations need to make policies by blending both traditional and nontraditional perks and employee-friendly policies for retaining their workforce.

9.2.2 OPPORTUNITY FOR ADVANCEMENT

Money is not only the primary motivator for retention, other factors like opportunity for advancement in the workforce also play a crucial role in retention. In postpandemic situation, organizations should focus on developing different strategies for the growth and development of employees in the organization. Growth and development are the integral part of an individual's career, so organizations must provide importance on employees' growth. This type of work profile enhancement sometimes is cost efficient also. It does not always require putting money in line from an organizational perspective. The main concern for organizations here is to how to pave the path for employee development. Different strategies like training, coaching, mentoring, etc., should be adapted for this purpose. But before implementing strategies, organizations should assess different levels of need. Need assessment is a very pivotal part for the advancement of organizations as well as employees. Orthodox level of need assessment provides us a general outlook, but in postpandemic situation needs assessment varies in nature. There are mainly three levels of need assessment, organizational, task, and person.

Now due to pandemic situation most of the organization hit rock-bottom, so the inclusion of advancement strategies for employee also need to include organizational benefit as well as it needs to be cost effective. For this purpose, all these three levels of need assessment need to be rigorous and have to be rewarding from organizational perspective. So, the major focus of organizations during this time should be on the following.

9.2.3 TRAINING

In general terms, training refers to the different methods organizations implement for enhancing the knowledge, experience, and skills of the employees (Walsh and Taylor, 2007). Organizations in postpandemic situation should focus on the in-house training facility, online training programs as it reduces the cost of training as well as employees get ample opportunity for their advancement even when they feel safe at home. Employees in general are trainable and as stated by Gohain et al. (2017) employees' success also depends on organizational training.

9.2.4 COACHING

Coaching involves practical, goal-focused forms of one-on-one learning and behavioral change, it can also be conducted in groups as the preferred tool for behavior and performance enhancement. In coaching process, most of the time coaches are selected from the same organization where the employee belongs. In postpandemic situation, this type of opportunity for advancement of the employees where organization needs not invest time or money distinctly will be the need of the hour.

9.2.5 MENTORING

Mentoring is another process organizations that should focus on for the advancement of employees. Mentoring is much more a one-to-one employee development process; here the concerned mentor not only guides the mentee in resolving different organizational puzzles, besides he/she guides the mentee in different spheres of life toward professional and personal development (Megginson, 2006). Mentor–mentee relation establishment is the most crucial role here and every organization should try to engage in this most intensively at this phase. More specifically, it is the responsibility of the HR professional to select proper mentor for an employee for his or her betterment. One of the most crucial drawbacks of mentoring is that it is a very time-consuming procedure, so patience is very much needed to get the outcome of this program. Those strategies also need to assess to understand the effective outcome of those programs. Though pandemic creates some sort of organizational constraints for advancement of employees, still organizations need to assess employee needs and engage employees in those programs. In a nutshell, organizations have immensely benefitted from mentoring programs (Wilson and Elman, 1990), and during the postpandemic period, it is expected that mentoring would help employees' mental health and work performance (Luis and Vance, 2020).

9.2.6 ORGANIZATIONAL COMMUNICATION

Another important factor for employee retention is organizational communication (Downs and Adrian. 2004). It is quite evident from exit reports of employees from different organizations that almost 40% of employees leaving the organization feel disappointed with the communication within the organization. Considering the current situation, the necessity of proper communication within the organization appears to be high. It was shown by various different studies that where the employees had good communication with the management, they were less likely to leave the organization. This type of organizational communication is very much needed in postpandemic situation for retention of employees. Communication within the organization has been found to be more effective when it is bottom-up. This type of communication provides employees a sense of responsibility and belongingness which further leads to retention (Erickson, 2015). Organizational communication is the solution to various problems within the organization. Mainly in the current sociocultural context, it is the most apt because most of the employees are working from home. It is the biggest challenge that the organizations are facing during the pandemic days. One-to-one communication is very important for retention of employees (Sanders et al., 2020) because we do communicate not only verbally but nonverbally also. So, it is of utmost importance that constant connection with the employees in different mediums becomes more important from the organizational perspective (Chakraborty et al., 2021). This enhances interpersonal relationships as well. Organizations should adapt a clear and open channel of communication with the employees, which not only develops trust but is considered as the best foundation for employees perspective. Employees not only feel trusted but they also feel less marginalized, it boosts their self-esteem also.

9.2.7 ORGANIZATIONAL SUPPORT

Lack of support from management and from the coworkers can serve as a reason for lack of employee retention. Support from the supervisors and support from the coworkers are immensely important for employee retention (Chakraborty and Ganguly, 2019). It was quite evident from the different research works that an employee's view toward the organization majorly depends on the relationship with the supervisors (Paille, 2012). Especially after the pandemic situation, employee's intention to leave the organization will be impacted by the support they get during the crisis days from the organization. This can be one of the biggest challenges organizations faced because of lockdown. It not only hinders organization's growth but also inhibits the relational mechanism between employee and employer. In many sectors, like IT and ITes, marketing, education, etc., still operates from the home, so it will be big challenge organizations will be facing. Different organizations take different measures to resolve this issue, some of them are employee assistance programs, employee counseling, etc. It not only helps organization to reach its goal but also inculcates organizational support and values among employees. Social distancing during the pandemic troubles the mental health of the employees and they are more anxious (Chakraborty et al., 2021). Employers can support their employees in different ways. A few are enumerated here:

i. By providing positive feedback regarding their job. Instead of criticizing for the negative outcome, organization's positive attitude motivates employees.
ii. By recognizing good work and rewarding employees if possible. Reward them not always in materialistic ways but organizations also can take unconventional ways for this purpose.
iii. Provide emotional and social support. Postpandemic situation not only is depressing for organizations but also quite hazardous for employees. So if organizations help employees to overcome their emotional baggage through counseling or other measures, then employees would feel more connected with the organization.

From different reports, it was also found that many organizations have already established different programs for the wellness of employees (Wu et al., 2020; Amaya and Melnyk, 2020). But organizations must consider that this is not a short-term war rather we have to fight it for many days, so those programs must continue until the pandemic is completely over.

9.2.8 WORK ENVIRONMENT

The challenge for organizations today is not only about managing retention, it is about managing people. Sectors like healthcare and pharmaceuticals are still working under an immense pressure. Employees of these sectors work tirelessly and also live with the fear of virus contamination. So for those organizations, it is a very big challenge to maintaining its workforce with a suitable and safe work environment. The primary focus is not only on the healthcare sectors but also on the heavy and midscale manufacturing sectors. With different phases of unlocking, organizations are now starting their operations gradually by maintaining standard operating procedures. Though guidelines are there but it is the biggest constraint that organizations are facing to operate within the safe environment. Organizations should focus on managing the work environment to make better use of the available human asset. Previously employees preferred to stay with the organizations where they felt like a second home. Now in this phase of paradigm shift, employees are more concerned about their safety in the organization. So it is the responsibility of the organizations to provide a safe environment within the organization. So now the important environmental factors that organizations need to focus on are as follows:

a. Near contamination-free environment.
b. Proper sanitization in the workplace.
c. Regular health check-up of employees in the organizational setup.
d. Encourage employees to use preventive measures.
e. Provide essential commodities like mask, sanitizer, etc., in the workplace also.

If organizations adapt those measures in their organizational setup, employees would feel safe and confident, which boost their esteem as well as trust toward the

9.2.9 ORGANIZATIONAL LEADERSHIP

Leadership is important in any organization or in every people-related activities. It is another most important factor for retention of the employees in an organization. Firstly, it is needed to understand leadership. Sharma and Jain (2013) define leadership as a process by which a person influences others to accomplish an objective and directs the organization in a way that makes it more cohesive and coherent. According to Zaccaro and Klimoski (2001), the positions of leadership are established in work settings to help organizational subunits to achieve the purposes for which they exist within the larger system. In a study done by Nwokocha and Iheriohanma (2015) in Nigeria that aimed at examining nexus between leadership styles, employee retention, and employee performance, it was found that effective leadership style is crucial for achieving organizational goals as well as employee retention. Managers or supervisors are not only trained to develop their managerial skills rather it is their main responsibility to take care of the needs of the employees as well. Pandemic creates the imbalance in the organization, now the role and responsibility of the leaders are becoming more crucial. Pandemic situation has changed the organizational dynamics, so the leader's role has also changed to a large extent. In a study by Mills (2007), it was found that transformational leadership is the most effective leadership style while considering employee retention. Transformational leadership focuses on real-time problems, defines new benchmarks, builds understanding, motivates, and shapes the behavior of subordinates to achieve organizational goals effectively (Manshadi et al., 2014; Nagy and Edelman, 2014; Jiang et al., 2017). It was evident that transformational leadership enhances moral values and ideas as well as significantly improves employee commitment toward the organization (Deichmann and Stam, 2015). It is also essential to note that it is the responsibility of the leaders to effectively communicate with the employees. Especially in a pandemic situation, leaders also need to motivate the employees and push the employees for fulfilling the organizational goals.

9.2.10 ORGANIZATIONAL SECURITY

Pandemic hits hard the organization in different spheres, so it is quite hard for organizations to retain their workforce fully. Recent reports from several sources anticipate a huge job loss from several sectors (Crayne, 2020; Posel et al., 2021; Saenz and Sparks, 2020). As job insecurity is gradually on the rise day-by-day during the pandemic, it is important that organizations make endeavors to stand by the side of their employees and create a sense of security. More specifically as evidenced among the tourism industry and hotel managers COVID-19 has taken a toll on employee job security (Filimonau et al., 2020).

9.3 INDIVIDUAL-LEVEL FACTORS OF EMPLOYEE RETENTION

Employee retention is an organizational phenomenon but it has two sides always. Individuals come to an organization with own individuality. Retention of the employee through an organizational concern, still individual factors also play a crucial role in retention. It needs to consider that human capital is quite different from other capitals, they have thinking and emotional brain which discriminate them from other capitals in an organization. So from an organization's perspective, it is also very important to understand an employee's individual perspective. Because a clear understanding of its employee helps an organization and HR professionals to develop strategies to retain its workforce. So it is pertinent that individual factors need to be discussed along with the organizational factors.

9.3.1 PERSONALITY

The first and foremost individual factor that needs to be considered is human personality. The most used definition of personality is that by Gordon Allport that defines personality as "a dynamic organization within the individual, of those psycho-physical systems that determine its unique adjustment to the environment." From that definition, it might extract that personality represents the combination of stable and dynamic psychological attributes that capture the unique nature of a person. In literature, personality has several definitions and different approaches to understand it. Trait theorists and trait type theorists were able to explore personality in a holistic approach. On the other hand, psychoanalytic theorists take a completely different approach to understand personality. So from different literatures, it is quite evident that personality is a very complex phenomena and a bit complex to understand completely. It is the feature that differentiates an individual from another like fingerprint. So complete understanding of an employee's personality is quite impossible from organizational perspective. Still, organizations need to at least explore different facets of the personality of their employees for better understanding of them, which contribute in organizational growth and development.

Several research works in personality psychology showed that personality is a key predictor of employee's intention to leave or stay in the organizations (Hong and Kaur, 2008). There exists a significant relationship between personality and employee retention (Barrick et al., 1998). So understanding of personality is very much helpful for employee retention. As discussed previously, there are several approaches to understand human personality but every approach is not suitable for organizations. Like psychoanalytic approach deals with the unconscious mind of an individual, but from organizational perspective, it is not very suitable. Because it does not only require rigorous and more time to understand human personality through psychoanalytic approach but is also not very cost efficient. So organizations are relying on more easy and reliable approaches to understand personality. Majorly, organizations rely on trait and trait-cum-type approaches to understand and predict individual's personality. By reviewing several research works, researchers are able to identify some traits to predict employee's intention to stay or leave.

9.3.2 NEUROTICISM

Neuroticism represents individual differences in adjustment among individuals and explains why individuals differ in terms of emotional stability. Individuals high on neuroticism have a slight probability to experience negative emotions like anxiety, impulsiveness, etc. (Costa and McCrae, 1992). Different research works showed that individuals high on neuroticism were less likely to make a change in their job (Cheng et al., 2004), as they have slight likelihood to stay in an organizations for a longer period of time. Sudden changes in the pattern of livelihood might increase their anxiety and stress. So it is a predictor of personality that is positively related to intention to stay (Lambert, 2001). The pandemic time is a time marked with anxiety. So, people who are already neurotic or on the higher side of neuroticism, would display more anxiety and stress. Pandemic uncertainties will draw a huge impact on them. Under such circumstances, it is likely that they feel more sense of instability and in a short while might leave their jobs also. These kinds of employees need additional levels of organizational support so that they stay with the organization and perform smoothly.

9.3.3 EXTRAVERSION

Extraversion describes the extent to which people are assertive, sociable, dominant, energetic, and active. Generally, extraverted people are cheerful in nature and able to communicate with the others in a more convenient manner (Howard et al., 1996). In general terms, salespersons are very much prototypical example of extraversion, though exceptions are there. Research indicates that people who have high score on extraversion are more likely to change their job. They need more impulses for gratification and new environment, new ventures gratify their needs optimally (Sengupta and Ray, 2016).

9.3.4 OPENNESS TO EXPERIENCE

It is the disposition to be imaginative, nonconforming, unconventional, and autonomous. Includes traits like having wide interests being imaginative and insightful (Feist, 1998). As this particular trait is a good predictor for turnover intention of the employees. Those who are high on this trait showed a marked inverse specificity with retention. Those individuals are constantly driven by new experience and explorations.

9.3.5 AGREEABLENESS

Agreeableness measures how able individuals are to get along with others. Agreeable individuals are generally decent and cheerful and therefore tend to be more involved in their tasks. They are friendly, courteous, altruistic, helpful, and they attempt to compromise their personal interests with others. Costa and McCrae (1992) argued that agreeableness should be related to happiness because agreeable individuals have greater motivation to achieve interpersonal intimacy, which should lead to greater levels of well-being. Agreeableness has significant inverse impact on turnover intention (Salgado, 2002; Zimmerman, 2008). Several studies showed that those who are high on agreeableness showed a less intent to leave an organization (Jeswani and Dave, 2012).

Those four individual traits might consider as a great predictor for employees intention to leave. Some shows a direct and some shows an inverse relationship with individual's intention to leave. But it also needs to consider that personality assessment is a very rigorous process. So more research works from different contextual background help organizations to understand its relation with retention.

9.3.6 PERCEIVED JOB SATISFACTION

In an article published in Harvard Business Review (1973), written by Vincent Flower and Charles Hughes, they tried to explore retention of employees from different perspectives. They tried to understand why people stay, instead of why people leave an organization. In their study, they are able to find out different important individual factors to predict employees intention to stay. And one of the most important predictor was found to be job satisfaction. It is much easier for organizations to retain its workforce when they are satisfied with their current job. Hoppock (1935) defined job satisfaction as any combination of psychological, physiological, and environmental circumstances that cause a person truthfully to say I am satisfied with my job. One of the most cited definitions of job satisfaction defined it as how the employee feel about the organization and its various aspects. Different literature and research works showed that job satisfaction mostly leads to retention of employees in the workforce. Job satisfaction is a multifaceted phenomenon, it includes several spectrums, like economical, psychological aspects. So for the better understanding of job satisfaction, organizations need constant monitoring. Especially in postpandemic situation, it is very important to focus upon different factors that might lead to employee job dissatisfaction. It is very important to consider that job satisfaction is not only the feeling that an employee has toward the organization, rather it also encompasses the expectation from the organization. Different factors that impact job satisfaction are compensation, job content, relationship with supervisor and other employees, opportunity for advancement, etc. Now in this pandemic situation, other factors might add to the list like health benefits, increments, etc. Right now all issues, which lead to job dissatisfaction, might not be taken care of but constant support and communication might help organization to reduce the level of dissatisfaction.

9.3.7 PERCEIVED WORK-LIFE BALANCE

Work-life balance is the state of equilibrium where a person equally prioritizes the demands of one's career and the demands of one's personal life. A good work-life balance has a significant impact on several dimensions of an employee's life. A good work-life balance reduces stress and burnout (Chakraborty et al., 2020), reduces absenteeism at workplace, etc. So, it plays an important role in predicting retention in workforce also. Employers who are committed to providing environments that support work-life balance for their employees can save on costs, experience fewer cases of absenteeism, and enjoy a more loyal and productive workforce. A successful balance between work life and family does not only provide an employee satisfaction but it is also beneficial from the organizational perspective. A state of disequilibrium has arises in work-life balance due to the COVID-19 pandemic. Employees across the globe have found their work-life balance impacted detrimentally due to pandemic. Healthcare sectors, police even those in academia even if they are not the front line warriors suffered most in terms of their work-life balance. IT sector which is one of the largest sector is encouraging work from home. Those desperate measures due to pandemic create an imbalance in their work-life balance also. While some employees are working for day and night, others find it difficult to manage their work schedule properly. So the conventional way to look into the matter has changed now. Though the discussion on work-life balance is not gender specific, but it needs to be considered that female employees suffer the most. So organizations that enhance and provide different measure to maintain a good work-life balance, attracts the employees' attention, and leads to employee retention. Different measures should be taken from organizational side as well as from individual's side, like:

a. Flexible work timing.
b. Use of communication tool to indicate employees online and offline hours.
c. Getting ready for the work same way like offline mode.
d. Setting boundaries in work hours.
e. Prioritizing health issues of own and other family members.
f. Taking care of the mental health also.
g. Accommodating time for recreational activities.
h. Working in a space that is distinct from the rest of the home, if possible.
i. Developing good eating and lifestyle habits.
j. Trying to make some time for physical activities, like exercises, yoga, etc.
k. Organization must provide holidays and other benefits for better work-life balance.

Those measures not only help employees to cope up with their burden and stress but also help organizations to have a productive employee who would feel positive about work and organization, and hence encourage employee retention.

Previous factors regarding organization and individual have helped to chalk out the probable causes of retention. But it needs to be considered that COVID-19 pandemic has turned the world upside down and completely changed our outlook toward almost everything. So the orthodox and conventional analysis helps us to understand employee retention, but organizations need to develop new strategies to retain its workforce in new normal.

9.4 EMPLOYEE RETENTION STRATEGIES IN THE NEW NORMAL

Employee retention is a pressing topic in COVID-19 pandemic and it is a tough challenge as well. A static workforce provides stability to the organization and helps organization to maintain its productivity in an efficient manner. So organizations should develop some new strategies for effective employee retention.

9.4.1 EMPLOYEE ASSISTANCE PROGRAM (EAP)

In India, EAP is not a new concept, but in reality implementation and use of EAP was less encouraging. Providing a good EAP is beneficial for employees and it builds trust and sense of worthwhileness within them. A good EAP in the postpandemic era should include factors, like:

a. Health and wellness spot where employees can communicate about their health issues and get recommendations from experts.
b. Encouraging employees to discuss about the work-related issues with the experts.
c. Supporting health and wellness programs virtually and encouraging employees to become a part of those programs.
d. Allowing employees to work in flexi hours. Encouraging them to spend quality time with family in a safe way.
e. Trying to provide medical and nonmedical support if any employee or family member is infected by the virus.

9.4.2 MENTAL HEALTH WELLNESS SERVICES

The primary focus in this pandemic is to save ourselves from the virus. But in this battling time, our mental health also gets compromised by the impact of COVID-19. In a report published by National Institute of Mental Health and Neuroscience, India in July 2020 showed that a consistent and substantial growth in several mental health issues like anxiety, depression, substance abuse, suicide, poor life satisfaction among frontline workers as well as in general population. Desperate time needs desperate measures, so mental health interventions at work have reported best effectiveness for mental health promotion and prevention strategies. Workplaces are optimal settings to create a culture of fostering mental health. From organizational perspective, it also needs to be considered that in general stigma toward mental health issues is very much relevant in our culture. So promotion of mental health wellness programs must include sensitization of employees to reduce their stigma regarding mental health issues. Measures that need to be taken regarding this are as follows:

a. Sensitization and encouraging employee to opt for mental health wellness program.
b. Set up an effective team of mental health experts along with the organizations representative to look into the mental health issues of employees.
c. Regular and constant monitoring.
d. Effective communication needs to be encouraged with supervisors or managers to understand the underlying issues if present.
e. Arrange virtual mental health programs like seminar or workshops at an episodic interval.
f. Try to include family members of employees in mental health wellness program, if possible.
g. Empathetic attitude from the organizational authority need to be promoted.

Through those measures organizations not only help their workforce, besides they are also able to gain trustworthiness and loyalty of their employees. This sense of trust helps the organization in their long run to retained its workforce intact.

9.4.3 BRIDGING COMMUNICATION GAPS

In this pandemic situation, most of the workforce structure relies on effective communication. In some sectors, a strong grievance arises because of the workload and in other sectors the mode of communication completely relying on virtual medium. So an effective communication with the employees at regular intervals helps organizations to understand employee's individual perspective. It is very much important and needed to establish a regular cadence of communication, like:

a. Establishing individual monthly touchpoints between managers and their direct reports.
b. Establishing an open screen policy in organizational setup. This way organization encourage team members to set up time with the managers if they have concern.

c. Encouraging teams to engage in get-together activities virtually or in a safe environment, if possible.
d. Ensuring effective communication and a good leadership role is also very much expected. So organizations also need to invest in leadership programs for the managers.

9.4.4 SAFETY MEASURES

The primary concern for all organizations is that because of the pandemic, majors employee concerns are now around the health of the employees. Organizations need to take suitable and appropriate measures to maintain healthy environment for employees. The cost of employee retention is now equated with the cost of health of the employees. Organizations must ensure to provide different safety equipment to their workforce.

9.5 CONCLUSION

This overall discussion enables us to understand the future of retention and engagement from several perspective. Postpandemic era is a testing time for organizations also for the workforce. It needs to consider that most organizations, specifically in India, are in an economic crisis. But organizations require to consider that attrition has both soft and hard costs. So retention of the existing workforce is not only helpful for reducing those costs but also makes organizations more productive. So for better retention, organizations must consider those domains of new normal along with the conventional ways must implement those interventions to create a better organizational culture. In this testing, world changes are inevitable. Changes in technical, infrastructural, social, and economic spheres modified the organizational scenario. Due to the unpredictability and manpower crunch, in some sectors, difficulty bar has risen high. Through this chapter, organizations will envisage the opportunity to understand more deeply about the matter of concern. Employee attrition has always been hazardous, so better understanding of the factors of employee retention is very much required. Through this chapter, organizations have the chance to understand different individual level as well as organizational level motivators of employee retention. This understanding helps organizations to make policies and take preventive measure to retain its workforce. Thus the chapter, (1) provides an empirical basis for HR practitioners for a better retention management, (2) provides a strong basis for developing an organizational culture in the new normal, and (3) helps organizations to build strategies for retention considering the economic downturn.

KEYWORDS

- employee retention
- factors of retention
- new normal

REFERENCES

Amaya, M.; Melnyk, B. M. Leveraging System-Wide Well-Being and Resiliency in Higher Education during the Covid-19 Pandemic. *Build. Healthy Acad. Communities J.* **2020,** *4* (1), 7–16.

Barrick, M. R.; Stewart, G. L.; Neubert, M. J.; Mount, M. K. Relating Member Ability and Personality to Work-Team Processes and Team Effectiveness. *J. Appl. Psychol.* **1998,** *83* (3), 377.

Chakraborty, T.; Ganguly, M. Crafting Engaged Employees through Positive Work Environment: Perspectives of Employee Engagement. In *Management Techniques for Employee Engagement in Contemporary Organizations*; IGI Global, 2019; pp. 180–198.

Chakraborty, T.; Mishra, N. Appreciative Inquiry: Unleashing a Positive Revolution of Organizational Change and Development. *Int. J. Econ. Com. Busi. Manage.* **2019,** *6* (2), 32–37.

Chakraborty, T.; Gohain, D.; Saha, R. What Comes in the Way of Engagement? Moderation Analysis of Stress on Women Marketing Executives' Work Life Balance. *Int. J. Human Resour. Dev. Manage.* **2020,** *20* (3–4), 349–368.

Chakraborty, T.; Kumar, A.; Upadhyay, P.; Dwivedi, Y. K. Link between Social Distancing, Cognitive Dissonance, and Social Networking Site Usage Intensity: A Country-Level Study during the COVID-19 Outbreak. *Internet Res.* **2021,** *31* (2), 419–456. DOI: 10.1108/intr-05-2020-0281

Chakraborty, T.; Tripathi, M.; Saha, S. The Dynamics of Employee Relationships in a Digitalized Workplace: The Role of Media Richness on Workplace Culture. In *Critical Issues on Changing Dynamics in Employee Relations and Workforce Diversity*; IGI Global, 2021; pp. 175–205.

Costa, P. T.; McCrae, R. R. *Revised NEO Personality Inventory (NEO-PI-R) and NEO Five-Factor Inventory (NEO-FFI) Manual*; Psychological Assessment Resources: Odessa, FL, 1992.

Crayne, M. P. The Traumatic Impact of Job Loss and Job Search in the Aftermath of COVID-19. *Psychol. Trauma: Theor. Res. Pract. Policy* **2020,** *12* (S1), S180.

Deichmann, D.; Stam, D. Leveraging Transformational and Transactional Leadership to Cultivate the Generation of Organization-Focused Ideas. *Leadersh. Q.* **2015**, *26*, 204–219. DOI: 10.1016/j.leaqua.2014.10.004

Desai, M.; Majumdar, B.; Chakraborty, T.; Ghosh, K. The Second Shift: Working Women in India. *Gender Manage. Int. J.*, **2011**.

Downs, C. W.; Adrian, A. D., Eds. *Assessing Organizational Communication: Strategic Communication Audits*; Guilford Press, 2004.

Erickson, R. A. Communication and Employee Retention. *Int. Encyclopedia Interpersonal Commun.* **2015**, 1–10.

Feist, G. J. A Meta-Analysis of Personality in Scientific and Artistic Creativity. *Personality Soc. Psychol. Bull.* **1998**, *2* (4), 290–309.

Filimonau, V.; Derqui, B.; Matute, J. The COVID-19 Pandemic and Organisational Commitment of Senior Hotel Managers. *Int. J. Hosp. Manage.* **2020**, *91*, 102659.

Gohain, D.; Chakraborty, T.; Saha, R. Are Entrepreneurs Trainable Towards Success: Reviewing Impact of Training on Entrepreneurship Success, 2017.

Hong, L. C.; Kaur, S. A Relationship between Organizational Climate, Employee Personality and Intention to Leave. *Int. Rev. Busi. Res. Papers* **2008**, *4* (3), 1–10.

Howard, P. J.; Medina, P. L.; Howard, J. M. The Big Five locator: A Quick Assessment Tool for Consultants and Trainers. *Annu.-San Diego-Pfeiffer Co.* **1996**, *1*, 107–122.

Jeswani, S.; Dave, S. Impact of Individual Personality on Turnover Intention: A Study on Faculty Members. *Manage. Labour Stud.* **2012**, *37* (3), 253–265.

Jiang, W.; Zhao, X.; Ni, J. The Impact of Transformational Leadership on Employee Sustainable Performance: The Mediating Role of Organizational Citizenship Behavior. *Sustainability* **2017**, *9*, 1567. DOI: 10.3390/su9091567

Lambert, E. G. To Stay or Quit: A Review of Literature on Correctional Officer Turnover. *Am. J. Criminal Justice* **2001**, *26* (1), 61–76.

Luis, C.; Vance, C. A Pandemic Crisis: Mentoring, Leadership, and the Millennial Nurse. *Nurs. Econ.* **2020**, *38* (3), 152–163.

Manshadi, M. D.; Ebrahimi, F. P.; Abdi, H. M. A Study of the Relationship between Transformational Leadership and Organizational Learning. *Eur. J. Exp. Biol.* **2014**, *4*, 12–20.

Megginson, D. Mentoring in Action: A Practical Guide. *Human Resour. Manage. Int. Digest* **2006**.

Mills, G. E. *Transformational Leadership and Employee Retention: An Exploratory Investigation of the Four Characteristics*; Capella University, 2007.

Nagy, B.; Edelman, D. J. Transformational Leadership in Planning Curricula. *Curr. Urban Stud.* **2014**, *2*, 198–211. DOI: 10.4236/cus.2014.23020

Nwokocha, I.;& Iheriohanma, E. B. J. Nexus between Leadership Styles, Employee Retention and Performance in Organisations in Nigeria. *Eur. Sci. J.* **2015**, *11* (13), 185–209.

Paille. Employee Retention: Exploring the Relationship between Employee Commitment, Organizational Citizenship Behaviour and the Decision to Leave the Organization. *Int. J. Human Resour. Dev. Manage.* **2012**, *12* (1/2), 140–157.

Posel, D.; Oyenubi, A.; Kollamparambil, U. Job Loss and Mental Health during the COVID-19 Lockdown: Evidence from South Africa. *PloS One* **2021**, *16* (3), e0249352.

Saenz, R.; Sparks, C. The Inequities of Job Loss and Recovery amid the COVID-19 Pandemic, 2020.

Salgado, J. F. The Big Five Personality Dimensions and Counterproductive Behaviors. *Int. J. Selection Assess.* **2002**, *10* (1–2), 117–125.

Sanders, K.; Nguyen, P. T.; Bouckenooghe, D.; Rafferty, A.; Schwarz, G. Unraveling the What and How of Organizational Communication to Employees during COVID-19 Pandemic: Adopting an Attributional Lens. *J. Appl. Behav. Sci.* **2020,** *56* (3), 289–293.

Sengupta, S.; Ray, A. *Employee Retention: An Indian Perspective*; Lambert Publishing, Germany, 2016.

Sharma, M. K.; Jain, S. Leadership Management: Principles, Models and Theories. *Global J. Manage. Busi. Stud.* **2013,** *3* (3), 309–318.

Walsh, K.; Taylor, M. S. Developing In-House Careers and Retaining Management Talent: What Hospitality Professionals Want from Their Jobs. *Cornell Hotel Restaurant Admin. Quart.* **2007,** *48* (2), 163–182.

Wilson, J. A.; Elman, N. S. Organizational Benefits of Mentoring. *Acad. Manage. Persp.* **1990,** *4* (4), 88–94.

Wu, A. W.; Connors, C.; Everly, Jr, G. S. COVID-19: Peer Support and Crisis Communication Strategies to Promote Institutional Resilience, 2020.

Zaccaro, S. J.; Klimoski, R. J., Eds. The Nature of Organizational Leadership: An Introduction. The Nature of Organizational Leadership, 2001; pp 3–41.

Zimmerman, R. D. Understanding the Impact of Personality Traits on Individuals' Turnover Decisions: A Meta-Analytic Path Model. *Personnel Psychol.* **2008,** *61* (2), 309–348.

CHAPTER 10

Preserving Employees' Well-Being: An Organization's Post-Pandemic Imperative

S. SABESAN* and M. A. S. VASANTH

Bharathiar University, Coimbatore, India

*Corresponding author. E-mail: swaminathansabesan@gmail.com

ABSTRACT

The entire world is witnessing the worst effects of chaos caused by the COVID-19 pandemic. Outspread of pandemic is disrupting the lives and livelihood of many and has affected the job and works-style of employees in all industrial setups. Work from home has become norm of every single day. Given the sedentary and stressful life, employees are prone to develop lifestyle diseases. Moreover, employees with pre-existing lifestyle diseases are at greater risk of getting health complications early that could lead to the perceived loss of well-being among the employees. Considering the above, the present authors conceptualized and developed a proprietary "integrated employee well-being intervention framework." This framework is aimed to aid organizations to preserve the employees' overall well-being, which will enable them to become self-aware, feel alive, stay engaged, and remain energized. This framework is a symbiotic blend of embedding knowledge (about disease, wellness, and well-being) and demonstration of behaviors (wellness-related behaviors and well-being related behaviors), followed by deep practice and sustenance of new behaviors (through daily reflection and journaling) by the employees. It pivots around the enhancement of health-related behaviors, proactive prevention of diseases, and enduring promotion of holistic health of employees to embrace a culture of well-being within organizations. The potential benefits are drawn out as follows:

- Demystifying wellness and well-being.
- Integrated employee well-being intervention framework.
- Embedding disease-related knowledge in employees.
- Factors contributing to employees' wellness.
- Embedding well-being-related knowledge in employees.
- Importance of deep practice, reflection, journaling, and sustenance of new behaviors.
- Role of employee well-being champion (EWC) in embedding a culture of well-being within the organization.

10.1 INTRODUCTION

The entire world is witnessing the worst effects of chaos caused by the COVID-19 pandemic. Outspread of pandemic have disrupting the lives and livelihood of many and have affected the job and works-style of employees in all industrial set-ups, work from home has become norm of the day. It is also imposing an existential threat to many employees in terms of survival, retaining the job, salary, timely promotion, and payment of increments and perquisites. This has brought out changes in the working environment drastically.

The compliance to workplace precautions (sanitation, mask, and social distance) and doing official work from their residences have become very common. Given the new reality, employees have become vulnerable to develop lifestyle diseases. Moreover, employees with pre-existing lifestyle diseases are at higher risk of getting health complications. This may affect the well-being of the employees.

Therefore, it becomes necessary that every organization must endeavor to preserve the employees' well-being. To preserve employee well-being, organizations need to define, design, develop, and deliver an integrated and holistic employee well-being intervention. This initiative will empower employees to become self-aware, feel alive, stay engaged, and gain fulfillment personally and professionally. The perspectives offered will enable the reader to acquire a deep understanding of "employee well-being"—its meaning, importance, and ways for preservation by using "integrated employee well-being intervention framework."

10.2 DEMYSTIFYING WELLNESS AND WELL-BEING

The constructs "wellness" and "well-being" are used interchangeably. However, one should not miss the wood for trees. The subtle distinction between wellness and well-being needs to be clearly understood. Our medical community views an individual's health through the lens of physical health rather than mental and emotional health. Generally, the definition of good health is largely confined to the absence of diseases or infirmity. This has got relevance to seeking remedies for the physical ailments and conditions. The term wellness generally relates to intention, action, and activities relevant to disease prevention, early diagnosis, and disease management.

However, well-being is related to an individual's emotional and mental dimensions. Well-being is broader and more expansive than wellness, encompasses physical, mental, and emotional health.

10.3 EVALUATION OF THE EXISTING WELLNESS INITIATIVES

In the Indian context, the employee wellness initiatives offered by the major corporations in different sectors like healthcare, IT, manufacturing, and pharmaceuticals cover the following activities:

- Health check-ups (blood test, ECG, scans, etc.).
- Counseling sessions (personal & tele counseling).
- Smoking & alcohol cessation programs.
- Stress/sleep management sessions.
- Recognition program connected with the achievement of health parameters.

It is found that the existing employee wellness programs across sectors predominantly cover the above activities in isolation and therefore it falls short of addressing the overall well-being of the employees. Moreover, the wellness programs rarely result in bringing enduring behavioral change in them. Most of them are siloed or one-off initiatives in the organization.

10.4 THE RATIONALE BEHIND EMPLOYEE WELL-BEING INTERVENTIONS

Employees are the indispensable resource for any organization. They help organizations to achieve optimum productivity and profitability. Those employees with unhealthy lifestyles are more likely to develop lifestyle diseases. With the onset of such diseases, they become stressful. They will find it difficult to demonstrate engagement and productivity at work. They also incur a lot of expenses for regaining their normal health. To regain their health, they must modify their unhealthy lifestyle. This is possible only through organization-led employee-well-being intervention.

10.5 INTEGRATED EMPLOYEE WELL-BEING INTERVENTION FRAMEWORK

The employee well-being intervention must go beyond reactive treatment. It should lay emphasis on proactive prevention of diseases with a thrust on the promotion and preservation of employees' well-being. Such type of intervention empowers employees to stay healthy, remain happy, keep engaged, and become productive for achieving improved quality in living. It pivots around the enhancement of health-related behaviors, proactive prevention of diseases, and the advancement of holistic health of employees across the year. The framework is a mix of embedding knowledge (about disease, wellness, and well-being) and demonstration of behaviors (wellness-related behaviors and well-being related behaviors), followed by deep practice and sustenance of new behaviors (through daily reflection and journaling) by the employees (Figure 10.1).

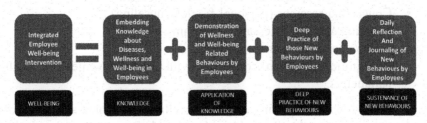

FIGURE 10.1 Integrated employee well-being intervention framework.

10.5.1 NEED FOR THE FRAMEWORK

10.5.1.1 TO ENHANCE AND PRESERVE THE EMPLOYEES' WELL-BEING

Organizations should seek the professional services of behavioral health and positive psychology practitioners (PPPs) for embedding knowledge about diseases, wellness, and well-being among the employees. Such knowledge can be disseminated through digital platforms. The intervention encompasses preparatory work, learning events, action learning (which includes deep practice, reflection, journaling), and sustenance of new behaviors with the support from the employees' supervising managers.

10.5.1.2 TO EMBRACE A CULTURE OF WELL-BEING

EWC from the Human Resource Department should lead these initiatives under the employee assistance program. EWC, behavioral health practitioner, and PPP should cocreate and customize the design, development, delivery, duration, frequency, and evaluation of such sessions, keeping the organizational context in mind. An attempt is made here to help readers to gain a flavor of the knowledge about lifestyle diseases, employee wellness, and employee well-being.

10.6 EMBEDDING DISEASE-RELATED KNOWLEDGE IN EMPLOYEES

The disease-related knowledge includes definition, classification, causes, symptoms, complications, management, and treatment of the major lifestyle diseases. Knowledge of these aspects is important for the avoidance of diseases and advancement of holistic health.

Disease-related knowledge motivates individuals to pursue preventive self-health care. Numerous studies (Vasanth & Sabesan 2019, Alhaik et al., 2019) have revealed that disease-related knowledge helps patients to overcome depression, stress, low self-efficacy, anger, mood swing, learning impairment, and guilt. In fact, Moradi et al. (2019) concluded in their study that the fasting blood glucose levels of the participants got significantly reduced after the diabetic education intervention. Likewise, Bukhsh et al. (2018) found that the diabetic educational intervention significantly improved the self-care behaviors and glycemic management of the participants. In contrast, inadequate, or low disease-related knowledge resulted in nonadherence to health-related behaviors and poor self-efficacy (Table 10.1).

10.6.1 DIABETES MELLITUS MANAGEMENT FOR IMPROVED WELLNESS

The persistent elevation of blood sugar level above the normal (American Diabetic Association, 2020-Fasting Plasma Glouse-126 mg/dl or a 2-h plasma glucose level of 200 mg/dl) is referred to as diabetes mellitus (Table 10.2).

TABLE 10.1 Lifestyle Diseases.

An attempt is made here, to help readers, gain knowledge about various lifestyle diseases in the form of definition, classification, causes, symptoms, complications, management, and treatment protocol of the chronic or lifestyle diseases 	**Major lifestyle diseases** Diabetes mellitus Hypertension Cardiovascular diseases Arthritis Kidney diseases Respiratory diseases

TABLE 10.2 Diabetes Mellitus Related Symptoms, Causes, Complication.

Symptoms	Causes	Complications of poorly managed diabetes	Overview of treatment
• General tiredness • Unexplained weight loss • Excessive urination/thirst/hunger • Relapse of infections • Delayed wound healing	• Obesity • Sedentary lifestyle • Poor health-related behaviors • Stress • Anxiety	• Cardiovascular disease • Kidney diseases • Stroke • Eye diseases • Foot gangrene & vascular disease	Healthy diet & regular exercise Improve diabetic-related knowledge along with coping strategies to manage stress and anxiety Periodic glucose and health monitoring & Adherence to medication Foot care Avoid smoking, reduce alcohol consumption

The treatment for diabetes mellitus calls for addressing the insulin resistance in the patient. Various studies (Bains & Egede, 2011; Al-Qazaz et al., 2011) have consistently shown that improved health-related behaviors (healthy diet, regular exercise, periodic glucose monitoring, foot care, regular adherence to medication, and avoidance of smoking/alcohol/drugs) significantly alleviate the symptoms and reduce the risk of the early development of complication of diabetes mellitus.

10.6.2 HYPERTENSION MANAGEMENT FOR IMPROVED WELLNESS

Hypertension or high blood pressure is indicated by the consistent elevation of blood pressure beyond the normal level (American Heart Association, 2020 – ≥140/90 mmHg). It seldom shows clear symptoms, unlike other diseases. If left unidentified and not treated appropriately may result in serious complications like heart attack, stroke, etc.

Hypertension is classified into primary and secondary hypertension. High blood pressure without an identifiable cause is referred to as primary hypertension. The increase in blood pressure is due to an identifiable underlying condition like diabetes, kidney diseases, thyroid diseases, tumors in the adrenal gland, sleep disorders, alcohol abuse, etc., which is classified as secondary hypertension (Table 10.3).

TABLE 10.3 Hypertension-Related Symptoms, Causes, Complication.

Symptoms	Causes	Complications of poorly managed hypertension	Overview of treatment
• Headache • Shortness of breath or nose bleeds • Visual disturbances	• Obesity • Sedentary lifestyle, diabetes, high blood lipid levels • Poor health-related behaviors • Fear, anxiety, & stress	• Cardiovascular disease • Kidney diseases • Stroke • Eye diseases	Healthy diet & regular exercise Improve hypertension-related knowledge along with coping strategies to manage fear, stress, and anxiety Periodic blood pressure monitoring & adherence to medication Avoid smoking, reduce alcohol consumption

10.6.3 CARDIOVASCULAR DISEASES MANAGEMENT FOR IMPROVED WELLNESS

Cardiovascular diseases are a cluster of diseases that involve the heart and/or blood vessels. Cardiovascular diseases affect the flow of oxygen-rich blood to body cells and returning of carbon dioxide rich blood to the heart and lungs for oxygenation. The cardiovascular diseases are broadly classified into coronary artery disease, cardiac arrhythmia, heart failure, myocardial infarction, stroke, and peripheral artery diseases (Table 10.4).

10.6.4 ARTHRITIS MANAGEMENT FOR IMPROVED WELLNESS

The term arthritis is an inflammation of one or more joints, which affects the mobility of patients. The arthritis is broadly classified into mechanical and inflammatory arthritis. Mechanical arthritis is the damage or inflammation of the joints due to injury. Inflammatory arthritis is a condition in which the hyperactive immune system attacks or damages the joints through the hypersecretion of inflammatory fluids (Table 10.5).

TABLE 10.4 Cardiovascular Diseases Related Symptoms, Causes, Complication.

Symptoms	Causes	Complications of poorly managed cardiovascular disease	Overview of treatment
• Chest discomfort • Pain, nausea, fatigue, abdominal pain • Shortness of breath • Numbness, coldness in the legs or arms	• Obesity • Sedentary lifestyle, diabetes, high blood lipid levels, Hypertension • Poor health-related behaviors • Fear, anxiety, & stress	• Worsening chest discomfort & pain • Myocardial infraction • Heart failure • Emergency ward admission	Healthy diet & regular exercise, cardiac rehabilitation Improve disease-related knowledge along with coping strategies to manage fear, stress, and anxiety Periodic health monitoring, adherence to medication, lifestyle management counseling, & comorbidities counseling Avoid smoking, reduce alcohol consumption

TABLE 10.5 Arthritis-Related Symptoms, Causes, Complication.

Symptoms	Causes	Complications of poorly managed Arthritis	Overview of treatment
• Pain • Heat sensation in the joints • Swelling, redness, and tenderness in joints • Stiffness in joints	• Obesity • Sedentary lifestyle • Lack of exercise • Malfunctioning of immune system (inflammatory arthritis)	• Irreversible damage to the joints • Restriction of mobility	Healthy diet, regular exercise, & reduction of weight Joint rehabilitation (physiotherapy) Periodic joint monitoring, adherence to medication Avoid smoking

10.6.5 *KIDNEY DISEASES MANAGEMENT FOR IMPROVED WELLNESS*

Kidney diseases mean the gradual or sudden loss of kidney functions, which result in the accumulation of fluids and waste products in the body. Kidney disease is broadly classified into acute kidney diseases and chronic kidney diseases. Acute kidney diseases are indicated by the sudden deterioration of kidney function due to a known cause. Chronic kidney diseases refer to the slow deterioration of kidney function because of diabetes mellitus, hypertension, and other chronic conditions (Table 10.6).

TABLE 10.6 Kidney Disease Related Symptoms, Causes, Complication.

Symptoms	Causes	Complications of poorly managed Kidney disease	Overview of Treatment
• Most of the patients with chronic kidney disease do not have any symptoms until the late stage of the disease • Tiredness, weakness, elevated blood pressure, loss of hunger, water-electrolyte imbalance, fluid accumulation in the body and lungs, swelling, low urine production, itching, and weight loss	Poorly managed diabetes mellitus and hypertension, which account for two-thirds of kidney disease cases	Multiorgan disturbance and damage	Effective diabetes management Effective hypertension management Regular exercise, fluid intake management Avoid smoking & alcohol

10.6.6 RESPIRATORY DISEASES MANAGEMENT FOR IMPROVED WELLNESS

Respiratory diseases are lung diseases that negatively alter airflow and make it difficult for the individual to breathe (Table 10.7).

TABLE 10.7 Respiratory Diseases Related Symptoms, Causes, Complication.

Symptoms	Causes	Complications of poorly managed respiratory disease	Overview of treatment
Shortness of breath, wheezing, chronic cough, fatigue, inability to exercise, chest pressure, and loss of muscle or weight loss	Infection, smoking, air pollution, and malfunctioning immune system	Severe respiratory infections, heart failure and heart attack, hypertension, lung collapse	Exercise, aerobic activity and diaphragmatic breathing, pulmonary rehabilitation, immunization against infections, and oxygen therapy

10.7 FACTORS CONTRIBUTING TO EMPLOYEE WELLNESS

Employee wellness comprises of diet, exercise, sleep, and health monitoring. Every employee who attends the learning event on wellness-related knowledge will understand the efficacy of exercise, diet, sleep, and health monitoring.

10.7.1 EFFICACY OF EXERCISE

Regular exercise can reduce body weight and the accumulation of fat in the body. It improves calorie-burning potential, oxygen consumption, and overall cardiovascular health. It regulates blood pressure, blood glucose, and blood lipid levels. It reduces the risk of developing lifestyle diseases.

Benefits of exercise
Improve calorie burning
Increases oxygen consumption
Boosts immunity
Reduce blood glucose/fat level
Reduce bodyweight
Strengthen bones/joints

Exercise helps people to manage and prevent the early development of complications of lifestyle diseases. It enhances the immune system's capability to fight against infections. Finally, it improves the life expectancy of people. It becomes very clear that regular exercise improves the holistic health of employees.

10.7.2 EFFICACY OF HEALTHY DIET

Health regulatory bodies (American Diabetic Association, American Heart Association, European Association for the Study of Diabetes, etc.) strongly recommend that a healthy diet prevents lifestyle diseases. The term healthy diet refers to "an intake of vegetables and fruits over animal food and whole grains over refined carbohydrates."

Benefits of healthy diet
Regulate blood glucose/fat/pressure
Prevent lifestyle diseases
Reduces body weight
Boost energy levels

High consumption of red meat, oil fried foods, carbonated drinks, pastries leads to obesity and related lifestyle diseases. Frequent eating or snacking also intensifies the risk of weight gain and worsening of lifestyle diseases.

10.7.3 EFFICACY OF GOOD SLEEP

Benefits of Good Sleep
Boost immune system
Improves energy
Improves concentration/memory
Improves learning agility
Reduces weight gain

Sleep enables maintaining good health. It facilitates the body to repair itself and the brain to consolidate memories and process information. It increases the life expectancy of employees.

10.7.4 EFFICACY OF HEALTH MONITORING

Benefits of health monitoring
Provide opportunity for early diagnosis
Provide opportunity for lifestyle modification
Offer insight on current health status
Reduce reactive healthcare cost
Reduce the risk of progression of diseases
Increases life expectancy

Periodic health monitoring offers actionable insights about health status and facilitates corrective measures on health issues and lifestyle modifications.

10.8 EMBEDDING WELL-BEING RELATED KNOWLEDGE IN EMPLOYEES

The construct "well-being" embraces more than just physical health. Well-being connotes a positive mindset, emotions, and moods along with physical health. These are critical points, overlooked and ignored much in today's employee wellness programs by many organizations (Figure 10.2).

FIGURE 10.2 Demystifying the construct well-being.

Employees with well-being become healthy and productive with improved quality of life, immunity, and increased life expectancy.

Benefits of employee well-being
Improve employee engagement at work
Reduce employees stress
Improve employee quality of life
Improve employee's problem-solving ability
Increase employee life expectancy
Improve employee's physical health

Embedding the learnings from positive psychology (science and practice of happiness) helps employees, enhance, and preserve their well-being. In this regard, actionable insights drawn from the PERMA model (Seligman, 2013) assume significance.

This model comprises of the five core elements of well-being. These five core elements of the PERMA model can be contextually applied in organizations to improve the holistic well-being of employees.

10.8.1 APPLYING THE CORE ELEMENTS OF PERMA MODEL AT WORK

An attempt is made here to define each core element of PERMA and how employees can embrace these core elements daily.

10.8.2 EMBEDDING POSITIVE EMOTIONS RELATED KNOWLEDGE IN EMPLOYEES

Positive emotion is about "feeling good" and provides the best path to well-being. It helps people to augment positivity about the past (e.g., practicing gratitude and forgiveness), the present (e.g., by savoring physical pleasures and mindfulness), and the future (e.g., by building hope and optimism). It also strengthens relationships, builds resilience, and that can pave way for success. Employees can build and practice positive emotions such as gratitude, forgiveness, savoring, mindfulness, and hope/optimism at work. More importantly, deep practice and sustenance of these positive emotions will improve the employee's well-being.

Among the positive emotions, practicing gratitude is efficacious in bringing enduring happiness and improved well-being. This was validated by Komase et al. (2019), in their study on the effectiveness of a gratitude intervention program among 835 employees (Table 10.8).

10.9 DEMONSTRATION OF DISEASE, WELLNESS, AND WELL-BEING RELATED KNOWLEDGE

The responsibility of EWC does not end with organizing learning events concerning the dissemination of wellness and well-being related knowledge for employees. In order to bring an enduring impact of building well-being among employees, EWC should mandate and facilitate every employee to demonstrate all the aforementioned behaviors daily both at home and at workplace. The role of supervising managers in encouraging and empowering employees (team members) can be sought to reinforce the practice of new behaviors daily.

10.9.1 DEEP PRACTICE, REFLECTION, JOURNALING, AND SUSTENANCE OF NEW BEHAVIORS

The persistent and consistent practice of learned behaviors will lead to any great achievement in any field. With the deep practice of following the 10,000 h rule, the individual employee becomes an expert and gains complete mastery. While achieving mastery, an individual employee can deploy the framework of tiny habits (Fogg, 2020)/atomic habits (Clear, 2018) daily.

TABLE 10.8 Positive Emotions and the Recommended Practices.

a) Gratitude at work	Action ideas to practice gratitude at workplace
• O'Leary (2013) defined gratitude as "an affirmation of goodness and good things in the world (such as gifts and benefits that one received from significant others) and the source of goodness is always outside of oneself." He also viewed it as a "relationship strengthening emotion."	1. Reflect and write down three good things that happened at work that you are grateful for each day. 2. Write a letter of gratitude to your mentor, boss, friend. 3. Express thanks instantly for every help you receive from others.
• People who show gratitude acknowledge and appreciate the goodness of life such as their health, family, friends, belonging, etc.	4. Make a point to go out of your way to express thanks to someone who is not typically recognized. 5. Offer customized "Thank you cards" to the team for their accomplishment.
• They remain thankful for what they had/what they have.	6. Make a gratitude wall at the workplace and encourage people to articulate their gratitude there.
• They count their blessings daily and feel that they are lucky and privileged to live.	7. Inspire people to create and maintain gratitude journal daily.
• The practice of gratitude results in improved well-being, enhanced life satisfaction, a greater sense of connectedness, and enriched physical health (Emmons and McCullough, 2013).	8. Begin emails with a gratitude note. 9. Start meetings with genuine gratitude and a thanks note. 10. Count your blessings when things go wrong.

b) Forgiveness at work	Action ideas to practice forgiveness at workplace
• Forgivingness is referred to as a deliberate decision to let go of feelings and thoughts of one's anger, hurt, and desire for vengeance forever.	1. Think of someone who wronged you recently at work. Put yourself in their shoes and understand their perspectives. 2. Stop brooding on negative feelings as it is a sheer waste of time.
• It involves not only the cancellation of negative emotions and attitudes but also the development of positive emotions and attitudes.	3. Ask yourself what you need to do for salvaging the situation. 4. Practice forgiveness by treating it as a gift to yourself, so that you can regain peace.
• It also means restoring basic goodness and faith in oneself.	5. Make a list of individuals against whom you hold a grudge. Choose one person and decide to meet personally to discuss your grudge with him per week.
• Forgiveness has a positive impact on the overall well-being of the employees.	

TABLE 10.8 (Continued)

• It brings positive health outcomes such as lowered blood pressure, reduced anxiety, better sleep, and improved self-esteem.	6 Hold an open conversation with a person with whom you have a grudge and listen with empathy. Practice forgiveness and letting go.
• Organizations with forgiving culture, experience more trusting alliances, humanness in the workplace, the attraction of best talent, improved engagement, better productivity, superior customer care, and improved quality of life.	7 Establish rules to agree and disagree. Accept if possible. Otherwise, acknowledge the individual differences.
• The practice of forgiveness helps employees to gain a sense of inner strength, allowing them to let go of the past hurts, making peace with the past, traversing in life with purpose, and finally hope and freedom to create a new future.	8 Create positive memories by celebrating the best of the experiences and move on.

c) Savoring at work

Action ideas to practice savoring at workplace

- The term savoring is referred to as "the conscious and mindful attempt to attend, appreciate, fully feel, enjoy and extend one's own positive experiences to make the most of a good moment."
- The common savoring techniques include savoring the past (reminiscing), savoring the present, and savoring the future (anticipating).
- The employees can be encouraged to reminisce the happy memories of the workplace such as successful completion of the project, recognition obtained, awards won, appreciation received, and success stories of the past.
- Employees can also imagine and anticipate their future career growth, power, and leadership position they are going to occupy in the future.
- Employees who savor are happier, show higher self-esteem, improved physical health, better creativity, coping skills to manage work-related stress, and live a superior quality of life.

1 Pay attention to every positive experience and share it with others.
2 Reflect on your good fortune at a particular moment.
3 Jump and shout with joy if good happens to you.
4 Pat on your back for your good work.
5 Practice mindfulness to enjoy most of the positive moment.
6 Photograph your positive experiences for building a memory bank.
7 Reflect and journal your positive experiences daily.

TABLE 10.8 (Continued)

d) Mindfulness at work	**Action ideas to practice mindfulness at workplace**
• American Psychological Association (APA.org, 2012) defined mindfulness as "a moment-to-moment awareness of one's experience without judgment."	1 Take a few minutes from your workday to focus on your breathing.
	2 Follow the sensation of your breath as it goes out and goes in.
	3 Go for a walk and pay attention to the lifting and falling of your feet.
• Moreover, "it is the practice of paying attention in a way that creates space for insight" (Salzberg, 2020).	4 Ask yourself: How can I make an impact on my key stakeholders? What mindset do I need to strengthen and develop relationships? What should I do differently to take better care of myself? How will I be more compassionate to others and myself during hard times? How will I feel more connected and fulfilled with others?
• In other words, mindfulness is about being aware of what is going on around us.	
• The practice of mindfulness can help employees deal with anxiety, cope with stress, overcome the obsessive-compulsive disorder, depression, mood disorder, emotional reactivity.	
• It also improves working memory, attentional skills, well-being, resilience, and self-compassion.	5 Take minibreaks during work hours and think about how you are feeling in the moment.
	6 Create a journal and write down how you are feeling each day.
	7 Avoid doing too many things at once.
e) Hope at the workplace	**Action ideas to practice hope at workplace**
• The COVID-19 times call for a high level of hope from every employee to navigate the uncertainty and the hard times.	1 Look back on wins and gains of the past to get a feeling that you are continuously making progress.
• In his book "Making Hope Happen" Shane (2013), mentions, "less-hopeful people are more concerned with 'surviving the now' than preparing for the future.	2 List your successes and strengths that will make you feel more hopeful.
• On the other hand, the most hopeful people are more likely to create a picture of a meaningful goal that expands their sense of what they can accomplish."	3 Make the most of self-reflection on the positive events of your life such as, what was good about today, what is there to be thankful for today, and what positive events are making me feel hopeful about the future?

TABLE 10.8 (Continued)

- The construct "hope" is setting positive expectations about one's future. It embodies positive thinking and concentrating on good things to come. It does not appear magically from an external source. Hope, if practiced, increases one's self-esteem, health, life span, and well-being.

4. Pray daily by believing that good things will happen one day.
5. Refrain from consuming "News" as most of them appear to be toxic.
6. Discipline yourself to avoid hopeless thoughts and for which you must believe that interpretation of events makes you feel either good or miserable.
7. Wear a positive outlook on life.
8. Remember to practice gratitude daily.
9. Surround yourself with people who breathe positivity as hope thrives in the right company.
10. Focus on what you can control and on what you can do will help you move forward.

f) Engagement at work

- Engagement is referred to as "bringing the whole self to work or task."
- Employees who are engaged are often completely absorbed in what they do, lose track of time, and get so involved in activities that they forget about everything else.
- The engaged employees bring their best physical, emotional, and cognitive efforts to their work.
- When employees are completely engrossed in a task, totally at the moment, deploying all the strengths to meet the challenge at hand, positive psychologists, call that state "flow."
- Csikszentmihalyi (1998) describes it as "being completely involved in an activity for its own sake. The ego falls away. Time flies.

Action ideas to practice engagement at workplace

1. Identify activities that you love most at work.
2. Pursue those activities out of positive emotions.
3. Learn to deploy those activities daily for their own sake.
4. Leverage your top strengths and apply them at work.

TABLE 10.8 (Continued)

- Every action, movement, and thought follow inevitably from the previous one, like playing jazz. Your whole being is involved, and you're using your skills to the utmost."

g) Relationship at work

- It is found that people with close social relationships stay healthy and optimistic about the future.
- "Relationship" in the PERMA model refers to all the relationships that each employee has including one's relationship with his/her boss, friends, and family. It is the cornerstone of everything an employee does in his/her daily life.
- It has a positive influence on the overall well-being of the employees.
- Employees with good relationships are healthier, have a positive mindset about the future, learn the work-related skills faster, communicate effectively at the workplace, handle workplace conflicts in a positive way, actively participate in social activities, and perform better at the workplace.

Action ideas to practice relationship at workplace

1. Show genuine interest in other people.
2. Initiate and maintain eye contact.
3. Be an empathetic listener without judgment.
4. Speake politely but firmly
5. Use encouraging body language.
6. Acknowledge and celebrate individual differences.
7. Practice Gratitude and keep connections alive and active.
8. Commit to meet new people and build enduring relations.

h) Meaning at work

- The construct "Meaning" is defined as "connecting and contributing to something bigger and beyond oneself."
- People with meaning believe that their lives matter most; feel driven by a sense of purpose wherein they invest time to contribute to the world and finally understand that their lives as a coherent part of a larger narrative rather than random and disconnected.
- Frankl (1984), in his "In the search for Meaning" explains "Man does not simply exist but always decides what his existence will be, what he will become the next moment.

Action ideas to practice meaning at workplace

1. Be self-aware.
2. Discover your life purpose.
3. Know what matters most to you.
4. Identify and put your passion to work.
5. Make sure that you live your passion and purpose for your organization and community.
6. Go for experiences than possessions.
7. Live life with generosity and compassion.

TABLE 10.8 *(Continued)*

- By the same token, every human being has the freedom to change at any instant." Embedding a sense of meaning benefits employees in several ways like increased satisfaction, better cardiovascular health, freedom from cognitive impairment, greater resilience, and improved engagement and well-being at work.
- The four building blocks of meaning include "Purpose," "Belonging," "Storytelling," and "Transcendence." (Smith, 2017) "Purpose" is using your signature strengths to serve others.
- "Belonging is about relationships where you are valued for who you are intrinsically and where you value others as well," "Storytelling" is the act of taking one's life experiences and weaving them into a narrative that explains who you are and where you came from.
- "Transcend" is to rise above, and transcendent experiences are ones in which one feels lifted above the hustle and bustle of daily life and feels connected to a higher reality.

i) Accomplishment at work

- This forms the last element of the PERMA model. It is not uncommon to find that employees take pride in something that they have done or accomplished at work.
- These accomplishments drive individuals to achieve more and make them feel good. This accomplishment strengthens their self-esteem and confidence.
- The ability to practice grit (passion and perseverance) also adds to the sense of achievement, something that can be savored and recalled for motivation when facing a new challenge (Duckworth, 2016).

Action ideas to practice accomplishment at workplace

1. Make your goals into subgoals.
2. Craft them as SMART—specific, measurable, achievable, relevant, and time-bound.
3. Adopt a growth mindset approach.
4. Seek the help of a mentor or coach.
5. Pursue and achieve the goals by using grit.

TABLE 10.8 *(Continued)*

- Employees who have goals that target personal growth and connections with others experience improved well-being.
- Those who say "I will never be able to do this, or I am bound to fail" are less likely to pursue and persist with goals.

Therefore, every employee can draw inspiration from these frameworks and should start demonstrating those microbehaviors daily.

Every employee should reflect deeply, on what went well and what did not go well concerning the demonstration of new microbehaviors concerning wellness and well-being, what lessons they can draw, and do it differently the next day. They are required to journal these reflections daily by using a journaling template. This will help them to track the progress made on their well-being journey. Supervising managers' support can be sought, for having a fortnightly call with every employee and offer support in case employees face any challenges regarding the sustenance of those new behaviors.

10.10 CONCLUSION

With this "integrated employee well-being intervention framework" in place, organizations can seamlessly enhance and preserve the employees' holistic well-being. To make this happen, continuous support of the senior management and the regular review of the supervising managers are very critical. More importantly, EWC should take a proactive leadership role and influence the sponsors to build a "holistic well-being culture" within the organization's eco-system.

The key takeaways can be summed up as below:

- ✓ Acquire knowledge about the importance of wellness and well-being.
- ✓ Obtain perspectives on various lifestyle diseases and health-related behaviors.
- ✓ Gain an understanding on "integrated employee well-being intervention framework."
- ✓ Achieve clarity on various action ideas for the well-being of employees in organizations.
- ✓ Understand the role of reflection, journaling, and sustenance of well-being of employees in organizations.

While all the above are relevant for preserving the well-being of the employees, it becomes an organizational imperative in challenging situations arising out of such pandemic.

KEYWORDS

- wellness
- wellbeing
- life style diseases
- disease-related knowledge
- wellness and wellbeing-related behaviors
- physical health and psychological health

REFERENCES

Alhaik, S.; Anshasi, H. A.; Alkhawaldeh, J.; Soh, K. L.; Naji, A. M. An assessment of Self-Care Knowledge among Patients with Diabetes Mellitus. *Diab. Metabol. Syndr.: Clin. Res. Rev.* 2019, *13* (1), 390–394.

Al-Qazaz, H. K.; Sulaiman, S. A.; Hassali, M. A.; Shafie, A. A.; Sundram, S.; Al-Nuri, R.; Saleem, F. Diabetes Knowledge, Medication Adherence and Glycemic Control among Patients with Type 2 Diabetes. *Int. J. Clin. Pharm.* **2011,** *33* (6), 1028–1035.

Bains, S. S.; Egede, L. E. Associations between Health Literacy, Diabetes Knowledge, Self-Care Behaviors, and Glycemic Control in a Low Income Population with Type 2 Diabetes. *Diab. Technol. Therap.* **2011,** *13* (3), 335–341.

Bukhsh, A.; Nawaz, M. S.; Ahmed, H. S.; Khan, T. M. A Randomized Controlled Study to Evaluate the Effect of Pharmacist-Led Educational Intervention on Glycemic Control, Self-Care Activities and Disease Knowledge among Type 2 Diabetes Patients: A Consort Compliant Study Protocol. *Medicine (Baltimore)* Mar **2018,** *97* (12), e9847. DOI: 10.1097/MD.0000000000009847. PMID: 29561461; PMCID: PMC5895327.

Clear, J. *Atomic Habits: Tiny Changes, Remarkable Results: An Easy & Proven Way to Build Good Habits & Break Bad Ones*; Avery, an imprint of Penguin Random House: New York, 2018.

Csikszentmihalyi, M. *Flow: The Psychology of Optimal Experience*; Harper & Row: New York, 1990.

Duckworth, A. *Grit: The Power of Passion and Perseverance*; Scribner/Simon & Schuster, 2016.

Fogg, B. J. *Tiny Habits*; Houghton Mifflin Harcourt: Boston, 2020.

Frankl, V. E. Man's Search for Meaning: An Introduction to Logo Therapy; Simon & Schuster: New York, 1984.

Komase, Y.; Watanabe, K.; Imamura, K.; Kawakami, N. Effects of a Newly Developed Gratitude Intervention Program on Work Engagement among Japanese Workers: A Pre- and Posttest Study. *J. Occup. Environ. Med.* Sep **2019,** *61* (9), e378–e383. DOI: 10.1097/JOM.0000000000001661. PMID: 31306267.

Lopez, S. J. *Making Hope Happen*; Atria Paperback: New York, 2013.

Moradi, A.; Alavi, S. M.; Salimi, M.; Nouhjah, S.; Shahvali, E. A. The Effect of Short Message Service (SMS) on Knowledge and Preventive Behaviors of Diabetic Foot Ulcer in Patients with Diabetes Type 2. *Diab. Metab. Syndr.* Mar–Apr **2019,** *13* (2), 1255–1260. DOI: 10.1016/j.dsx.2019.01.051. Epub 2019 Feb 1. PMID: 31336474.

O'Leary, K. Gratitude Works! A Twenty-One-Day Program for Creating Emotional Prosperity, 2013.

Seligman, M. E. P. *Flourish: A Visionary New Understanding of Happiness and Well-being*; Free Press: New York, 2013.

Sharon, S. *Real Change: Mindfulness to Heal Ourselves and the World*; Flatiron Books, 2020.

Smith, E. E. The Power of Meaning: Finding Fulfillment in a World Obsessed with Happiness; Crown, 2017.

Vasanth, M. A. S.; Sabesan, S. (2019). A Study on Related Cognition of T2DM among Primary School Teachers. *IRHRW Int. J. Soc. Sci.* **2019,** *7* (2), 276–279.

CHAPTER 11

Employee Well-Being under the Work-from-Home Culture: Toward an Alternative Framework

SUDDHABRATA DEB ROY*

University of Otago, Aotearoa, New Zealand

*E-mail: suddhabratadeb.debroy@otago.ac.nz

ABSTRACT

The Covid-19 pandemic has enforced a global shift in organizational culture and workspace management. It has created a scenario where most of the "office-work" has shifted "home" and in doing so, has provided a unique opportunity to study two concurrent processes—the large-scale transformation of the "home" into a "workspace" and the alterations resulting from the same in the domains of employee and resource management.

The present chapter primarily emphasizes the various aspects of the works of social philosophers, Giles Deleuze, and Félix Guattari, on automation and its impact on the life of employees, along with Robert Tiqqun's theory of *The Cybernetic Hypothesis*. The various facets and derivatives of Deleuze and Guattari's theories, which are taken as conceptual tools in the chapter include their own concept of the *minor* and its relationship with "confined spaces," Thomas Nail and Manuel DeLanda's theory on *assemblages*, and Nicholas Thoburn's analysis of *machinic* relations. By interrelating these conceptual formulations, in the context of the contemporary widespread culture of "work from home," the chapter explains the processes through which companies have been engaging in employee management and resource utilization during the pandemic, and its potential impacts in a post-Covid world.

Human Resource Management in a Post-Epidemic Global Environment: Roles, Strategies, and Implementations.
Tanusree Chakraborty, Nandita Mishra, Madhurima Ganguly, & Bipasha Chatterjee (Eds.)
© 2023 Apple Academic Press, Inc. Co-published with CRC Press (Taylor & Francis)

By using the above-stated conceptual tools along with qualitative data collected through in-depth interviews conducted in Bengaluru, India, the chapter analyzes the contemporary relationship between labor, capital, machines, and employee well-being (EWB). The chapter particularly emphasizes the importance of mental well-being in employee management and the ways in which, it can be incorporated within the mechanisms put in place for managing remote work. By maintaining a value-neutral approach, the present work also focuses on the usage of human–machine networks and their role in making global capital function, along with their possible utilization to ensure higher job satisfaction and well-being of the employees.

11.1 INTRODUCTION

The Covid-19 pandemic has enforced unprecedented alterations within the global economy. Although human history is not oblivious to plagues and pandemics, the Covid-19 pandemic, it cannot be denied, has struck at a point in human history where the involvement of technology within the everyday lives of the global population stands at an extremely high level. The Indian economy is also not an exception to this. It had been dominated by agriculture for a long time but the agricultural sector, today, has fallen behind other sectors and the service sector has taken the lead both in public and private modes of employment and revenue. With the onset of the Covid-19 pandemic, which had its first case in India on the 30th of January, the workers within the software industry found themselves in a precarious situation. In India, the first lockdown was brought into effect in March 2020, it was followed by strict measures taken by the government with a view to curbing the spread of the Coronavirus in the country. While most of the nonessential government offices were shut down, the private sector kept on functioning. Lockdowns along with the drive to resist any spread of the virus within their employees had forced these organizations to change how they work. In turn, it has also changed how workers live, even in the confinements of their homes, especially in the case of the information technology and software workers (ITSW). The ITSW find themselves in the middle of a crisis, where they have had to alter the way they live in addition to the way they work. Along with the implementation of lockdowns, these workers did not find themselves "being" at home but rather found themselves working from home, creating a situation that has been extremely difficult for them to live through in comparison with the prepandemic phase. The *Work from*

Home Culture *(WFHC)* has become the "new normal" for these workers, which has affected not only how they work, but also how they live.

Under these circumstances, the element of well-being becomes a particularly important part of the sustenance of the organization itself, if it has to retain the productivity of its employees. EWB is a crucial part in the functioning of any organization and Human Resource Management (HRM) practices are intimately related to EWB and organizational performance (Van de Voorde et al., 2012). The importance of academic studies related to EWB has been established today with an increasing number of employees becoming aware of the benefits of employee-centered well-being practices within the organizations (Pradhan and Hati, 2019; Chakraborty and Ganguly, 2019). The primary subjects of the present study are the ITSW in Bengaluru and Kolkata. The paper takes an approach developed by Delbridge and Keenoy (2010), which takes into account the weaknesses of the unitarist and mainstream contemporary HRM studies. Delbridge and Keenoy (2010) argue that in order to bring forward meaningful and significant HRM scholarship, it is necessary to situate HRM within the existing sociopolitical reality. In that regard, the first step toward framing effective strategies toward EWB is to understand the state and nature of the social structure within which these employees work. They argue for the construction and expansion of the theoretical paradigm of *critical HRM (CHRM)* studies (Delbridge and Keenoy, 2010: 800), which addresses the concerns of both critical management studies (Adler et al., 2007) and the *internal critical literature,* which has attempted to critique the mainstream normalized theoretical understandings of HRM (Delbridge and Keenoy, 2010: 807). In addition to situating HRM within contemporary sociopolitical reality and challenging normalized structures of theory, CHRM also talks about the inclusion of marginalized voices within HRM studies and including within its paradigm, smaller organizations, and cooperatives, which are otherwise excluded by mainstream HRM studies (Delbridge and Keenoy, 2010).

The present chapter begins with an analysis of the literature and contemporary research on EWB in both management studies and the social sciences, critically examining and analyzing some of their deficiencies. The chapter follows it up by arguing that EWB needs to be theorized today taking into consideration that the complete contemporary social structure itself functions as a production unit. The paper argues that in order to analyze the well-being of the employees within the contemporary society, it is necessary to overcome the traditional boundaries of analytical and theoretical constructs, both within management research and the social sciences. Taking cue from that, the chapter brings forward the necessity of theorizing the well-being of the ITSW as a different kind of workers, who have been socialized within the production process. The current chapter also highlights the relationship between the experiences of employees in different urban centers within WFH culture. The chapter finally ends with an argument advocating for a more humanist and subjective approach toward EWB of the ITSW.

The chapter relates HRM practices to the broader changes in the society noting that even within HRM, there is an inter-relationship between different strategies and practices (Boon et al., 2019), which in turn, gets affected by social events and dynamic processes. The chapter tries to reiterate the idea put forward by Wang et al. (2020) that there is a difference between how employees and managers perceive existent HRM policies and practices.

11.2 METHODOLOGY

The current study is based upon the ITSW in Bengaluru and Kolkata. The selection of the cities was based upon the growth of the IT industry in the two cities, which have been along different developmental trajectories (Mitter and Sen, 2000). Another reason behind the selection of these two cities was to understand and analyze whether there were any differences between the experiences of the employees working in these two cities caused due to their differing histories and work cultures. Snowball sampling method was used for determining the respondents for the study. The total number of respondents who were selected for the study were ten, five each from Bengaluru and Kolkata, taking into consideration the intended length of the present chapter. The interviews were conducted only after receiving the consent of the interviewees and the anonymity of the interviewees was assured prior to conducting the interviews. The qualitative data that has been used in the study was collected through semistructured interviews with the respondents. The questions in the interviews revolved around four primary topics:

- WFHC from the perspective of an employee.
- The role of HR in the WFHC.
- The Question of Personal Growth.
- EWB within the WFHC.

Both the terms *employee* and *worker* have been used in the chapter. The term *worker* has been used whenever references are made to the working class as a whole. The term *employee* has been used to refer particularly to the ITSW and emphasize their uniqueness.

11.3 EWB AND CONTEMPORARY HRM

The world of business today is far more complicated than the previous century. The service industry, which according to Pradhan and Hati (2019), involves both knowledge and information-based work, is highly demanding in nature—both physically and psychologically—for the employees and the organizations involved therein. The complexity within the world of business and global capitalist structures, did not evolve out of a vacuum but rather, have complemented and have been complemented by a growing complexity within the society as well. Along with this multiplying complexity, multiple factors play important roles if the ITSW are to achieve success within the industry (Panda and Rath, 2017; Pradhan and Hati, 2019), which can also have an impact on their social lives. Within contemporary society, there cannot be a well-being strategy, which treats all employees as a single homogenous unit—either physically or psychologically. Instead, EWB has to be a highly segmented domain of subjective analysis. With a constantly expanding range of operations, EWB is intimately associated with the mental and physical health-related costs incurred by the organizations (Grawitch et al., 2006) and the productivity and performance of the employees (Wright, 2010), both of which are important factors in the growth and sustenance of the organizations.

It is essential for the employees and the management that the structure and functioning of the employees within their work-from-home scenarios remain as employee-friendly as possible. It should be managed in a manner that allows the employees to voice their concerns regarding the same within the organizational structure. Shantz et al. (2014) opine that this inability to voice concerns constitutes a critical part of becoming alienated from one's work, which has a negative impact on one's overall productivity (Shantz et al., 2015). The Marxist formulation of alienation is about the process in which the worker loses control and "ownership" over the products of his/her labor and the laboring process (Marx, 1844/1975). Within contemporary society and workplace management, alienation can be an important factor in the overall performance of the organization because it impacts multiple dimensions of organizational and employee relationship (Shantz et al., 2014, 2015). For effective management of the employees, the centrality of the employees within the structure has to be taken into cognizance. Autonomism can play an important role in the construction of such conceptual structures as it acknowledges the centrality of the workers within the society (Witheford, 1994). This also requisites an employee-centered HRM practice and theory, which understands the inherently conflicting nature of the employee–employer relationship (Edwards, 1986) and intervenes into processes that direct the functional operation of the organizations which in turn, directly affect the employees (Edwards, 2005).

There are two mainstream perspectives that attempt to understand EWB within contemporary management literature—hedonic and eudemonic approaches (Ryan and Deci, 2001). While the hedonic approach is based upon the conception of happiness being the only determining factor of EWB, the eudemonic approach takes the realization of complete human potential to be a desired goal of EWB. Juniper et al. (2011) have already established that EWB is subjective in nature and is multidimensional in outlook. It encapsulates processes of both the physical and psychological well-being (PWB) of the employees (Warr, 1999). The PWB of the employees had been also highlighted by Ryff and Keyes (1995) in their multi-dimensional well-being model, which incorporated within itself the emotional, social, and PWB. EWB, again, can be divided into two components—context free well-being revolving around the general all-encompassing EWB and domain-specific/job-specific EWB centered upon a specific aspect of their lives (Pradhan and Hati,3-4). The well-being of the employees within any structure has to be about the all-encompassing well-being of the employees, including but not restricted to those factors influenced by work and the workspace (Juniper et al., 2011). This becomes a crucial component of contemporary well-being strategy because the employees today do not exist as a homogenous whole.

> *"The organization does not understand that I might have my own set of problems, which might be different than others."*
> (Respondent Location [RL]: Bengaluru)
>
> *"There are people for whom face-to-face conversation is very important for effective performance. The expectation from the organization that everybody can manage their performance equally from home results in additional pressure."* (RL: Bengaluru)
>
> *"Under the WFHC, the organization does not do much for my personal growth. Although I know that some of my colleagues have been able to learn new skills and manage their work-life balance very well, it has been difficult for me, very difficult actually."*
> (RL: Kolkata)

The pandemic induced WFHC has brought into effect a multiplicity of contingent factors within the domain of EWB, resulting from the extension of the office or the factory beyond its previously specified boundaries (Negri, 1989b) resulting in the usage of the society as a means of production thus establishing a social factory (Tronti, 1962/2019) and the socialized worker (Negri, 1989a). These socialized workers can be said to be a creation of the machinic relationships (Deleuze and Guattari, 1988), which have been put in place by various organizational structures. The task of the management, in the age of Covid-19, is to ensure that the employees do not have to suffer from the responses toward the pandemic, which various governments have initiated, and that each employee is treated in a manner, which does not undermine their human existence. This becomes extremely important when the employees have been confined to their homes with minimal *actual* social interaction, which makes the role of the HRM department within the organization more important than ever. The technical managers within the organizations might not always be the best available resource for managing EWB within these situations.

> *"The technical manager cannot handle the humanitarian aspect of an employee's life because he or she is not trained to do so."*
> (RL: Kolkata)
>
> *"The manager does not understand the importance of communication within the work process."*
> (RL: Bengaluru)
>
> *"The HR has been rendered powerless and that is affecting many employees as we cannot talk freely with technical managers."*
> (RL: Kolkata)

11.4 THE SOCIAL FACTORY AND EWB

The development of the software industry in India has been the subject of numerous studies over the last couple of decades (Srinivas, 1998; D'Costa and Sridharan, 2004). With an ever-increasing and differentiated population, the cities that harbor these industries have been bringing forward societal alterations both at macro and micro levels. These alterations are again, intimately related to the production of commodities and information, which today is not only about simple production, but rather, entails within itself, aspects of consumptionthat are equally important for the sustenance of the overall system. Contemporary society is about the management of the entire process in which capital is reproduced (Tronti, 1973). This in turn creates a condition where the organic and dynamic relationship between living and dead labor exists in a form widely different from the industrial age (Tronti, 1962/2019). EWB, within CHRM, has to take these alterations into account. The primary argumentative vantage point of a contemporary theory of well-being has to be one based upon the conceptualization that the entire society has been incorporated under the aegis of the means of production.

The alterations within the workspaces and more importantly, the constantly varying idea of the "workspace," also has a huge impact on the employees as in the contemporary world, workspaces not only include offices and factories, but also households that have been internalized within the system of value production. With the WFHC becoming a common phenomenon in the lives of the ITSW, these processes have been instrumental to the construction of the cybernetic domination of employees, without a proper well-being strategy in place for them. The antihumanist philosophy within which these employees are managed contribute to the maintenance of the *general order of things while priding itself of having gone beyond the human* (Tiqqun, 2020: 27). Contemporary society has been characterized by numerous machines, machines that have been granted a particular autonomy and have been merged with the dominant social order (Tiqqun, 2020). The employees entrenched within these machines find themselves in a socially precarious condition, which transcends their designated workspace and penetrates into their total social existence, because the networks that drive these machines creating material and psychological precarity are intimately related to the wider sociopolitical reality, which often are not favorable toward EWB.

> *"The society as a whole has become depressing and more demanding in nature. How can I work in peace knowing that I might be infected anytime, and that there is nobody to care for me and my family's health beside myself?"*
> (RL: Bengaluru)

> *"The organization pays for my internet, but the maintenance costs like electricity and furniture, which come with working from home have to be borne by me personally. With a rising cost of living, I remain worried about those costs which would otherwise be borne by my organization."*
> (RL: Kolkata)

Zheng et al. (2015) argued that the PWB of the employees needed to take into cognizance both the workspace and nonworkspace associated psychological experiences of the employees. Within the social factory, when the very existence of nonworkspace places is under jeopardy, it becomes crucial to analyze EWB in a holistic manner, which takes the entire society into its fold, with a focus on the employee whose productivity and well-being is determined by his/her entire social existence and not only by the workspace. In other words, EWB needs to take into account the technical composition of the workers that revolves around theorizing the relationship between productivity and wage levels and the processes in which this relationship determines the division of labor within the organization (Marks, 2012). Employees form and maintain the system that sustains capital and thus, a theory of EWB that puts more emphasis upon capital than the employees, tends to create problems for both the organization and the employees. A contemporary and comprehensive strategy toward EWB demands the analysis of the technical composition of the employees as against the dominant model based upon the analysis of the composition of capital. When, "...the whole of society becomes an *articulation* of production, the whole of society lives in function of the factory and the factory extends its exclusive dominion over the whole society" (Tronti, 1962/2019: "Factory and Society"), well-being strategies cannot continue seeing the official workspace as the only site of theorizing EWB.

The Covid-19 has enabled the sustained usage of the household space for waged activities, where the "productive" and "unproductive" labor, using the terms in a classical sense, have for all purposes, fused with each other. Within the WFHC, the home has become an extension of the office or rather it has mutated into becoming the

> *"Earlier, it took me a few minutes to get assistance for a problem. Today, it takes me a few hours. It not only hampers my own productivity but also impacts the overall performance of my team. The organization has to look into these aspects while talking about EWB."* (RL: Kolkata)
>
> *"The fear that I might not get help from my team or my colleagues immediately, has put me under tremendous pressure. I cannot concentrate easily on working anymore because of the fear of getting stuck at something. Not everybody knows everything."*
> (RL: Bengaluru)

"office" itself. This process has reiterated Hardt and Negri's (1994) argument that contemporary laboring processes are no longer constrained within the physical boundaries of a factory. The WFHC has further ensured that the employees, locked within their homes due to the pandemic, keep on working. But, in the process, it has created a problem for the employees by completely subsuming them within the digital spaces. Under such circumstances where the employee also loses his/her channels of direct communication, the individual employee is at a greater risk of being alienated from his/her work because they tend to lose their decision-making autonomy along with their task identity (Shantz et al., 2015). Both these processes are the results of the fact that within WFHC, the employees do not get to exert their spontaneous human instincts while interacting through digital modes of communication, which not only affects the flow of the entire laboring process and the psychological state of the employee, but also has a significant impact on the overall productivity of the organization itself.

Shantz et al. (2014) argue that there is an inversely proportional relationship between the meaningfulness of work and alienation. However, detailed studies into the concerns of the individual employees within the employee–employer relationship are scarce (Shantz et al., 2014: 2350). The conceptualization of the entire society as a production unit will enable theories of EWB to take into account the totality of the human existence of the employees and thus, will also enable HRM scholars to theorize concepts like alienation in a holistic manner. Under the highly developed contemporary capitalism, when the society itself has emerged as a means of production and has become an extension of the factory (Tronti, 1962/2019), a strategy for well-being has to engage with the employees' life outside their "official working-spaces" as well. Both the employees and the organizational structures today are in a phase of constant evolution, where everyday realities based on economic and social factors determine the alterations within their mutated workspaces, similar to Tronti's (2019) theorization. The Covid-19 pandemic has been excruciatingly brutal to the ITSW, who have been living through numerous rapid mutations within their lives with little changes to the structural models of EWB within their organizations. With the fusion of the office and the home, the official workspace or the factory of the yesteryears has lost its special ascription within the society. The tangibility of the prepandemic phase enabled the organizations to regularly assess the EWB through informal behavioral analysis and interactions. But during the pandemic, with a return to prepandemic normality still being a distant reality, organizations now have to come up with new strategies regarding EWB.

11.5 WELL-BEING OF THE SOCIALIZED WORKERS AND EMPLOYEES

The employees today are socialized to a large extent. However, in the context of India, the process of socialization is contingent upon multiple factors related to social attributes and the social condition of the employee. Most of the social scientific research in India on EWB has emphasized what Negri (1988) calls the *mass worker*—a term that he used to define the semiskilled workers working in the huge factories (Witheford, 1994). But the concept of the mass worker cannot be used to theorize a large section of the working class today, which includes the ITSW as well, as they are not managed homogenously through mere Taylorist management strategies but rather heterogeneously through a combination of Taylorism, Fordism, Keynesianism and general governmental planning (Negri, 1989a). They have become socialized in the sense that the relationship they share with capital is not only about their labor power but about their social existence itself (Negri, 1989a). The socialized worker today, thus, cannot be expected to be responding to EWB strategies formed keeping in mind the mass workers of the previous era, which remain inadequate to address the ITSW's concerns.

The socialized worker today operates out of cramped spaces, which do not provide him/her with "ready-made structures of history, narrative, and tradition, that would enable the easy passage of a demarcated autonomous identity through a culture" (Thoburn, 2003: 19). Their entire social existence within contemporary WFHC is mediated by a process of social alienation, within which they become minors. The usage of "minor" here is not to refer to a minority subgroup, but instead conceptualizes processes "...seen in the movement of groups, in their variations, mutations, and differences and hence has no membership, coherence, identity, or constituency in itself. It is becoming of which no one has an ownership... " (Thoburn, 2003: 7). In other words, they are put into "impossible positions" (Thoburn, 2006: 44) within which the essence of their existence becomes *not identity but creation* (Thoburn, 2003: 15). The task for HRM scholarship and practitioners within this juncture is to analyze the potential *deminorization* of these employees through effective EWB methods. EWB is important because it affects how the employees take decisions related to their organizations (Pradhan and Hati, 2019). It has a dynamic relationship with the manner in which the employees react toward the management or toward the organization in general.

The mass worker of the industries was objectively determined by a relationship with production mechanisms resulting in similar social behavior and objective social characteristics (Battaggia and Campanile, 1981). But the worker today is heterogeneous in nature, with numerous subjectivities (Hardt and Negri, 2012) and is different from the classical notions of the worker (Hardt and Negri, 2004). Within the socialized workers, the ITSW is further unique because they mostly do not work on direct physical matter but rather their jobs revolve around creating mechanisms or services. Cooperation within themselves in the process of creating the product or the service assumes a significantly important place in the work process because they do not work through assembly lines but through lines of communication making both communication and coordination central to the creation of the final product (Negri, 1989a). In other words, productive cooperation is a precondition of the labor process for them (Hardt and Negri, 1994), which creates the basis for the creation of the socialized workers through the massive involvement of the workers in the broader process of value creation. The socialized worker, thus created within the social factory, a result of the end of the regime of the industrial factory, works within previously unexplored zones of analysis and activity, which become normalized under accelerated social development (Witheford, 1994).

Contemporary organizational dynamics are social in nature (Negri, 1989b) and the management of human labor is not only about managing the forms of "productive" labor but rather is about the management of the various modes of contemporary laboring activities within the society, which have become productive with the rapid usage of technology (Hardt and Negri, 1994). Previously, marginalized aspects of the production process are being utilized within the production circuit. It was within a paradigm informed by this mode of thought that Negri visualized the socialized worker as an attempt to alter the traditional theories regarding the nature of labor power (Witheford, 1994). The ITSW represents the physical manifestation of Negri's Socialized Worker in the Indian context, whose job descriptions emphasize coordination and communication within and outside the designated workspaces.

> "I am not very comfortable with the organization knowing about the content of my interactions with my colleagues or my team, which are at times very personal in nature."
> (RL: Kolkata)

> "The problem now is that the manager thinks he can call me at midnight even though my shift ends in the evening. I have no issues with being told what to do but I don't like being under constant surveillance."
> (RL: Bengaluru)

Contemporary society produces new forms of social relationships (Hardt and Negri, 2000), which are utilized within the production process and dissolve the heretical distinctions between productive and unproductive labor. They bring forward the new dimension of social labor, which is highly cooperative in nature making the biopolitical nature of the workspace an integral part of the EWB associated with the ITSW.

The restrictions imposed upon by the pandemic have completely stopped the physical interaction between the workers and have shifted the interaction online onto digital spaces, which can be put under surveillance. The employees today, are completely subsumed under Deleuzian machinic relationships, "where the technical, social and human relations have been integrated into a machinic whole" (Thoburn, 2003: 76).

> *"I would really want my organization to understand that being at home during the pandemic is a challenging task. Practically, there is no difference between my home and office now, which has made it very difficult to find work-life balance."* (RL: Bengaluru)
>
> *"I am not comfortable working from my home. Additionally, now I have to work regularly during weekends which is making it very difficult to address concerns which are outside my official domain but deeply affect my productivity."* (RL: Kolkata)

However, these machinic relationships have not developed automatically, because technology, which plays role in the creation of these relationships, is a manifestation of human social practices (Thoburn, 2003) that are representative of the state of the society. The machinic whole, characterized by networked cybernetics (Tiqqun, 2020), is a creation of the human society as "machines are social before being technical" (Deleuze and Guattari, 1988: 39). Contemporary EWB has to reinvent the relationship between the social and the technical, which will enable it to address the dual concerns of both technical and social issues pertaining to the employees within the organization. Within a networked and interconnected systematic structure, most of the problems tend to attract solutions that are applicable to the entire system in a teleological fashion (Thomson and Sluckin, 1953). As a result, there occurs a lack of emphasis on the individual well-being of different components of the system. While the strategies address the concerns of the overall technical system quite well, it does not address the social concerns of the individual employees effectively, which affects the efficacy of the EWB techniques employed.

11.6 CONCLUSION: TOWARD A HUMANIST THEORY OF EWB

The role of human cooperation has come to occupy a central position in the lives of the ITSW during the pandemic. With public spaces remaining closed, people have been forced to restrict their social existence to digital spaces, which has had an impact on their overall PWB, in addition to their physical well-being within a society under lockdown. The combined effects of these processes increase the probability of work alienation, whose primary causal factor is the separation of an individual's labor from his/her social being (Shantz et al., 2014). EWB has to address this general social process, which has become accelerated within the WFHC. Hedonic approaches within the contemporary society cannot address the overall EWB because of its unilateral approach focusing on the factors, which are supposed to make the employees happy rather than those which actually make them happy (Segal, 2017).

Eudemonic approaches, however, can be relatively more successful within the WFHC because they can go beyond the aims of hedonic approaches toward EWB. Well-being today, however, cannot be essentialized by eudemonic approaches as well because of its psychologically essentialist nature that at times, tends to undermine the material basis of human existence. EWB has to encompass the entire gambit of factors, which determine the social existence of the employees including, as Page and Vella-Brodrick (2009) opine, PWB, well-being within the workspace and overall subjective well-being (SWB). The SWB of employees cannot, however, be only about issues and factors related to their work but also has to address the concerns of the factors, which drive the employees to work including their personal well-being and their social well-being outside the workspaces. The importance that an employee focused well-being strategy possesses has been highlighted by numerous scholars (Scott, 1994; Legge, 1995).

The dominant practice of HRM, both with social science and management, has been to theorize keeping in line the view that the interests of the employee and the employer are aligned (Hannon, 2010). However, this one-dimensional perspective, fails to take into cognizance the inherent struggle between the two, which is a characteristic feature of all industrial relations. One-dimensional approach toward EWB, fails to acknowledge the gradual evolution of the workers and the relation between existent social dynamics and EWB. The employees today, apart from their objective interests, also have subjective interests, prominently embedded within their social existence. In addition to the already existing subjectivities, the workers today, produce new forms of subjectivity everyday through their social and individual activities (Hardt and Negri, 2000), which impact the reception of the EWB-related strategies of the organization. Taking cue from this, some of the major arguments that have been highlighted by this chapter can be summarized as noted below:

- The experiences of the ITSW, both in Bengaluru and Kolkata remain similar under WFH culture even though their experiences might have been different in the pre Covid-19 era.
- The interests of the employee and the employer cannot be clubbed together under all circumstances.
- The altering dynamics of the lives of the employees have to be considered while devising effective EWB strategies.
- WFH has explicitly converted the social structure and private lives of the ITSW into a part of the production unit.
- EWB strategies need to move away from objective dehumanizing vantage points and engage more with the subjective selves of the ITSW.

The development of the IT industry is contingent upon EWB, and as such, holistic approaches toward EWB cannot be homogenous in all social contexts. The well-being of the employees is critical to the functioning of the company. The companies today have to adequately fund HRM departments and employ effective scholars and practitioners (DeNisi et al., 2014). Some of the basic steps that companies can take toward devising more effective HRM practices is to formulate their HRM strategies through a vantage point informed by the employees and not algorithms. The indeterminacy surrounding the objectives of HRM and the relationship of those objectives with EWB (Boon et al.., 2019) can be resolved by taking into account the perspectives of the employees into account. The over-reliance on routinized tactics and top-down approach of organizations are difficult to be converted into successful strategies of EWB (Beurden et al., 2021). Instead, the requirement is of a more democratized and decentralized methods of achieving EWB where the feedback from the employees and the employees' perspectives of their own well-being becomes a central vantage point. Employee perspectives and their perceptions of HRM practices, as Wang et al. (2020) and Beurden et al. (2021) inform, can be highly varied in nature based on differing methods of evaluation, the groups formed by the employees, etc. These variations could again contribute to a significant gap between HRM research and effective organizational practices, which can be bridged by more nuanced and dynamically evolving approaches toward existing problems, both within academia and workplaces.

The EWB strategies adopted by most of the organizations within the Indian milieu have been based upon the heretical conceptualization of the ITSW as a single homogenous unit with a uniform objectivity, the existence of which is debatable within contemporary society. Within the WFHC, the cooperation and coordination between employees have become one of the most significant components of sustaining the organization itself. The contemporary social structure is one that has been established with communication being the central component of social existence (Tiqqun, 2020). It has become increasingly dependent upon collaborative relationships between the employees (Chakraborty and Mishra, 2019; Chakraborty et al., 2020), regulated and managed through the utilization of technology, which have made certain influential EWB strategies such as "digital detoxification" redundant. Contemporary well-being strategies cannot negate or refuse technological innovations but rather should be about the usage of technology for the benefit of the entire organization and the employees therein. Technology has been the cause of many problems in the socio-biological lives of human beings (Chakraborty et al., 2021), but without the important intervention of modern technology, some of the very basic characteristics of contemporary human existence would not have been possible (Hardt and Negri, 2017). The vulnerabilities, both of the overall technosocial system and the employees, exposed by the pandemic are expected to have long-term effects. This can be addressed through a re-engineering of the social factory from a perspective taking into account the multiple subjectivities of the employees therein by focusing on more employee-centered humanist HRM practices.

11.7 LIMITATIONS OF THE STUDY

The sample size of employees taken for the chapter, which has been dictated by the intended length and scope of the chapter, is not sufficient to exhaustively theorize the condition of employees. Also, the theorization of the relationship between the conditions of employees in two urban centers and its impact on EWB, which has been discussed only tangentially in this chapter, demands a much larger engagement, which is beyond the scope of this chapter.

KEYWORDS

- Covid-19
- assemblage
- machinic relations
- cybernetic hypothesis
- labor
- employee relations

REFERENCES

Adler, P.; Forbes, L.; Willmott, H. Critical Management Studies: Premises, Practices, Problems and Prospects. *Ann. Acad. Manage.* **2007,** *1*, 119–180.

Battaggia, A.; Campanile, F. Mass Worker and Social Worker. *No Politics Without Inquiry* **1981,** 1.

Beurden, J. V.; Voorde, K. V. D.; Veldhoven, M. V. The Employee Perspective on HR Practices: A Systematic Literature Review, Integration and Outlook. *Int. J. Human Resour. Manage.* **2021,** *32* (2), 359–393.

Boon, C.; Den Hartog, D. N.; Lepak, D. P. A Systematic Review of Human Resource Management Systems and Their Measurement. *J. Manage.* **2019,** *45* (6), 2498–2537.

Chakraborty, T.; Ganguly, M. Crafting Engaged Employees through Positive Work Environment: Perspectives of Employee Engagement. In *Management Techniques for Employee Engagement in Contemporary Organizations*; IGI Global, 2019; pp 180–198.

Chakraborty, T.; Mishra, N. Appreciative Inquiry: Unleashing a Positive Revolution of Organizational Change and Development. *Int. J. Econ. Com. Busi. Manage.* **2019,** *6* (2), 32–37.

Chakraborty, T.; Gohain, D.; Saha, R. What Comes in the Way of Engagement? Moderation Analysis of Stress on Women Marketing Executives' Work Life Balance. *Int. J. Human Resour. Dev. Manage.* **2020,** *20* (3–4), 349–368.

D'Costa, A. P.; Sridharan, E. *India in the Global Software Industry*; Palgrave: London, 2004.

Delbridge, R.; Keenoy, T. Beyond Managerialism? *Int. J. Human Resour. Manage.* **2010,** *21* (6), 799–817.

Deleuze, G.; Guattari, F. *A Thousand Plateaus*; Minneapolis: University of Minnesota Press, 1988.

DeNisi, A. S.; Wilson, M. S.; Biteman, J. Research and Practice in HRM: A Historical Perspective. *Human Resour. Manage. Rev.* **2014,** *24* (3), 219–231.

Edwards, P. *Conflict at Work*; Basil Blackwell: Oxford, 1986.

Edwards, P. The Challenging But Promising Future of Industrial Relations. *Ind. Relat. J.* **2005,** *36* (4), 264–282.

Grawitch, M. J.; Gottschalk, M.; Munz, D. C. The Path to a Healthy Workplace: A Critical Review Linking Healthy Workplace Practices, Employee Well-being, and Organizational Improvements. *Consult. Psychol. J.* **2006**, *58* (3), 129–147.

Hannon, E. Employee-Focused Research in HRM. *Int. J. Human Resour. Manage.* **2010**, *21* (6), 818–835.

Hardt, M.; Negri, A. *Labor of Dionysus: A Critique of the State-Form*; University of Minnesota Press: Minneapolis, 1994.

Hardt, M.; Negri, A. *Empire*; Harvard University Press: Cambridge, 2000.

Hardt, M.; Negri, A. *Multitude*; Penguin: New York, 2004.

Hardt, M.; Negri, A. *Declaration*; Agro-Navis, 2012.

Hardt, M.; Negri, A. *Assembly*; Oxford University Press: London, 2017.

Juniper, B. A.; Bellamy, P.; White, N. Testing the Performance of a New Approach to Measuring Employee Well-being. *Leadership Organ. Dev. J.* **2011**, *25* (4), 344–357.

Legge, K. *Human Resource Management: Rhetorics and Realities*; Palgrave Macmillan: Basingstoke, 1995.

Marks, B. Autonomist Marxist Theory and Practice in the Current Crisis. *ACME* **2012**, *11* (3), 467–491.

Marx, K. Economic and Philosophical Manuscripts of 1844. In *Marx and Engels Collected Works: Volume 3*; London: Lawrence and Wishart, 1844/1975; pp 329–348.

Mitter, S.; Asish Sen. Can Calcutta Become Another Bangalore? *Econ. Polit. Wkly* 2000, *35* (26), 2263–2268.

Negri, A. Archaeology and the Project: The Mass Worker and the Social Worker. In *Revolution Retrieved: Selected Writings on Marx, Keynes, Capitalist Crisis and New Social Subjects 1967–1983*; London: Red Notes, 1989a; pp 199–228.

Negri, A. *The Politics of Subversion*; Polity: Cambridge, 1989b.

Page, K. M.; Vella-Brodrick, D. A. The 'What', 'Why' and 'How' of Employee Well-being: A New Model. *Soc. Indicat. Res.* **2009**, *90* (3), 441–458.

Panda, S.; Rath, S. K. Modelling the Relationship between Information Technology Infrastructure and Organizational Agility. *Global Busi. Rev.* **2017**, *19* (8), 424–438.

Pradhan, R. K.; Hati, L. The Measurement of Employee Well-being: Development and Validation of a Scale. *Global Busi. Rev* **2019**. https://doi.org/10.1177/0972150919859101

Ryan, R. M.; Deci, E. L. On Happiness and Human Potentials. *Annu. Rev. Psychol.* **2011**, *52* (1), 141–166.

Ryff, C. D.; Keyes, C. L. The Structure of Psychological Well-being. *J. Personal. Soc. Psychol.* **1995**, *69* (4), 719–727.

Scott, A. *Willing Slaves? British Workers under Human Resource Management*; Cambridge University Press: Cambridge.

Segal, L. *Radical Happiness*; Verso: London, 2017.

Shantz, A.; Alfes, K.; Truss, C. Alienation from work: Marxist ideologies and twenty-first-century practice. *Int. J. Human Resour. Manage.* **2014**, *25* (18), 2529–2550.

Shantz, A.; Alfes, K.; Bailey, C.; Soane, E. Drivers and Outcomes of Work Alienation: Reviving a Concept. *J. Manage. Inquiry* **2015**, *24* (4), 382–393.

Srinivas, S. *The Information Technology Industry in Bangalore* (TBDPU Working Paper No. 89). The Bartlett Development and Planning Unit, 1998. https://www.ucl.ac.uk/bartlett/development/sites/bartlett/files/migrated-files/WP89_0.pdf

Thoburn, N. *Deleuze, Marx and Politics*; Routledge; London, 2003.

Thoburn, N. Vacuoles of Noncommunication. In *Deleuze and the Contemporary World*; Buchanan, I., Parr, A., Eds.; Edinburgh University Press: Edinburgh, 2006; pp 42–56.
Thomson, R.; Sluckin, W. Cybernetics and Mental Functioning. *Br. J. Phil. Sci.* **1953**, *4* (14), 130–146.
Tiqqun, R. *The Cybernetic Hypothesis*; Semiotext(e): Massachusetts, 2020.
Tronti, M. Factory and Society. In *Workers and Capital*; Tronti, M., Ed.; Verso: London [Unpaginated eBook], 1962/2019.
Tronti, M. *Workers and Capital*; Verso: London [Unpaginated eBook], 1971/2019.
Tronti, M. Social Capital. *Telos 1973*, *17*, 98–121.
Van De Voorde, K.; Paauwe, J.; Van Veldhoven, M. Employee Well-being and the HRM–Organizational Performance Relationship. *Int. J. Manage. Rev.* **2012**, *14*, 391–407.
Wang, Y.; Kim, S.; Rafferty, A.; Sanders, K. Employee perceptions of HR practices: A critical review and future directions. *The International Journal of Human Resource Management*, *31*(1), 128–173.
Warr, P. Well-being and the Workplace. In *Well-being: The Foundations of Hedonic Psychology*; Kahneman, D., Diener, E., Schwarz, N., Eds.; Russell SAGE Foundation: New York, 1999; pp 392–412.
Witheford, N. Autonomist Marxism and the Information Society. *Capital Class* **1994**, *18* (1), 85–125.
Wright, T. A. More Than Meets the Eye: The Role of Employee Well-being in Organizational Research. In *Oxford Handbook of Positive Psychology and Work*; Linley, P. A., Harrington, S., Garcea, N., Eds.; Oxford University Press: Oxford, 2010; pp 143–154.
Zheng, X.; Zhu, W.; Zhao, H.; Zhang, C. Employee Well-being in Organization. *J. Organ. Behav.* **2015**, *36* (5), 621–644.

CHAPTER 12

Post-Pandemic Employee Wellness Focus: An Empirical Study on the Well-Being Aspects of Healthcare Sector Employees

TAHIR MUMTAZ AWAN[1*] and ZAKIA KHURSHID KAYANI[2]

[1]Department of Management Sciences, COMSATS University Islamabad, Pakistan

[2]Tazeen Group of Companies, Islamabad, Pakistan

*Corresponding author. E-mail: tahir_mumtaz@comsats.edu.pk

ABSTRACT

Coronavirus (COVID-19) as told by the World Health Organization is said to be more Spartan than terrorism (Farham, 2020). Terrorism attacks deeply upset well-being and mental health by the distressing emotional and psychological outlook of human mental health like pandemics (Fischer and Ai, 2008). Prior studies (e.g., Bader and Berg, 2014; De Clercq et al., 2017; Raja et al., 2020) proposed that the intimidations related to pandemic would affront the wellness of employees, their performance, attitude, and behaviors. It intensifies stress, anxiety, and emotional enervation among them. Employee wellness indicates their rendezvous at the workplace and emotional anguish destructively influences them. The social environment is changing brusquely because of COVID-19 and its threat has affected emotional and psychological well-being. Considering the above evidence, the purpose of this chapter is to evaluate employee wellness after the COVID-19 pandemic by adapting appropriate scale(s), as a means of investigating the impact

---

Human Resource Management in a Post-Epidemic Global Environment: Roles, Strategies, and Implementations.
Tanusree Chakraborty, Nandita Mishra, Madhurima Ganguly, & Bipasha Chatterjee (Eds.)
© 2023 Apple Academic Press, Inc. Co-published with CRC Press (Taylor & Francis)

on the psychological and emotional operative. Surveys were conducted among medical staff of Pakistan using online and offline questionnaires. Appropriate analysis techniques using SPPS were conducted to confirm the results. The findings of the study suggested that it is important to focus on employee wellness after the pandemic. The finding of the study supports making employee wellness programs, policies, and plans. Furthermore, the study explains that different wellness measures (i.e., availability of safety measures, the role of traveling option, the presence of healthcare facilities at the workplace) play a vital role in ensuring employee well-being. Based on these findings, organizations need to provide proper well-being programs to address employee concerns. Further, organizations need to revisit their health programs and must include provisions for pandemics like COVID-19.

12.1 INTRODUCTION

In today's environment, jobs are an important part of an individual's life. People work to meet their living expenses. The working habitat exerts a great impression on their well-being. The situations at the workplace differ from regular situations; hence, the employee's wellness should be differentiated from general wellness. There is no consent on the definition of employee well-being so far (Page and Vella-Brodrick, 2009). The term employees' well-being can be understood by everyone but nobody can provide an exact definition (Lyubomirs, 2001). Employee well-being is a concept that refers to the psychological wellness of an employee and contains numerous components including job satisfaction, anxiety and burnout, and affective well-being (Warr, 1990; Daniels, 2000; Holman, 2004). The concept of wellness emerged after World War II where employees faced difficult working situations and had effects on their health subsequently. The early wellness concept focused on "wellness as not only absence of illness but overall well-being of individuals" (Panelli and Tipa, 2007).

The two main proxies of employee well-being used in literature are psychological wellness and subjective well-being (Ryan and Deci, 2001). The emphasis of subjective wellness is on the hedonic perspective of well-being, which is the search for happiness and satisfying life (Diener, 1984). Whereas, psychological well-being perspective relates to the eudemonic wellness, which is the completion of human potential and an evocative life. Psychological well-being includes perceived success in the challenges of life, for example, pursuing meaningful objectives, growth, and development as an individual and creating quality ties to others (Ryff and Keyes, 1995; Ryff and Singer, 2008). Differentiating the conceptual grounds of these two types is still under debate by researchers. One school of thought argues that subjective well-being and psychological well-being address different aspects of well-being, although these two are related to the subjective nature of well-being (Keyes et al., 2002). The viewpoint of Kashdan et al. (2008), however, differs from the other school of thought. They propose that subjective and psychological well-being reflect two traditions in research rather than two different concepts as they are more similar than different.

Busseri et al. (2007) have proposed three major components of subjective well-being including, high-level positive emotions, low-level negative emotions, and overall satisfaction with life. Organizations should foster positive work environment (Chakraborty and Ganguly, 2019). Subjectivity is considered as one important feature of subjective well-being which implies that well-being is assessed based on one's values rather than the values of others (Diener, 1984). Nevertheless, in a communist culture, individuals are willing to forego their desires and prefer group requirements to improve the group's wellness. Ryff and Keyes (1995) suggested a framework of psychological wellness with six dimensions including self-acceptance, personal growth, purpose in life, positive relations with others, environmental control, and sovereignty. Though psychological wellness is derived from western culture, the general structure of psychological well-being could be applied to other cultural settings as well (Markus and Kitayama, 1998).

12.1.1 OBJECTIVE OF STUDY

Employee's well-being is a serious issue for the survival of the organization around the globe (Spreitzer and Porath, 2012) and is always an important concept for researchers in organizational behavior. Between the years 2011 and 2012, researchers were focused on the dimension of employee's job satisfaction (Dimotakis et al., 2011), negative affect (Vandenberghe et al., 2011), and work attitude (Leavitt et al., 2011). Recent research works have focused on the measurement of employee's well-being as a subject matter (Hernandez et al., 2018). But still there exists gap regarding employee well-being from pandemic perspective. Keeping that in mind, this study aims to identify the post-pandemic organizational concern of employee well-being.

12.1.2 EMPLOYEE'S WELL-BEING AND ORGANIZATIONS

Lifestyle behaviors related to health like insufficient diet and less physical activity result in lowering the quality of life. This leads to the risk of many mental as well as physical diseases including stress, obesity, depression, and other cardiac problems (Davis et al., 2005). These health issues are of grave concern for the organizations as they may cause a decline in productivity and healthcare costs (Mattke et al., 2013a, 2013b). These issues can be addressed by forming employee wellness programs. The employee's wellness programs have the potential to significantly participate in this scenario and help to reduce the chances of severe medical conditions, improving productivity, and finally vindicating the possible increase in the cost of healthcare (Hill-Mey et al., 2015; Dement et al., 2015).

Workplace wellness programs are those which are provided by the employer to increase the well-being of the employees, increases awareness, change behavior, and create a conducive environment that is supportive of employee's health (Aldana, 2001). Employees get benefitted from the employer in terms of healthcare, childcare, flexible work schedules, and paid vacation, etc. Employee wellness programs can be defensive or curative in their design. Increasing the wellness of employees can include the personal stressor's assessment, stress management techniques, and may include an old social support system (Sulphey, 2014). Pipe et al. (2012) explored that wellness programs can improve teamwork and communication (Chakraborty et al., 2021a, 2021b) for preventing stress, reduce errors in the workplace, improve employee safety, increasing employee satisfaction, improving staff retention, and reducing hiring costs that may incur on fresh hiring. Further, it may lead the organization toward increasing performance.

Deloitte (2017) recognized the concept of well-being as an important issue for the employees as well as the employer and the whole society at large. It is important to identify that how organizations can use this concept to achieve a competitive advantage as employee well-being is recognized as the source of various performance forces like job satisfaction, productivity, anxiety, and work-life stability, and employee turnover (Keeman et al., 2017). Moreover, the concept of well-being is not only related to employee overall well-being but also affects the nation as well (Bowling et al., 2010; Goh et al., 2015).

12.1.3 COVID-19 AND EMPLOYEE PERSPECTIVES

COVID-19 caused by the severe acute respiratory syndrome (SARS)-Cov-2 virus results in world disasters, leaving long-lasting impacts on an individual level as well as on the global economy. The disease started from the Wuhan city of China in December 2019 and as of November 16, 2020, more than 5.5 crore people are infected with this virus and around 1.3 million died in over 200 countries (Wordmeter, 2020). Employees at different stages have faced multiple issues like job insecurity, health issues, and unemployment around the globe (Godinic et al., 2020). The world has faced many consequences of this pandemic which included international and domestic travel bans, empty shopping centers, and controlled social gatherings. Due to this, organizations moved to the work from home modules except those who had to render services from their work stations like doctors, etc. The situation of COVID-19 led many issues to initiate. One of the important issues is employee wellbeing including both mental- as well as physical health-related issues. At stated by Chakraborty et al. (2021a, 2021b), social distancing due to the pandemic creates a mental challenge among common people. Martins et al. (2020) reported that the workers in the services industry faced devastating hardships during the pandemic. As a direct result of COVID-19, 50 million jobs in the hospitality industry are at risk as warned by the World Travel and Tourism Council (Nicola et al., 2020).

The ongoing pandemic is a foundation of intense anxiety for the world populace. The ongoing pandemic of COVID-19 may relate to many stressors that can trench employee's mental health, throughout and even after the pandemic. The torment felt by an individual is not the problem rather it is the outcome of the problem (Mirowsky and Ross, 2003). Consequently, to reduce mental health risks, understanding this problem is more important. Hamouche (2020) identified several stressors during a pandemic with the perception of safety, threat and risk of contagion, quarantine and confinement, disgrace and social barring, infobesity, and the unknown, financial loss, and job insecurity. Moreover, the outbreak of pandemics has significantly influenced the business world which results in an individual's feeling of job insecurity. This has a greater impact on the mental health of employees, especially those who are being affected by the organization's policies of closure and reduced working time during the pandemic. Job insecurity negatively affects the mental health of employees at the workplace (Strazdins et al., 2004).

COVID-19, as told by the World Health Organization (WHO), is said to be more Spartan than terrorism (Farham, 2020). Terrorism attacks deeply upset wellness and psychological health by the distressing emotional and psychological outlook of human mental health (Fischer and Ai, 2008). Prior studies (e.g., Bader and Berg, 2014; De Clercq et al., 2017; Raja et al., 2020) proposed that the intimidations related to terrorism would affront the wellness of employees, their performance, attitude, and behaviors. It intensifies stress, anxiety, and emotional enervation among them. Employee wellness indicates their rendezvous at the workplace and emotional anguish destructively influences them. The social environment is changing brusquely because of COVID-19 and its threat has affected emotional and psychological well-being.

The issue of employee well-being becomes more relevant during the situation of a pandemic like COVID-19. On one side, employees who are providing the essential services like grocery stores, healthcare, quarantine centers, long-term care homes, and pharmacies are facing a direct encounter with visitors and ultimately are at higher risk of getting infected, stress, anxiety, and mental sickness (Sim, 2020). On the other side, also reflects a dramatic situation where abrupt shift to work from home, self-isolation, less social interaction has serious impacts on the mental health of employees. It may cause depression, loneliness, and anxiety (Braverman, 2020; Staglin, 2020) which is headed toward the rise in substance abuse and even suicide (Higgins-Dunn, 2020). Further, employers faced damaging situations for their reputation as they were called on social media for not providing employee well-being (Cassidy, 2020). Employee well-being, as discussed earlier, is studied in the context of employee mental health, stress, and personality traits (Danna and Griffin, 1999; Hayman, 2010). Later on, the other dimensions were evolved including psychological, physiological, and social (Grant et al., 2007; Ponting, 2020). In context to the deleterious impacts of COVID-19, Tuzovic and Kabadayi (2018) included different dimensions of employee well-being: physical, mental, social, and financial. According to the job demands-resources (JD-R) model, which determines employee well-being, "the job demand and resources levels are influenced by external factors (e.g., economic and industrial factors and government policies and technological factors" technology (Bakker et al., 2003; Bakker and Demerouti, 2007). Moreover, the changes in external forces lead to the change in demands and resources for employees, which creates implications for employee wellness in turn (Brauchli et al., 2013). The organizational efforts in response to the COVID-19 pandemic, like social distancing, services hibernation versus service continuity, the employee wellness issue became even more critical (Tuzovic and Kabadayi, 2018).

COVID-19 has changed the whole scenario at the decision making of an organization. The research works show that some factors have an impact on individuals even after the outbreaks of pandemic and have lifelong effects (Brooks et al., 2020). For example, the SARS pandemic caused stigma, increased stress, and effects on the psychological health of employees.

Researchers, such as Siu (2008), witnessed that workers experienced stigmatization even after the pandemic. Similarly, job insecurity, financial loss, life-threatening illness could also be considered as the post-COVID-19 effect on employees' life (Hamouche, 2020; Monica, 2020).

12.2 METHODOLOGY

The purpose of this chapter is to identify the post-pandemic organizational concern of employee well-being, to achieve this aim data was collected from 165 respondents through an online scenario-based survey from the basically health and related sectors from major cities in Pakistan. This study used a mixed-method approach, that is, quantitative, and qualitative. The quantitative part of the study was analyzed by using SPSS and the qualitative part was analyzed by thematic analysis and narrate style was used to illustrate them. The questionnaire was based on 15 independent fact variables and 33 dependent measure variables. The first part of the questionnaire was demographics, knowledge questions, Personal Protection Equipment (PPE), ability to work, willingness to work, and health and safety was a measure on five points Likert scale, the other measurements were descriptive.

12.2.1 DEMOGRAPHIC PROFILE OF RESPONDENTS

Demographic statistics of data show that mostly 64% of respondents were doctors, 18% were nurses, 12% were professionals related to the healthcare sector, 4% were from other management departments of health sectors, and 2% were scientists related to health sector. Whereas age demographics show that 30% belong to age group 18–25, 51% belong to age group 26–35, 12% were from age group 36–45. While 3% of respondents age were between 46 and 55 and 4% were above 56. In this dataset, 56% female respondents, and 44% were male respondents. Among all respondents, 39% were doing a full-time permanent job, while 34% were doing a full-time contractual job, whereas 24% people were doing a part-time job and 3% people have not mentioned their nature of the job. Among all respondents, 18% of people had direct contact with five patients, 12% with four patients, 18% had direct contact with three patients, and 18% had direct contact with two patients. Only 34% of respondents had direct contact with one patient only.

12.2.2 ANALYSIS

Considering the post-COVID-19 impacts, the organization's concern over employee well-being is of more importance. Addressing this phenomenon, this chapter is an effort to identify the post-pandemic organizational concern of employee well-being. For that purpose, data were collected from the employees of the health sector working in different cities of Pakistan. A total of 165 responses were collected from the major cities of Pakistan. Results show that most respondents had sufficient knowledge of COVID-19. Most respondents (43%) revealed that cases were normal, while 24% of respondents said that cases were the cause of corned and further result is shown in Table 12.1. Only 17% of respondents were highly agreed to work during the COVID-19 situation in the country. While 13% also agreed to work, 21% were neutral, whereas 25% and 24% were disagreed to strongly disagree, respectively. Similarly, the respondent's willingness to work during the COVID-19 situation in their city was also not very high. As 47% were not consented to work and 35% agreed and 18% were neutral. All these results are also depicted in Table 12.1.

TABLE 12.1 Opinion About COVID-19.

About COVID-19	Percentages				
	Strongly disagree	Disagree	Neutral	Agree	Strongly agree
At present, I have sufficient knowledge about COVID-19 Pandemic	7.9%	6%	21.7%	41.2%	23%
The prospect of cases being treated in the trust is a cause for concern	6.1%	13.3%	43%	25.5%	12.1%
If COVID-19 arrived in your country, I would come to work as normal	23.6%	24.8%	20.6%	13.3%	17.6%
If COVID19 arrived in your city I would come to work as normal.	21.8%	24.8%	18.2%	15.2%	20%

Personal Protection Equipment

Provision of PPE for staff in the presence of COVID-19 in the city was not in the hospital. Respondents were asked about provisions of PPE for staff members in the presence of COVID-19 in the city but not at their workplace. They agreed to the provision of PPE in all conditions having contact with an infected patient or not. If they have contact with an infected patient or travel on public transport in all cases PPE should be provided (see Table 12.2).

TABLE 12.2 Provision of PPE for Staff in Presence of COVID-19 in the City Not in Hospital.

Personal protection equipment (PPE) If there were cases of COVID-19 in your city, but not in the Hospital, I would expect:	Percentages				
	Strongly disagree	Disagree	Neutral	Agree	Strongly agree
Provision of PPE for all staff who have direct contact with known infected patients.	5.5%	9.1%	23.6%	7.3%	54.5%
Provision of PPE for all staff who have a direct contract with all patients	6.7%	9.7%	26.7%	20%	37%
Provision of PPE for all trust staff irrespective of direct patient contact	4.8%	19.4%	33.3%	16.4%	26.1%
Provision of PPE for traveling to work on public transport	17%	24.8%	29.1%	16.4%	12.7%

Provision of PPE for All Staff in Presence of COVID-19 in Hospital

Respondents were asked about provisions of PPE for staff members in the presence of COVID-19 in the hospital. In that case, they agreed to the provision of PPE in all conditions having contact with an infected patient or not. If they have contact with an infected patient or travel on public transport in all cases, PPE should be provided (see Table 12.3).

TABLE 12.3 Provision of PPE for All Staff in the Presence of COVID-19 in Hospital.

Personal protection equipment (PPE) If there were cases of COVID-19 in the Hospital, I would expect	Percentages				
	Strongly disagree	Disagree	Neutral	Agree	Strongly agree
Provision of PPE for all staff who have direct contact with known infected patients.	5.5%	7.3%	17%	21.8%	48.5%
Provision of PPE for all staff who have direct contract with all patients	5.5%	6.7%	18.2%	31.5%	38.2%
Provision of PPE for all trust staff irrespective of direct patient contact	8.5%	14.5%	30.9%	26.1%	20%
Provision of PPE for traveling to work on public transport	21.2%	21.2%	27.3%	19.4%	10.9%

Ability and willingness to work

Respondents were asked how far they live from the workplace or distance of their workplace. They were asked to tell from 1 to 10 km scale and the result depicts that most respondents have 10 km distance, followed by 1, 2,7, 4, and 5 km, as shown in Table 12.4. The use of transport type data showed that most people used public transport shared 69%, few used individual public transport 11%, whereas less percentage use own transport 17% and only 3% people do not use any transport as they preferred to walk, as shown in Table 12.4. Then the people's behavior related to care arrangement settings in the workplace was measured by examining their concern about effective care arrangement for children and elders. Most of the respondents show their concern about children's cares arrangement at the workplace. While 30% of respondents showed a neutral response and 25% were not worried about arrangements. Similarly, for elder care arrangements most respondents were concerned about elderly care arrangement setting at the workplace. Respondents were asked about the number of children at home. Most of the 53% were having three kids, followed by 14% kids, 13% only one child, 12% two children, and 8% said they have five children at home. These results are shown in Table 12.4.

TABLE 12.4 Ability and Willingness to Come to Work.

Ability & willingness to come to work	Percentages				
How far away from your main hospital base do you live?	< 5 miles	6–10 miles	11–15 miles	16–20 miles	>20 miles
	13.3%	17.7	40%	23%	6%
	Walk	Public transport		Private transport	
What travel option do you have to get to work?	10.9%	69.1%		20%	
My ability to come to work depends on:	Strongly disagree	Disagree	Neutral	Agree	Strongly agree
Use of public transport	29.1%	27.3%	28.3%	9.7%	5.5%
Effective child care arrangement	12.1%	13.3%	30.9%	31.5%	12.1%
Effective elderly care arrangement	10.3%	15.2%	31.5%	29.1%	13.9%

Willingness to work and health and safety concerns

Respondents were also asked about their willingness to come to work is influenced by different factors, that is, reliance on public transport, personal health, and family health. Results show that most people's willingness is affected by

Post-Pandemic Employee Wellness Focus

public transport as above it was discussed that most of them use public transport either shared or individual. In both cases, the unavailability of public transport affects their willingness to come to work. Moreover, respondents show their concern about personal health and family health. Proper healthcare arrangements at the workplace increase their sense of personal care and ultimately family health. Willingness to come to the workplace is affected by personal and family health if an employee himself/herself is not feeling well or any member in the family is affected by the virus then definitely their willingness will decrease (Table 12.5 shows the detailed results).

TABLE 12.5 Respondents' Willingness, Health, and Safety.

My willingness to come to work, in the event of COVID-19 will be adversely influenced by:	Percentages				
	Strongly disagree	Disagree	Neutral	Agree	Strongly agree
My reliance on the use of public transport	18.2%	15.8%	9.7%	29.7%	26.7%
My concern about public health	12.1%	8.5%	10.3%	44.2%	24.8%
My concerns about my family's health	3.6%	12.1%	23%	40.6%	20.6%
Health & safety If there were cases of COVID-19 in the Hospital, I would like the provision of:	Strongly disagree	Disagree	Neutral	Agree	Strongly agree
Health Monitoring	1.2%	4.2%	18.8%	34.5%	41.2%
Rapid access diagnosis and treatment for COVID-19	5.5%	5.5%	13.9%	29.7%	45.5%
Prophylactic treatment for COVID exposures	5.5%	4.2%	13.3%	33.9%	43%

Further, the results revealed that in the case of COVID-19 in the hospital, the provision of health monitoring is important and most respondents agreed to it. They further added that rapid diagnosis and treatment are also important and if there is any case in the case of COVID-19 in the hospital then immediately these actions should be taken. Graphical representation of these results is also given in Table 12.5.

Fear of staff catching the virus

Lastly, the hospital staff was asked to report their responses in case of diagnoses of COVID-19 in any member of staff. It was suggested that the patient should be quarantined and shifted to other places by most respondents. While another question was that patients should be treated and quarantined in the hospital. On this question, mix response was observed. The majority of respondents were agreed, whereas 30% were not agreed with it. Respondents were not agreed to keep the patients at home and get treated there. They showed mixed behavior while most of them were not in favor of keeping patients at home (see Table 12.6). Additionally, the medical staff was in favor of social and eating restrictions on all staff members. The majority agreed to have the restriction, 28% were neutral and 28% were not agreed to have social restrictions on all staff for socialization. Lastly, respondents said that all staff members should be given knowledge and counseling during the pandemic. As stress factors may increase during a pandemic that is why counseling is important to tackle situations. Most respondents agreed to have counseling sessions as depicted in Table 12.6.

TABLE 12.6 Fear of Staff Catching COVID-19.

If staff develop COVID-19	Percentages				
	Strongly disagree	Disagree	Neutral	Agree	Strongly agree
They should be quarantined and treated in the hospital	6.7%	4.2%	25.5%	29.7%	33.9%
They should be quarantined and treated elsewhere	12.7%	15.8%	17.6%	29.1%	24.8%
They should be quarantined and sent home	60%	11.5%	12.1%	8.5%	7.9%
There should be eating and social restrictions on all staff to prevent cross-infection	10.9%	17%	28.5%	24.2%	19.4%
The hospital should provide anonymized updates on the number of staff affected by COVID	6.7%	9.1%	21.8%	27.9%	34.5%
There should be rapid access counseling for staff during the epidemic	4.2%	6.1%	19.4%	27.3%	43%

Finally, in the end, a few open-ended questions were asked about "If you would wish to see the provision of treatment of staff then what treatment they like to have"?

The identified themes of the result are as follows:

Get treatment according to set protocol.
Plasma Therapy.
Vaccination.

Based on common themes in data, it was identified that most respondents agreed to have treatment according to set protocols and person should be shifted to the hospital when needed. The second most preferred treatment is plasma therapy. While vaccination is also suggested by many healthcare specialists, but it has not developed yet.

Secondly question was about how frequent treatment should be given?
Right after diagnosis
On need

Further, about the frequency of treatment, it was suggested that treatment should be given right after the diagnosis while others suggest giving a treatment on need. Thirdly, medical specialists were asked about the patient's residence then most respondents agreed to keep the patient in the hospital or separate isolation center. Some of them also suggest taking care of the patient at home if possible. Otherwise, it is good and safe to keep patients at the hospital or in an isolation center. Lastly, respondents exposed that all patients should be taken care of by doctors, authorized medical staff, or any trained specialist.

12.3 DISCUSSION AND CONCLUSION

This chapter aimed to measure the employees' well-being during the pandemic and their behavior toward different situations. For that purpose, a survey was conducted in major cities of Pakistan. The result of the study revealed that respondents preferred to have PPE) in the case of COVID-19 in the city not in the hospital. Whereas in the presence of COVID-19, in hospital, PPE must be provided to staff for the well-being of employees (Tuzovic and Kabadayi, 2018). Data revealed that there were very less respondents who use personal transport. Most of them are relying on public transport either shared or individual. Respondents showed their concern about protection arrangements at the workplace for children and elders. They show more willingness to come to the workplace if proper care arrangements are available at the workplace.

Moreover, employees were concerned about healthcare facilities for them at the organization and revealed that rapid diagnosis and treatment of the patient is necessary. Additionally, they suggested that if any staff member is diagnosed with COVID-19, he/she should be treated according to set protocols immediately and shifted to an isolation center or kept in the hospital. They are not in favor of keeping the patient at home. The presence of PPE and other protection protocols is important for employees to be followed by the organization and provide a safe and healthy environment for them. As it creates an employee sense of well-being, organizations must think over the same lines and their focus must be the wellness of employees working within or outside the organization even after the pandemic (Prasad et al., 2020). Based on these findings, organizations need to provide proper well-being programs to address employee concerns. Further, organizations need to revisit their health programs and must include provisions for pandemics like COVID-19.

12.4 KEY TAKEAWAYS

- Employees show concern about healthcare facilities by organization.
- Patient with positive COVID-test should be treated immediately.
- The presence of PPE and other protection protocols is important for employees to be followed by the organization and provide a safe and healthy environment for them.
- All patients should be taken care of by doctors, authorized medical staff, or any trained specialist.
- People should get vaccinated after its development.
- People need counseling during corona to handle the corona fatigue.
- Finally, organizations need to revisit their health programs and must include provisions for pandemics like COVID-19.

KEYWORDS

- **well-being**
- **COVID-19**
- **employee wellness**

REFERENCES

Aldana, S. G. Financial Impact of Health Promotion Programs: A Comprehensive Review of the Literature. *Am. J. Health Promo.* **2001,** *15* (5), 296–320.

Bader, B.; Berg, N. The Influence of Terrorism on Expatriate Performance: A Conceptual Approach. *Int. J. Human Resour. Manage.* **2014,** *25* (4), 539–557.

Bakker, A. B.; Demerouti, E. The Job Demands-Resources Model: State of the Art. *J. Manage. Psychol.* **2007.**

Bakker, A.; Demerouti, E.; Schaufeli, W. Dual Processes at Work in a Call Centre: An Application of the Job Demands–Resources Model. *Eur. J. Work Organ. Psychol.* 2003, *12* (4), 393–417.

Bowling, N. A.; Eschleman, K. J.; Wang, Q. A Meta-Analytic Examination of the Relationship between Job Satisfaction and Subjective Well-being. *J. Occup. Organi. Psychol.* **2010,** *83* (4), 915–934.

Brauchli, R.; Schaufeli, W. B.; Jenny, G. J.; Füllemann, D.; Bauer, G. F. Disentangling Stability and Change in Job Resources, Job Demands, and Employee Well-Being—A Three-Wave Study on the Job-Demands Resources Model. *J. Vocation. Behav.* **2013,** *83* (2), 117–129.

Braverman, B. The Coronavirus Is Taking a Huge Toll on Workers' Mental Health across America. *CNBC,* April 6. https://www.cnbc.com/2020/04/06/coronavirus-is-takinga-toll-on-workers-mental-health-across-america.html (accessed Nov 5, 2020).

Brooks, S. K.; Webster, R. K.; Smith, L. E.; Woodland, L.; Wessely, S.; Greenberg, N.; Rubin, G. J. The Psychological Impact of Quarantine and How to Reduce It: Rapid Review of the Evidence. *Lancet* **2020.**

Busseri, M.; Sadava, S.;.;DeCourville, N. A Hybrid Model for Research on Subjective Well-being: Examining Common-and Component-specific Sources of Variance in Life Satisfaction, Positive Affect, and Negative Affect. *Soc. Indicators Res.* 2007, *83* (3), 413.

Cassidy, F. Caring for Employee Mental Health: A Coronavirus Guide. *Raconteur,* March 31. https://www.raconteur.net/business-innovation/mental-health-coronavirus-guide (accessed Oct 4, 2020).

Chakraborty, T.; Ganguly, M. Crafting Engaged Employees through Positive Work Environment: Perspectives of Employee Engagement. In *Management Techniques for Employee Engagement in Contemporary Organizations*; IGI Global, 2019; pp 180–198.

Chakraborty, T.; Kumar, A.; Upadhyay, P.; Dwivedi, Y. K. Link between Social Distancing, Cognitive Dissonance, and Social Networking Site Usage Intensity: A Country-level Study during the COVID-19 Outbreak. *Internet Res.* 2021, *31* (2), 419–456. DOI: 10.1108/intr-05-2020-028

Chakraborty, T.; Tripathi, M.; Saha, S. The Dynamics of Employee Relationships in a Digitalized Workplace: The Role of Media Richness on Workplace Culture. In *Critical Issues on Changing Dynamics in Employee Relations and Workforce Diversity*; IGI Global, 2021; pp 175–205.

Daniels, K. Measures of Five Aspects of Affective Well-being at Work. *Human Relat.* **2000,** *53* (2), 275–294.

Danna, K.; Griffin, R. W. Health and Well-being in the Workplace: A Review and Synthesis of the Literature. *J. Manage.* **1999,** *25* (3), 357–384.

Davis, E.; Waters, E.; Wake, M.; Oberklaid, F.; Williams, J.; Mehmet-Radji, O.; Goldfeld, S. Population Health and Wellbeing: Identifying Priority Areas for Victorian Children. *Australia and New Zealand Health Policy* **2005,** *2* (1).

De Clercq, D.; Haq, I. U.; Azeem, M. U. Perceived Threats of Terrorism and Job Performance: The Roles of Job-related Anxiety and Religiousness. *J. Busi. Res.* **2017**, *78*, 23–32.

Deloitte. *At a Tipping Point? Workplace Mental Health and Wellbeing*; Deloitte Centre for Health Solutions: London, 2017.

Dement, J. M.; Epling, C.; Joyner, J.; Cavanaugh, K. Impacts of Workplace Health Promotion and Wellness Programs on Health Care Utilization and Costs: Results from an Academic Workplace. *J. Occup. Environ. Med.* **2015**, *57* (11), 1159–1169.

Diener, E. Subjective Well-being. *Psychol. Bull.* **1984**, *95*, 542–575.

Dimotakis, N.; Scott, B. A.; Koopman, J. An Experience Sampling Investigation of Workplace Interactions, Affective States, and Employee Well-being. *J. Organ. Behav.* **2011**, *32* (4), 572–588.

Farham, B. 'More Dangerous Than Terrorism'-the Media versus the Facts. *SAMJ: SA Med. J.* **2020**, *110* (3), 169–169.

Fischer, P.; Ai, A. L. International Terrorism and Mental Health: Recent Research and Future Directions. *J. Interpersonal Violence* **2008**, *23* (3), 339–361.

Godinic, D.; Obrenovic, B.;.;Khudaykulov, A. Effects of Economic Uncertainty on Mental Health in the COVID-19 Pandemic Context: Social Identity Disturbance, Job Uncertainty and Psychological Well-Being Model. *Int. J. Manage. Sci. Busi. Admin.* **2020**, *6* (1), 61–74.

Goh, J.; Pfeffer, J.; Zenios, S. A.; Rajpal, S. Workplace Stressors & Health Outcomes: Health Policy for the Workplace. *Behav. Sci. Policy* **2015**, *1* (1), 43–52.

Grant, A. M.; Christianson, M. K.; Price, R. H. Happiness, Health, or Relationships? Managerial Practices and Employee Well-being Tradeoffs. *Acad. Manage. Persp.* **2007**, *21* (3), 51–63.

Hamouche, S. COVID-19 and Employees' Mental Health: Stressors, Moderators and Agenda for Organizational Actions. *Emerald Open Res.* **2020**, *2* (15), 15.

Hayman, J. Flexible Work Schedules and Employee Well-being. *New Zealand J. Employment Relat.* **2010**, *35* (2), 76.

Hernandez, R.; Bassett, S. M.; Boughton, S. W.; Schuette, S. A.; Shiu, E. W.; Moskowitz, J. T. Psychological Well-being and Physical Health: Associations, Mechanisms, and Future Directions. *Emotion Rev.* **2018**, *10* (1), 18–29.

Higgins-Dunn, N. Coronavirus Crisis Creates 'Perfect Storm' for Suicide Risk as Job Losses Soar and People Are Isolated at Home *CNBC*, May 12. https://www.cnbc.com/2020/05/12/coronavirus-crisis-creates-perfect-storm-for-suicide-risk-as-job-losses-soar-and-peopleremain-isolated-at-home.html (accessed Nov 12, 2020).

Hill-Mey, P. E.; Kumpfer, K. L.; Merrill, R. M.; Reel, J.; Hyatt-Neville, B.; Richardson, G. E. Worksite Health Promotion Programs in College Settings. *J. Educ. Health Prom.* **2015**, *4*.

Holman, D. Employee Well-being in Call Centres. In *Call Centres and Human Resource Management*. Palgrave Macmillan: London, 2004; pp 223–244.

Kashdan, T. B.; Biswas-Diener, R.; King, L. A. Reconsidering Happiness: The Costs of Distinguishing between Hedonics and Eudaimonia. *J. Positive Psychol.* **2008**, *3* (4), 219–233.

Keeman, A.; Näswall, K.; Malinen, S.; Kuntz, J. Employee Wellbeing: Evaluating a Wellbeing Intervention in Two Settings. *Front. Psychol.* **2017**, *8*, 505.

Keyes, C. L.; Shmotkin, D.;.;Ryff, C. D. Optimizing Well-being: The Empirical Encounter of Two Traditions. *J. Person. Soc. Psychol.* **2002**, *82* (6), 1007.

Leavitt, K.; Fong, C. T.; Greenwald, A. G. Asking about Well-being Gets You Half an Answer: Intra-Individual Processes of Implicit and Explicit Job Attitudes. *J. Organ. Behav.* **2011**, *32* (4), 672–687.

Lyubomirs, S. Why are Some People Than Other. *The Role of Cognitive and Motivational Processes in Well-Being American*, 2001.

Markus, H. R.; Kitayama, S. The Cultural Psychology of Personality. *J. Cross-Cultural Psychol.* **1998**, *29* (1), 63–87.

Martins, A.; Riordan, T.; Dolnicar, S. A Post-COVID-19 Model of Tourism and Hospitality Workforce Resilience, 2020.

Mattke, S.; Liu, H.; Caloyeras, J.; Huang, C. Y.; Van Busum, K. R.; Khodyakov, D.; Shier, V. (2013a). Workplace Wellness Programs Study. *Rand Health Quart.* **2013a**, *3* (2).

Mattke, S.; Schnyer, C.; Van Busum, K. R. A Review of the US Workplace Wellness Market. *Rand Health Quart.* **2013b**, *2* (4).

Mirowsky, J.; Ross, C. E. *Social Causes of Psychological Distress*; Transaction Publishers, 2003.

MONICA, D. B. Impact of Work From Home on Employee Wellbeing during Pandemic. *J. Contemp. Issues Busi. Govern.* **2020**, *26* (2), 442–446.

Nicola, M.; Alsafi, Z.; Sohrabi, C.; Kerwan, A.; Al-Jabir, A.; Iosifidis, C.; Agha, R. The Socio-Economic Implications of the Coronavirus Pandemic (COVID-19): A Review. *Int. J. Surg. (London, England)* **2020**, *78*, 185.

Page, K. M.; Vella-Brodrick, D. A. The 'What', 'Why' and 'How' of Employee Well-being: A New Model. *Soc. Indicat. Res.* **2009**, *90* (3), 441–458.

Panelli, R.; Tipa, G. Placing Well-being: A Maori Case Study of Cultural and environmental specificity. *Eco Health* **2007**, *4* (4), 445–460.

Pipe, T. B.; Buchda, V. L.; Launder, S.; Hudak, B.; Hulvey, L.; Karns, K. E.; Pendergast, D. Building Personal and Professional Resources of Resilience and Agility in the Healthcare Workplace. *Stress Health* **2012**, *28* (1), 11–22.

Ponting, S. S. A. Organizational Identity Change: Impacts on Hotel Leadership and Employee Wellbeing. *Service Ind. J.* **2020**, *40* (1–2), 6–26.

Prasad, K. D. V.; Vaidya, R. W.; Mangipudi, M. R. Effect of Occupational Stress and Remote Working on Psychological Wellbeing of Employees: An Empirical Study during Covid-19 Pandemic with Reference to Information Technology Industry around Hyderabad. *Indian J. Com. Manage. Stud* **2020**, *2*, 1–13.

Raja, U.; Azeem, M. U.; Haq, I. U.; Naseer, S. Perceived Threat of Terrorism and Employee Outcomes: The Moderating Role of Negative Affectivity and Psychological Capital. *J. Busi. Res.* **2020**, *110*, 316–326.

Ryan, R. M.; Deci, E. L. On Happiness and Human Potentials: A Review of Research on Hedonic and Eudaimonic Well-being. *Annu. Rev. Psychol.* **2001**, *52* (1), 141–166.

Ryff, C. D.; Keyes, C. L. M. The Structure of Psychological Well-being Revisited. *J. Personality Soc. Psychol.* **1995**, *69* (4), 719.

Ryff, C. D.; Singer, B. H. Know Thyself and Become What You Are: A Eudaimonic Approach to Psychological Well-being. *J. Happiness Stud.* **2008**, *9* (1), 13–39.

Sim, M. R. The COVID-19 Pandemic: Major Risks to Healthcare and Other Workers on the Front Line, 2020.

Siu, J. Y. M. The SARS-Associated Stigma of SARS Victims in the Post-SARS Era of Hong Kong. *Qual. Health Res.* **2008**, *18* (6), 729–738.

Spreitzer, G.; Porath, C. Creating Sustainable Performance. *Harv. Busi. Rev.* **2012**, *90* (1), 92–99.

Staglin, G. When Home Becomes the Workplace: Mental Health and Remote Work. *Forbes*, March 17. https://www.forbes.com/sites/onemind/2020/03/17/when-home-becomesthe-workplace-mental-health-and-remote-work/#73acf4761760 (accessed Nov 5, 2020).

Strazdins, L.; D'Souza, R. M.; Lim, L. L. Y.; Broom, D. H.; Rodgers, B. Job Strain, Job Insecurity, and Health: Rethinking the Relationship. *J. Occup. Health Psychol.* **2004,** *9* (4), 296.

Sulphey, M. M. Construction & Validation of Employee Wellness Questionnaire. *Indian J. Ind. Relat.* **2014,** 690–700.

Tuzovic, S.; Kabadayi, S. The Influence of Social Distancing on Employee Well-being: A Conceptual Framework and Research Agenda. *J. Serv. Manage.* **2018,** *32* (2), 145–160.

Vandenberghe, C.; Panaccio, A.; Bentein, K.; Mignonac, K.; Roussel, P. Assessing Longitudinal Change of and Dynamic Relationships among Role Stressors, Job Attitudes, Turnover Intention, and Well-being in Neophyte Newcomers. *J. Organ. Behav.* **2011,** *32* (4), 652–671.

Warr, P. The Measurement of Well-being and Other Aspects of Mental Health. *J. Occup. Psychol.* **1990,** *63* (3), 193–210.

CHAPTER 13

Work-Life Issues and Stress: Challenges and Coping in the Post-Pandemic Period

NITESH BEHARE*, ANUP SHIVANECHARI, and SHRIKANT WAGHULKAR

Balaji Institute of International Business, Sri Balaji University, Pune, India

Corresponding author. E-mail: beharenb@gmail.com

> "It's not the load (stress) that breaks you down,
> it's the way you carry it"
>
> —Lou Holtz

ABSTRACT

WHO (2020) had noted that "Anxiety, uneasiness, and stress are usual reactions to perceived threat or real threats, as well as it also occurs when we experience any uncertainty or unfamiliar situation(s)." Thus, it is very much expected that individuals may experience the fear of losing their job during pandemic situation. As global GDP is continuously shrinking and many businesses are facing financial crises, which is also reflected in employee turnover. So many employees are struggling for retaining their jobs which in turn exceeds their working hours, inflexible weekly holidays, excessive workload, etc. (Nicholas Bloom, 2020), which is hampering employees' work-life balance (Kang, 2020) and resulting in stress (Hamouche Salima, 2020). So to keep the employee's morale high and keep them stress-free business, professionals specifically HR personnel have strategically planned their employees' activities to achieve business targets without challenging employees' physical and mental fitness. This chapter has given a detailed

---

Human Resource Management in a Post-Epidemic Global Environment: Roles, Strategies, and Implementations.
Tanusree Chakraborty, Nandita Mishra, Madhurima Ganguly, & Bipasha Chatterjee (Eds.)
© 2023 Apple Academic Press, Inc. Co-published with CRC Press (Taylor & Francis)

outline about how corporates were taking care of their employees with respect to managing their work-life and occupational stress, different activities which they planned during pandemic to keep their employees happy and stress-free, also implementation of NEW NORMAL in the current working environment.

13.1 INTRODUCTION

These days everyone of us is pulled in many directions because of simultaneous responsibilities at work as well as at home. Fulfilling these responsibilities creates drowsiness which results in stress that is a normal and inseparable part of everyone's life. Many events which happen around individuals create physical as well as mental stress. Sometimes it goes beyond the limit where our body starts signaling that we are feeling stressed about our day-to-day life. In our daily routine, we might be dealing with many problems like financial problems, job uncertainty, personal problems, separation of loved ones from us, etc., which can cause stress. So we can say that stress is a constantly changing condition where an individual is provoked with demands, opportunities, or various resources associated with the desire of an individual where the result is perceived to be dynamic as well as unreliable.

Many psychologists around the globe have the same opinion and all of them consider stress as a complex phenomenon and can be described as "it is the wear and tear of everyday life" (UKEssays, 2018). Hans Selye (1956), a well-known personality who is also considered as the father of stress theory, defined stress as "a general reaction of body to any demand made upon it." (Lopamudra Pattnaik, 2018) Hans Selye, the first psychologists, assimilated stress into medical terminologies which consider stress as "for *any demand stress is a usual and uncertain response."* Managing stress in today's world is key concern in the individuals' life (Siang Yong Tan, 2018). According to Gale Encyclopaedia of Medicine (2008), "stress management is a well-designed programs and bunch of scientific practices proposed effectively to deal with stress by evaluating specific stress creating factors and minimizing their effects by taking positive actions in individuals' life" (Amba Brown, 2020).

13.2 PRECOVID STRESS MANAGEMENT

Before the COVID-19 outbreak, most of us were working from offices even organizations were asking their employees to do so. So employees were having a regular routine at their workplaces and after that, they were free to spend their time as per their preferences. At their workplaces, employees have to meet the deadlines which may result in workplace stress. There may be many reasons for workplace stress that can affect employees and employers both. Sometimes it is okay to have a little stress (generally which is termed as "positive stress"); however, when the stress level increases and unbearable, then chances of change in mental and physical health may occur.

Susic Paul (2013) opined that "stress management is application of vide range of techniques in psychoanalyses intended to manage stress level of an individual typically for improving their everyday functioning."

Destructive physical and emotional responses could be the outcome of workplace stress which may happen when there is a gap between individuals' performance and employees' level of control over meeting these performances. Effective management of the stress helps to break the stress burden so that individuals can be happy, healthy, and more productive (WHO, 2020). Managing stress at the workplace is about controlling individuals' thoughts, emotions, workplace environment, and the way an individual deal with their problems. Ultimately, stress management has to balance individuals' life, interpersonal relationships, with time for work, relaxation from the work, and sparing time for fun—and creating flexibility of bearing pressure and meet the organizational challenges (Lawrence Robinson, 2019).

Work-Life Balance

So to manage workplace stress, the term *work-life-balance* came into existence which means for work and personal life both an individual needs time. So for the better productivity of the employee, organizations were taking care of their employees with respect to managing stress at workplace. According to the proven studies on work-life balance, to reduce stress at workplace, a good work-life balance can substantially help (Maxwell, n.d.). Many studies have also revealed that employees with a positive work-life balance can perform better at workplaces, so promoting this balance of work life is very much favorable to create win–win situation for individuals as well as to the company. So for the organizations, it is a challenging task to create a balance between both work and individuals' life. Properly balanced individuals' career and personal life keeps them healthier, mentally and physically both. So with the help of a properly managed work-life balance, any individual will be equipped to manage better which will positively impact various spectrums of his life. Organizations who achieve a status for encouraging work-life balance draw excellent candidates for new job openings which turned to higher retention rates, more dedication, and ample availability of in-house expertise (Doris Stout, 2017).

On the other hand, Harvard Business School came up with the study mentioning that 94% (Deborah Jian Lee, 2014) of employees were working more than 50 h per week, whereas half of the respondents were working more than 65 h (Deborah Jian Lee, 2014) per week, which is an alarming situation for many organizations. One of the reasons for such situation is the extensive use of technology which makes them available around the clock also lesser job availability and stress of losing their existing job had incentivized extended working hours. Many psychologists have agreed that multifactorial stress is destructing employees' physical and mental health (Deborah Jian Lee, 2014).

Stress Management Techniques on and Off the Workplace

We already discussed that stress is very much harmful with regard to both physical and emotional responses, which occur when there is a difference between job demands of employees and their over meeting of such demands. Altogether, the amalgamation of high expectations from the job and a less control over such type of situation can turn into stress. So workplace stresses can have many origins which can influence both employees and employers alike. Many studies have proved that to boost employee performance some stress is *okay* but when stress load increases and employee is unable to handle, changes in both, mental and physical appearance, may occur.

According to the National Association of Mental Health (NAMH), individual employee "personality and handling strategy" can have direct, moderating, or perceptual effects on outcomes of the stress. For example, an employees' past experience, personality traits, and resources appear to affect how that employee interprets and manages particular situations. The report generated by NAMH had also pointed out the difference between pressure and stress. Pressure is a subjective feeling of tension that is prompted by the potential stressful situation which rouses mental vigilance and motivation, pressure may also lead to have positive impression on employee satisfaction and their performance. However, when this pressure increases (which turns into stress) may lead to fear, irritability, aggression, frustration, and stress, and may even contribute to physical and mental illnesses. HSE has recognized six major categories of potential workplace stressors. But Mr. Palmer noted that organizational culture is the seventh driver of stress that is not recognized as an explicit factor of stress by the HSE (Smruti Rekha Sahoo, 2016).

Many scholars have described that occupational life is connected to stress. Spark and Cooper (1999) claimed that there is a substantial relation in workplace factor and negative symptoms of health or mental syndrome like irritation, depression, and anxiety. On the other hand, many people are more comfortable with remote working which will ultimately save their valuable resources like time and money. As they do not have to spend time in traveling to office, they will have more time for themselves which can be utilized for any kind of activity like spending time for gardening, or spending with family, and even it be used for extra office work. Also, they remote working will give them "convenience" of working from wherever they feel convenient to work. Additionally, as per their convenience, employees can decide when to rest and when to work as they are under less stress which will help them in giving out better performance to tasks. Along with the benefits, there are many challenges associated with remote working. Same as their in-office counterparts' workplace stress can also influence the employees who are working remotely. Though the form as well as the reason of the stress would be different and can be even more challenging to distinguish than typical in-office workplace stress. Because of this COVID-19 pandemic, many organizations had pushed their employees to work remotely and that employees are undergoing through huge stress which is also a critical issue to solve. In fact, in many developed countries, it was found that 41% (Elizabeth Scott, 2021) of "highly mobile" employees (who regularly work remotely) felt stressed comparing to only 25% of those employees who work on-site (Elizabeth Scott, 2021).

13.3 STRESS MANAGEMENT IN PANDEMIC SITUATION

COVID-19 pandemic has changed everyone's routine globally which caused stress and increased the predicaments for the employees who were already surrounded by various other stressors in their life (AJ Horch, 2020). With the increase in COVID-19 cases, many of us are apprehensive about ourselves as well as the people we care most. No matter from where we are working, remotely or from workplace, fear and anxiety may become a part of our life. For a prolonged period of time, when people are under stress, it can cause or exacerbate a many health problems. So considering these facts many organizations came online/digital stress management programs, such as e-workshops, live yoga and meditation sessions, councilors, many entertainment programs to keep their employee engaged and stress-free so as to keep them motivated and enthusiastic.

Stress Management and Management Leadership

In January 2020, WHO declared COVID-19 as a Public Health Emergency of International Concern. Considering the impact of COVID-19 on societal health was termed as an astonishing worldwide crisis on humanitarian and because of which everything was locked down. Therefore, organizational leaders were consistently under pressure due to worldwide financial crises which also exaggerated their stress. Though it was a stressful situation for everyone, effective leaders learned to manage stress when making crucial decisions and motivating their other employees. These leaders had set the example if leaders can follow healthy stress management practices then why not others. Organizational leaders are convinced about these practices and agreed that by doing so, any organization can become healthier and will be ready to deal with any stressful situation and can manage future crises in a better way (American Psychological Association, 2020)

Today everyone has too much expectations from others which may create superfluous psychological burden that results in stress on the individual. NICK (2019) in his analysis suggested five stages in stress management pyramid, such as alarm, resistance, possible recovery, adaptation, and burnout. As per his opinion, everyone may not go through all stages sequentially—but by disseminating these stages individual will probably to take encouraging action to accelerate retrieval poststressful phase of a life or that individual will be capable enough to be ready with the plan for dealing with any level of stress. Let us discuss these stages of stress management pyramid in detail.

1. Alarm (Fight-or-Flight)

Young Diggers (2010) in his research claimed that when individuals are stimulated to a probable situation stress, human body goes with some temporary hormonal changes, and due to which blood pressure elevates and heart rate increases, enhancing supplies of our energy to deal with a perceived threat. It is broadly supposed that response of *fight-or-flight* came into existence as a usual need for initial human families, and individuals' spontaneous reaction to the potential situation of stress in a similar way. These normal signals such as cooler skin, sweating, dilated pupils, warm breathing, and dry mouth can help individual to identify if they may belong to this stage.

2. Resistance

According to Lumen Candela (2019) whatever would be the individuals, initial response to stress, his/her body may have the capability to deal with situation which is resulting in a reaction toward stress when we move to resistance stage. This specifies stage can be considered as a stressful situation. So by liberating "anti-inflammatory hormones," human body is struggling to become normal and ease out the side effects of stress. To deal with the stress, Lumen Candela (2019) in her research article recommended effective strategies such as notice and understand the root causes of stress, take necessary action, and accordingly plan for the future to move through the second stage, that is, resistance stage.

3. Coping (Recovery)

Possibly this is the most fundamental stage of the individuals' cycle of stress because retrieval from the stress is a fundamental part to improve from a stressful phase to return to a balanced state. This can be achieved by carrying out a precise assessment. As everybody has different experiences of going through stressful situation and recovering in many different ways, but there are few techniques such as daily exercise/yoga, meditation, healthy diet, consistent sleep (Healthy Sleep, 2007), dancing, and laughter therapy by assuring you that you are offering yourself a best chance that you can (Debra Fulghum Bruce, 2020).

4. Adaptation

After undergoing through a stressful situation, people may take some time to recover (as stage 3) or familiarize to the situation which an individual experienced. Sometimes, human being acclimates to a stressful situation considering that they would not fight the stressful condition so their body will always remain in stress, which may have enduring adverse effects like insomnia, fatigue, may gain/lose weight, lower confidence, as well as difficulty in dealing with your emotions (N Cole, 2018). There are a few strategies that an individual can use when they experience ongoing stress by exploring the possibilities and absolution of expectations (Stress Less, 2015), as well as making yourself compassionate and to others.

5. Burnout

According to Joe Robinson (2015) when someone is prompted in a stressful condition, it is suggested that they have to take time to recover from it. If any individual, despite any reason, is not capable to agree sufficient retrieval or naïvely adjusted to a situation that has occasioned in being deferred in a discriminating stage of stress, probably the individual will experience burnout that comprises cynicism, severe exhaustion, lacking positivity, facing shattering thoughts, feeling emotionally drained, and a disinterestedness from others. Strategies like "take moments to slow your mind and body, reassess your values and goals, rest, recover and reward" (Melanie Greenberg, 2016) for your hard work will help in long-lasting retrieval as well as aid your speedy mental recovery.

13.4 STRESS MANAGEMENT IN REMOTE WORKING ENVIRONMENT

As COVID-19 spread around the globe, organizations as well as their employees demanded the remote working wherever possible. MNCs like Microsoft, Google, IBM, Accenture, Wipro, etc., have initiated and acted to address their employees' most immediate employment concerns upraised due to pandemic. Consequently, many of the employees are experiencing new feelings and thoughts which is causing stress to them. So how can organizations manage stress when working remotely? So as to minimize the anxiety of uncertainty of job and professed threat, it is expected that communication from the organization should be enriched therefore framing a positive perception amongst all the employees. Consequently, regular communication with remote employees as well as counseling them on how to achieve their performance goals by adjusting their behavior is a very effective way of increasing their engagement. According to one of the reputed HR consultancy, employees who often meet their superiors are three times more involved than their subordinates, and also they are highly innovative and agile (Dr. Jolly Sahni, 2020). That is why employee empowerment is crucial component of successful teams.

There are a few modern stress management techniques that organizations are suggesting to their employees such are work-life balance, stay socially connected, be kind to others, and schedule, plan, and diarize. Few employers initiated online cultural programs and fun games for their employees to divert their employees from work stress. Some employers have offered paid leaves for a few days with OTT platform subscriptions. All these actions had created a positive environment for their employees who are working remotely.

Modern Stress Management Techniques

Stress prevention at the workplace is most efficacious but when employees are working remotely it becomes very much complex. Organization has to take additional efforts to deal with it. One of the best ways to reduce stress of remote working employees is to imitate the recommendations of those who work in office. Resting for appropriate duration, consuming less caffeine content and doing enough exercise, these practices are all good ideas to deal with workplace stress. Whereas remote workers should also follow different set of practices such as prioritize the tasks in the morning, schedule time for unanticipated collaboration, move around, green walk (walk on lawn), set a schedule, change your surroundings (by playing favorite music or by dancing), be compassionate with yourself, talk to your friends, do not overwork, get comfortable in saying "no" to the things you do not want to do, do not be too hard on yourself, spent time with family and friends, be flexible with your time, put time on the calendar to exercise, set up an after-work ritual, make time for social interaction, etc.

E-stress Management (Using Artificial Intelligence (AI), Deep Learning, Machine Learning, Mobile Apps)

Technology played a significant role in managing stress using various techniques. One of the researches by Mohammed (2019) suggested that a portable sensor platform can monitor numerous physiological gestures like skin conductance, variation in heart rate, and irregularities in breathing pattern. On the other hand, Bobade (2020) revealed that when an individual gets stressed, prominent changes can be observed in different biosignals such as impedance, thermal, acoustic, electrical, optical, etc., which will also be helpful in recognizing individuals' stress levels. For individual's stress, detection is possible using various electronics tools, a multimodal data recorded from electronic wearable such as motion sensors and physiological gadgets, which can helpful in averting many stress-related health problems. Various studies have proved that on an average, the employee drops 7.1 days because of extraordinary stress at workplaces, whereas 35% of occasions of high-stress situations are related to mental health issues. It gives clear idea that organizations are losing direct cost from temporary leaves, which amounts to over $13 million (Staff Writer, 2019). Therefore, with the use of AI, organizations can supervise employees' data and can understand the various reason of stress. It can also intrude at exact moment, by managing employees with various activities where employees are remotely working and/or working on-site, stress management techniques, such as meditation or mind relaxation music with yoga will be really helpful. There are other techniques that are assisting employees in managing stress. One of the techniques is mental health chatbots, like Moodkit, Wysa, and Woebot, which can offer intellectual insights and behavioral change in employees on the basis of cognitive-behavioral techniques.

13.5 WORK-LIFE BALANCE DURING PANDEMIC

Globally, due to pandemic, many people are trying harder to retain their work-life balance. COVID pandemic has distracted everyone's routine because many organizations asked their employees either to go fully or partially remote, schools are also working remotely so kids are also at home, many businesses have closed their operations, conversely life events (like marriages) and social gatherings, which used to happen in normal situations, are also either constrained or canceled. However, in doing so, the pandemic overturned the work/life balances of many individuals. In other words, COVID-19 has made individual to forget "how was good work-life balance?". The employees who are working remotely, experiencing it more difficult to differentiate between work life from personal life. Nowadays, dining tables turned into office work stations and online calls, conference calls and office meetings are disturbed by pets and family members and/or outsiders.

Work-life balance before COVID outbreak was never been challenging, but the worse thing is nobody has an idea when things will become *normal*. Everyone in the normal life ecology is redefining their balance between personal life and professional life. While managing the new remotely working environment, to improve work-life balance, many individuals are trying hard to improve their work-life balance notwithstanding the said challenges, it is well possible to stay positive and healthy. Many workplaces have suggested a few techniques, such as find new ways to exercise, set strict boundaries at home, stay socially connected, know when to unplug, find outlets for laughter, focus on mental health (Team, 2020), embrace flexibility, have a designated workspace, setting appropriate break time during the working hours, shutting down their computer at the end of working hours, and at last allowing yourself to enjoy the weekend (Randolph Matusky, 2020).

13.6   E-STRESS MANAGEMENT AND ITS CHALLENGES FOR HR PERSONNEL DURING PANDEMIC

Online stress management

The augmentation of technology has led to a fast-paced life where prompt indulgence is predominant and it is easier to get involved with family members, friends, and even strangers. Technology has brought several benefits which we pointed earlier, but along with that technology is also helping employees and management to understand the level of stress and its remedies to release the stress. Nowadays, many stress management consultancies and institutions (like www.e-stressmanagement.com, www.mylatherapy.com, www.webmd.com, and www.mayoclinic.com) playing pivotal role E-stress management during this pandemic. These agencies are offering many stress management courses/programs for a specified duration which helps to develop the required skills to deal with stress in such a way that supports your happiness.

These consultancies/institutions help individuals to meet their objective of reducing stress when working remotely through their expert-tailored exercises. This program emphasizes on making sure, how an individual understands about dealing with stress. Knowing the way, an individual can deal with particular stressors which can help them to develop particular skill so that it reduces the effect that stress.

The program offered by these consultancies/institutions includes offering information on various topics like stress tips, lore about stress, and how to get help from experts (psychologist). They also give specific tools by offering additional insight about stress symptoms. They use the particular quiz to understand individuals' acquaintance of illnesses and diseases that are related to stress, physical reaction toward the stress, and how particular physical activity can help them to manage their stress.

App-based stress management

To deal with stress in the technological edge, workplaces are also offering mobile app based stress management techniques. These apps are taking inputs from the employee/user to obtain stress responses based on a scanning mechanism. The app-based system operated by putting the index finger on phone's back camera (Siddhesh Keshkamat, Survey: Stress Management

Using Artificial Intelligence, 2016), and when flashlight of the phone turned on, based on the blood flow heartbeat intervals of an individual can be measured (Siddhesh Keshkamat, Survey: Stress Management Using Artificial Intelligence, 2016). After calculating blood pressure values, temperature values, this mechanism proves to be a valuable benefit for examining and enumerating responses related to the stress. These mobile-based apps will help the organization to generate more precise outputs for the stress responses of their employees. The more precise research is going on in this field to make stress management more simple and powerful.

Day-by-day, the use of AI is increasing in stress mapping, managing, and assisting employees to get relief from the stress. These days, case-based reasoning (CBR), which is a subfield of AI, is used. CBR focuses on how new practices and their proficiencies help the system to overcome the complications that were faced when dealing with stress in earlier circumstances (Siddhesh Keshkamat, Survey: Stress Management Using Artificial Intelligence, 2016). As everybody knows that past experiences have distinctive physiognomies to elaborate particular problems and can be presented in different ways. So to offer a solution to a new case; these previously studied cases can be represented using a problem and a solution structure. For the assessment of a present case, earlier one can contain its outcome. This system takes the measurement values for the physiological signals for computing the stress levels to categorized from highly stressed to deeply relaxed so that appropriate suggestions can be made to employees.

Challenges of E-Stress Management for HR Personnel during Pandemic

During this pandemic, cogently, workplaces are moved from offices to home. Prior to COVID outbreak, many people were working from office and did not had any experience working remotely and now they may not be comfortable with remote working. Primarily employees may have faced problems of network connectivity, lack of IT infrastructure, unavailability of PC/laptop, etc., so because of these technical issues, it was difficult for the employees and HR personnel to be in touch during pandemic. Anyhow, both had managed the situation but other aspects of managing stress are still missing because pandemic has fundamentally limit physical interaction. Even employees may not be putting the right data when asked for app-based stress evaluation.

13.7 APPLICATION OF NEW NORMAL IN THE WORK ENVIRONMENT

Everyone knows that COVID-19 disrupted the workplaces as employers, across the globe, forced their employees for working remotely to avoid the spread of novel coronavirus. As government is lifting up the lockdown gradually across geographies, a crucial challenge is also knocking the door of the workspace, that is, optimum productivity along with prime workplace safety. According to the report (Cristopher Wolf, 2020), 47% of professionals worldwide felt more productive when working remotely, whereas 76% prefer to avoid on-site work when they have to concentrate on a specific project. This gives a clear idea that pandemic has given us the opportunity to positively reengineer the culture of workplace. So instead of having traditional corporate culture now we may have *hybrid workplace/ flexible culture/Flexible and connected workplace* where employees are allowed to work remotely or from the office. Or in other words, only the required amount of employees will work from office and the rest will work remotely (Debolina Biswas, 2020). Under this, *New Normal* workplaces are turned into *Virtual Corporate Offices* where all meetings are now conducted using video conferencing through various platforms such as GoToMeeting, Airmeet and MeetFox, JioMeet, Zoom Meeting, Google meet, MS Teams Meeting, etc.

New normal has the opportunity of quick implementation of emergent technologies across the industries. Aggressive use of AI had benefitted virtual workplace by enlightening employees' productivity. Routine and monotonous work is automated with the use of AI, for instance, many voice process are now converted into *AI-powered chatbots*.

Key challenge in front of the workforce is to match the global job expectations. Because of the economic slowdown and aggressive use of advanced technology, the employment market became more competent. One most effective way is *upskilling and reskilling* of an individual because according to NASSCOM, 40% of domestic employees are required to be reskilled by 2022 (Debolina Biswas, 2020). Another possible way of meeting this challenge is talent optimization and employee retention where the required skill set of the employees to be advanced and engaging them with the new pool of recruits. Under this pandemic crisis, *health and safety* of the employees are key concerns of every workplace. Many organizations are asking their employees for regular check-ups by allocating specific financial provisions. This is the best step taken by many workplaces that have emotionally, physically, as well as financially supported their employees that gained the confidence and loyalty of employees.

13.8 POST-COVID STRESS MANAGEMENT CHALLENGES

The antiquity of the COVID-19 is still being written. When this pandemic ends, a *new normal* may last for a few months, years, or may be forever. For the next few years, wearing a mask, keeping social distance, avoiding social gatherings, preference for remote working, virtual meetings (even with friends, relatives), aggressive use of AI may be the most noticeable changes. Someone rightly said that "today's solutions are future's problems." Visors, masks, and facial protection will be integrated with the new working environment. Tea and coffee may get replaced with "immunity booster Kadha" and keeping sanitizers in the pocket may be the compulsory action for every employee working on the floor. On the other hand, these *new normal changes* with respect to technology will lead to create new challenges in the corporate world. When corporate will aggressively adopt AI-based technology for their routine work, it will reflect more in employee turnover. Those employees who will be associated with workplaces will always be under the stress of job insecurity. Though e-stress management is possible these days but in the future possibilities of *manipulation* of these practices are also expected. As it is also expected that workplaces may adapt more technological changes where employees may be asked to compromise the remuneration which in turn increases the possibility of getting less compensation.

13.9 CONCLUSION

The COVID-19 outbreak has drastically impacted from all sides where employer and employee both are struggling with unprecedented situations and much of it is related to the mental health of employees. Unfortunately, partial and inappropriate inflow of coronavirus-related information, isolation of an individual from society, sudden technological advancement, preference of remote working, aggressive use of AI, layoffs, pay-cut, extended working hours, economic recession, and a sense of helplessness are all adversely affecting people's mental well-being, creating stress, depression, anxiety, and many other mental health issues.

So to deal with the situation, corporates came with many business solutions to retain their employees' mental health. Such as, along with giving tips to the employees for adjusting to remote work, also educated their managers to imply best practices when dealing with employees working remotely, so that both will be better able to support their teams with quality performance. More precisely, both were advised to keep themselves engaged and emotionally healthy, also to maintain the standards for staying connected, retaining, and/or rebuilding healthy work culture of team, and focusing toward achieving long-term objectives of the company rather than short term output to avoid stress.

HR personnel has also planned accordingly to deal with employee stress management. They also started giving fitness allowances and remote working benefits for its employees (Mint, 2020). HR personnel are also tracking the employees' health with the help of technology and trying their best to keep employees work-life balanced. On the other hand, employees are also trying their best to cope up with the remote working challenges.

Under this chapter, author had tried to elaborate how workplaces were taking care of their employees for managing their balance in work-life and stress at work, what activities they planned during pandemic to keep their employees stress free, also what would be their plan with respect to NEW NORMAL on the current pandemic situation. As the pandemic is yet to over the future scope of the research is yet opened in many aspects such as employee behavior with respect to remote working, effects of new normal at workplaces, e-stress management, etc.

KEYWORDS

- stress management pyramid
- COVID-19
- stress in pandemic
- occupational stress
- E-stress management
- new normal

REFERENCES

Horch, A. J. *How to Manage Stress and Avoid Work Burnout during the Pandemic*, Aug 4, 2020 (CNBC, Ed., & CNBC). Retrieved October 6, 2020, from www.cnbc.com: https://

www.cnbc.com/2020/08/04/how-to-manage-stress-and-avoid-work-burnout-during-the-pandemic.html

Brown, A. *Positive Psychology*, Sept 01, 2020. Retrieved Sept 29, 2020, from https://positivepsychology.com/: https://positivepsychology.com/stress-management-techniques-tips-burn-out/

American Psychological Association. *How Leaders Can Maximize Trust and Minimize Stress During the COVID-19 Pandemic*, Mar 2020 (APA, Ed.). Retrieved Oct 08, 2020, from www.apa.org: https://www.apa.org/news/apa/2020/03/covid-19-leadership.pdf

Cristopher Wolf, I. S. *The New Normal Is... Reinventing Work Culture*, Oct 12, 2020 (Capgemini). Retrieved Dec 4, 2020, from www.capgemini.com: https://www.capgemini.com/2020/10/reinventing-work-culture/

Biswas, D. *The Future of Work in the New Normal: Hybrid, Flexible, More Productive*, Aug 5, 2020. Retrieved Dec 21, 2020, from www.yourstory.com/: https://yourstory.com/2020/08/workplace-future-new-normal-hybrid-coronavirus#:~:text=The%20'new%20normal'%20has%20brought,and%20upskilling%2C%20and%20rethink%20workspaces.&text=COVID%2D19%20disrupted%20the%20workplace%20as%20we%20knew%20it

Lee, D. J. *Fobes*, Oct 20, 2014 (Lee, D. J., Editor). Retrieved Nov 02, 2020, from https://www.forbes.com/: https://www.forbes.com/sites/deborahlee/2014/10/20/6-tips-for-better-work-life-balance/#6ab078b729ff

Bruce, D. F. *Exercise and Depression*, Feb 18, 2020 (Bhandari, S., Editor). Retrieved Nov 30, 2020, from www.webmd.com: https://www.webmd.com/depression/guide/exercise-depression#1

Stout, D. *Healthy Work Life Balance* (Stout, D., Ed.). Retrieved Nov 1, 2020, from www.linkedin.com: https://www.linkedin.com/pulse/healthy-work-life-balance-doris-stout?articleId=6265245626741637120

Sahni, J. Impact of COVID-19 on Employee Behavior: Stress and Coping Mechanism During WFH (Work From Home) Among Service Industry Employees. *Int. J. Operat. Manage.* Oct **2020**, *1* (1), 35–48. Retrieved Nov 30, 2020, from https://researchleap.com/impact-of-covid-19-on-employee-behavior-stress-and-coping-mechanism-during-wfh-work-from-home-among-service-industry-employees/

Scott, E. *Very Well Mind*, Apr 07, 2021 (Morin, L. A., Ed.). Retrieved Apr 16, 2021, from https://www.verywellmind.com/: https://www.verywellmind.com/the-stress-of-working-from-home-4141174

Salima, H. COVID-19 and Employees' Mental Health: Stressors, Moderators and Agenda for Organizational Actions. *Emerald Open Res.* Apr 20, 2020, 1–11. DOI: 10.35241/emeraldopenres.13550.1

Healthy Sleep. *Sleep and Mood. Division of Sleep Medicine at Harvard Medical School*, Dec 07, 2007. Retrieved Nov 30, 2020, from www.healthysleep.med.harvard.edu/: http://healthysleep.med.harvard.edu/healthy/getting/overcoming/tips

Robinson, J. *The 7 Signs of Burnout*, Apr 24, 2015. Retrieved Dec 03, 2020, from www.worktolive.info: https://www.worktolive.info/blog/bid/357306/the-7-signs-of-burnout

Kang, M. *People Matters*, Jun 29, 2020. Retrieved Nov 15, 2020, from www.peoplemattersglobal.com: https://www.peoplemattersglobal.com/article/employee-relations/covid-19-has-been-both-good-and-bad-for-work-life-balance-26159

Robinson, L. *Stress Management*, Oct 2019. (Robinson, L., Ed.) Retrieved Sept 29, 2020, from www.helpguide.org/: https://www.helpguide.org/articles/stress/stress-management.

htm#:~:text=Effective%20stress%20management%20helps%20you,and%20meet%20 challenges%20head%20on.
Lee, D. J. *6 Tips for Better Work-Life Balance*, 2015. Retrieved Sept 29, 2020, from www.forbes.com: https://www.forbes.com/sites/deborahlee/2014/10/20/6-tips-for-better-work-life-balance/#208018329ff5
Candela, L. *Stress: The Stress Response*, 2019. Retrieved Nov 30, 2020, from www.courses.lumenlearning.com: https://courses.lumenlearning.com/boundless-ap/chapter/stress/
Maxwell. *Work Life Balance and Stress Management*, (n.d.). Retrieved Oct 2, 2020, from https://www.maxwell.cz/: https://www.maxwell.cz/training-solutions/personal-effectiveness/work-life-balance-and-stress-management/
Greenberg, M. *6 Proven Ways to Recover from Stress*, Mar 31, 2016. (Greenberg, M., Ed.) Retrieved Oct 31, 2020, from /www.psychologytoday.com: https://www.psychologytoday.com/au/blog/the-mindful-self-express/201603/6-proven-ways-recover-stress
Mint. *Kotak Mahindra Bank Introduces Fitness Allowance for Employees*, Dec 8, 2020. Retrieved Dec 11, 2020, from www.livemint.com: https://www.livemint.com/industry/banking/kotak-mahindra-bank-introduces-fitness-allowance-for-employees-11607411033976.html
Mohammed, M. K. Modeling Mental Stress Using a Deep Learning Framework. *IEEE Access* **2019**, *1*. DOI: 10.1109/ACCESS.2019.2917718
Pattnaik, L. *Effect of Workplace Stress: A Study in Indian Context*. Sambalpur University, Dept of Business Administration; The international Seminar: Sambhalpur, 2018. Retrieved Nov 15, 2020, from https://www.pdffiller.com/jsfiller-desk10/?projectId=6101793ca104095621366c62&lp=true#f543d9b4e3584dcb94bb14864eab33e8
Cole, N. *The 5 Stages of Stress (It's Important to Know Which One You're In)*, Apr 22, 2018. Retrieved Nov 30, 2020, from www.artplusmarketing.com: https://artplusmarketing.com/the-5-stages-of-stress-its-important-to-know-which-one-you-re-in-28f16e9f1950
Nicholas Bloom, A. G. *Standfoard News*, Mar 30, 2020. Retrieved Nov 10, 2020, from news.stanford.edu: https://news.stanford.edu/2020/03/30/productivity-pitfalls-working-home-age-covid-19/
NICK. *USQ Social Hub*, Oct 28, 2019. Retrieved Dec 11, 2020, from www.social.usq.edu.au: https://social.usq.edu.au/wellbeing/articles/5-stages-of-stress-article#:~:text=In%20fact%2C%20it%20has%20five,recovery%2C%20adaptation%2C%20and%20burnout.
Bobade, P. M. V. Stress Detection with Machine Learning and Deep Learning Using Multimodal Physiological Data. In *Second International Conference on Inventive Research in Computing Applications (ICIRCA)*; IEEE, Ed., Vol. 1; IEEE: Coimbatore, India, 2020; pp 51–57. DOI: 10.1109/ICIRCA48905.2020.9183244
QLG. *Queensland Government*, Nov 22, 2013. Retrieved July 15, 2021, from https://www.qld.gov.au/: https://www.qld.gov.au/health/mental-health/lifestyle
Matusky, R. *Association for Talent Development*, Apr 14, 2020. Retrieved Dec 1, 2020, from www.td.org: https://www.td.org/user/content/randolphmatusky/finding-a-work-life-balance-during-a-pandemic-04-14-20-12-46
Repici, A.; M. R. Coronavirus (COVID-19) Outbreak: What the Department of Endoscopy Should Know. *Gastrointest Endosc.* **2020**, 192–197.
Scott, E. *How to Handle the Stress of Working from Home*, Mar 17, 2020. Retrieved October 6, 2020, from www.verywellmind.com: https://www.verywellmind.com/the-stress-of-working-from-home-4141174
Siang Yong Tan, A. Y. Hans Selye (1907–1982): Founder of the Stress Theory. *Singapore Med. J.* Apr **2018**, *59* (4), 170–171. DOI: 10.11622/smedj.2018043

Siddhesh Keshkamat, S. K. Survey: Stress Management Using Artificial Intelligence. *Int. Adv. Res. J. Sci. Eng. Technol.* **2016**, *3* (3), 18–19. DOI: 10.17148/IARJSET.2016.3304

Sahoo, S. R. Management of Stress at Workplace. *Global J. Manage. Busi. Res.: Admin. Manage.* **2016**, *16* (6), 1–9. Retrieved Dec 1, 2020, from https://globaljournals.org/GJMBR_Volume16/1-Management-of-Stress-at-Workplace.pdf

Soetikno, R.; T. A. Considerations in Performing Endoscopy during the COVID-19 Pandemic. *Gastrointest Endosc.* **2020**, 176–183.

Staff Writer, C. B. *HR Technologists*, Nov 15, 2019. Retrieved Oct 30, 2020, from www.hrtechnologist.com: https://www.hrtechnologist.com/articles/culture/can-ai-help-with-workplace-stress-management/

Stress Less. *How to Prepare Yourself for Potentially Stressful Situations*, 2015. Retrieved Nov 19, 2020, from www.stresslessworkshops.com: https://stresslessworkshops.com/how-to-prepare-yourself-for-potentially-stressful-situations/

Paul, S. Stress Management: What Can You Do? *St. Louis Psychologists and Counseling Information and Referral*, Jan 24, 2013. Retrieved Nov 15, 2020.

Team, G. P. *Georgetown*, Sept 23, 2020. Retrieved Nov 20, 2020, from https://georgetownpsychology.com/: https://georgetownpsychology.com/2020/09/how-to-manage-work-life-balance-during-the-pandemic/

Tekeste, N. N. *A Qualitative Study on the Causes of Stress and Management Mechanisms at Volvo Trucks AB, Umeå*; Umeå: Umeå School of Business and Economics, 2013. Retrieved from http://www.diva-portal.org/smash/get/diva2:693132/FULLTEXT01.pdf

UKEssays. *Introduction to Stress Management*, Aug 1, 2018. Retrieved Sept 25, 2020, from https://www.ukessays.com/: https://www.ukessays.com/essays/management/introduction-to-stress-management.php

Warn, F. K. Workplace Dimensions, Stress and Job Satisfaction. *J. Manager. Psychol.* **2003**, 8–21.

WHO. Retrieved Nov 5, 2020, from www.who.int: https://www.who.int/teams/mental-health-and-substance-use/covid-19

WHO. *Occupational Health: Stress at the Workplace*, 2020, Oct 19 (W. TEAM, Ed.). Retrieved Nov 10, 2020, from www.who.int: https://www.who.int/news-room/q-a-detail/ccupational-health-stress-at-the-workplace

Work/Life Balance and Stress Management. Nov 22, 2013. Retrieved Oct 02, 2020, from https://www.qld.gov.au/: https://www.qld.gov.au/health/mental-health/lifestyle#:~:text=Work%2Dlife%20balance%20is%20adjusting,greater%20focus%20and%20concentration

Diggers, Y. *The Fight or Flight Response: Our Body's Response to Stress*; Feb 2010. Retrieved Nov 30, 2020, from https://youngdiggers.com.au/: https://youngdiggers.com.au/sites/default/files/Fight%20or%20flight%20response.pdf

CHAPTER 14

Self-Development among College Teachers during a Pandemic: A Qualitative Study with Reference to West Bengal, India

RITUPARNA BASAK[1*] and SENJUTI BANDYOPADHYAY[2]

[1]Muralidhar Girls' College, Kolkata, India

[2]Mrinalini Datta Mahavidyapith, Kolkata, India

*Corresponding author. E-mail: rtprnb@gmail.com

ABSTRACT

The present unprecedented scenario caused by the Novel Corona Virus pandemic has hard hit the education sector. From the end of March to till date, the educational institutions are shut down, causing the students, teachers, and the administration to adopt new strategies to survive in this changing situation.

The present study aims to understand how the college teachers are evolving themselves in this demanding environment. Qualitative analysis of semistructured interviews, taken from 40 undergraduate college teachers from different colleges of West Bengal, was done for this purpose.

The analysis suggests that all the teachers have acquired new technological knowledge, though mostly for professional purposes. Initiating a personal YouTube channel or blog is also observed. The previous exposure and knowledge of technology have worked as a major contributing factor to the perception of skill enhancement.

Human Resource Management in a Post-Epidemic Global Environment: Roles, Strategies, and Implementations.
Tanusree Chakraborty, Nandita Mishra, Madhurima Ganguly, & Bipasha Chatterjee (Eds.)
© 2023 Apple Academic Press, Inc. Co-published with CRC Press (Taylor & Francis)

For professional upgradation, all teachers have participated in various web-based activities, like Webinars, Workshops, etc., and few of them have started new research projects also.

For personal development, most teachers have mentioned that their additional time is devoted to their preferred activity, which ranges from book reading to watching web series. A significant number of teachers have resumed their long-lost hobby in this homebound time.

An interesting finding was that female teachers have participated in more professional activities than personal ones, as they perceived time constraints mostly due to familial responsibilities.

14.1 INTRODUCTION

In the present scenario, the pandemic and lockdown due to the Novel Corona virus have greatly impacted the whole world. This virus caused a complete change in all the levels whether physical or psychological, in all the sectors like social, economic, educational, or environmental. These changes had either some positive outcome like family members got the chance to spend more time together or affected in a negative way like Indian economic growth has seen negative figures after more than two decades. The whole education system was on sudden brake from the second week of March, 2020 because of the complete shutdown of the schools and colleges as a preventive measure for containing the spread of Covid-19. The Chief Minister of West Bengal on March 22 announced a complete lockdown in West Bengal to impose a complete safety from the spreading of Covid-19. The Prime Minister of India announced a nationwide lockdown on March 24 (The Hindu Net Desk, 25 March 2020). This unprecedented situation has suddenly raised multiple questions for education globally (Kidd and Murray, 2020) and pushed the educators to reinvent themselves to reshape the mechanisms of whole system for imparting lessons.

Across the world, there is a trend of remodeling the education system to ensure that the students from all areas including last corner of the country get the proper education during this pandemic situation. However, the shifting from a physical classroom to a virtual classroom was unexpected and rapid due to Covid-19 and it confronted the educators and the students a great challenge for which both the groups required skills, knowledge, tools, and technology to run this virtual teaching–learning process smoothly. This transitioning phase from offline to online mode suddenly imposed the importance on some impertinent issues. From the professional perspectives like use of internet whether on computer or mobile phone, application of different online educational apps, and use of mobile for other than calling, were rapidly increased for smooth running of the system in online mode. The use of ICT (information and communication technology) was very limited before the pandemic, which suddenly received the prime importance during this Covid-19 period. From the personal ground, teachers started utilizing the time with their preferred activity ranging from book reading to web series watching. Many started resuming long-lost hobby in this homebound time.

The Government of India with the Chief Ministers of the states declared the lockdown throughout the country as a logical solution to enforce the social distancing among the people. In the educational field, the sudden shut down of institutions brought the disruption in the academic progress of the students. To think for the betterment of the students, the Ministry of Human Resource Development (MHRD) in their press release (March 21, 2020) shared various free digital e-learning platforms like National Programme on Technology Enhanced Learning, Study Web for Active Young Expiring Minds (SWAYAM), e-Pathshala, DIKSHA portal, SWAYAM Prabha, National Repository of Open Educational, etc. to run the system continuously during this lockdown period (MHRD, 2020a). The ministry also issued an advisory for educational institutions to continue teaching through online mode and requested teachers to teach from home. The traditional teaching method was suddenly changed to the educational technology method due to Covid-19, where teachers and students were exposed to new innovative educational methodologies (Joshi et al., 2020). This transformation of the classroom provided teaching, learning, debate, discussion, quiz, and evaluation to that online platform and made the learning equitable, convenient, lifelong, and accessible (Gupta and Gupta, 25 September 2020).

In West Bengal, before lockdown most of the college teachers were not very expert and trained in online teaching–learning system as it was not mandatory for teaching. Covid-19 pandemic compelled the teachers to develop themselves to adapt with the demanding situation and to learn and use technology in the digital platform for the successful accomplishment of online teaching and learning. Initially, they faced lots of challenges like unavailability of advanced technological system like laptop or desktop, unlimited internet connection, suitable video and audio system for giving lectures, or taking assignments through online mode. They mostly had to deal with the technological problems by themselves as there was no one who could directly help them with these technical issues during the online classes time or assignment time. However, the teachers had to accept these challenges with no other choice in hand, and eventually they had learned and perfected the art of innovative impartation of knowledge through online mode.

Gradually, teachers have grasped the system by developing themselves with skills and technologies and have built the rapport with the students in the online world and are giving service to the nation ceaselessly. Now teachers give lectures online and upload the study materials and the lecture videos both in English and regional languages to the online portal for the continuous availability of the resources for the students. The educators have also developed the online assignment and evaluation procedures especially for the college students to ensure their academic progress without any year loss. They have started to develop their own online portal for uploading the e-contents for the benefit of the students so that the students can access the materials with their own pace of time.

Apart from the professional struggles, the sudden lockdown has posed a great deal of challenges in personal domain too. The abrupt halt though initially caused a lot of uncertainty but later was eventually adjusted with and utilized by the educators in their own preferred ways. The unforeseen condition has altered the regular schedule of life leaving some spare time in hand, which was utilized by the educators to explore and exercise activities of their choice that contributed to their personal development and wellness. This study also tried to understand the efforts of teachers in practical and effective use of the spare time available due to homebound lockdown.

Studies showed the major challenges faced by the teachers during amid this lockdown phase to resume this teaching–learning system in digital platform (Arora and Srinivasan, 2020). Therefore, it is very important to study that during this pandemic situation how teachers' competence and various opportunities contributed to teachers' self-development and mastery during this specific situation. This study focused on the opportunities teachers have taken to upgrade themselves during this evolving pandemic situation.

The key highlights of the chapter are, the unforeseen health emergency caused by novel corona virus or Covid-19, affected most of the nations across the globe by March 2020, resulting in temporary shutting down of most organizations including educational institutions, to contain the spread of the disease. As per the need of the moment, the knowledge sector shifted from the physical to the virtual world with much preparation. Following the decision of lockdown, the teaching fraternity faced difficulty in adapting with the increasing demand of this transformation, from enhancing skills to fulfill the professional duty to managing personal demand. This chapter tries to address the issues faced by the college teachers of West Bengal to give the readers better understanding of the impact of the pandemic on the lives of teachers.

14.2 LITERATURE REVIEW

March 2020 was a great landmark in the history of humanity, which changed the whole world from a physical world to a digital world. In the educational field, teachers faced a significant challenge to adapt to online teaching during this Covid-19 pandemic situation. Before March 2020, the typical teaching environment of educational institutions was characterized by students forgathered in classroom following the timetables for listening the lectures and teachers came to teach their respective course contents through formal lecturing (König et al., 2020a, 2020b). Teachers were used to chalk-and-talk method and students were used to follow them teaching on the board. At a particular time period, students were asked to give their assignment or do projects either individually or in group and teachers were appointed to evaluate those works. The use of technology was very limited to some particular subjects and students and teachers from other background were least familiar to the ICT system. The lockdown compelled the teachers, students, and parents to encounter an unprecedented situation where online mode is the only possible way for teaching and learning. Teachers had to adapt online teaching, enabling them to use different tools and techniques for solving various online problems related to teaching–learning system (Eickelmann and Gerick, 2020).

Digitalization in educational institutions especially in colleges was started before the Covid-19 pandemic situation in a limited way. For conducting quality online courses in no time, supports and financial helps were received from many institutions (Taylor, 2002). The ICT was restricted in a limited subjects and situations depending upon the course curriculum. Teachers of those particular subjects were specialized in ICT and used to apply it in teaching and students of those subjects got the opportunities to use the digital tools and resources for their learning. Studies reported different factors like lack of time, ICT competence, lack of technical skills, and less computer knowledge are the causal factors for the rigidity toward accepting online teaching for some faculties (Prottas et al., 2016; Keengwe et al., 2008; Chen, 2010; Yuen and Ma, 2008). Many research studies encouraged the importance and emergence of ICT in the educational system to cope with the digital opulence all over the world (Kozma, 2011). Research showed that new opportunities can be open in teaching and learning through digital resources and indicated the effectiveness of technology for different subjects (Chauhan, 2017). ICT that had restricted accessibility to limited people suddenly become user friendly and open to all due to this pandemic situation. Therefore, it is significant to notice the principles and guidelines followed for successful implementation of teaching and learning in digital classroom and teachers' competencies bridged the gap between the physical and digital system with the help of technology.

During the Covid-19 pandemic situation, an urgent need of digitalization emerged, especially in higher education both students and teachers were required to adept the digital tools and resources for keeping the education system active and progressive. Research stated that new online teaching is rearranging the students learning with adaptation and management of the whole practice (Moorhouse, 2020). Teachers have learnt and adapted themselves with the digital competence to integrate the technology with the pedagogy (Baker et al., 2018). Kaup et al. (2020) studied the challenges related to technology, training, and student involvement for continuing academic in this lockdown period. Another research studied the complicacies of teachers of many institutions who do not even have sufficient infrastructure to conduct online classes (Verma et al., 2020). They also instructed old-aged teachers who are technologically challenged to take classes online (Sharma, 2020). During this sudden challenging time of pandemic, the college teachers have evolved drastically from knowing merely subject knowledge to coherent understanding and application of technologies to the teaching and learning both in professional and personal level.

Self-development of teachers is closely connected with the opportunities they have exposed during this lockdown period both in quality and quantity and the application of those opportunities in the right place. It is also significant matter to notice how the teachers utilized their knowledge, skills both academic and technological for professional and personal development. Teachers who used to get less time for their own learning related to researches have started resuming that habit. The lectures given through online mode was a great challenge for the teachers to involve the whole class in teaching–learning interactive sessions and also enabling students to access learning contents from home. The provision of different assignments through online offered a means to reach all students during this lockdown phase for attending education (König et al., 2020a, 2020b). In response to the challenge caused by Covid-19, teachers extended their knowledge capacity by incorporating technology in teaching–learning system to bring the whole class in the virtual classroom. It is for sure that without the endeavors and involvement of teachers this new online teaching system would not be possible.

With the rapid growth of online teaching during this unprecedented pandemic situation, there is a significant rise of researches studying the impact of various aspects of online teaching on the education system. It is necessary to study how much teachers have succeeded in encountering the challenges they faced with the emergence of Covid-19 pandemic situation. In a study in Los Angeles, it is found that teachers informed their lack of skills for online teaching and lack of time for content preparation showing their resistance to change to a new system (Gratz and Looney, 2020). Different other issues related to online teaching like internet network, lack of skills and training, lack of interaction, etc. were mentioned in the research study by Arora and Srinivasan (2020). Joshi et al. (2020) found that in India teachers who got technical support and proper direction from the institutions faced no problem in online teaching, whereas teachers belonging to the institutions who did not have any licensed teaching did not get much support from the institutions. Teachers faced problems teaching some specific courses like numerical, practical online while in physical classroom they interact with the students face to face where language is the prime way of communication for teaching and learning.

14.3 METHODOLOGY

The focus of the present qualitative research is specifically on the competence and development of teachers who faced multiple challenges arising from the college and university shutdowns. Tradition teaching in colleges was completely dismissed and a new forms of system emerged. This study was conducted to see how teachers transformed that unprecedented situation to an active and useful one where they utilized the skills and technology for their overall progression. This involved the challenges of remodeling the teaching competencies, which was implemented in a novel way with the integration between teachers' cognition and technology. This study threw light upon the various activities practiced by the teachers to upgrade them both professionally and personally.

Research Question: How college teachers are keeping themselves updated, both professionally and personally, during this homebound Pandemic situation?

Interpretative Phenomenological Analysis (IPA): In the present study, IPA has been used to explore and understand the experiences of 40 college teachers and their perception of progression during this lockdown. IPA was first proposed by Jonathan Smith, it emphasizes on convergence and divergence of experiences, as well as it involves a detailed examination of the participant's life experiences; it attempts to explore personal experience and is concerned with an individual's personal perception or account of an object or event, as opposed to an attempt to produce an objective statement of the object or event itself (Smith and Osborn, 2003).

Another distinctive feature of IPA is the concept of "double hermeneutic." Smith and Osborn (2003) used the term "double hermeneutic" to emphasize the two layers of interpretation that are involved in IPA.

- Participant's meaning making (interpreting their own experience),
- Researcher's sense making (interpreting the participant's account) (Smith et al., 2009).

Thus there is an inevitable circularity in the process involving questioning, uncovering meaning, and further questioning; this circular process of understanding a phenomenon is called the "hermeneutic circle" (Smith et al., 2009).

Sample

The study was conducted among the teachers working in the government and private under graduation colleges of West Bengal, India. To ensure appropriate representation teachers from different age groups and varied subject background were taken for the study. Telephonic interview was conducted with 40 teachers who has shown interest and has given their consent for participation in the study. The study population had 19 male and 21 female teachers with an age range of 30–58 years. All the participants were teaching for at least 3 years and were conducting online classes during the course of the study. Academically two participants had postdoctorate degree, 21 participants held doctorate degree, 12 were pursuing their doctoral research during the course of study, and 5 teachers were postgraduates. Out of 40 participants 9 were teaching in private colleges and 31 were associated with government colleges.

Procedure

Semistructured in-depth interviews were conducted to collect data from the teachers to gather information regarding their different activities and pursuits during the lockdown. The questions were open ended in nature, giving the interviewer the freedom to probe for details. The semistructured questions were verified by five experts for assessing reliability and validity and the modifications were incorporated as per the suggestions. The revised final set of questions was given to five others experts to confirm the construct validity.

Interviews were conducted through telephonic medium and were recorded in the form of audio clips. All conversations were then transcribed and thoroughly read and coded autonomously by both the researchers.

Terminologies that provided insight about the themes were marked and then similar themes were clustered to get higher order arguments. To confirm the transparency and accuracy of the analysis process, Ryan and Bernard (2000) cutting and sorting techniques were used. In this process codes or themes with an internal consistency of 86% were accepted. Only those themes were sustained where mutual agreement was received from both the researchers.

14.4 FINDINGS

The IPA of interviews taken from undergraduate college teachers of West Bengal has revealed the following aspects of their "lived experience" in the difficult time of the pandemic. For better understanding of their strategies and challenges in successfully adapting in this situation, the findings of the study are presented in 4 themes, which were obtained from clustering the rudimentary themes that emerged from the analysis.

14.5 ACQUIRING NEW TECHNOLOGICAL SKILLS

"Change is constant. Embrace, adapt, and learn. It is must for growth and success."

As soon as lockdown was announced, educational institutes were closed to contain the spreading of the infectious disease. Following that many educational institutions started online teaching to ensure the continuation of learning. Because of this situational demand, all teachers had to learn or increase their technological expertise, especially in different online teaching platforms like Zoom, Google Meet, Google Classroom, Teamlink, etc. In addition, working knowledge of different file sharing and file storage mediums like Google Drive, Google Cloud, etc. was also demanded to ensure smooth delivery of study materials to the students. The factors that influenced this learning process were Prior Exposure and Learning of Technologies, Availability of Technical Support, and Perception of future prospect:

i) **Prior Exposure and Learning of Technology**—In the present technology dependant time, all teachers had basic understanding of gadgets and applications, but what was evident from the present study is that the level of prior knowledge has impacted the learning and perception of learning of new technologies. Teachers, who have stated that they had moderate to good command on technologies before the lockdown struck, informed that during this time their learning was primarily limited to certain online teaching and assessment applications. Whereas teachers with limited prior exposure to technologies and gadgets have expressed that their proficiency has increase in a notable way. They were previously unaware of various online faculties, which they have learned to operate and have utilized for their professional and personal needs. The perception of increased mastery was quite evident for this group of teachers.

ii) **Availability of Technical Support**—The unprecedented situation has posed a great challenge in front of the institutions, teachers as well as the whole educational system. In the initial days after lockdown, efforts were devoted to chalk out certain ways in which learning can be extended to maximum number of student within limited resources in hand, and online classes using certain video calling applications and certain software for assessments emerged as a feasible solution. Prior to this online classes or meetings were conducted in a very few organizations, which eventually became integral to delivery of learning, and this has demanded collective endeavor.

As found in the present study, teachers who have received certain amount of institutional guidance such as technical assistance, real-time address of technical problems faced by teachers or had received direct technical support from family members (especially spouse or children) or colleagues, have stated that the adjustment to the "new normal" was "manageable." Whereas teachers who had to work out the technical issues almost alone have expressed the process of adaptation as "chaotic," "frustrating," and "worrisome."

iii) **Perception of Future Prospect**—An interesting observation was that the comprehension of relevance of online teaching and Internet-based activities in future academic progress has played an important role in broadening the learning activities in teachers. Those who have felt that different online courses or applications currently used will have much importance for their academic aspirations have expanded their acquirement of technological knowledge to fields beyond their immediate necessity, such as "learning new programming language" (Participants 3, 11, 29, 31), "Artificial Intelligence" (Participant 36, 37).

In this context, it was observed that teachers with more than 30 years of teaching experience in conversational method and with few years left in their service have shown rigid attitude toward learning new technologies. They were more convinced with the limitations of online teaching methods, for which their technological learning was restricted to only those platforms that were suggested by their institutes and were serving the basic requirements of teaching and checking assessments.

14.6 ENHANCING KNOWLEDGE BASE

"Teaching requires continuous evolution." As everything that happens around are not just the matters of observation but also they eclectically accumulate our learning sources. A teacher thus requires continuous upgradation of their knowledge, both horizontally and vertically, to enhance and enrich understanding of their surrounding as well as their own subject matter, which in turn influences their students' learning.

It was evident from the analysis that during the lockdown all participant teachers have utilized their available time and resources in various ways for their academic as well as professional progress.

i) **Attending Different Web-Based Programs**—All 40 participants of the present study have attended different Webinars, Workshops, and Faculty Development Programs according to their need and interest, from institutes around the globe, for the purpose of self-development as well as the betterment of their presentation of knowledge. As in this era of digitization, these programs were available from one's home without any actual need for transport, which made it easier for the educators to participate in numerous web-based initiatives without hampering their schedule. For this reason, all participants have stated that during this lockdown they have attended more number of such programs than they did in the last academic year.

ii) **Conducting Different Web-Based Programs**
"Knowledge is the only treasure that increases on sharing"
In the study, 33% of the participants have conducted different sessions in webinars or workshops in their field of expertise to ensure that their knowledge reaches beyond their regular students. When asked about these experiences, they have mentioned that these activities not just contribute to their professional advancement but also to their personal growth, as in preparing and delivering these special programs they have often chosen subjects, which are "otherwise not included in the syllabus" (Participant 12) or "often

not elaborated in the curriculum followed but are equally relevant" (Participant 23) or "are of practical value" (Participants 2, 37).

Here, a significant observation was noticed that teachers of private institutions were engaged in conducting webinars, workshops more in number and with longer duration of time while the teachers from government institutions the number and the duration of these programmes were comparatively short.

iii) **Broadening One's Perspective**—An interesting observation in the study was that 25% of the participants have enrolled themselves in at least one online certificate course from web-based platform, which is totally based on their own interest and is not reinforced by any professional valuation system. Among them, 10% of the educators have even enrolled themselves in courses that are not from their own subject matters. Further investigation has revealed that increased awareness of courses available and additional time in hand during homebound lockdown has given the educators a chance to "explore interests" and to expand their perspectives.

iv) **Engagement in Research Activities**—Research is an integral part of higher education system and the desire to find answers to unknown is what greatly motivates teachers to excel and expand their academic prowess. During the lockdown, such initiatives were observed in the participants. 33% of the educators stated that they have written and submitted papers for upcoming publications, whereas 30% of the participants, who are presently pursuing their doctoral research, mentioned that they have devoted additional time to progress the completion of their research work as well as documentation. Interestingly, 15% of the teachers have started conducting new investigations during this lockdown period owing to the corresponding changes of the pandemic.

14.7 ENGAGING IN PREFERRED ACTIVITIES

"Personal development is the belief that you are worth the effort, time, and energy needed to develop yourself."

Initially, after declaration of lockdown, the whole education system in India was temporarily halted. Activities resumed after few weeks, giving little warm-up time to different stake holders to face the upcoming challenges. On the other side, this unprecedented situation automatically generated immense stress, uncertainties, and anxiety in most of the people including educators, and these reactions were required to be addressed and managed. Also being homebound saved people some traveling time, giving them chance to explore and engage in things that were otherwise left aside. What was evident from the study is that all participants said to have utilized additional times according to their preferences, which has eventually contributed in their personal development and wellbeing.

i) **Recreational Activities**

Individual proclivity has determined their choice of recreational activity. In this study 48% of the participants have said that their book reading habit has increased in this time, various newspaper reports also has affirmed that the lockdown brings back the love for reading (Martin, 21 July, 2020).

"I have almost completed my long pending wish list." (Participant 17)

Here, 25% of the participants have informed that they have purchased new books in this period. An interesting trend was observed that out of this book-loving group of educators, almost 50% of have either shifted to or simultaneously using digital medium for reading and purchasing books.

Over-the-Top platforms have also emerged as another common choice among educators where 63% has stated that they are using at least one such platform for entertainment purpose and 28% of the participants have started using or have subscribed to at least one OTT platform for the first time during this lockdown. The study suggests that educators have preferred to watch different online shows in their leisure time.

ii) **Resuming an Old Hobby or Discovering New Ones**

Another striking observation was that 40% of the participants have stated that in the spare time they have restarted exploring and nurturing some old hobbies, which were previously abandoned due to time constrain. Singing, painting, dancing, and creative writing emerged as the most commonly mentioned hobbies that were resumed during this time by the participants.

In the study, 13% of the participants have also mentioned that they have started new pastime activity in their leisure time. YouTube has been mentioned by all of them as the reference point for instructions and ideas. Cooking, Gardening, and Crafting were the most frequent choices of new hobbies among the participants.

iii) **Familial Responsibilities**
A salient feature that was quite prevalent in the study was the perception of additional familial responsibilities by female candidates. When probed, it was revealed that, as in the lockdown period most of them had no additional domestic help as a result the burden of household chores increased, leading to a feeling of shortage of time available for personal and professional growth. For male participants, although being more active in household errands was mentioned, but no such feeling of constrain was stated by them.

14.8 INNOVATIVE APPLICATION

"Innovation is the ability to see change as an opportunity, not as a threat"

Difficult times demand innovative solutions and as it is evident from the study that teachers have presented some novel ways to deal with the challenged in hand.

i) **Creative use of study materials**—Creative use of internet and computer applications for the purpose of better delivery of learning material especially practical curriculum has been mentioned by the participants. For lab-based subjects, 13% of the teachers have planned and converted the curriculum to more feasible assignments. One participant has mentioned about using animated materials to ensure better grasp of concepts for the students.

ii) **New online enterprise**—Alternatively, 10% of the participants have created new YouTube channel and related website for anytime availability of lectures and notes for students beyond their classrooms. They have elucidated that this initiative has potential for their future growth as they are being able to get recognition from a larger number of viewers, which may "eventually open better doors of opportunities."

iii) **Online Whiteboard**—Here, 12% of the teachers mentioned about some new innovative techniques they have adopted for their online teaching during this lockdown period. Digital whiteboard is one of those innovations that teachers would use for writing anything, doing mathematics, statistics, drawing, painting everything for making the class more interactive, enjoyable, and interesting and made the students more engaged and attentive in the class. They have installed different whiteboard or blackboard apps in mobile and software in laptop or desktop to make the class more lively, which became actually very beneficial for both the teachers and the students. So the teachers actually transformed the traditional chalk-and-talk method into the digital chalk-and-talk system.

iv) **Evaluation process**—The teachers had to change the evaluation processes from the physical to digital medium during this lockdown phase. They used to evaluate the exam scripts physically before lockdown, which was common and came under official rules and regulations. After lockdown, to maintain the social distance and to be safe from the transmission of the virus they were compelled to change the system and evaluate the exam scripts through online mode. They learnt different techniques for checking the copies in document, image through different software like PDF, Acrobat reader, etc. to win this serious challenge. Apart from the conventional paper-pencil method of assessment, teachers came up with other ways of evaluation, which also required more active participation from the students, for instance online presentation of given topic, poster competition, and online quiz were few of them mentioned by the teachers.

14.9 CONCLUSION

The outbreak of Covid-19 stands the world in front of a great challenge since World War II. Every sector around the world is badly affected by this pandemic situation. The study showed how the teachers upgraded themselves both for professional and personal development during this unprecedented situation.

In the professional field, the educators across the country have acquired new technological skills to run the teaching–learning process smoothly have enrolled in a number of courses, webinars, workshops to equip with this digitalization and to provide the best facilities and resources to the students. They transformed the traditional classroom to the digital platform for the betterment of the system taking references from different online sources like YouTube, various websites for teaching as well as for other personal growth in professional field like developing own music YouTube channel, blog writing, and personal website.

In personal level, they started resuming their long-lost hobbies like singing, painting, and dancing, and discovered new interests like blog writing, developing new habits like cooking, gardening, etc. during this pandemic period.

In research field, many of the teachers conducted webinars, online research surveys, and started writing research papers or book chapters to increase their academic or research excellence. During the normal time, teachers used to get less time for their own and family, which were compensated during this time period.

According to the National Education Policy (NEP)-2020 proposed by The MHRD, Government of India online teaching and learning is given importance for the enhancement in near future and a budget is also allotted for different online technologies like LMS, Moodle, Google Suite, MOOC, and so on. In the NEP-2020, an emphasis is given for the promotion of advanced teaching–learning system through upgraded and advanced technologies like artificial intelligence, big data, 3D printing, and robotics (MHRD, 2020b).

This study was conducted during the initial months of the lockdown, as the colleges are yet to reopen; one concern that prevails is that whether in the following days materialization of opportunities would continue in same pace and fervor. Another scope of further investigation lies in observing how the school teachers who are dealing with younger student population, especially elementary school teachers, are confronting the professional challenges posed by the transformation of educational sector.

This pandemic situation taught us that change is evitable and has to be accepted with the time and situation. The abrupt transformation from traditionalism to digitalism in education sector has only been possible because of this catalyst called Covid-19. This new digitalization in education system is more optimist and best solution for the progress of the future citizens of the country, where teachers play an essential role.

14.10 SUMMARY

The article highlighted the challenges faced by college teachers of West Bengal and shed light on the ways they are utilizing this lockdown period for self-development, in both personal and professional sphere.

Interviews conducted on 40 college teachers of West Bengal and following IPA revealed their "lived experience" in the period of lockdown and virtual delivery of education.

Firstly, increased exposure to ICT has resulted in better learning and perceived expertise of different technological tools. Certain factors such as prior knowledge, external technical support, and perceived future prospect influenced the skill acquiring process of the teachers.

Secondly, the teachers broadened and enriched their knowledge base by attending as well as conducting web-based programs, enrolling in online certificate courses, and devoting more time in research activities.

Thirdly, participants revealed that the additional time in home is utilized in preferred recreational activities, nurturing hobbies, and assuming familial responsibilities.

Fourthly, the critical situation demanded some innovative initiatives, such as creative virtual delivery of learning materials, ingenious utilization of online platforms and resources, which were observed in the investigation

The sudden transition of education delivery system from physical medium to virtual one seems like a moderating phase toward a proximate era of digitization of education.

KEYWORDS

- **self-development**
- **college teachers**
- **technological skill**
- **professional up gradation**

REFERENCES

Arora, A.K.; Srinivasan, R. Impact of Pandemic COVID-19 on the Teaching-Learning Process: A Study of Higher Education Teachers. *Prabandhan: Indian J. Manage.* **2020,** *13* (4), 43–56.

Baker, J. P.; Goodboy, A. K.; Bowman, N. D.; Wright, A. A. Does Teaching with PowerPoint Increase Students' Learning? A Meta-analysis. *Comput. Educ.* **2018,** *126,* 376–387. DOI: 10.1016/j.compedu.2018.08.003.

Chauhan, S. (2017). A Meta-analysis of the Impact of Technology on Learning Effectiveness of Elementary Students. *Comput. Educ.* **2017,** *105,* 14–30. DOI: 10.1016/j.compedu.2016.11.005

Chen, R. J. Investigating Models for Preservice Teachers' Use of Technology to Support Student-Centered Learning. *Comput. Educ.* **2010,** *55* (1), 32–42.

Eickelmann, B.; Gerick, J. Learning with Digital Media: Objectives in Times of Corona and under Special Consideration of Social Inequities. *Die Deutsche Schule* **2020,** *16,* 153–162. DOI: 10.31244/9783830992318.09

Gratz, E.; Looney, L. Faculty Resistance to Change: An Examination of Motivators and Barriers to Teaching Online in Higher Education. *Int. J. Online Pedagogy Course Design (Design)* **2020,** *10* (1), 1–14.

Gupta, A.; Gupta, V. Reshaping Learning. *The Hindu*, Sept 25, 2020. https://www.thehindu.com/education/how-the-pandemic-has-changed-some-elements-of-teaching-learning-permanently/article32694224.ece

Joshi, A.; Vinay, M.; Bhaskar, P. Impact of Coronavirus Pandemic on the Indian Education Sector: Perspectives of Teachers on Online Teaching and Assessments. In *Interactive Technology and Smart Education*; Emerald Publishing Limited. DOI: 10.1108/ITSE-06-2020-0087

Kaup, S.; Jain, R.; Shivalli, S.; Pandey, S.; Kaup, S. Sustaining Academics during COVID-19 Pandemic: The Role of Online Teaching-learning. *Indian J. Ophthalmol.* **2020**, *68* (6), 1220–1221.

Keengwe, J.; Onchwari, G.; Wachira, P. The Use of Computer Tools to Support Meaningful Learning. *AACE J.* **2008**, *16* (1), 77–92.

Kidd, W.; Murray, J. The Covid-19 Pandemic and Its Effects on Teacher Education in England: How Teacher Educators Moved Practicum Learning Online. *Eur. J. Teacher Educ.* **2020**, *43* (4), 542–558. https://www.tandfonline.com/doi/full/10.1080/02619768.2020.1820480

König, J.; Bremerich-Vos, A.; Buchholtz, I.; Fladung, C.; Glutsch, N. Pre-service Teachers' Generic and Subject-specific Lesson-planning Skills: On Learning Adaptive Teaching during Initial Teacher Education. *Eur. J. Teacher Educ.* **2020a**, *43* (2), 131–150. DOI: 10.1080/02619768.2019.1679115

König, J.; Jäger-Biela, D. J.; Glutsch, N. Adapting to Online Teaching during COVID-19 School Closure: Teacher Education and Teacher Competence Effects among Early Career Teachers in Germany. *Eur. J. Teacher Educ.* **2020b**, *43* (4), 608–622. https://www.tandfonline.com/doi/full/10.1080/02619768.2020.1809650?src=recsys

Kozma, R. B. ICT, Education Transformation, and Economic Development: An Analysis of the US National Educational Technology Plan. *E-Learn. Digit. Media* **2011**, *8* (2), 106–120. DOI: 10.2304/elea.2011.8.2.106

Martin, K. A. Lockdown Brings Back the Love for Reading. *The Hindu*, July 21, 2020. https://www.thehindu.com/news/national/kerala/lockdown-brings-back-the-love-for-reading/article32154415.ece

MHRD. Students to Continue Their Learning by Making Full Use of the Available Digital E-Learning Platforms—Shri Ramesh Pokhriyal 'Nishank'. pib.gov.in., 2020a. https://pib.gov.in/PressReleasePage.aspx?PRID=1607521

MHRD. National Education Policy 2020. In Press Information Bureau, 2020b; pp 33–49. https://static.pib.gov.in/WriteReadData/userfiles/NEP_Final_English_0.pdf

Moorhouse, B. Adaptations to a Face-to-face Initial Teacher Education Course 'Forced' Online Due to the COVID-19 Pandemic. *J. Educ. Teach.* **2020**, *42* (4). DOI: 10.1080/02607476.2020.1755205

Prottas, D. J.; Cleaver, C.M.; Cooperstein, D. Assessing Faculty Attitudes towards Online Instruction: A Motivational Approach. *Online J. Distance Learn. Admin.* **2016**, *19* (4). https://www.learntechlib.org/p/193257/

Ryan, G. W.; Bernard, H. R. Data Management and Analysis Methods. In *Handbook of Qualitative Research*; Denzin, N., Lincoln, Y., Eds., 2nd ed.; Thousand Oaks, CA: Sage, 2000; pp 769–802.

Sharma, A. K. COVID-19: Creating a Paradigm Shift in India's Education System. *Economic Times Blog*, Apr 15, 2020. https://economictimes.indiatimes.com/blogs/et-commentary/covid-19-creating-a-paradigm-shift-in-indias-education-system/

Smith, J. A.; Osborn, M. Interpretative Phenomenological Analysis. In *Qualitative Psychology: A Practical Guide to Research Methods*; Sage Publication: Thousand Oaks, CA, 2003.

Smith, J. A.; Flowers, P.; Larkin, M. *Interpretative Phenomenological Analysis: Theory, Method And Research*; London, 2009.

The Hindu Net Desk. Morning Digest. *The Hindu*, Mar 25, 2020. https://www.thehindu.com/news/morning-digest-march-25-2020/article31157325.ece

Tuffour, I. A Critical Overview of Interpretative Phenomenological Analysis: A Contemporary Qualitative Research Approach, 2017. www.researchgate.net

Verma, G.; Campbell, T.; Melville, W.; Park, B. Y. *Science Teacher Education in the Times of the COVID-19 Pandemic*, 2020.

Yuen, A.H.; Ma, W.W. Exploring Teacher Acceptance of E-learning Technology. *Asia-Pacific J. Teacher Educ.* 2008, *36* (3), 229–243.

CHAPTER 15

Mental Health and Economic Downturn: Are Post-Pandemic HR Roles and Responsibilities Changing?

DEBRAJ DATTA[*]

Management Department, Sister Nivedita University, West Bengal, India

[*]E-mail: debraj.datta@gmail.com

ABSTRACT

COVID 19 outbreak created a huge change in our socioeconomic structure. The orientation toward life of common people changed significantly because of growing health-related and economic concern arising out of pandemic situation. The pandemic is also causing great level of stress and anxiety because of a number of factors such as fear of infection, loss of livelihood, and prevailing uncertainty. This chapter used secondary and primary research involving Focus Group Discussion (FGD) technique and Questionnaire Survey with Hamilton Anxiety Rating Scale (HAM-A) and Rating Scale to explore the relationship between age, gender, occupational profile, and work experience with anxiety level of working professionals and students. It also tried to find out the impact psychological disturbance could have on the productivity, quality of work, interpersonal communication, relationship, motivation, and self-esteem among the professionals during pandemic period. The findings revealed that professionals suffered from stress and anxiety because of pandemic situation. It also explored the level of anxiety and workplace factors for different profiles. This chapter then discussed about the roles that HR professionals could play to overcome such problems.

15.1 INTRODUCTION

The first known case of COVID-19 infection was a Wuhan resident surnamed Chen, which was reported on December 8, 2019 (Page et al., 2021). On January 11, 2020, the first known death was reported by the Chinese state media (The Guardian, 2020). On January 20, the first confirmed cases outside mainland China that occurred in Japan, South Korea, and Thailand were reported. The first case in United States was reported on the very next day. On January 30, India witnessed its first COVID-19-positive case in Thrissur district, Kerala, with a student of Wuhan University who was on vacation to India (Perappadan, 2020). Such cases compelled World Health Organization (WHO) to declare COBID-19 as a global health emergency. From March 24, the Indian government announced first country-wide lockdown that was extended a number of times (Table 15.1).

TABLE 15.1 The Lockdown Phases in India.

	Lockdown phases		
Phase #	Start date	End date	Duration (days)
1	March 25, 2020	April 14, 2020	21
2	April 15, 2020	May 3, 2020	19
3	May 4, 2020	May 17, 2020	14
4	May 18, 2020	May 31, 2020	14

Source: https://en.wikipedia.org/wiki/COVID-19_pandemic_lockdown_in_India

As the situations improved, a number of unlock phases were implemented until now, as shown in Table 15.2.

The primary ways of containing a pandemic—individual, organizational, and governmental, however, did not create the expected impact in India. At the time of writing this chapter, India stands second just after USA in terms of total number of infections and third after USA and Brazil in terms of total number of deaths (Table 15.3).

Such a rapid spread created a huge impact in health, education, and corporate sectors. Various developed and developing economies have suffered heavily in terms of the Gross Domestic Product, which could be understood from the following figure (Figure 15.1).

In the last few months, thanks to mass vaccination programmes, the prospects for the world economy have brightened a bit (OECD report, 2021), but still a lot of uncertainties prevail. The critical factors will be proper

TABLE 15.2 The Lockdown and Unlock Phases in India.

Phase #	Unlock phases Start date	End date	Duration (days)
1	June 1, 2020	June 30, 2020	30
2	July 1, 2020	July 31, 2020	31
3	August 1, 2020	August 31, 2020	31
4	September 1, 2020	September 30, 2020	30
5	October 1, 2020	October 31, 2020	31
6	November 1, 2020	November 30, 2020	30
7	December 1, 2020	December 31, 2020	31
8	January 1, 2021	January 31, 2021	31
9	February 1, 2021	February 28, 2021	28
10	March 1, 2021	March 31, 2021	31
11	April 1, 2021	April 30, 2021	30
12	May 1, 2021	May 31, 2021	31
13	June 1, 2021	June 30, 2021	30
14	July 1, 2021	July 31, 2021	31

TABLE 15.3 Situation of Top Five Infected Countries and Worldwide as on July 8, 2021.

#	Country	Total cases	Total deaths	Total recovered	Total active cases
1	USA	34,676,896	622,213	29,203,308	4,851,375
2	India	30,752,108	405,967	29,880,724	465,417
3	Brazil	18,962,786	530,344	17,422,854	1,009,588
4	France	5,799,107	111,284	5,641,613	46,210
5	Russia	5,707,452	140,775	5,143,255	423,422
	World total	186,320,571	4,026,417	170,467,757	11,826,397

Source: https://www.worldometers.info/coronavirus/

implementation of vaccination programmes, drafting and executing public health policies and economic stimulus packages, effectiveness of vaccine against continuously mutating strains of virus, and willingness of common people to follow general health protocols such as wearing mask, washing hands, and maintaining physical distancing. The sign of economic recovery is evident, but the rate varies across the economies. United States and South Korea are expected to reach pre-pandemic per capita income levels after about 18 months, whereas this figure is expected to be nearly 3 years for most of the European economies and between 3 and 5 years for countries such as Mexico and South Africa (OECD report, 2021). The following table explains with details (Table 15.4).

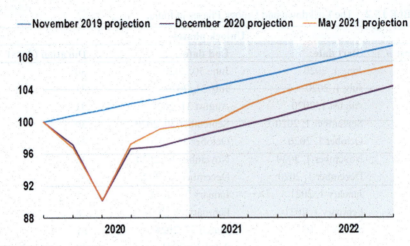

FIGURE 15.1 OECD economic outlook projections.

Source: OECD Economic Outlook 106, 108, and 109 database and projections.

TABLE 15.4 OECD Economic Outlook Projections (YoY % Change).

	2020	2021	2022
World	−3.5	5.8	4.4
Australia	−2.5	5.1	3.4
Canada	−5.4	6.1	3.8
Euro area	−6.7	4.3	4.4
Germany	−5.1	3.3	4.4
France	−8.2	5.8	4.0
Italy	−8.9	4.5	4.4
Spain	−10.8	5.9	6.3
Japan	−4.7	2.6	2.0
Korea	−0.9	3.8	2.8
United Kingdom	−9.8	7.2	5.5
United States	−3.5	6.9	3.6
G20	−3.1	6.3	4.7
Argentina	−9.9	6.1	1.8
Brazil	−4.1	3.7	2.5
China	2.3	8.5	5.8
India	−7.7	9.9	8.2
Indonesia	−2.1	4.7	5.1
Mexico	−8.2	5.0	3.2
Russia	−2.6	3.5	2.8
Saudi Arabia	−4.1	2.8	3.8
South Africa	−7.0	3.8	2.5
Turkey	1.8	5.7	3.4

Source: OECD economic outlook 109 database.

The pandemic has an adverse impact on various sectors, which was highlighted in recent RBI monthly update:

Highlights of RBI Monthly Update—May, 2021

- COVID-19 second wave has a devastating impact in India following the global trend.
- Although Central and State Governments have started working to curb surge, the result may take time as country-wise full-time lockdown is not tenable any more considering economic situations.
- Demand shock is the biggest impact of 2nd COVID-19 wave, which includes loss of mobility, discretionary spending, and employment, besides inventory accumulation.
- The aggregate supply is less impacted because of 2nd COVID-19 wave.
- The second wave of COVID-19 has halted but not derailed the momentum of economic activity as on the first half of the first quarter of the current financial year.
- The loss of momentum is less critical than the last year.

Source: May 17, 2021 issue of Business Standard.

However, such reports indicate only the impact of COVID-19 on economy, but undermine the impact of health condition of workforce. This chapter will explore the ramification of this unforeseen crisis on the mental health of the professionals and students who are preparing to enter into work life.

The chapter focusses on the following:

- The rapid spread of COVID-19 outbreak in various countries including India compelled the governments across the globe to implement lockdown in multiple stages, which created a huge change in our socioeconomic structure.
  - The orientation toward life of common people changed significantly because of growing health-related and economic concern arising out of pandemic situation.
  - The pandemic is also causing great level of stress and anxiety because of a number of factors such fear of infection, loss of livelihood, and prevailing uncertainty.

- A number of secondary and primary research techniques were used to:
  - Explore the relationship between age, gender, occupational profile, and work experience with anxiety level of working professionals and the students.
  - Find out the impact of psychological disturbance on the employees in terms of:
    - Productivity
    - Quality of work
    - Interpersonal communication and relationship
    - Motivation and self-esteem
- The research found significantly high impact of pandemic situation on professionals in terms of stress and anxiety and also explored the level of anxiety and workplace factors for different profiles.
- On the basis of these findings, the following areas of HR professionals were recommended, where HR department must look into and come out with proper strategy
  - Adjusting recruitment methods
  - Equipping and training the workforce
  - Recognizing employee efforts
  - Ensuring employee wellness
  - Developing learning environment
  - Employee upskilling
  - Applying innovative practices
  - Adopting proactive approaches
  - Fostering culture of openness
  - Framing new normal policies

15.2 BACKGROUND

Although the above table depicts the grave situation of India in the context of global pandemic situation, the table given below explores many reasons why Indians must not worry considering the overall global conditions (Table 15.5).

However, most of the news outlets are sensationalizing the whole situation and creating unnecessary panic. It is further fueled by a barrage of so-called authentic news or scientific revelation news snippets that are circulating among the millions through WhatsApp, Facebook, and other social media outlets, which resulted in overspread phobia and anxiety. Although there have been attempts by the central and state governments to flatten the curve, no attempt on curbing such media-induced triggers and stressors has been noticed, probably because mental health still is not considered with due importance and hence has not been considered a priority. This might lead to a different kind of disaster—a chronic psychological disorder at the mass level leading to huge mental health crisis (Chakraborty et al., 2021).

TABLE 15.5 Comparative Data of West Bengal, India, and World as on July 8, 2021.

Indicators	West Bengal	India	World
Total case per million	16,769	22,035	23,938
Total recovery per million	16,391	21,409	21,907
Total death per million	199	290	517
Total active case per million	179	335	1514
Fatality rate (%) of closed cases	1.20	1.34	2.31
Fatality rate (%) of total cases	1.18	1.32	2.16
Recovery rate (%) of total cases	97.75	97.16	91.52
Daily increase (%) of new case	0.07	0.15	3.97
Weekly increase (%) of new case	0.53	0.98	6.04
Daily increase (%) of recovery	0.10	0.15	0.22
Weekly increase (%) of recovery	0.81	1.20	1.52
Daily increase (%) of death	0.10	0.20	0.22
Weekly increase (%) of death	0.74	1.39	1.36
Daily change (%) of active cases	−3.07	0.08	0.83
Weekly change (%) of active cases	−19.97	−11.79	2.64

Source: For West Bengal: https://www.wbhealth.gov.in/pages/corona/bulletin
For India: https://www.covid19india.org/
For World: https://www.worldometers.info/coronavirus/

Various researches on the people who were in isolation or quarantine during previous pandemic outbreak such as Severe Acute Respiratory Syndrome (SARS) found that most of them developed significant and long-term complications of distress, anxiety, suicidal tendency, addiction issue, anger, depression (Duan and Zhu, 2020; Serafini et al., 2020). Personal hygiene, isolation, and distancing protocols could halt the physical spread of this disease, but still continuous discussion and incessant exposure to pandemic-related news via social and traditional media outlets could create a long-lasting impact on mental health and subsequently lead to physical disorders (Frankenhauser, 1980; Turner and Lloyd, 1995; Cohen et al., 1995;

McEwen, 2002; Singh, 2020), especially among the childless (Miller, 2020) and single (Smith, 2020) people. Multiple studies found profound adverse psychological and social impact of COVID-19 on people (Puri, 2020; Saladino et al., 2020; Sher, 2020; Kopp, 2020; Robinson, 2020). Stress-related psychiatric conditions lead to substance use disorders (Newcomb and Bentler, 1988; Wills et al., 1992; Riggs and Whitmore, 1999) and suicidal behavior. Pandemic brought huge amount of fear of an uncertain future that is driving people toward such drastic steps and some patients with chronic depression who had been improving relapsed since the lockdown created limited access to mental healthcare (Das, 2020). As per a study conducted in the last year, distress triggered by the nationwide lockdown increased the occurrence of suicide across the country (PTI report, 2020). Hence, there should be continuous effort to promote awareness about mental health by the governments, NGOs, special interest groups, and practitioners (psychiatrists and psychologists) using traditional and digital media vehicles (Datta, 2020). Various studies suggested that COVID-19 pandemic could have a far-reaching impact even beyond year 2021 (Akkermans et al., 2020; Regmi and Lwin, 2020). There is also no proper idea of the nature and time period of adversity on socioeconomic environment and business institutions (Bartik et al., 2020), although a number of vaccines have been developed and mass inoculation programmes have started (Yu et al., 2021). This makes the job more difficult for the HR professionals while developing and implementing an appropriate strategic planning framework that could alleviate the fear of uncertainty in the mind of the employees about the future course of action (Elsafty and Ragheb, 2020) and consequently could decrease employees' stress level and increase their motivation and confidence (Wong et al., 2020).

The COVID-19 pandemic because of its high infection rate and high mortality rate posed huge challenges to healthcare systems and public health policies globally (Chandra, 2020; Stratton, 2020). This could be accentuated by the increase in alcohol consumption and substance user disorders (SUD) as a result of pandemic-induced adverse clinical, psychological, and psychosocial conditions (Abrams, 1983; deGoeij et al., 2015; Lagisetty et al., 2017; Peacock et al., 2018), and hence specific strategies for prevention and treatment must be discussed (Lagisetty et al., 2017; Bojdani et al., 2020). It is widely known that the state and the severity of tobacco and alcohol consumption are associated with the clinical and psychological conditions (Meyerholz et al., 2008; Schulte and Hser, 2014; Lagisetty et al., 2017; Godoy et al., 2018; Sureshchandra et al., 2019; Volkow, 2020). The substance users could invite more health hazards with their habit of using combination of multiple drugs (Sinha et al., 2009; Kuerbis et al., 2014; Serafini et al., 2016).

Such cases will increase vulnerability of a large population with various clinical comorbidities such as diabetes, Chronic Obstructive Pulmonary Disease (COPD), and hypertension (Chand et al., 2019; Dolapsakis and Katsandri, 2019; Hulin et al., 2019; Cascella et al., 2020, Cherian et al., 2020). The role of prevalence of comorbidity conditions in mortality is quite evident in the data published by the Health Department of West Bengal Government (Figures 15.2 and 15.3).

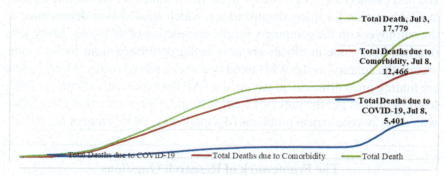

FIGURE 15.2 Prevalence of comorbidity factor in COVID-19 mortality in West Bengal as on July 8, 2021.

Source: https://www.wbhealth.gov.in/pages/corona/bulletin

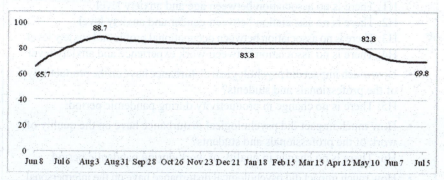

FIGURE 15.3 % prevalence of comorbidity factor in COVID-19 mortality in West Bengal as on July 8, 2021.

Source: https://www.wbhealth.gov.in/pages/corona/bulletin

Social distancing protocol and isolation or quarantine are considered to be the most essential measures to help prevent corona virus transmission. But such isolation and continuous exposure to negative news could elicit a number of negative emotions such as irritability, sadness, anger, anxiety, fear, or boredom along with fear, anxiety, and uncertainty, collectively known as trigger relapse (Ornell et al., 2020). Deteriorating economic condition, loss of livelihood, rampant salary cut, and future uncertainties are amplifying the situations. There is an estimated loss of 12.2 crore jobs because of COVID-19 which shot up India's unemployment rate to a staggering 27.1% since the beginning of the lockdown (India Today, 2020). The worst COVID-19-affected sectors include travel, door-to-door sales, recreation, fitness, wellness, and real estate (PTI report, 2020). Work-from-home (WFH) became an only available option for many organizations, which created over-dependence of the employees on the computers for the completion of their jobs. Many jobs that had been done in offices are now being performed from living rooms around the country, as the WFH trend becomes a forced reality. Many people are finding great difficulty in paying the EMI for home, educational, or other loans, which as per the previous studies would trigger addiction issue along with other psychological problems (deGoeij et al., 2015; Dom et al., 2016).

The Framework of Research Questions

- How much impact did pandemic have on mental health of the professionals and students?
  The first set of hypotheses aims to capture this.
  H1: There is no association between age and anxiety level
  H2: There is no association between gender and anxiety level
  H3: There is no association between occupational profile and anxiety level
  H4: There is no association between work experience and anxiety level

- How much impact did psychological disturbance have on the productivity of the professionals and students?
  H5: There is no change in productivity during pandemic period.

- How much impact did psychological disturbance have on the quality of work of the professionals and students?
  H6: There is no change in quality of work during pandemic period.

- How much impact did psychological disturbance have on the interpersonal communication and relationship amongst the professionals and students?
  H7: There is no change in extent of interpersonal communication during pandemic period.

- How much impact did psychological disturbance have on the motivation and self-esteem of the professionals and students?
  H8: There is no change in motivation and self-esteem during pandemic period.

Research Problem

In the context of pandemic crisis, economic downturn, and ensuing psychological problems, HR function faces severe challenge while recruiting and managing workforce. It must consider the following questions to handle such predicament.

Apart from collecting secondary data on the impact of pandemic on mental health from a number of published resources such as newspapers, magazines, journals, websites, a mix of exploratory and descriptive research was conducted on a sample of final-year MBA students and working professionals, obtained from the database of current students and alumni of author's institution and also with collaboration with www.mycoolguru.com—the career and life ecosystem of career aspirants and professionals.

In the first part, the FGD technique was used. A focus group is defined as a group of individuals selected and assembled by researchers to discuss and comment on the subjects, which could range from brand perception to consumption pattern of products especially of complex or emotive in nature, on the basis of personal experience (Davies, 1999). Focus group discussion enables researchers to listen to myriad voices, explore newer dimensions of complex issue, and consequently gather meaningful insights that might not have been possible had the discussion not initiated (Palomba and Banta, 1999). Considering various opinions regarding the ideal size for a focus group (Morgan, 1998; Crabtree and Miller, 1999; Blackburn and Stokes, 2000; Fern, 2001), size of all the groups was kept at 6. The homogeneity of group was ensured keeping same demographic, sociocultural, and economic profiles to avoid conflicts and wayward interactions as suggested by the researchers (Greenbaum, 1988, 2000; Puchta, 2004). The number of groups was also a relevant issue. No research suggested any fixed number of groups required. For the present research, two occupation profiles were chosen as primary factors of differentiation viz. student and professionals, which were further differentiated in gender and age. In total, three groups were formed of students and four groups were formed of professionals. But, for these homogeneous groups, groupthink could be a problem where group members could try to minimize conflicts and reach to a unanimous decision without considering individual opinions or even rationally testing or evaluating the so-called consensus, which could compel dissenting members to suppress their opinions or concepts outside the comfort zone of unilateral thinking, which could compel the group members to make hasty, irrational, and self-comforting decisions (Whyte, 1952; Janis, 1972). Hence, two heterogeneous groups were formed by including a mix of people from students and working professionals of varying age group and gender. All the 9 FGD sessions were conducted on Zoom. The group structure is shown as follows.

TABLE 15.6 Sampling Design for Descriptive Research.

FGD group #	Composition	Group size
1	Students	6
2	Students	6
3	Students	6
4	Professionals	6
5	Professionals	6
6	Professionals	6
7	Professionals	6
8	Students and professionals	6
9	Students and professionals	6
Total		54

It was followed by conducting descriptive research by considering 2 (Occupational Profile: students vs. professionals) * 3 (Age: 21–25 vs. 25–35 vs. 35–40) * 2 (Gender: males vs. females) mixed design with a sample of 413 respondents as described below.

TABLE 15.7 Sampling Design for Descriptive Research.

	21–25			25–35			35–45			Total
	Male	Female	Total	Male	Female	Total	Male	Female	Total	
Students	126	115	241							241
Professionals	15	14	29	45	34	79	34	30	64	172
Total	141	129	270	45	34	79	34	30	64	413

The survey used the Hamilton Anxiety Rating Scale (HAM-A) to understand the impact of pandemic on mental health of the professionals.

Hamilton Anxiety Rating Scale (HAM-A)

The Hamilton Anxiety Rating Scale (HAM-A) consists of the following 14 items designed to assess the severity of the respondent's anxiety on a scale of 0–4 (0 = least, 4 = most).

1. Anxious mood: Worries, anticipation of the worst, fearful anticipation, irritability.
2. Tension: Feelings of tension, fatigability, startle response, moving to tears easily, trembling, feelings of restlessness, inability to relax.
3. Fears: Of dark, of strangers, of being left alone, of animals, of traffic, of crowds.
4. Insomnia: Difficulty in falling asleep, broken sleep, unsatisfying sleep and fatigue on waking, dreams, nightmares, night terrors.
5. Intellectual: Difficulty in concentration, poor memory.
6. Depressed mood: Loss of interest, lack of pleasure in hobbies, depression, early waking, diurnal swing.
7. Somatic (muscular): Pains and aches, twitching, stiffness, myoclonic jerks, grinding of teeth, unsteady voice, increased muscular tone.
8. Somatic (sensory): Tinnitus, blurring of vision, hot and cold flushes, feelings of weakness, pricking sensation.
9. Cardiovascular symptoms: Tachycardia, palpitations, pain in chest, throbbing of vessels, fainting feelings, missing beat.
10. Respiratory symptoms: Pressure or constriction in chest, choking feelings, sighing, dyspnea.
11. Gastrointestinal symptoms: Difficulty in swallowing, wind abdominal pain, burning sensations, abdominal fullness, nausea, vomiting, borborygmi, looseness of bowels, loss of weight, constipation.
12. Genitourinary symptoms: Frequency of micturition, urgency of micturition, amenorrhea, menorrhagia, development of frigidity, premature ejaculation, loss of libido, impotence.
13. Autonomic symptoms: Dry mouth, flushing, pallor, tendency to sweat, giddiness, tension headache, raising of hair.
14. Behavior at interview: Fidgeting, restlessness or pacing, tremor of hands, furrowed brow, strained face, sighing or rapid respiration, facial pallor, swallowing, etc.

The scores could vary between 0 and 56; score less than 17 indicates mild severity, 18–24 mild to moderate severity and 25–30 moderate to severe. (Hamilton, 1969; Maier et al, 1988).

15.3 FINDINGS AND INTERPRETATION

The findings for all the nine focus groups are described below.

Groups 1 to 3: Only students

The participants more or less agreed on the adverse impact of pandemic on their health and mind. They showed their concern regarding their studies and preparation. They believed their preparation was not up to the mark since all of them did their summer internship working from home and all their third semester classes were conducted online, which might not be enough for the recruiters. They also felt that the job opportunity would have shrunk because of pandemic and many of them would not be able to get the job. Some of them expressed the need to upskill themselves and also informed that they already made investment in a few such courses.

Groups 4 to 7: Only professionals

The participants narrated the situation they were facing at their workplace. Many of them informed that their organization had been implementing salary-cut policy for the last few months. Some mentioned that some people in their organization even lost their job because of pandemic. They unanimously agreed that they were going through uncertainty and stressful situations. The professionals belonging to 35 to 45 years age group have shown more concern in this regard.

Groups 8 to 9: Mixed group of students and professionals

In such cases, the students interacted freely with the professionals many of whom were their alumni. Some of these professionals even were engaged in recruiting through campus interviews. All of them agreed how the anxiety and uncertainty had intensified in their life during the pandemic period.

In the descriptive research, the HAM-A scale scores were obtained from the 413 respondents to analyze the impact of pandemic on mental health across demographic profiles. The descriptive statistics (Mean = 47.31, Median = 47, Standard Deviation = 5.02, Skewness = −0.01, Kurtosis = −1.15, coefficient of variation = 10.614%) suggested a quite high anxiety score. The t-test was found to be significant (t-statistic = 9.23, $p<0.5$) and it may be concluded that there a was significantly high anxiety score because of the pandemic.

To test H1: There is no association between age and anxiety level. One-way Analysis of Variance (ANOVA) was conducted for three age groups, namely 21 to 25, 25 to 35, and 35 to 45 on HAM-A scale scores. The ANOVA test (F-statistic = 0.443, df = 2, $p>.05$) was found to be nonsignificant. Hence, the hypothesis might be accepted and it may be concluded that pandemic created a similar impact on mental health across the age groups.

To test H2: There is no association between gender and anxiety level; the t-test was conducted for two gender groups on HAM-A scale scores. The t-test (t-statistic = 0.0441, df = 411, $p>.05$) was found to be nonsignificant. Hence, the hypothesis might be accepted and it may be concluded that pandemic created a similar impact on mental health irrespective of the gender.

To test H3: There is no association between the occupational profile and the anxiety level; the t-test was conducted for two occupational profiles, namely students and professionals on HAM-A scale scores. The t-test (t-statistic = 0.355, df = 411, $p>.05$) was found to be nonsignificant. Hence, the hypothesis might be accepted and it may be concluded that pandemic created a similar impact on mental health irrespective of occupational profiles.

To test H4: There is no association between work experience and anxiety level. One-way ANOVA was conducted for three levels of work experience as per the age group, viz. little work experience for the 21–25 age group, reasonable work experience for the 25–35 age group, and significant work experience for the 35–45 age group on HAM-A scale scores. The ANOVA test (F-statistic = 0.662, df = 2, $p>.05$) was found to be nonsignificant. Hence, the hypothesis might be accepted and it may be concluded that pandemic created a similar impact on mental health among the professionals irrespective of their work experience and career phase.

To test H5: There is no change in productivity during the pandemic period, all the 413 respondents were asked to self-assess their change in level of productivity at their workplace (academic activity for students and professional activity for the working executives) on a 0 to 10 rating scale, where 0 denoted no change and 10 denoted maximum possible change. The descriptive statistics (Mean = 6.53, Median = 7, Standard Deviation = 2.48, Skewness = −0.65, Kurtosis = −0.002, coefficient of variation = 38.01%) suggested significant change in productivity. The t-test was found to be significant (t-statistic = 53.46, $p<0.5$), and it may be concluded that there was change in productivity during the pandemic period. While conducting further analysis on age, the ANOVA test (F-statistic = 6.56, df = 2, $p<.05$) was found to be significant. Tukey post-hoc analysis revealed that the 21–25 age group was quite high in their self-assessment score and significantly different from the other two age groups. While conducting further analysis on gender, the t-test (t-statistic = 0.277, df = 412, $p>.05$) was found to be nonsignificant meaning similar impact irrespective of gender. While conducting analysis on occupational profile, the t-test (t-statistic = 6.319, df = 411, $p<.05$) was found to be significant with very high scores from the students as compared with that from the professionals. While conducting further analysis on work experience, the ANOVA test (F-statistic = 9.802, df = 2, $p<.05$) was found to be significant. Tukey Post-hoc analysis revealed that the 21–25 age group is quite low in their self-assessment score and significantly different from the other two age groups.

To test H6: There is no change in quality of work during pandemic period; all the 413 respondents were asked to self-assess their change in quality of work at their workplace (academic activity for students and professional activity for the working executives) on a 0 to 10 rating scale, where 0 denoted no change and 10 denoted maximum possible change. The descriptive statistics (Mean = 7.85, Median = 8, Standard Deviation = 1.2, Skewness = −0.12, Kurtosis = −0.99, coefficient of variation = 15.36%) suggested significant change in quality of work. The t-test was found to be significant (t-statistic = 32.32, $p<0.5$), so null hypothesis may be rejected and it may be concluded that there was change in quality of work during pandemic period. While conducting further analysis on age, the ANOVA test (F-statistic = 39.97, df = 2, $p<.05$) was found to be significant. Tukey post-hoc analysis revealed that all the age groups differed on their level of response. While conducting further analysis on gender, the t-test (t-statistic = 0.277, df = 412, $p>.05$) was found to be nonsignificant meaning a similar impact irrespective of gender. While conducting analysis on occupational profile, the t-test (t-statistic = 1.21, df = 412, $p>.05$) was found to be nonsignificant. While conducting further analysis on work experience, the ANOVA test (F-statistic = 20.51, df = 2, $p<.05$) was found to be significant. Tukey post-hoc analysis revealed that all the age groups significantly differed from each other.

To test H7: There is no change in the extent of interpersonal communication during pandemic period; all the 413 respondents were asked to self-assess their change in the extent of interpersonal communication at their workplace (academic activity for students and professional activity for the working executives) on a 0 to 10 rating scale, where 0 denoted no change and 10 denoted maximum possible change. The descriptive statistics (Mean = 7.71, Median = 8, Standard Deviation = 1.51, Skewness = −0.53, Kurtosis = −0.15, coefficient of variation = 19.53%) suggested significant change in extent of interpersonal communication. The t-test was found to be significant (t-statistic = 23.05, $p<0.5$); so null hypothesis may be rejected and it may be concluded that there was change in extent of interpersonal communication during pandemic period. While conducting further analysis on age, the ANOVA test (F-statistic = 1.02, df = 2, $p>.05$) was found to be nonsignificant. While conducting further analysis on gender, the t-test (t-statistic = 4.62, df = 412, $p<.05$) was found to be significant indicating more impact among the women. While conducting analysis on occupational profile, the t-test (t-statistic = 0.36, df = 411, $p>.05$) was found to be nonsignificant. While conducting further analysis on work experience, the ANOVA test (F-statistic = 10.22, df = 2, $p<.05$) was found to be significant. Tukey post-hoc analysis revealed that the 21–25 age group was quite high in their self-assessment score and significantly different from the other two age groups.

To test H8: There is no change in motivation and self-esteem during pandemic period; all the 413 respondents were asked to self-assess their change in level of motivation and self-esteem at their workplace (academic activity for students and professional activity for the working executives) on a 0 to 10 rating scale, where 0 denoted no change and 10 denoted maximum possible change. The descriptive statistics (Mean = 8.29, Median = 8, Standard Deviation = 1.19, Skewness = −1.82, Kurtosis = 10.03, coefficient of variation = 14.4%) suggested significant change in motivation and self-esteem. The t-test was found to be significant (t-statistic = 38.99, $p<0.5$), and it may be concluded that there was change in level of motivation and self-esteem during pandemic period. While conducting further analysis on age, the ANOVA test (F-statistic = 23.98, df = 2, $p<.05$) was found to be significant. Tukey post-hoc analysis revealed that all the age groups differed from each other in the level of change in motivation and self-esteem although all reported higher values. While conducting further analysis on gender, the t-test (t-statistic = 5.74, df = 412, $p<.05$) was found to be significant indicating more impact among the men. While conducting analysis on occupational profile, the t-test (t-statistic = 7.17, df = 411, $p<.05$) was found to be significant with very high scores from the students as compared with that from the professionals. While conducting further analysis on work experience, the ANOVA test (F-statistic = 3.45, df = 2, $p>.05$) was found to be nonsignificant.

TABLE 15.8 Summary of Findings.

Factor	Overall	Age	Gender	Occupational profile	Work experience
Anxiety Level: HAM-A scale scores	Significantly high	Similarity in impact	Similarity in impact	Similarity in impact	Similarity in impact
Change in productivity	Significant	Quite high score for 21–25 age group; significantly different from other two age groups	Similarity in impact	Very high score for the students	Quite low score for 21–25 age group; significantly different from other two age groups
Change in quality of work	Significant	All the age groups differed from each other	Similarity in impact	Similarity in impact	All the age groups differed from each other
Change in extent of interpersonal communication	Significant	Similarity in impact	More impact for women	Similarity in impact	Quite high score for 21–25 age group; significantly different from other two age groups
Change in motivation and self-esteem	Significant	All the age groups differed from each other	More impact for men	Very high score for the students	Similarity in impact

Source: Developed by the author based on his primary survey data and analysis.

15.4 CONCLUSION

As seen above, the COVID-19 situation created a paradigm shift in the mindset of the people as well as the processes and structures (Giurge and Bohns, 2020; Fetters, 2020). It became imperative for all the employees to adjust their way of working since according to the health experts, not only is the adverse impact of current pandemic far from over (Hixon, 2020), but the risk of future health hazards arising out of this pandemic situation is fairly certain (Desmond-Hellmann, 2020). The career aspirants must attune to such changes occurring in corporate practices and hence should upskill themselves. The HR hence must make subsequent changes in its strategies with long-term perspective, in terms of recruitment, employee engagement and communication, performance appraisal, competency mapping, training and development, compensation, and benefits to ensure business continuity during and post-COVID-19 (Maurer, 2020; Chawla et al., 2020). Fostering a climate of positivity helps employee engagement in general (Chakraborty and Ganguly, 2019; Chakraborty and Mishra, 2019). HR department must strive to induce resilience in organizational framework to create sustainable workforce management model that will insulate the organization in the future from the shocks, challenges, and uncertainties arising from pandemic-like situations (Ngoc Su et al., 2021).

The employee communication and engagement will become very important in building more trust and transparency to help them overcome the feelings of uncertainty, isolation, depression, stress, and anxiety (Tensay and Singh, 2020; Barreiro and Treglown, 2020). The employees might struggle with feelings of alienation and banishment for the implementation of work-from-home policy in professional life and social distancing norms in personal life, thus posing an unprecedented challenge for HR professionals since they could not refer to any standard or previously tested strategy, structure, system, process, and policies.

Below mentioned are some of the areas where HR department must look into.

Adjusting recruitment methods: The recruiters must appreciate the fact that the students could not get the regular exposure to classroom discussion, live projects, and internship. Their morale is also quite down with bleak news regarding economy. Recruiters must consider these factors and subsequently tweak the recruitment parameters, tools, and processes.

Equipping and training the workforce: Pandemic situation brought a lot of changes at workplace; WFH requires a lot of changes in the way employees work. One major aspect is digital mode of work. The various activities such as client interaction and departmental meetings are being conducted online, which would require employees to develop the skill and also to get out of comfort zone and obliterate the inertia. HR must regularly arrange technical training sessions and motivational sessions to uphold this culture.

Recognizing employee efforts: Crisis situations create anxiety and increase self-doubt and depression as found in the study. HR department hence must accentuate its employee recognition initiatives and efforts. In addition to monetary rewards or some recreational packages (which are any way not meaningful or motivating currently due to travel restrictions and mandatory quarantine procedures for foreign travel), there could be some initiatives what Hertzberg called "motivators," such as announcement of WFH warrior for a certain time period (month or quarter), upskilling opportunities, flexi-time work environment, acknowledgment and appreciation for innovative practices adopted to name a few.

Ensuring Employee Wellness: HR department must have true concern for the physiological and psychological well-being of the employees. It must include regular check of health condition of employees and their family members. Some relevant webinars with the doctors, psychiatrist/ psychological counselors, and yoga/meditation experts must be organized to keep them informed about do's and don'ts during this horrid time. The functional heads also must have been persuaded by HR to take care of their team members on a day-to-day basis and must accommodate for employees who are affected because of pandemic.

Developing learning environment: Pandemic situation made it evident that employees need to learn, unlearn, and relearn. HR managers must ensure learning environment. The philosophical statement made in Latin by René Descartes "Cogito, ergo sum" eons ago translated into English as "I think, therefore I am" could be the motto of such initiatives. There should be a structured guideline of how andragogy and heutagogy learning could be initiated and practiced with proper enabling of technology.

Employee upskilling: Pandemic situation compels employees and career aspirants to upskill. Responsible HR managers must motivate employees to avail these facilities. Some arrangements, if needed in terms of work schedule adjustment, must be made accordingly. Necessary financial support, even if partial, may be considered. Some tie-ups with educational institutions before campus recruitment must be made to enhance the employability of the students before the induction into the company.

Applying innovative practices: HR department must be innovative and disruptive in regards with sustainable, scalable, and holistic employee engagement. More and more opportunities must be created for process improvements and incremental and exponential innovation.

Adopting proactive approaches: HR professionals must be proactive in understanding the need and requirement of the employees and should come out with necessary solution to the problem they might face, thus ensuing engagement and relationship with them.

Fostering culture of openness: HR must also ensure a heterarchical environment of openness, transparency, and camaraderie, where the employees could discuss on various sensitive subjects arising out of COVID-19 pandemic, such as skill obsolescence, job insecurity, job rotation, productivity in alternative work practices and models, or remote interpersonal communication in the virtual workplace.

Framing New Normal Policies: Considering all the above factors, the HR department must review and make necessary change in the policies, procedures, and practices. The goal must be to create a framework that will cater to the changes as demanded by post-pandemic situation. Special emphasis must be given on flexibility of workplace and work hours while designing remote working (Vyas and Butakhieo, 2021), technology-embedded work processes, gig economy (Umar et al., 2020), consultant mode and contractual staffing, review parameters, and compensation plan.

While these initiatives seem to be imperative for post-pandemic era, it needs to be understood that all these might not necessarily work for every company in every sector. Customization must be made considering the challenges and dynamics. For an example, contact-based sectors such as tourism, restaurant, gym, beauty parlors, and multiplexes must come with significant modification, as required. However, the bottom line is that every employee must have different approaches in a post-pandemic work environment and the challenge for HR professionals will be how to shift toward a more dynamic, human-focused, flexible approach.

Key Takeaways of the Chapter are

- This chapter revealed that despite the grave situation of India in the context of global pandemic situation, there are many reasons why people living in West Bengal state where the research was conducted and India as a whole must not worry considering the overall global conditions. This chapter explored how most of the news outlets have been sensationalizing the whole situation and a barrage of so-called authentic news or scientific revelation news snippets have been

widely circulated through Whatsapp, Facebook, and other social media outlets, which resulted in unnecessary phobia, panic, anxiety, depression, and paranoia. This chapter mentioned a lot of research findings that corroborated such prevalence of chronic psychological disorder.
- This chapter explained how in the context of pandemic crisis, economic downturn, and ensuing psychological problems, HR function would face severe challenges while recruiting and managing workforce and formed the research problem that was based on the following questions that HR professionals must handle under such perilous situations.
  - How much impact did pandemic have on mental health of the professionals and students?
  - How much impact did psychological disturbance have on the productivity of the professionals and students?
  - How much impact did psychological disturbance have on the quality of work of the professionals and students?
  - How much impact did psychological disturbance have on the interpersonal communication and relationship among the professionals and students?
  - How much impact did psychological disturbance have on the motivation and self-esteem of the professionals and students?
- This chapter contained the findings of a mix of exploratory and descriptive primary research, which were conducted on a sample of students and working professionals using the Focus Group Discussion technique and the descriptive research method by administering a survey using the Hamilton Anxiety Rating Scale.
- The studies found that the COVID-19 situation created a paradigm shift in the mindset of the people as well as the processes and structures. It became imperative for all the employees to adjust their way of working. The career aspirants must attune to such changes occurring in corporate practices and hence should upskill themselves. The HR hence must make subsequent changes in its strategies with long-term perspective, in terms of:
  - Recruitment
  - Employee engagement and communication
  - Performance appraisal
  - Competency mapping, training, and development

- ○ Compensation and benefits to ensure business continuity during and post-COVID-19.
- The chapter described how the employee communication and engagement will become very important in building more trust and transparency to help them overcome the feelings of uncertainty, isolation, depression, stress, and anxiety. The employees might struggle with feelings of alienation and banishment for the implementation of work-from-home policy in professional life and social distancing norms in personal life, thus posing an unprecedented challenge for HR professionals since they could not refer to any standard or previously tested strategy, structure, system, process, and policies.
- The chapter explored a number of areas where HR department must look into and come out with proper strategy. Those are:
  - ○ Adjusting recruitment methods
  - ○ Equipping and training the workforce
  - ○ Recognizing employee efforts
  - ○ Ensuring Employee Wellness
  - ○ Developing learning environment
  - ○ Employee upskilling
  - ○ Applying innovative practices
  - ○ Adopting proactive approaches
  - ○ Fostering culture of openness
  - ○ Framing New Normal Policies

KEYWORDS

- **pandemic**
- **anxiety**
- **stress**
- **uncertainty**
- **self-esteem**
- **focus group discussion**
- **Hamilton Anxiety Rating Scale**
- **HR role**

REFERENCES

Abrams, D. B. Alcohol and Stress Interactions. In *Stress and Alcohol Use*; Pohorecky, L. A.; Brick, J., Eds.; Elsevier: New York, 1983.

Akkermans, J.; Richardson, J.; Kraimer, M. The Covid-19 Crisis as a Career Shock: Implications for Careers and Vocational Behavior. *J. Vocational Behav.* **2020**, *119*, 1–6. DOI: 10.1016/j.jvb.2020.103434

Barreiro, C. A.; Treglown, L. What Makes an Engaged Employee? A Facet-Level Approach to Trait Emotional Intelligence as a Predictor of Employee Engagement. *Personality Individual Differences* **2020**, 159.

Bartik, A. W.; Cullen, Z. B.; Glaeser, E. L.; Luca, M.; Stanton, C. T. What Jobs Are Being Done at Home during the COVID-19 Crisis? Evidence from Firm-Level Surveys (No. w27422). National Bureau of Economic Research, 2020.

Blackburn, R.; Stokes, D. Breaking Down the Barriers: Using Focus Groups to Research Small and Medium-Sized Enterprises. *Int. Small Busi. J.* **2000**, *19* (1), 44–63.

Bojdani, E.; Rajagopalan, A.; Chen, A.; Gearin, P.; Olcott, W.; Shankar, V.; Cloutier, A.; Solomon, H.; Naqvir, N. Z.; Batty, N.; Festin, F. E. D.; Tahera, D.; Chang, G.; DeLisi, L. E. COVID-19 Pandemic: Impact on Psychiatric Care in the United States, a Review. *Psych. Res.* **2020**, *289*.

Cascella, M.; Rajnik, A.; Cuomo, S.; Dulebohn, C.; Di Napoli, R. *Features, Evaluation and Treatment Coronavirus (COVID-19) StatPearls [Internet]*; StatPearls Publishing: Treasure Island, Jan 2020.

Chakraborty, T.; Ganguly, M. Crafting Engaged Employees through Positive Work Environment: Perspectives of Employee Engagement. In *Management Techniques for Employee Engagement in Contemporary Organizations*; IGI Global, 2019; pp 180–198.

Chakraborty, T.; Mishra, N. Appreciative Inquiry: Unleashing a Positive Revolution of Organizational Change and Development. *Int. J. Econ. Com. Busi. Manage.* **2019**, *6* (2), 32–37.

Chakraborty, T.; Kumar, A.; Upadhyay, P.; Dwivedi, Y. K. Link between Social Distancing, Cognitive Dissonance, and Social Networking Site Usage Intensity: A Country-Level Study during the COVID-19 Outbreak. *Internet Res.* **2021**, *31* (2), 419–456. DOI: 10.1108/intr-05-2020-0281

Chand, H. S.; Muthumalage, T.; Maziak, W.; Rahman, I. Pulmonary Toxicity and the Pathophysiology of Electronic Cigarette, or Vaping Product, Use Associated Lung Injury. *Front. Pharmacol.* 2019, *10*, 1–7. https://doi.org/10.3389/fphar.2019.01619

Chandra, J. *Stress and Anxiety Rise amid Coronavirus Pandemic*, Apr 23, 2020. Retrieved Nov 05, 2020, from https://www.thehindu.com/sci-tech/health/stress-and-anxiety-rise-amid-coronavirus-pandemic/article31409223.ece

Chawla, N.; MacGowan, R. L.; Gabriel, A. S.; Podsakoff, N. P. Unplugging or Staying Connected? Examining the Nature, Antecedents, and Consequences of Profiles of Daily Recovery Experiences. *J. Appl. Psychol.* **2020**, *105* (1), 19.

Cohen, S.; Kessler, R. C.; Gordon, L. U. Strategies for Measuring Stress in Studies of Psychiatric and Physical Disorders. In *Measuring Stress: A Guide for Health and Social Scientists*; Cohen, S.; Kessler, R. C.; Gordon, L. U., Eds.; Oxford University Press: New York, 1995; pp 3–26.

COVID19INDIA. Retrieved November 25, 2020 from https://www.covid19india.org/

Crabtree, B. F.; Miller, W. L. *Doing Qualitative Research*, 2nd ed.; Sage Publications: Thousand Oaks, CA, 1999.

Das, M. *Suicides See a Sharp Rise in Kolkata amid Lockdown, over Half Are 40 Years or Younger*, July 4, 2020. Retrieved Nov 11, 2020 from https://theprint.in/india/suicides-see-a-sharp-rise-in-kolkata-amid-lockdown-over-half-are-40-years-or-younger/453853/

Datta, D. Impact of COVID-19 on Mental Health. In *Mental Health Strategies and Psychosocial Challenges in the Post COVID-19 Pandemic*; Shukla, A., Ed.; Eureka Publication Pvt. Ltd: Bangalore, India, 2020; pp. 45–71.

Davies, R. *Focus Groups in Asia*. Retrieved November 12, 2020 from http://www.orientpacific.com/focusgroups.htm

deGoeij, M. C.; Suhrcke, V.; Toffolutti, D.; van de Mheen, T. M.; Schoenmakers, A.; Kunst, E. How Economic Crises Affect Alcohol Consumption and Alcohol-Related Health Problems: A Realist Systematic Review. *Soc. Sci. Med.* **2015**, *131*, 131–146. https://doi.org/10.1016/j.socscimed.2015.02.025

Desmond-Hellmann, S. Preparing for the Next Pandemic, Apr 3, 2020. Retrieved April 17, 2020, from https://www.wsj.com/articles/preparing-for-the-next-pandemic-11585936915.

Dolapsakis, C.; Katsandri, A. Crack Lung: A Case of Acute Pulmonary Cocaine Toxicity. *Lung India* 2019, *36* (4), 370–371. https://doi.org/10.4103/lungindia.lungindia_193_19

Dom, G.; Samochowiec, J.; Evans-Lacko, S. Wahlbeck, K.; Van Hal, G.; McDaid, D. The Impact of the 2008 Economic Crisis on Substance Use Patterns in the Countries of the European Union. *Int. J. Environ. Res. Public Health* **2016**, *13* (1), 122. https://doi.org/10.3390/ijerph13010122

Duan, L.; Zhu, G. Psychological Interventions for People Affected by the COVID-19 Epidemic. *Lancet Psych.* 2020, *7* (4), 300–302. https://doi.org/10.1016/S2215-0366(20)30073-0.

Elsafty, A. S.; Ragheb, M. The Role of Human Resource Management towards Employees Retention during Covid-19 Pandemic in Medical Supplies Sector—Egypt. *Busi. Manage. Stud.* **2020**, *6* (2), 5059–5059.

First Death from China Mystery Illness Outbreak, Jan 11, 2020. Retrieved July 10, 2021 from https://www.theguardian.com/world/2020/jan/11/china-mystery-illness-outbreak-causes-first-death

Fern, E. H. *Advanced Focus Group Research*; Sage Publications: Thousand Oaks, CA, 2001.

Fetters, A. We Need to Stop Trying to Replicate the Life We Had. *The Atlantic*, Apr 10, 2020.

Frankenhauser, M. Psychobiological Aspects of Life Stress. In *Coping and Health*; Levine, S.; Ursin, H., Eds.; Plenum Press: New York, 1980; pp 203–223.

Giurge, L. M.; Bohns, V. K. 3 Tips to Avoid WFH Burnout, Apr 3, 2020. Retrieved Apr 13, 2020, from https://hbr.org/2020/04/3-tips-to-avoid-wfh-burnout.

Godoy, P.; Castilla, J.; Soldevila, N.; Mayoral, J. M.; Toledo, D.; Martin, V.; Astray, J.; Egurrola, M.; Morales-Suarez-Varela, M.; Dominguez. A. Smoking May Increase the Risk of Influenza Hospitalization and Reduce Influenza Vaccine Effectiveness in the Elderly. *Eur. J. Public Health* 2018, *28* (1), 150–155. https://doi.org/10.1093/eurpub/ckx130.

Greenbaum, T. L. *The Practical Handbook and Guide to Focus Group Research*; Lexington, MA: D. C. Heath and Company, 1988.

Greenbaum, T. L. *Moderating Focus Groups: A Practical Guide for Group Facilitation*; Sage Publications: Thousand Oaks, CA, 2000.

Hamilton, M. Diagnosis and Rating of Anxiety. *Br. J. Psych.* **1969,** Special Publication No 3, 76–79.

Health & Family Welfare Department, Government of West Bengal. *Corona Bulletin*, 2020. Retrieved Nov 25, 2020, from https://www.wbhealth.gov.in/pages/corona/bulletin

Hixon, T. Get Ready to Live with COVID-19, Mar 16, 2020. Retrieved Apr 23, 2020, from https://www.forbes.com/sites/toddhixon/2020/03/12/get-ready-to-live-with-covid-19/#26f55d347824.

Hulin, J.; Brodie, A.; Stevens, J.; Mitchell, C. Prevalence of Respiratory Conditions among People Who Use Illicit Opioids: A Systematic Review. *Addiction* **2019**, *115*, 832–849. https://doi.org/10.1111/add.14870

India Today Web Desk. *India to Lose 130 Million Jobs Due to Covid-19 Pandemic: Report*, June 16, 2020. Retrieved Nov 14, 2020 from https://www.indiatoday.in/education-today/latest-studies/story/india-to-lose-130-million-jobs-due-to-covid-19-pandemic-report-1689590-2020-06-16

Janis, I. L. *Victims of Groupthink*; Houghton Mifflin Company: Boston, MA, 1972.

Kopp, D. Opinion|Loneliness Is a Health Hazard, Too, Mar 22, 2020. Retrieved April 10, 2020, from https://www.wsj.com/articles/loneliness-is-a-health-hazard-too-11584906625.

Kuerbis, A.; Sacco, P.; Blazer, D. G.; Moore, A. A. Substance Abuse among Older Adults. *Clin. Geriatric Med.* **2014**, *30* (3), 629–654. https://doi.org/ 10.1016/j.cger.2014.04.008

Lagisetty, P. A.; Maust, D.; Heisler, M.; Bohnert, A. Physical and Mental Health Co-morbidities Associated with Primary Care Visits for Substance Use Disorders. *J. Addict. Med.* **2017**, *11* (2), 161–162. https://doi.org/10.1097/ADM.0000000000000280

Maier, W.; Buller, R.; Philipp, M.; Heuser, I. The Hamilton Anxiety Scale: Reliability, Validity and Sensitivity to Change in Anxiety and Depressive Disorders. *J. Affect. Disord.* **1988**, *14* (1), 61–68. https://doi.org/10.1016/0165-0327(88)90072-9

Maurer, R. Virtual Happy Hours Help Co-Workers, Industry Peers Stay Connected, 2020. Retrieved April 18, 2020, from https://www.shrm.org/hr-today/news/hr-news/pages/virtual-happy-hours-help-coworkers-stay-connected.aspx.

McEwen, B. S. Protective and Damaging Effects of Stress Mediators: The Good and Bad Sides of the Response to Stress. *Dialogues Clin. Neurosci.* 2002, *8* (4), 367–381. https://doi.org/10.31887/DCNS.2006.8.4/bmcewen.

Meyerholz, D. K.; Edsen-Moore, M.; McGill, J.; Coleman, R. A.; Cook, R. T.; Legge, K. L. Chronic Alcohol Consumption Increases the Severity of Murine Influenza Virus Infections. *J. Immunol.* **2008**, *181* (1). 641–648. https://doi.org/10.4049/jimmunol.181.1.641

Miller, A. M. People Who Got Sick with the Coronavirus While Living Alone Describe Their Panic: 'I Could Be Dead and Decaying and No One Would Know', May 5, 2020. Retrieved May 20, 2020, from https://www.businessinsider.com/what-its-like-to-get-covid-19-when-living-alone-2020-5.

Ministry of Health & Family Welfare, Government of India, 2020. Retrieved Nov 25, 2020 from https://www.mohfw.gov.in/

Morgan, D. L. *The Focus Group Guidebook: Focus Group Kit 1*; Sage Publications: Thousand Oaks, CA, 1998.

Newcomb, M. D.; Bentler, P. M. Impact of Adolescent Drug Use and Social Support on Problems of Young Adults: A Longitudinal Study. *J. Abnormal Psychol.* 1988, *97* (1), 64–75. https://doi.org/10.1037/0021-843X.97.1.64

Ngoc Su, D.; Luc Tra, D.; Thi Huynh, H. M.; Nguyen, H. H. T.; O'Mahony, B. Enhancing Resilience in the Covid-19 Crisis: Lessons from Human Resource Management Practices in Vietnam. *Curr. Iss Tour.* **2021**, 1–17. DOI: 10.1080/13683500.2020.1863930

OECD Economic Outlook. *Global Prospects Are Improving But Performance Diverges Strongly across Countries*, May 2020. Retrieved July 10, 2021 from https://oecd.org/economic-outlook

Ornell, F.; Schuch, J. B.; Sordi, A. O.; Kessler, F. H. P. "Pandemic Fear" and COVID-19: Mental Health Burden and Strategies. *Braz. J. Psych.* **2020**, *42* (3). https://doi.org/10.1590/1516-4446-2020-0008

Page, J.; Hinshaw, D.; McKay, B. In Hunt for Covid-19 Origin, Patient Zero Points to Second Wuhan Market—The Man with the First Confirmed Infection of the New Coronavirus Told the WHO Team That His Parents Had Shopped There. *Wall Street J*, 2021. Retrieved Feb 27, 2021.en who fell sick on Dec. 8, 2019.

Palomba, C. A.; Banta, T. W. *Assessment Essentials: Planning, Implementing, and Improving Assessment in Higher Education*; John Wiley & Sons: San Francisco, 1999.

Peacock, A.; Leung, J.; Larney, S.; Colledge, S.; Hickman, M.; Rehm, J.; Giovino, G. A.; West, R.; Hall, W.; Griffiths, P.; Ali, R.; Gowing, L.; Marsden, J.; Ferrari, G. A.; Grebely, J.; Farrell, M.; Degenhardt. L. Global Statistics on Alcohol, Tobacco and Illicit Drug Use: 2017 Status Report. *Addiction* **2018,** *113* (10), 1905–1926. https://doi.org/10.1111/add.14234

Perappadan, B. S. India's First Coronavirus Infection Confirmed in Kerala. *The Hindu*, Jan 30, 2020. https://www.thehindu.com/news/national/indias-first-coronavirus-infection-confirmed-in-kerala/article30691004.ece

PTI report. *Suicide Leading Cause for over 300 Lockdown Deaths in India, Says Study*, May 5, 2020. Retrieved Nov 12, 2020 from https://economictimes.indiatimes.com/news/politics-and-nation/suicide-leading-cause-for-over-300-lockdown-deaths-in-india-says-study/articleshow/75519279.cms

PTI report. *Job Loss Most Severe Immediate Impact of COVID-19: Survey*, June 11, 2020. Retrieved Nov 11, 2020 from https://economictimes.indiatimes.com/jobs/job-loss-most-severe-immediate-impact-of-covid-19-survey/articleshow/76323649.cms?from = mdr

Puchta, C. *Focus Group Practice*; Sage Publications: Thousand Oaks, CA, 2004.

Puri, N. *Age of Anxiety: Mental Health Is the Next Looming Crisis in Covid-19 Times*, Apr 12, 2020. Retrieved Oct 29, 2020 from https://www.business-standard.com/article/health/age-of-anxiety-mental-health-is-the-next-looming-crisis-in-covid-19-times-120041001208_1.html

RBI Highlights Demand Shock As Biggest Impact Of Second Covid-19 Wave, May 17, 2021. Retrieved July 9, 2021 from https://www.business-standard.com/article/news-cm/rbi-highlights-demand-shock-as-biggest-impact-of-second-covid-19-wave-121051701058_1.html

Regmi, K.; Lwin, C. M. Impact of Social Distancing Measures for Preventing Coronavirus Disease 2019 [COVID-19]: A Systematic Review and Meta-Analysis Protocol. medRxiv. DOI: 10.1101/2020.06.13.20130294

Riggs, P. D.; Whitmore, E. A. *Substance Use Disorders and Disruptive Behavior Disorders*; APA Press: Washington, DC, 1999.

Robinson, B. What Studies Reveal about Social Distancing and Remote Working during Coronavirus, Apr 4, 2020. Retrieved Apr. 10, 2020, from https://www.forbes.com/sites/bryanrobinson/2020/04/04/what-7-studies-show-about-social-distancing-and-remote-working-during-covid-19/#1bfe20ca757e.

Saladino, V.; Algeri, D.; Auriemma, V. *The Psychological and Social Impact of Covid-19: New Perspectives of Well-Being*, Oct 2, 2020. Retrieved Nov 3, 2020 from https://www.frontiersin.org/articles/10.3389/fpsyg.2020.577684/full

Schulte, M. T.; Hser, Y. I. Substance Use and Associated Health Conditions throughout the Lifespan. *Public Health Reviews* **2014,** *35* (2), 1–23. https://doi.org/10.1007/BF03391702

Serafini, K.; Toohey, M. J.; Kiluk, B. D.; Carroll, K. M. Anger and Its Association with Substance Use Treatment Outcomes in a Sample of Adolescents. *J. Child Adolescent Substance Abuse* **2016,** *25* (5), 391–398. https://doi.org/10.1080/1067828X.2015.1049394

Serafini, G.; Parmigiani, B.; Amerio, A.; Aguglia, A.; Sher, L.; Amore, M. The Psychological Impact of COVID-19 on the Mental Health in the General Population. *QJM: Int. J. Med.* **2020,** *113* (8), 531–537. https://doi.org/10.1093/qjmed/hcaa201

Sher, L. The Impact of the COVID-19 Pandemic on Suicide Rates. *QJM: Int. J. Med.* **2020**, *113* (10), 707–712. https://doi.org/10.1093/qjmed/hcaa202

Singh, P. K. *Promote Hand Hygiene to Save Lives and Combat COVID-19*, May 4, 2020. Retrieved Oct 30, 2020 from https://www.who.int/southeastasia/news/detail/04-05-2020-promote-hand-hygiene-to-save-lives-and-combat-covid-19

Sinha, R.; Fox, H. C.; Hong, K. A.; Bergquist, K.; Bhagwagar, Z.; Siedlarz, K. M. Enhanced Negative Emotion and Alcohol Craving, and Altered Physiological Responses Following Stress and Cue Exposure in Alcohol Dependent Individuals *Neuropsychopharmacology* **2009**, *34* (5), 1198–1208. https://doi.org/10.1038/npp.2008.78

Smith, R. A. Single Life and the Coronavirus, Apr 5, 2020. Retrieved May 20, 2020, from https://www.wsj.com/articles/single-life-and-the-coronavirus-11586088001.

Spring, A.; Earl, C. 'Just Not Blond': How the Diversity Push Is Failing Australian Fashion. *The Guardian: Australia Edition*, May 22, 2018. https://www.theguardian.com/fashion/2018/may/22/just-not-blonde-how-the-diversity-push-is-failing-australian-fashion

Stratton, S. J. COVID-19: Not a Simple Public Health Emergency. *Prehospital Disaster Med.* **2020**, *35* (2), 119. https://doi.org/10.1017/S1049023X2000031X

Sureshchandra, S.; Raus, A.; Jankeel, A.; Ligh, B. J. K.; Walter, N. A. R.; Newman, N.; Grant, K. A.; Messaoudi, I. Dose-Dependent Effects of Chronic Alcohol Drinking on Peripheral Immune Responses. *Sci. Rep.* **2019**, *9* (1), 7847. https://doi.org/10.1038/s41598-019-44302-3

Tensay, A. T.; Singh, M. The Nexus between HRM, Employee Engagement and Organizational Performance of Federal Public Service Organizations in Ethiopia. *Heliyon* **2020**, *6* (6), e04094. DOI: 10.1016/j.heliyon.2020.e04094

Turner, R. J.; Lloyd, D. A. Lifetime Traumas and Mental Health: The Significance of Cumulative Adversity. *J. Health Soc. Behav.* **1995**, *36* (4), 360–376. https://doi.org/10.2307/2137325

Umar, M.; Xu, Y.; Mirza, S. S. The Impact of Covid-19 on Gig Economy. *Econ. Res.- Ekonomska Istraživanja* **2020**, 1–13. https://www.tandfonline.com/doi/abs/10.1080/1331677X.2020.1862688

Volkow, N. D. Collision of the COVID-19 and Addiction Epidemics. *Ann. Internal Med.* **2020**, *173* (1), 61–62. https://doi.org/10.7326/M20-1212

Vyas, L.; Butakhieo, N. (2021) The Impact of Working from Home during COVID-19 on Work and Life Domains: An Exploratory Study on Hong Kong. *Policy Design Practice* **2021**, *4* (1), 59–76. DOI: 10.1080/25741292.2020.1863560

Whyte, W. H. Groupthink. *Fortune Magazine*, Mar 1952.

Wills, T. A.; Vaccaro, D.; McNamara, G. The Role of Life Events, Family Support, and Competence in Adolescent Substance Use: A Test of Vulnerability and Protective Factors. *Am. J. Community Psychol* **1992**, *20*, 349–374. https://doi.org/10.1007/BF00937914

Wong, E.; Ho, K.; Wong, S.; Cheung, A.; Yeoh, E. Workplace Safety and Coronavirus Disease (COVID-19) Pandemic: Survey of Employees. *Bull World Health Organ.* E-pub **2020**, 20.

Worldometer. *COVID-19 Coronavirus Pandemic*, 2020. Retrieved Nov 25, 2020 from https://www.worldometers.info/coronavirus/

Yu, Z.; Wang, G.; Goldman, E.; Zangerl, B.; Xie, N.; Cao, Y.; Maida, M. COVID-19 Vaccine: Call for Employees in International Transportation Industries and International Travelers as the First Priority in Global Distribution. *Open Med.* **2021**, *16* (1), 134–138.

CHAPTER 16

Covert Casualty in a Crisis: Gender Equity—Empowering Human Resources via Learning, Authenticity, and Resilience

TUSHARIKA MUKHERJEE[*]

Work and Organizational Psychologist, Lecturer, Trainer, Justus Liebig University Giessen, Germany

[*]*E-mail: tusharikamukherjee@gmail.com*

ABSTRACT

A crisis, as we witnessed during the 2020 pandemic, challenges society and individuals in unprecedented ways and initiates an urgent need for survival. As our work systems also become vulnerable, the impact of a crisis is perceived disproportionately by the different segments. Workplace inequity, exclusion, and discrimination against women emerge as the contagion effect of the synchronous economic downturn. It often includes calculated institutive action aimed at enduring the crunch as well as reviving the fragile organizations. In this chapter, we unravel the subtle ways of gender-based discrimination that has persisted even in modern workplaces with contemporary work values and has inadvertently become a means of leveraging the economic crisis. Inclusivity mandated by law has been partially successful in deflating the diversity resistance seen across sectors. A more accommodative response comprises learning from the critical situation, initiative taking, and proactive restructuring of skills and innovation in transforming crisis management from an emergency response to a sustainable process. Whether the post-pandemic rhetoric vis-à-vis the human resources strategies can evolve into a global and inclusive order rests on the authenticity of the equity measures, supportive leadership, and an inclusion fostering organizational climate. We further discuss resilience as an organizational competency that enables crisis anticipation, coping, and an effective adaptation, more so when supported by a diversity of reflection and collective sense making.

16.1 INTRODUCTION

As our society and business environments continue to evolve, they make our work organizations vulnerable to crisis and change. The COVID-19 pandemic created an unprecedented situation impacting our social behavior and posing a challenge for our economy and the work sector. The initial response to the pandemic primarily involved public health policies, which over time translated into the questions of people's livelihood and future security. The subsequent uncharted transformation in our work organizations has now merged with the unpredictability of the efficacy of human resource management (HRM). As the consequences of this crisis are more likely to outlast its duration, the necessity in the post-pandemic era is to reinvent organizations through learning and innovation, competent handling of the critical issues, and preparing for challenges that might surface as we embrace the new normal.

Ordinarily perceived as a standoff, an organizational crisis can alternately accelerate revival. The chosen path is contingent upon the cognizance of the situation as either a threat or an opportunity (Milburn et al., 1983). When an organization's survival and continuity is the most compelling issue, the leadership, the mood of the state, and the political intention determine which activities of the organization or workforce will be encouraged and which others will be undervalued and sanctioned, or even impaired for a longer time to come. The range of impact of the pandemic on organizational processes highlights several organizational challenges during the COVID-19 pandemic, including health and safety in the workplace, mental health and well-being, lack of connectivity and belongingness, work–life conflict, altered opportunities of advancement, workplace fairness and equity, and job insecurity. A study carried out in Australia, Brazil, Canada, China, France, Germany, India, Ireland, Mexico, UK, and the US reported that people in emerging economies experienced a greater amount of crisis on these grounds (McKinsey, 2020). A significant finding that emerged from this study is that women, LGBTQ+, and people of color experienced a greater crisis in the workplace particularly with their mental health, growth opportunities, fair assessment of performance, and job security. The UN Department of

Economic and Social Affairs noted that the gender gap in workforce participation that had marginally reduced in the past two decades has widened during the pandemic (UNDESA, 2020). It raises several fundamental questions regarding the inadequate economic empowerment of women even in a highly globalized work environment. It also underlines the continued gender bias embedded in the warped diversity management practices and inclusion practices.

In this chapter, we review workplace gender-based discrimination in its most noted forms for decades. We also look at the factors contributing to the perennial overriding of human rights and equality and examine its present modes exacerbated by the global crisis of 2020. Further, we explore crisis management strategies embedded in organizational learning, the creation of authentic workplace diversity, and organizational resilience. It is imperative at this juncture to discern and predict the decisions leaders will make in moving forward and spearheading transformative changes.

With this background the current chapter highlights on (1) how workplace discrimination against women finds new dimensions in the pandemic, (2) how workplace vertical discrimination in the form of the glass ceiling and glass cliff continues to be a reality in 2021, (3) how crisis management through austerity measures finds women at the receiving end, (4) how diversity flourishes when an organization moves from resistance to learning and finally (5) a brief on how authentic inclusion and organizational resilience are the steps forward in the post-pandemic era.

16.2 THE ROAD TO GENDER PARITY TILL 2020

The social and economic inequality between man and woman has traversed through numerous evolutionary changes over time. The ubiquitous gendering of organizations and their practices has continually reinforced the demarcation set by social norms and power distributions (Acker, 2006). Crusading against the universal patriarchal order, women empowerment and feminist movements have proliferated salient initiatives for abating gender-based inequalities (Connell and Messerschmidt, 2005). The unprecedented participation of women in the workforce succeeded in transforming the unbalanced representation into a more socially justified and equitable one, albeit partially. Nevertheless, women globally continue to be marginalized and predominantly regarded as an outsider to the hegemonic masculinity. Acker asserts, "systematic disparities between participants in power and control over goals, resources, and outcomes; in workplace decisions such as how to organize work; in opportunities for promotion and interesting work; in security in employment and benefits; in pay and other monetary rewards; in respect and pleasures in work and work relations" comprise the pervasive forms of discrimination in organizations (2006, p. 443). Much of the discrimination that receives attention is overt injustice (Welle and Heilman, 2007), while a more covert and powerful barrier to developmental aspirations of women (microinequities) sustains in the work sector and intercepts women's advancement merely because "they are women" (Morrison et al., 1987, in Baxter and Wright, 2000).

The illusory claims of contemporary organizations concerning their transition from gender-biased to anti-discriminatory establishments have many dimensions. A principal sequel to gender discrimination is the underrepresentation of women in leadership positions in organizations (Chakraborty and Mishra, 2019). Hymowitz and Schellhardt (1986) noted this as the glass ceiling phenomenon or the latent barriers women face in their attempts to climb the leadership ladder. The existence of glass ceiling in organizations was formally acknowledged in the United States first through the legislation of the Glass Ceiling Act within the Civil Rights Act of 1991 (for protection against gender and race-based discrimination), as a step toward reinstating social justice (Boyd, 2008). Equal opportunity initiatives and affirmative action (reverse discrimination; Levinson, 2011) across organizations and countries enabled substantive proportions of women to enter the workplace and attain managerial positions, yet the numbers are far from observable equity. The acutely fewer number of women at top positions in organizations is an aftereffect of the systemic buildup of hurdles women face relative to men in their upward mobility in the hierarchy (Baxter and Wright, 2000).

Glass ceiling prevents women from gaining access to the top positions in the organizational hierarchy (Ryan and Haslam, 2007), a form of vertical discrimination (Cotter et al., 2001). Elucidating the expanse of glass ceiling, Boyd (2008) called the phenomenon the stained glass ceiling to describe the advancement difficulties of women in ministries, as grass-ceiling in the field of agriculture, and as political glass ceiling in politics. The effects observed are across sectors, with manufacturing industries, clerical and service jobs, civil services, social work, and journalism not remaining unaffected (e.g., Tabak, 1997; Harlan and Berheide, 1994; Naff and Thomas, 1994; Gibelman and Schervish, 1995; Tan, 1990; Maume, 2004). Though glass ceiling effects are visible even at entry levels, Cotter and colleagues (2001) see a relative increase in discrimination at higher levels as the primary indicator of glass ceiling. Wright and Baxter (2000) propose that glass ceiling is not equivalent to generic gender discrimination because the term represents a "particular pattern of hierarchically organized disadvantage." The advancement hurdles systematically contributing to the glass ceiling effect are artificially created (Cotter et al., 2001). In other words, this discrimination rests on factors other than skills, abilities, work orientation, or productivity-relevant predictors of work outcomes. Further, the occupancy of higher positions by women is conditional on the attrition at lower levels. As women feel discouraged to seek advancement by the anticipated glass ceiling, premature withdrawals recurrently result in reinforcing glass ceiling (Alessio and Andrzejewski, 2000; Maume, 2004).

> *The Glass Ceiling Index 2021 published by the European Institute for Gender Equality showcases the environment for working women across 29 nations in Asia, Australia, Europe, and North America. Based on the year 2020 or later, Sweden (84.0*), Iceland (78.7*), and Finland (77.7*) held the top three spots, while Turkey (35.7*), Japan (31.0*), and South Korea (24.8*) ranked the lowest. Canada (65.9*), United States (58.2*), Britain (57.2*), and Germany (54.4*), ranked 11th, 18th, 20th, and 22nd, respectively.*
>
> *(*the scores are based on the share of women in management, on boards, and in parliament, where 100 represents the best score)*

The impact of glass ceiling magnifies with the paradoxical phenomenon of glass escalator or the relative ease and enhanced mobility experienced by men (Maume, 1999), even in female-dominated sectors (Ryan and Haslam, 2007). It represents discrimination against women through privileges in the form of rapid promotions to men (Ng and Wiesner, 2007). The glass ceiling effects are compounded by the independent or collateral presence of one or more appendages such as barriers encountered by women while entering an organization (glass door; Cohen, 1998), the restricted scope of promotion for women at the lowest levels of organization (glass floor; Barnet-Verzat and Wolff, 2008), unfair evaluation practices as discrimination against assertive women (chilly workplace climate; Fassinger, 2008), women being held back at lowest organizational levels with jobs of low remuneration (sticky floors; Kee, 2006), and women self-sabotaging their careers through implementing strategies that have severe backlashes on them (Smith et al., 2012).

Besides the three obvious pathways to leadership positions, viz., vacancies for which an aspirant is eligible, competition, and the decision makers' preference for individual characteristics in the incumbent (Gorman and Kmec, 2009), three additional mechanisms shape decision makers' bias and eventual preference of a male over a female candidate. First, decision makers may give credence to gender as a measure of competence. Inferences are drawn on social characteristics over and above the performance evidence, such that high competence is associated with male stereotypes and low competence with the female stereotype (e.g., Ridgeway 1997; Heilman et al., 1989). Qualitative evidence also suggests that decision makers employ gender and race-based inaccurate assumptions as additional information to objective observations (Moss and Tilly, 2001). Second, gender-stereotypical selection criteria may influence the perceived suitability of the candidate. Decision makers look for congruity between preconceived schema for desirable attributes and the incumbent, which may form the basis for selection. In occasions where the desired attributes are stereotypically masculine, male candidates are likely to be preferred over their female counterparts (Eagly and Karau, 2002). Empirical evidence reveals that leader/manager stereotypes are analogous to male stereotypes, which usually drive the "think manager— think male" heuristic. Third, the gender of the decision maker may allow in-group favoritism to function as a plausible determiner by influencing impressions and evaluations of same sex or opposite sex candidates. Male decision makers complying with the in-group perceptions are more likely to rate male candidates as more trustworthy and cooperative (Fiske et al., 2002; Beckman and Phillips, 2005). Furthermore, Gorman and Kmec (2009) assert that gender bias intensifies in higher positions, as decisions are intuitively made based on complex and relatively ambiguous information about the incumbent. Elucidating that gender discrimination can be unintentional, Motowidlo (1986, in Powell and Butterfield, 1994) argues that the fear of selecting an unsuitable candidate, personal similarities, and finding a match for a predetermined prototype, may be instrumental in making decisions based on gender differences.

Gender role stereotypes and gender-differentiated perceptions also frequently influence the career choices women make. For most, occupations that conform to societal expectations are preferred over and above their capabilities (Correll, 2001). Women reportedly occupy a higher proportion of leadership positions in service sectors, such as health, social service, retail, and banking (Haslam and Ryan, 2008). However, investigations in the glass ceiling phenomenon suggest that women are less likely to penetrate only some specific areas within the broad work sectors. A survey in the medical field in the United States revealed that 55% of women, as opposed to 42% male, practiced in lower paying specializations, such as pediatrics, general practice, and general internal medicine. Higher paying specialties, such as radiology, general surgery, anesthesiololgy, and subspecialty surgery, had a substantially lower representation of women practitioners (Longo and Straehley, 2008). Surgery was perceived to be a nonconforming gender role by 96% of female medical students. They deemed obstetrics/gynecology, pediatrics, radiology, and ophthalmology as more appropriate career choices. Respondents also revealed that male bias, competition, and lack of female mentors were crucial in disapproving surgery as an option (Lillemoe et al., 1994). Recent estimations somewhat validated earlier findings, where only 25% of female doctors considered surgery as a career option (as compared with 42% male doctors), with 68% citing surgery as a career unwelcoming of women (Fitzgerald et al., 2012).

> As per the European Parliament figures, women constituted 76% of the COVID-19 frontline workers, exposing them more to the virus. This is addition to the essential services which remained fully or partially open during the pandemic. Women make up over 80% of precarious jobs, such as domestic help (95%), childcare (93%), personal care workers in healthcare (86%), and cashiers (82%).
>
> Women faced greater job insecurity and job loss as most COVID-hit sectors, such as childcare, retail, and hospitality and tourism, employ large percentages of women (84% in the 15–64 years age group).
>
> In a February 2021 briefing, the European Parliament held that the pandemic has impacted men and women differently and called for a gender-sensitive response (Shreeves, 2021).

16.3 GENDER EQUITY DURING CRISIS MANAGEMENT

16.3.1 FROM DIVERSITY RESISTANCE TO LEARNING

Civil liberty leaders and social reformers have globally confronted socioeconomic and political discrimination against women over the decades. Though affirmative action has provided the basic infrastructure women needed to enter the work sector, inequity has continued to impede their progress by recurring in more subtle forms. The fact that contemporary organizational practices and literature is replete with discrimination testify to the pervasive resistance to diversity.

Whether inclusion is an imposition upon the management or emerged from an internalized choice becomes the principal criterion to identify the strategic organizational responses aimed at learning (Dass and Parker, 1999). Elucidating varied approaches to inclusion, Dass and Parker argue that ascribing diversity as a threat to homogeneity, status quo, and the "we"-"they" identity is more likely to elicit a reactive response to the questions of inclusion, which develops into diversity resistance. The approach grows defensive as the perspective of discrimination and fairness becomes driven by the argument that differences create disturbance leading to the belief that the in-groups must be protected and the entrant must assimilate. The defensive strategy involves negotiation and appeasement of stakeholders through more observable tactics like assigning minority representatives as leaders of affirmative action. Institutionalized measures of equity and fairness (e.g., quotas) can serve as the foundation for inclusivity but run the risk of being perceived as obstacles to the career advancement of others. Precisely, fairness for some is injustice for others. An accommodative response is a relatively new-age understanding of diversity issues, a position fueled by agreeing to the differences. The dissimilarities are valued, and the inclusion strategies are by choice. Managers begin to accept differences as legitimate and contributive to improved performance and turnover. What follows is a shift in the mindset from mere tolerance of dissimilarities to endorsement and patronage; nevertheless, it runs the risk of the nonmajority groups perceiving getting utilized for the advantage of the dominant groups (Dass and Parker, 1999).

The learning perspective, on the contrary, represents dynamism and initiative taking beyond any legal mandate. According to Dass and Parker (1999), this approach acknowledges the dichotomy of consensus disagreement within individuals and recognizes that a diverse workforce brings innovation, development, competency, and stability. The learning paradigm encompasses proactive engagement with diversity. A learning organization is "skilled at creating, acquiring, and transferring knowledge, and at modifying its behavior to reflect new knowledge and insights" (Garwin, 1993, p. 81). Whether adaptive to expected or unexpected constraints or generative through challenging existing assumptions about people and processes, convergent or involving problem-solving and decision-making through standardized competencies, or divergent by diversification and restructuring of skills, creativity, and innovation, organizational learning is the current benchmark for entrepreneurship and sustainability (Wang and Rafiq, 2009).

The unfolding of diversity management perspectives is analogous to the classic analysis of phases of organizational crisis, where an initial response of shock and disorganization gradually leads to defensive retreat or resistance to modification, succeeded by somewhat forced acknowledgment (Fink et al., 1971). The impact on intergroup relations also graduates from being fragmented and disconnected to being alienated and ritualistic, gradually developing into supportive and explorative initiatives. The progress over time leads to organic adaptation and change where the members experience trust, congruence, and interdependence in their handling of crisis (Fink et al., 1971). A collaborative learning system is equipped in anticipating challenges and more efficient in profiting from its strengths, thus enhancing its resilience in a crisis (More on organizational resilience in section Organizational Resilience).

16.3.2 AUSTERITY—AN INEQUITY AMPLIFIER

Organizational responses to economic crises like the global recession that started in 2008 have frequently involved a drastic reduction in the organizations' expenditures through austerity measures. A recurrent aftereffect of downgrading the costs has a disproportionate impact on women's employability and job security. Rubery and Raferty (2013) assert that a part of this gender difference can be attributed to the enduring sex-role stereotyping and the changes in the availability of male or female sex-typed jobs. As austerity measures bring in more buffer jobs, women are less likely to be regarded as flexible to adjust to these requirements. When women get employed in contracts, such as part-time, substitution, or voluntary work, it limits their advancement in the career ladder (Rubery and Raferty, 2013). The assumption of women being open to both voluntary and involuntary work during a crisis is principally a residue of perennial gender role stereotyping that places women as caregivers before a wage earner.

Much of the crisis response is motivated by the political will and agency in its defense of fiscal adversity (Cullen and Murphy, 2017). UN Human Rights report on the cascading effects of austerity measures on gender equality acknowledges a triagonal impact on women. First, reduced public expenditure directly impacts the state-funded care services, which inescapably amounts to women providing increased unpaid care, leaving less time for gainful employment or even recreational or self-care time. Second, crises bring higher prices of commodities and reduced incomes, creating additional pressure on women to run their households. Third, reduced public sector jobs leave women with lesser alternatives to find relatively stable jobs with equitable payments (OHCHR, 2018). For example, in analyzing the political culture of Ireland, Cullen and Murphy (2017) argue that austerity is gendered and dominated by the patriarchal standards of power and prestige. They further report that the longstanding efforts for gender equality have been severely damaged by austerity, including hefty budget reductions for organizations working toward gender equality like The Equality Authority and the Irish Human Rights Commission. Women's health institutes (Women's Health Council and Crisis Pregnancy Agency) faced depletion of their resources. Concurrently, the scholarly work on gender issues was majorly discouraged via the termination of agencies working with poverty, racism, and interculturalism in the last decade.

16.3.3 THE PARADOX OF WOMEN IN LEADERSHIP ROLES

It seems reasonable to assume that once women break through the glass ceiling or have the opportunity to move up the leadership ladder, the organizational hierarchy bestows equity. On the contrary, the workplace experiences of senior executives suggest distinct gender differentiation even beyond the glass ceiling. Positions occupied by women are more confining, allow restricted advancement, lack authority, and disburse limited rewards (Haslam and Ryan, 2008). While men reaching top positions experience challenge and self-development, women at corresponding positions report encountering obstacles masked as "challenges" (Ohlott et al., 1994). Women who can ascend the organizational hierarchy face a second form of subtle discrimination metaphorically termed the glass cliff (Ryan and Haslam, 2005). Ryan and Haslam assert that "... women may be being preferentially placed in leadership roles that are associated with an increased risk of negative consequences. As a result, to the extent that they are achieving leadership roles, these may be more precarious than those occupied by men" (2005, p. 83). Women advanced to higher positions, find themselves battling with the company's poor performance, failures, and organizational crisis.

One of the classic examples of the glass cliff phenomenon is the appointment of Kate Swann as the CEO of W.H. Smith (a UK firm) at the time of the company's severest crisis including lowered profits, reduced share prices, and major layoff (Ryan and Haslam, 2005). Likewise, Marissa Mayer was appointed the CEO of Yahoo (July 2012) when Yahoo was facing a strategic problem of massive competition and lack of innovation (Forbes, 2012). Ryan and Haslam stressed the existence of a glass cliff in politics (other than business), illustrating that Margaret Thatcher was appointed as the education minister (in Britain during the early 1970s) when the country confronted student radicalism and riots. Thatcher ultimately became the prime minister in 1979 when Britain underwent severe unemployment and economic recession (BBC, 2004). More recently, Theresa Mayer was elected as the UK Prime Minister soon after the Brexit referendum caused an economic downslide.

Ryan and Haslam (2007) identified several underlying processes to the glass cliff phenomenon. The predictors range from beliefs (prejudices) about distinct skills and competencies of men and women, to deliberate attempts at finding a weak scapegoat. The extent of male dominance in an occupational sector substantially impacts the presence of the glass cliff. Further, the perceived suitability of women for leadership positions is guided by two fundamental assertions: think manager—think male versus think crisis—think female; and hostile sexism versus benevolent sexism (Ryan and Haslam, 2007). While both these assertions reflect an impoverished integration of women into the workforce, they also have formidable implications for the management of diversity during crises.

Implicit theories of leadership and gender categorically dissociate attributes of a good leader from women (e.g., Agars, 2004; Eagly and Karau, 2002; Schein, 1975). The overarching stereotype that identifies management with men is the predominating impediment to women in management positions (Antal and Izreali, 1993; in Ryan and Haslam, 2007). Studies conducted on attributes of managers based on gender demonstrated that managers were stereotypically perceived to possess attributes similar to men, and rarely like women (Schein, 1975, 1973). Attributes, such as emotional stability, aggressiveness, leadership ability, self-reliance, competitiveness, self-confidence, objectivity, ambition, being well-informed, and being forceful, were frequently regarded as characteristics of both successful managers and men. Studies on manager and men stereotypes have validated the prevalent 'think manager – think male' relationship (Eagly, 2005; in Ryan and Haslam, 2007; Schein, 2001). A proximal consequence of inconsistency between manager stereotypes and women stereotypes is the discriminatory attitude toward women at the workplace (Eagly and Karau, 2002). Eagly and Karau also point out that stereotypes often lead to a less favorable evaluation of women in terms of both their potential and actual behavior as a leader (2002). Women leaders who do not conform to gender stereotypes are deprecated for the (in) appropriateness of their behavior. While a male manager is appreciated for his assertive behavior as a leader, a woman is criticized for not being adequately feminine for similar behavior. Negative evaluations automatically trigger perceptions of female leaders' unsuitability and expectations of failure (Ryan and Haslam, 2007).

Crises are stereotypically perceived to be associated with poor leadership. In a crisis, the leader is expected to behave or react in a manner different from routine. The attributes perceived to be crisis handling, such as being understanding, intuitive, and creative, are stereotypically associated with women (Ryan and Haslam, 2007; Schein, 1975). As a consequence, women frequently find themselves in positions designed to deal with a crisis. Think crisis—think female stereotypes drive decision makers to place women in positions with high emotional labor, rather than the positions demanding technical skills and knowledge. It runs as a counterargument to the think manager-think male proposition (Ryan et al., 2011). It also appears that these stereotypes associate male managers with successful organizations and female managers with unsuccessful ventures (Ryan et al., 2011).

Sexism constitutes a stereotypical gender–role attitude and discrimination in social or organizational contexts (Masser and Abrams, 2004). Sexism is an ambivalent and unified antipathy or hostility toward women (Swim et al., 1995) conceived to be emanating from two sources designated as hostile sexism and benevolent sexism (Glick and Fiske, 1996). Hostile sexism derives from the negative evaluation of women who do not conform to social norms, benevolent sexism, on the other hand, thrives upon idealization and positive appraisal of women in socially prescribed roles (Masser and Abrams, 2004). Those motivated by hostile sexism appoint women in precarious leadership positions with the maleficent motive of seeing them fail. On the contrary, benevolent sexists would reward women by selecting them for posts described as "challenging" but are risky in reality. Benevolent sexists assume that women are privileged by the opportunity to battle through the risks, regarded as equally precarious and unattractive by men (Ryan and Haslam, 2007). Such beneficence, Ryan and Haslam construe, is a conscious attempt to avoid outright discrimination against women. Glass cliffs are inadvertently sustained through subtle discriminations like offering a precarious leadership position to women, under the tag of golden opportunity. Secondly, the appointment of women to glass cliff positions is often supported because company management (in most cases men) normatively considers women to be more expendable. Intergroup networks work to the advantage of men, male decision makers saving attractive and steady positions for their in-group members (men) and prescribing problematic posts to women (Ryan and Haslam, 2007). Clearly, despite decades of affirmative action and equal opportunity practices, a multitude of factors contribute to the sustained gender inequity in our organizations. Kelly and Dobbin (1998) reviewing the efficiency of affirmative action argue that the institutionalized reforms are often prolonged even after their benefits can no longer be realized. One of the reasons for the redundancy of organizational strategies is the dynamic nature of discrimination which could not be arrested through legal compliance, formalized recruitment and training of women for their advancement, grievance redressal, targeted mentoring, etc. For example, despite anti-discriminatory statutes attempted to make the workplaces more balanced, they failed to remove the systemic barriers and project diversity as strength. (Kelly and Dobbin, 1998).

16.4 THE SOCIAL DISTANCING OF WOMEN AT WORK—ARE WOMEN PAYING A BIG PRICE IN 2020?

The global health crisis has evolved in a brief time into a human rights crisis in which women have been affected in multiple ways. The impact and the response to it have been grossly identified as gender regressive (Power, 2020). Some of the crucial issues are described in the following observations:

1. Workplace and business closures have impacted women more than men. The National Women's Law Center in the US noted that while women make up for 49% of the workforce, the job loss share in the first phases of the pandemic was 55%. The most impacted industries were education and health services (83%), retail trade (69%), leisure and hospitality (54%), and government positions (58%) (Ewing-Nelson, 2020).
2. School closures have forced many women to leave the workforce for childcare and homeschooling. Remote work via the home office, household work, and childcare has increased the risk of burnout. The evidence from Zika and Ebola showed depleted health care access for women, including antenatal and maternity services, along with disrupted child immunization programs. A large section of them who must continue working are in double jeopardy. Together, these factors have created this pandemic disproportionately more stressful and health degrading for women (Wenham, Smith, and Morgan, 2020).
3. Women in senior or leadership positions are 1.5% more likely than men to decelerate due to increased work pressure and burnout (Masterson, 2020). This has widened the unbalanced representation of women in key management positions. The 2020 Fortune 500 list revealed that only 37 CEO positions were held by women in contrast to the 463 CEO positions held by men (Catalyst, 2020).
4. Women with a disability or existing health conditions fear more discrimination due to perceived vulnerability. The Beijing Declaration and Platform for Action about 25 years ago upheld the nondiscrimination, equality, and freedom of women and girls with disabilities,

including their access to information and services regarding violence (unwomen.org, 1995). However, the lifetime prevalence of violence against women with disabilities continues to range from 26 to 90% (only marginally lower for disabled men, 28.7–86%), making them 1.5 times more vulnerable to experience abuse than those without disabilities (Lund, 2020; Hughes et al., 2012). The victimization has grown in magnitude during the COVID-19 pandemic owing to the public health measures of lockdown and quarantines.
5. Financial insecurity (due to job loss) and mobility restrictions are the two leading causes of the "shadow pandemic" of violence against women (UNWomen, 2020). McLaren and colleagues (2020) note that crisis (poverty, war, or disease outbreak) changes the power dynamics between man and woman. The pandemic has reinforced the enduring stereotype of the subordinate role of women in many households, thus compounding the burden on women.

Describing the nonsymmetrical distribution of household care shared by women during the COVID-19 pandemic, Wenham, Smith, and Morgan (2020) illustrate that

> *"In recent weeks, as the global workforce has moved online, meetings have been conducted from people's homes, making their routine domestic life visible. Whether this is the unmade bed in the background, the dirty cups on the sideboard, or a child interrupting the call, the reality of people's lives has been exposed. And while toddlers in the background can lighten a meeting, they also represent the stress of trying to balance work and family". (p. 1)*

The Global Gender Gap Report 2020 estimates that we need another 99.5 years, averaging globally, to reach gender parity in economic participation, political empowerment, education, and health and survival. The pandemic has put another obstacle in that course. It is pivotal to realize the role that organizations will have to play in the years to come. The advent and wide acceptance of remote working, even in traditional workplaces, such as universities and public offices, has infused optimism in the workforce not only in terms of more gender-neutral selections and more inclusive work environments but has also enabled flexible and remote working which is gaining more popularity and be normalized as desired work. It is undeniable that any progress in the direction of change and sustainable development should embed in the ability and willfulness of work organizations as pathfinders.

16.5 THE POST-PANDEMIC HRM DISCOURSE—EMERGING TRENDS

16.5.1 FOSTERING AUTHENTIC INCLUSION

Organizations in their sustainability efforts must recognize the structural impediments to gender-based/racial/cultural equality. Divergent from the traditional strategies of affirmative measures and stifling diversity resistance, contemporary workplaces can benefit abundantly from forging an organizational climate for inclusion. Defined as "a shared perception of the work environment comprising the practices, policies, and procedures that guide a shared understanding that inclusive behaviors, which foster a sense of belongingness and uniqueness, are expected, supported, and rewarded" climate for inclusion is primarily based on the learning perspective that endorses diversity as a resource and vital to organizational processes and actions (Boekhorst, 2015).

Challenging and critical situations call for authentic leadership driven by awareness of thoughts, actions, value orientations, knowledge, and competencies, alongside effective context appraisal and handling the crisis with optimism, resilience, and hope (Avolio et al., 2004) and appreciative leadership (Chakraborty and Mishra 2019). Evidence provides that authentic leadership can be instrumental in fostering workplace inclusion through trust-building, open and transparent communication, and authentic interpersonal relationships (Boekhorst, 2015). Verplanken and Holland (2002) contend that the high moral and ethical values of authentic leaders empower the inclusive organizational climate. Secondly, authentic leaders serve as role models enabling vicarious learning of appropriate inclusive behavior by other members (Boekhorst, 2015; Luthans and Avolio, 2003). Demonstration of such behavior operates at two levels; while it displays the expectation for inclusive behavior, it also creates an image of a climate for inclusion. The climate for inclusion enhances sharing of goals and an elevated cross-cultural exchange of information and skills, thus increasing performance (Boekhorst, 2015; Tjosvold et al., 2004).

16.5.2 ORGANIZATIONAL RESILIENCE

Organizations in the face of unexpected events maneuver their actions to circumvent a crisis, but they can rarely avoid being unscathed. The ones that survive must devise strategies to cope with its impact while continuing to grow. Adaptability and agility propel recovery from a setback, but resilience is the organizational competency that facilitates effective handling of unforeseen threats and crises (Lengnick-Hall et al., 2011). Organizational resilience is a dynamic capacity encompassing crisis prediction, coping, and learning from their impact to promote organizational change (Duchek, Raetze, and Scheuch, 2020; Duchek, 2014). Noteworthy in the present context, research suggests that diversity has a facilitating effect on resilience (Chakraborty et al, 2018). Diversity becomes a liability or opportunity, is promoted or discouraged, depends largely upon the organizations' perception of their resilience capacities and the factors contributing to it. Periods of high strain can push organizational resilience initiatives to traditional masculine leadership and decision-making, further widening the power gap between men and women. To avert gendered resilience practices, the management must identify and reorient the inherent structural hierarchies, actions, and communication (Witmer, 2019).

From the standpoint of the stage in a crisis, the process of resilience can be partitioned into anticipation, coping, and adaptation stages. The anticipation stage corresponds to the precrisis period and calls for recognizing plausible threats and proactive initiatives. This preparation is succeeded by problem-solving or coping. Finally, a resilient organization undergoes active adaptation via remodeling processes and relations and facilitating novel competencies (Duchek, Raetze, and Scheuch, 2020; Lengnick-Hall et al., 2011). Duchek, Raetze, and Scheuch further propose that group heterogeneity impacts anticipation positively by enhancing observation of the crisis environment and filtering the relevant information alongside initiating preparation for the impending damages and changes, and anticipatory innovation (e.g., de Oliveira Teixeira and Werther, 2013; Sutcliffe and Vogus, 2003). Secondly, a diverse team is more likely to engage in divergent thinking, facilitating coping with the crisis through sense-making and efficient problem-solving (e.g., Stephens et al., 2013; Weick et al., 2005). Lastly, diversity stimulates improved reflection and better learning based on previous crisis management. Heterogeneous experience sharing, differentiated skill sets, and interdependence in a diverse group lay the foundation for the evolution of resilience and effective crisis management. Resilience-enhancing diversity management will be valued in an organizational culture that incorporates an appreciation for diversity, openness, and communication (e.g., Dwertmann et al. 2016; van der Vorm et al. 2011).

16.6 CONCLUSION

In the wake of the global crisis, we are compelled to navigate through obscure and unpredictable events. From our initial response of self-protection, isolation, and sustained social distancing, we have reached a stage of the increasing vulnerability of economic decline which in turn contravenes our survival. The future of work now hinges on our collective sensemaking of the current global circumstances in terms of organizational and societal distress. Our social discourse will dictate whether we successfully adapt to the new environment or wither under its uncertainties (Stephens et al., 2020). The International Labor Organization (ILO, 2020) recognizes that lack of inclusiveness, underutilization of labor, stark inequalities in access to work, and deficiencies in work quality are the major challenges faced by our work sector. In response to the COVID-19 pandemic, ILO has delineated four priorities including a revival of the economy and employment, social protection and employee retention, security to workers including prevention against discrimination and exclusion, and strengthening organizations through social dialogue, capacity, and resilience building. The mission of achieving gender equity rests on an adjuvant macroeconomic environment and endogenous social stability. It is now imperative that we discover innovative social and economic policies, transform our organizational practices, and prepare for future risks through strategies that are both sustainable and inclusive.

KEY TAKEAWAYS

- The pandemic has posed unprecedented challenges for the human resource management policies around diversity issues and inclusion.
- The workplace discrimination against women vis-à-vis glass ceiling, glass cliff, and austerity drives have persisted in their new and subtler forms.
- Increasing health concerns, childcare, and elderly care demands, and the perceived mobility issues have enhanced the microinequities against women.
- A learning organization can withstand a crisis through its proactive engagement with diversity.
- Diversity management in the post-pandemic era should embrace trust-building, transparency in communication, and authentic leadership.

– Resilience-enhancing diversity management can herald as the effective human resource management strategy aimed at post-pandemic progress and sustainability.

KEYWORDS

- **gender equity**
- **organizational learning**
- **organizational resilience**
- **crisis management**
- **inclusion**

REFERENCES

Acker, J. Inequality Regimes Gender, Class, and Race in Organizations. *Gender Soc.* **2006,** *20* (4), 441–464.

Agars, M. D. Reconsidering the Impact of Gender Stereotypes on the Advancement of Women in Organizations. *Psychol. Women Quart.* **2004,** *28* (2), 103–111.

Alessio, J. C.; Andrzejewski, J. Unveiling the Hidden Glass Ceiling: An Analysis of the Cohort Effect Claim. *Am. Sociol. Rev.* **2000,** *65* (2), 311–315.

Antal, A. B.; Izraeli, D. N. A Global Comparison of Women in Management: Women Managers in Their Homelands and as Expatriates. In Ryan, M. K.; Haslam, S. A. The Glass Cliff: Exploring the Dynamics Surrounding the Appointment of Women to Precarious Leadership Positions. *Acad. Manage. Rev.* **2007,** *32* (2), 549–572.

Avolio, B. J.; Gardner, W. L.; Walumbwa, F. O.; Luthans, F.; May, D. R. Unlocking the Mask: A Look at the Process by Which Authentic Leaders Impact Follower Attitudes and Behaviors. *Leadership Quart.* **2004,** 15 (6), 801–823.

Barnet-Verzat, C.; Wolff, F. C. Gender wage gap and the glass ceiling effect: a firm-level investigation. *International Journal of Manpower*, 29 (6), 486–502.

Baxter, J.; Wright, E. O. The Glass Ceiling Hypothesis a Comparative Study of the United States, Sweden, and Australia. *Gender Soc.* **2000,** *14* (2), 275–294.

BBC Internet source: http://news.bbc.co.uk/2/hi/uk_news/magazine/3755031.stm

Beckman, C. M.; Phillips, D. J. Interorganizational Determinants of Promotion: Client Leadership and the Attainment of Women Attorneys. *Am. Sociol. Rev.* **2005,** *70* (4), 678–701.

Boekhorst, J. A. The Role of Authentic Leadership in Fostering Workplace Inclusion: A Social Information Processing Perspective. *Human Resour. Manage.* **2015,** *54* (2), 241–264.

Boyd, K. S. *Glass Ceiling. Encyclopedia of Race, Ethnicity, and Society*; Thousand Oaks, CA: SAGE, 2008; pp 549–552.

Catalyst. Quick Take: Women in the Workforce—United States, Oct 14, 2020. https://www.catalyst.org/research/women-in-the-workforce-united-states/

Chakraborty, T.; Mishra, N. Ontology Based Review of Corporate Board, Gender Diversity And Women Leadership. *Res. Directions* **2019**, *7* (1), 82–87.

Chakraborty, T.; Gupta, D.; Chatterjee, B. "Strong, Yet We Are Vulnerable": Role of Psychological Factors and Financial Affluence on Women's Entrepreneurial Success. *J. Global Busi. Advance.* **2018**, *11* (6), 726–752.

Chakraborty, T.; Mishra, N. Appreciative Inquiry: Unleashing a Positive Revolution of Organizational Change and Development. *Int. J. Econ. Com. Busi. Manage.* **2019**, *6* (2), 32–37.

Cohen, J. J. Time to Shatter the Glass Ceiling for Minority Faculty. *JAMA: J. Am. Med. Assoc.* **1998**, *280* (9), 821–822.

Connell, R. W.; Messerschmidt, J. W. Hegemonic Masculinity Rethinking the Concept. *Gender Soc.* **2005**, *19* (6), 829–859.

Correll, S. J. Gender and the Career Choice Process: The Role of Biased Self-Assessments. *Am. J. Sociol.* **2001**, *106* (6), 1691–1730.

Cotter, D. A.; Hermsen, J. M.; Ovadia, S.; Vanneman, R. The Glass Ceiling Effect. *Social Forces* **2001**, *80* (2), 655–681. DOI: 10.1353/sof.2001.0091

Cullen, P.; Murphy, M. P. Gendered Mobilizations against Austerity in Ireland. *Gender Work Organ.* **2017**, *24* (1), 83–97.

Dass, P.; Parker, B. Strategies for Managing Human Resource Diversity: From Resistance to Learning. *Acad. Manage. Persp.* **1999**, *13* (2), 68–80.

de Oliveira Teixeira, E.; Werther Jr, W. B. Resilience: Continuous Renewal of Competitive Advantages. *Busi. Horiz.* **2013**, *56* (3), 333–342.

Duchek, S. Growth in the Face of Crisis: The Role of Organizational Resilience Capabilities. *Acad. Manage. Proc.* **2014**, *2014* (1), 13487.

Duchek, S.; Raetze, S.; Scheuch, I. The Role of Diversity in Organizational Resilience: A Theoretical Framework. *Busi. Res.* **2020**, *13* (2), 387–423.

Dwertmann, D. J.; Nishii, L. H.; Van Knippenberg, D. Disentangling the Fairness & Discrimination and Synergy Perspectives on Diversity Climate: Moving the Field Forward. *J. Manage.* **2016**, *42* (5), 1136–1168.

Eagly, A. H.; Karau, S. J. Role Congruity Theory of Prejudice toward Female Leaders. *Psychol. Rev.* **2002**, *109* (3), 573.

Ewing-Nelson, C. After a Full Month of Business Closures, Women Were Hit Hardest By April's Job Losses. National Women's Law Center, 2020. https://nwlc-ciw49tixgw5lbab.stackpathdns.com/wp-content/uploads/2020/05/Jobs-Day-April-Factsheet.pdf

European Parliament, Understanding Covid-19's impact on women. 2021. https://www.europarl.europa.eu/news/en/headlines/society/20210225STO98702/understanding-the-impact-of-covid-19-on-women-infographics

Fassinger, R. E. Workplace Diversity and Public Policy: Challenges and Opportunities for Psychology. *Am. Psychol.* **2008**, *63* (4), 252.

Fawcett Society. 2009. http://www.fawcettsociety.org.uk/wp-content/uploads/2013/02/PRENANCY-DISCRIMINATION-2.pdf

Fink, S. L.; Beak, J.; Taddeo, K. Organizational Crisis and Change. *J. Appl. Behav. Sci.* **1971**, *7* (1), 15–37.

Fiske, S. T.; Cuddy, A. J.; Glick, P.; Xu, J. A Model of (Often Mixed) Stereotype Content: Competence and Warmth Respectively Follow from Perceived Status and Competition. *J. Personality Soc. Psychol.* **2002**, *82* (6), 878.

Fitzgerald, J. E. F.; Tang, S. W.; Ravindra, P.; Maxwell-Armstrong, C. A. Gender-Related Perceptions of Careers in Surgery among New Medical Graduates: Results of a Cross-Sectional Study. *Am. J. Surg.*, **2012**.

Forbes. 2012). http://www.forbes.com/sites/petercohan/2012/07/24/marissa-mayers-glass-cliff/

Garwin, D. A. Building a Learning Organization. *Harv. Busi. Rev.* **1993**, *71* (4), 73–91.

Gibelman, M.; Schervish, P. H. Pay Equity in Social Work: Not! *Social Work* **1995**, *40* (5), 622–629.

Glass Ceiling Index. 2021. https://www.economist.com/business/2021/03/06/is-the-lot-of-female-executives-improving

Glick, P.; Fiske, S. T. The Ambivalent Sexism Inventory: Differentiating Hostile and Benevolent Sexism. *J. Personality Soc. Psychol.* **1996**, *70* (3), 491.

Gorman, E. H.; Kmec, J. A. Hierarchical Rank and Women's Organizational Mobility: Glass Ceilings in Corporate Law Firms1. *Am. J. Sociol.* **2009**, *114* (5), 1428–1474.

Harlan, S. L.; Berheide, C. W. Barriers to Workplace Advancement Experienced by Women in Low-Paying Occupations. Center for Women in Government, University at Albany, State University of New York, 1994.

Haslam, S. A.; Ryan, M. K. The Road to the Glass Cliff: Differences in the Perceived Suitability of Men and Women for Leadership Positions in Succeeding and Failing Organizations. *Leadership Quart.* **2008**, *19* (5), 530–546.

Heilman, M. E.; Block, C. J.; Martell, R. F.; Simon, M. C. Has Anything Changed? Current Characterizations of Men, Women, and Managers. *J. Appl. Psychol.* **1989**, *74* (6), 935.

Hoobler, J. M.; Hu, J.; Wilson, M. Do Workers Who Experience Conflict between the Work and Family Domains Hit a "Glass Ceiling?" A Meta-Analytic Examination. *J. Vocational Behav.* **2010**, *77* (3), 481–494.

Hoobler, J. M.; Wayne, S. J.; Lemmon, G. Bosses' Perceptions of Family-Work Conflict and Women's Promotability: Glass Ceiling Effects. *Acad. Manage. J.* **2009**, *52* (5), 939–957.

Hughes, K.; Bellis, M. A.; Jones, L.; Wood, S.; Bates, G.; Eckley, L.;...Officer, A. Prevalence and Risk of Violence against Adults with Disabilities: A Systematic Review and Meta-Analysis of Observational Studies. *Lancet* **2012**, *379*, 1621–1629. http://dx.doi.org/10.1016/S0140-6736 (11)61851-5

Hymowitz, C.; Schellhardt, T. D. The Glass Ceiling. *Wall Street J. Special Report, the Corporate Woman (March)* **1986**, *D1*, 4−5.

ILO. 2020. World Employment and Social Outlook Trends 2020. https://www.ilo.org/wcmsp5/groups/public/—dgreports/—dcomm/—publ/documents/publication/wcms_734479.pdf

Kee, H. J. Glass Ceiling or Sticky Floor? Exploring the Australian Gender Pay Gap. *Econ. Record* **2006**, *82* (259), 408–427.

Kelly, E.; Dobbin, F. How affirmative action became diversity management: Employer response to antidiscrimination law, 1961 to 1996. *American Behavioral Scientist*, *41* (7), 960–984.

Kossek, E. E.; Lambert, S. J., Eds. *Work and Life Integration: Organizational, Cultural, and Individual Perspectives*; Psychology Press, 2012.

Lengnick-Hall, C. A.; Beck, T. E.; Lengnick-Hall, M. L. Developing a Capacity for Organizational Resilience through Strategic Human Resource Management. *Human Resour. Manage. Rev.* **2011**, *21* (3), 243–255.

Levinson, R. B. Gender-Based Affirmative Action and Reverse Gender Bias: Beyond Gratz, Parents Involved, and Ricci. *Harv. JL Gender* **2011**, *34*, 1.

Lewis, G. B.; Park, K. Turnover Rates in Federal White-Collar Employment: Are Women More Likely to Quit Than Men? *Am. Rev. Public Admin.* **1989**, *19* (1), 13–28. In Stroh, L. K.; Brett, J. M.; Reilly, A. H. Family Structure, Glass Ceiling, and Traditional Explanations for the Differential Rate of Turnover of Female and Male Managers. *J. Vocational Behav.* **1996**, *49* (1), 99–118.

Lillemoe, K. D.; Ahrendt, G. M.; Yeo, C. J.; Herlong, H. F.; Cameron, J. L. Surgery—Still an "Old Boys' Club"? *Surgery* **1994**, *116* (2), 255–259.

Longo, P.; Straehley, C. J. Whack! I've Hit the Glass Ceiling! Women's Efforts to Gain Status in Surgery. *Gender Med.* **2008**, *5* (1), 88–100.

Lund, E. M. Interpersonal Violence against People with Disabilities: Additional Concerns and Considerations in the COVID-19 Pandemic. *Rehab. Psychol.* **2020**, 65 (3), 199.

Masser, B. M.; Abrams, D. Reinforcing the Glass Ceiling: The Consequences of Hostile Sexism for Female Managerial Candidates. *Sex Roles* **2004**, *51* (9–10), 609–615.

Masterson, V. Why COVID-19 Could Force Millions of Women to Quit Work—and How to Support Them. *World Economic Forum*. https://www.weforum.org/agenda/2020/10/women-work-gender-equality-covid19/

Maume, D. J. Glass Ceilings and Glass Escalators Occupational Segregation and Race and Sex Differences in Managerial Promotions. *Work Occup.* **1999**, *26* (4), 483–509.

Maume, D. J. Is the Glass Ceiling a Unique Form of Inequality? Evidence from a Random-Effects Model of Managerial Attainment. *Work Occup.* **2004**, *31* (2), 250–274.

McKinsey COVID-19 and the Great Reset: Briefing Note #32, November 18, 2020.

McLaren, H. J.; Wong, K. R.; Nguyen, K. N.; Mahamadachchi, K. N. D. Covid-19 and Women's Triple Burden: Vignettes from Sri Lanka, Malaysia, Vietnam and Australia. *Soc. Sci.* **2020**, 9 (5), 87.

Milburn, T. W.; Schuler, R. S.; Watman, K. H. Organizational Crisis. Part I: Definition and Conceptualization. *Human Relat.* **1983**, *36* (12), 1141–1160. https://doi.org/10.1177/001872678303601205

Morrison, A.M.; White, R.P.; Velsor, E.V.; and the Center for Creative Leadership Breaking the Glass Ceiling. In Baxter, J.; Wright, E. O. The Glass Ceiling Hypothesis a Comparative Study of the United States, Sweden, and Australia. *Gender Soc.* **2000**, *14* (2), 275–294.

Moss, P. I.; Tilly, C. *Stories Employers Tell: Race, Skill, and Hiring in America*, Vol. 6; Russell Sage Foundation, 2001.

Motowidlo, S. J. Information Processing in Personnel Decisions. In Powell, G. N.; Butterfield, D. A. Investigating the "Glass Ceiling" Phenomenon: An Empirical Study of Actual Promotions to Top Management. *Acad. Manage. J.* **1994**, *37* (1), 68–86.

Naff, K. C.; Thomas, S. The Glass Ceiling Revisited: Determinants of Federal Job Advancement. *Rev. Policy Res.* **1994**, *13* (3–4), 249–272.

Ng, E. S.; Wiesner, W. H. Are Men Always Picked over Women? The Effects of Employment Equity Directives on Selection Decisions. *J. Busi. Ethics* **2007**, *76* (2), 177–187.

OHCHR United Nations Human Rights Report, 2018. https://www.ohchr.org/Documents/Publications/OHCHRreport2018.pdf

Ohlott, P. J.; Ruderman, M. N.; McCauley, C. D. Gender Differences in Managers' Developmental Job Experiences. *Acad. Manage. J.* **1994**, *37* (1), 46–67.

Power, K. The COVID-19 Pandemic has Increased the Care Burden of Women and Families. *Sustain.: Sci. Pract. Policy* **2020**, *16* (1), 67–73.

Ridgeway, C. L. Interaction and the Conservation of Gender Inequality: Considering Employment. *Am. Sociol. Rev.* **1997**, 218–235.

Rubery, J.; Rafferty, A. Women and Recession Revisited. *Work, Employ. Soc.* **2013**, *27* (3), 414–432.

Ryan, M. K.; Haslam, S. A. The Glass Cliff: Evidence That Women Are Over-Represented in Precarious Leadership Positions. *Br. J. Manage.* **2005**, *16* (2), 81–90.

Ryan, M. K.; Haslam, S. A. The Glass Cliff: Exploring the Dynamics Surrounding the Appointment of Women to Precarious Leadership Positions. *Acad. Manage. Rev.* **2007**, *32* (2), 549–572.

Ryan, M. K.; Haslam, S. A.; Hersby, M. D.; Bongiorno, R. Think Crisis–Think Female: The Glass Cliff and Contextual Variation in the Think Manager–Think Male Stereotype. *J. Appl. Psychol.* **2011**, *96* (3), 470.

Schein, V. E. Relationships between Sex Role Stereotypes and Requisite Management Characteristics among Female Managers. *J. Appl. Psychol.* **1975**, *60* (3), 340.

Schein, V. E. A Global Look at Psychological Barriers to Women's Progress in Management. *J. Soc. Iss.* **2001**, *57* (4), 675–688.

Schreeves, R. Covid-19: The Need for a Gendered Response, 2021. https://www.europarl.europa.eu/thinktank/en/document.html?reference=EPRS_BRI (2021)689348

Schwartz, F. N. Management Women and the New Facts of Life. In Stroh, L. K.; Brett, J. M.; Reilly, A. H. Family Structure, Glass Ceiling, and Traditional Explanations for the Differential Rate of Turnover of Female and Male Managers. *J. Vocational Behav.* **1996**, *49* (1), 99–118.

Smith, P.; Caputi, P.; Crittenden, N. A Maze of Metaphors Around Glass Ceilings. *Gender Manage. Int. J.* **2012**, *27* (7), 436–448.

Stephens, J. P.; Heaphy, E. D.; Carmeli, A.; Spreitzer, G. M.; Dutton, J. E. Relationship Quality and Virtuousness: Emotional Carrying Capacity as a Source of Individual and Team Resilience. *J. Appl. Behav. Sci.* **2013**, *49* (1), 13–41.

Stephens, K. K.; Jahn, J. L.; Fox, S.; Charoensap-Kelly, P.; Mitra, R.; Sutton, J.; Meisenbach, R. J. Collective Sensemaking around COVID-19: Experiences, Concerns, and Agendas for Our Rapidly Changing Organizational Lives. *Manage. Commun. Quart.* **2020**, *34* (3), 426–457.

Sutcliffe, K. M.; Vogus, T. J. Organizing for Resilience. *Positive Organ. Scholarship: Foundations New Discipline* **2003**, *94*, 110.

Swim, J. K.; Aikin, K. J.; Hall, W. S.; Hunter, B. A. Sexism and Racism: Old-Fashioned and Modern Prejudices. *J. Personality Soc. Psychol.* **1995**, *68* (2), 199.

Tabak, F. Women's Upward Mobility in Manufacturing Organizations in Istanbul: A Glass Ceiling Initiative? *Sex Roles* **1997**, *36* (1–2), 93–102.

Tan, A. S. *Why Asian American Journalists Leave Journalism and Why They Stay*; Asian American Journalists Association, 1990.

Tjosvold, D.; Tang, M. M. L.; West, M. Reflexivity for Team Innovation in China: The Contribution of Goal Interdependence. *Group Organ. Manage.* **2004**, *29*, 540–559.

UNDESA. Women and Men in the Labour Force, 2020. https://worlds-women-2020-data-undesa.hub.arcgis.com/app/27c1c1ad540347aabc70434238223919

UNWomen. 2020. https://www.unwomen.org/en/news/in-focus/in-focus-gender-equality-in-covid-19-response/violence-against-women-during-covid-19

unwomen.org. Beijing Declaration and Platform for Action, 1995. https://beijing20.unwomen.org/~/media/headquarters/attachments/sections/csw/pfa_e_final_web.pdf

van der Vorm, J.; van der Beek, D.; Bos, E.; Steijger, N.; Gallis, R.; Zwetsloot, G. Images of Resilience: The Resilience Analysis Grid Applicable at Several Organizational Levels. In *4th Resil. Eng. Assoc. Symp.* **2011**, 263e8.

Verplanken, B.; Holland, R. W. Motivated Decision Making: Effects of Activation and Self-Centrality of Values on Choices and Behavior. *J. Personality Soc. Psychol.* **2002**, *82* (3), 434.

Wang, C. L.; Rafiq, M. Organizational Diversity and Shared Vision: Resolving the Paradox of Exploratory and Exploitative Learning. *Eur. J. Innov. Manage.* **2009**, *12* (1), 86–101. https://doi.org/10.1108/14601060910928184

Weick, K. E.; Sutcliffe, K. M.; Obstfeld, D. Organizing and the Process of Sensemaking. *Organ. Sci.* **2005**, *16* (4), 409–421.

Welle, B.; Heilman, M. E. Formal and Informal Discrimination against Women at Work: The Role of Gender Stereotypes. In *Managing Social and Ethical Issues in Organizations*; Gilliland, S., Steiner, D. D., Skarlicki, D., Eds.; Information Age: Charlotte, NC, 2007; pp 229–252.

Wenham, C.; Smith, J.; Morgan, R. COVID-19: The Gendered Impacts of the Outbreak. *Lancet* **2020**, *395* (10227), 846–848.

Witmer, H. Degendering Organizational Resilience—The Oak and Willow against the Wind. *Gender Manage.* **2019**, *34* (6), 510–528.

Wright, E. O.; Baxter, J. The Glass Ceiling Hypothesis: A Reply to Critics. *Gender Society* **2000**, *14* (6), 814–821.

CHAPTER 17

A Perspective on Green Human Resource Management (GHRM) During the Post-Pandemic Era

UPAGYA RAI[1], ANURAG UPADHYAY[2*], and RICHA SINGH[3]

[1]IILM University, Gurugram 122003, Haryana, India

[2]Department of Psychology, Udai Pratap Autonomous College, Varanasi 221003, Uttar Pradesh, India

[3]Department of Psychology, Vasanta Collage for Women, Varanasi 221001, Uttar Pradesh, India

*Corresponding author. E-mail: dr.anuragwits@gmail.com

ABSTRACT

Green human resource management (GHRM) as a concept emerged with the initiation of the green evolution. The four basic principles of the green movement include environmentalism, sustainability, nonviolence, and social justice. Due to growing awareness about the green movement, management scholars from different areas started to focus on practices in the organization that can contribute to these environmental goals, at the same time keeping in mind the ecological sustainability along with human sustainability. During the pandemic COVID-19 and post-pandemic, organizations are seeing a sharp increase in green HR practices. With the virtual way of working during this time, green HRM has become a sheer necessity. There have been footprints of green HR practices in various sectors and practically all types of industries. This chapter is an attempt to understand the GHRM emergence, relevance, and scope in the future. This work will also explore the GHRM holistic application of this concept across organizations and their workforce, and how it has become more significant during the post-pandemic era.

17.1 INTRODUCTION: HISTORY AND ORIGIN OF GHRM

Since the Medieval Era, sustainable forestry management was known throughout Europe, and soil conservation, as well as sustainable agriculture practices were not known to Asian farming communities. Philosophers like Emerson and Thoreau (1962) wrote "In the wildness is the preservation of the world" and their followers were called transcendentalists who give credence to the fact that nature has a spiritual component that cut across the human usefulness. In the 1800s, early transcendentalists were trampled by the massive industrial revolution. Soon, there was a realization that industries are causing irreparable damage and endangering human health by causing harm to the wilderness, resulting in a conservatory effort like Yellowstone National Park in 1872. In 1892, the Sierra Club was created to do something for wilderness and make mountains glad. At the start of the 20th century, the conservation movement was hampered by the Great Depression and wars, but efforts to draw attention toward reckless use of chemicals causing damage to species of birds, fishes, insects, and animals continued. These efforts led to the celebration and introduction of Earth Day on April 22, 1970. The green movement solidifies the idea of environmental consciousness in the private and public sectors across the globe. Legislations in the form of acts were formed to protect environmental quality and natural resources, such as clean water, clean air, endangered species, pesticide, and national science act to name a few came into existence. Concerns related to the importance of environmental issues among developed and developing countries have grown in recent years. Organizations across the globe realized that it is time to integrate environmental management and human resource management (HRM) and form green human resource management (GHRM). Green HRM utilizes the HRM policies and promotes the businesses and organizations to use environmental resources in a sustainable manner (Lallanilla, 2020).

Promoting the sustainable use of resources within business organizations using HRM policies with the goal of environmental sustainability is referred to as GHRM. The present chapter focuses on the emergence of GHRM from the medieval era to the realization that industrialization is causing irreparable damage to nature. To repair the damage, efforts are required to preserve the ecosystem. GHRM is one among various efforts whose aim was to preserve the ecosystem by integrating environmental management and HRM. This chapter focuses on the purpose, relevance, and significance of GHRM and how various organizations outside and within India are implementing green practices. It also focuses on the numerous ways in which companies are creating awareness among employees by implementing GHRM practices. Finally, this chapter explains how GHRM has become a necessity as the world of work has transformed due to the COVID-19 pandemic.

17.2 GHRM: RELEVANCE AND SIGNIFICANCE

GHRM is a rather new expression. It was termed as green HRM by Wehrmeyer (1996) in his book which was an attempt to find a connection between management of Environmental and Human Resources. Another definition was given by Prasad (2013), who defined GHRM as the policies that Human Resource (HR) makes to protect and preserve natural resources. Sarode et al. (2016) believe that GHRM is an extension of HRM policies and practices devising strategies that are more sustainable and environment-friendly. Thus, it is safe to say that GHRM aims to manage human resources in a way that leads to sustainable environmental development. Ahmad (2015) and Nijhawan (2014) explain that the term GHRM is better understood by expanding the perspective. They emphasize that both organizations and their employees are engaging in the process of GHRM if they include social and economic well-being, cost reduction, attempts to enhance the efficiency of employees, and organization, or contribute by reducing carbon footprint. As explained by Opatha and Aruljarah (2014), green employees will have four primary roles: They must be preservationist, conservationist, nonpolluter, and green maker. GHRM is more important than ever before, with businesses expanding at a rapid rate in today's world, sustainability programs become crucial due to growing threats and uncertainty caused to our environment.

17.3 DEFINITION AND PURPOSE OF GHRM

GHRM deals with environment-friendly activities that promote the sustainable use of resources within organizations. Numerous definitions are given to the term GHRM by various researchers, thinkers and writers who are working in this field. Sharma and Grover (2018), in their paper, reported that Ramchandran, Director HR Vodafone Essar Ltd has defined Green HRM as the amalgamation of management at the level of environment and at the level of human resources. Whereas, Fortis Healthcare regional head Mr. Nath encapsulates GHRM as an HR initiative that is friendly to the environment that steers the organizations toward low cost, efficient employee association. Mandip (2012) emphasizes that practices that come under the umbrella of GHRM must transfer into practices followed by the HR department of various organizations as e-recruitment, e-training, e-compensation, etc. which will save the environmental resources efficiently and will consume less time in the HRM process.

GHRM has a unique purpose and that purpose is related to every employee, it makes sure that the green insight is created and enhanced with a maximum contribution on each of these areas which include green competencies, green attitude, green behavior, and green results. GHRM encourages these competencies to grow and flourish. Basically, GHRM is all about going green. For organizations to achieve their full potential in the field of GHRM, GHRM must become a part of its core processes, such as recruitment, selection, training, development, and evaluation as discussed by Muller-Carmen et al., in 2010. For example, green recruitment refers to hiring individuals who are aware and share the same passion and responsibility toward the environment and its preservation. Mandip (2012) expressed that the company website and the description for the job should mention their agenda and commitment toward GHRM. Mishra (2017) suggests that hiring of individuals can be done in an eco-friendly way by using tools like online application forms. Confirmation letters can also be given as a soft copy as much as possible. While selecting, it should be kept in mind that participants have prior habits, such as recycling the paper and other office supplies available, printing only if essential, and conserving energy by making sure that the lights are turned off when not working. GHRM practices can also be inculcated among employees through training and development after the recruitment process is done. A study done by Zoogah (2011) has focused on training and development to improve the awareness on environmental issues, to develop a constructive attitude far as the environment is concerned, encouragement to take proactive steps toward reducing the burden caused by the organization on the environment, and developing required knowledge and skills to make every employee competent and conscious to conserve the energy and reduce wastage. Mandip (2012) suggests that green orientation programs at regular intervals for the employees in an organization must be an essential part of their professional growth. These training sessions can also produce many useful propositions related to protecting the environment and natural ecosystem. If the green HRM initiative is attached to the performance management and appraisal of the employees, a positive result is resulted.

17.4 ADVANTAGES AND DISADVANTAGES OF GHRM

GHRM has many benefits for organizations and employees worldwide, particularly for developing economies. Listed below are a few advantages of GHRM from the perspective of the organization and employees.

1. Energy-efficient workspaces to minimize expenses.
2. Reduced cost to the company by effective utilization of resources.
3. Increased productivity, employee engagement, and job satisfaction.
4. Developing a culture of holistic well-being.
5. Carbon footprint reduction measures, such as carpool, teleconferencing, recycling, virtual interviews.
6. Online recruitment and training.
7. Brand building and reputation.

In his study on MBA students studying in the USA, Dolan (1977) reported that most of the graduates are ready to work at a significantly lower salary with an organization that is environmentaly responsible and practicing good GHRM policies.

Positive aspects of GHRM also come with certain shortcomings or disadvantages. As introduced below.

1. It can be costly to initially set up the GHRM practices and policies in place which an organization will have to incur.
2. Many organizations might experience a backlash from the employees as they are comfortable in the old ways of functioning.
3. GHRM in the initial days can also have a marginal impact which can lead to uneven competition and increased capital expenditure.

17.5 LITERATURE ON GHRM PRACTICES

Mishra (2017) expresses that performance appraisal can be a way to inculcate green behavior among employees. This will also ensure better adaptation of green human resource culture in an organization as everyone working in the organization also focuses on their personal growth and appraisal. Thus, by making these processes green we can ensure better adaptation and involvement of all green human resource practices. Mandip (2012) describes how companies such as Tata Group of Companies installed corporate-wide environmental performance standards to measure environment-friendly performance standards, and as a result have come up with green information systems and audits systems that provide valuable data on managerial environmental performance. Rewards and compensation are considered as potent tools to make sure the compliance to green habits as explained by Ahmad (2015). Another research was done by Phillips (2007) who estimated that 8% of the UK firms are now rewarding the green behavior of their employees with various rewards and financial incentives. Rewarding employees for their green performance in the form of financial and nonfinancial benefits is supported by Opatha and Arulrajah (2014). Organizations who consider these aspects while recruiting can achieve great success. This can empower the process and conscious awareness of green HRM. Various researches done in the area of GHRM suggest that in India, there is awareness among organizations about the greening of organizations, they are also mindful of the fact that this is tremendously beneficial in the long run for both organizations and the planet. A few researchers explored this topic and presented their findings. Mandip's (2012) findings revealed that ITC Limited is able to achieve 100% solid waste recycling. Popli (2014) studied at a firm in Nasik to understand how the organizations are aware about the green practices making the GHRM movement more prominent in India.

Environmental concern and human resource management is now integrated by many companies. The leader in this area is Google and is leading the way by hiring a director who works toward matching the company's environmental efforts and its business strategies. Tata group has gone green by pledging to do business that is consciously aware regarding reducing the toxic emission that harms the environment. Companies like ITC Ltd., The Associated Cement Companies Ltd. (ACC Ltd.) have been emphasizing the environment management practices and policies. Other companies which are going green include Honda, Johnson & Johnson, Goldman Sachs, Starbucks, Timberland, and General Motors (Lather et al., 2014).

17.6 GHRM CASE STUDIES BASED ON INDIAN COMPANIES

Lather et al. (2014), published case studies based on various organizations on how they are implementing GHRM and taking the initiative forward, for example, Gas Authority of India Limited (GAIL) green initiatives by Team GAIL for saving the Taj Mahal from environmental pollution. According to an internationally recognized survey done by Hewitt International, GAIL employees have shown the highest level of commitment at work, it is the safest company with no reported industrial hazards. GAIL contributes 2% of its Profit After Tax (PAT) to social causes. GAIL has most satisfied employees due to its good human resource management practices and contributed remarkably to the socioeconomic development of the country. Among the private sector companies, ITC is the frontrunner in adopting processes that are eco-friendly and eco-responsible (Lather et al., 2014). As a part of its eco-initiatives, ITC Ltd. took initiative to produce an environment-friendly universal paper which s branded by the name of "Paperkraft." During the production process this paper is treated with chlorine free technology. ITC's Green Leaf Threshing plant has bagged Social Accountability (SA 8000) certification which is among 10 unique units currently functional in the world. ITC is committed to protecting the environment in which it operates and provides the best working environment to its employees. ITC upholds HR philosophies, such as trust, teamwork, mutuality, objectivity, self-respect, and human dignity at its core, making ITC Ltd. a company that truly follows GHRM (Lather et al., 2014).

17.7 GHRM PRACTICES IN INDIA

GHRM practices are gaining momentum, there is awareness among stakeholders and employees that this is the way forward to a better, clean, and green future, but organizations are even now working on fundamentals and the details of implementing this at various aspects of GHRM and make them a part of their process. Another study was done by Mishra et al. (2014), which studied the Central Public Sector Enterprises (CPSE) and found that these sectors still have not implemented green HRM practices and there is a lot of scopes. Parida et al. (2015) studied the IT firms on awareness and implementation of GHRM practices and found that there are numerous ways these companies have adopted to implement GHRM which includes taking printouts on both sides of the paper, less use of paper, encouraging carpooling/providing transport to the employees an attempt to reduce vehicles on the road, switching off lights/sensor-based lightings in places, such as elevators, washrooms, staircases, and other places that are not in regular use and other power-consuming resources like air conditioner (AC) after 6 pm in the evening, encouraging online application for jobs and organizing interviews via video conferencing, etc. They also reported that employees' participation in green HR practices is voluntary and they are consciously aware of their contributions toward the environment. HR managers revealed that these practices have also given benefits at a monetary level and increased profit share. Some barriers noticed are the cost incurred by the organizations to implement these practices and maintain them. Sengupta and Sengupta (2015) in research done on various organizations, such as Information Technology (IT), Banking, Airlines, Telecom, Automobile, Manufacturing, and Healthcare indicates that there is awareness about the GHRM practices but a lot needs to be done regarding implementing and inculcating these practices among employees and managing them. Mishra (2017) investigated the manufacturing sector to understand the level of awareness and implantation of GHRM practices and found that this sector needs a stronger plan to create awareness and implement those practices among its employees. The above-mentioned researches indicate that in India, organizations are aware of GHRM practices but a lot needs to be done on the implementation front. Employees and their participation in GHR practices can be attained by creating an environment for individuals to make an independent decisions and should be allowed to take decision-making on matters that affect their jobs as suggested by Quagraine (2015). The process of employee involvement should be continuous. It should involve taking suggestions, feedback on all environmental strategies. This can help improve the existing environmental practices and add new and effective ones. Such continuous loops act as a motivation and ensure the involvement and cooperation from every employee in making the organization green. Philips (2007) explained that green HR practices help prevent pollution at workplaces. Employee involvement in the green initiatives can regulate economic, human, natural, and essential resources so that this initiative adds value to the organization (Mandip, 2012; Florida and Davison, 2001; May and Flannery, 1995; Denton, 1999). Bombiak and Marciniuk-Kluska (2018) conducted a study intending to explore the green HR initiatives followed by Polish enterprises. The result suggests that if an organization has a higher evaluation of the impact of the green activity, more frequently is the implementation of green activity in that organization. Thus, it can be concluded that the more the awareness and dissemination of information about GHRM, the more is the possibility that organizations will have sustainable development.

17.8 GHRM, HRM, AND COVID-19

The current pandemic situation is a BIG RESET, it is a human crisis. This reset brought the discussion of GHRM back to the basic discussion of HRM. The world of work is transformed due to the COVID-19 pandemic and it gives no time to adapt to the changing situation. The uncontrolled spread of the coronavirus altered and exposed the so-called efficient organizations and governments across the globe. COVID-19 compelled millions of workers to shift their workplace from office to working from home (virtual mode of working). Jobs that require physical presence and cannot be accomplished by working at home exposed those working to the risk of contracting the virus because of being physically present at work and minimizing social distancing. COVID-19 has affected marginalized individuals more than anyone else. Yancy (2020) reports that the mortality rate among Black counties was six times higher than that in White counties. The UK, Intensive Care National Audit and Research Center (2020) divulged the information that Black and Asian Communities reported more cases compared with White communities. Based on this international evidence, it can be concluded that three groups of people suffered most of the health burden during COVID-19 pandemic: socioeconomic disadvantaged, elderly, and minorities. A job that cannot accommodate the work from home option is one reason for susceptibility and exposure to COVID-19. In a survey done in the United Kingdom (UK), Atchison et al. (2020) reported that it is six times likely that a low-income job will not have a work from home option, no place to self-isolate, working on contract without any insurance or medical benefits, financially vulnerable. Schmitt-Grohe et al. (2020) reported that in New York, the percentage of positive cases of COVID-19 in the poor is 62% compared with the richest 35%. Laurencin and McClinton (2020) reported that the spread of myths and misconceptions was also prevalent in the minority community during the time of the pandemic. Apart from increasing the disparity among working classes and communities, the pandemic also affected working individuals as few lost their jobs, reduced working hours lead to dependence on government support for survival and work from home with a reduced salary. These changes shaped the workforce strategy around the world. As reported by Adams-Prassl et al. (2020), by April 2020, 20% of the workers in the United State of America and 17% of the workers in the United Kingdom lost their jobs. Since we all are in this together, It is the time no to evaluate our strategies and challenges. Stakeholders at all levels, including academics, workers, unions, managers, HR professionals, policy makers, and governments across the globe need to start a conversation keeping in mind what can be done to cater to the current situation and how can we come out of problems of Human Resource management that this pandemic has exposed us to. As Forde et al. (2020) and Warhurst and Knox (2020) report, it is important to bring in the policy and regulation that will decommodify the labor, improve job quality, and create HRM practices that focus on job security. Thus, the pandemic has to accommodate GHRM for the benefit of both the working individuals and the organizations. This has reduced physical contacts, mom-use of biometric machines, online attendance systems at work, online performance appraisals, and online training programs.

At banks, there has been a complete set of green practices (Mishra and Rath, 2021) in order to maintain the well-being of employees as well as customers. However, the authors also state that there have been challenges in implementing banking operations completely green. Hospitals have also taken their operations and HR practices green (Saifudin et al., 2020). As the need for learning persists across different types of organizations at all times, it is important to carry on the training and development functions of HR in a green mode. Online classes, virtual sessions, leadership development lectures are all required to go on making the need for GHRM more evident. This adoption of GHRM in organizations in the post-pandemic period has given organizations a more agile and flexible outlook. The gig economy has to survive with attached strings and that attachment is delivered by GHRM practices in organizations. Corporate sustainability has to be enhanced with best HR practices and green HR practices, in this era. Green HR practices make the job of connecting, locating recruiting, evaluation, and training possible even in times of social distancing. The sooner the companies can adopt GHRM, the better it is for their sustainability. Thus, it is important that during the post-pandemic phase, GHRM remains as a long-term commitment for organizations, there are strategic changes to ensure the success of GHRM in organizations. It is important for organizations to implement cost-effective GHRM as it has been understood to be the key to success. GHRM must be incorporated at every level—selection, training, evaluation, and appraisal. GHRM must be in the conscious awareness of every employee and part of the greater good in the post-pandemic period. Growing GHRM should be equivalent to the growth of organizations and individuals.

17.9 CONCLUSION

Thus, when we refer to GHRM, it should be expressed that this is a long-term process that takes strategic changes in corporate organizations. Post-pandemic HRM should actually be GHRM. There are ways to ensure this. Prepare an expenditure to be incurred to implement the policies and processes of GHRM, activities to start green selection, green training, green evaluation, green appraisal. All should be thought through before starting the process of GHRM, ways and means should be employed to ensure that GHRM is part of conscious awareness of every working individual in an organization and should be perceived as a part of the greater good, GHRM policies should be designed in a way that it adds to the profit-making part of the organization. The importance of GHRM should be explained to every individual and organization in the post-pandemic era and every employee who is a part of the organization should be engaged in GHRM practices, and they should view this as a part of their growth in the organization.

GHRM requires continual use of resources in organizations with the motive of environmental sustainability. It involves long-term commitment from the organizations and can be incorporated at every level from selection to training, evaluation, and appraisal of the employees. To ensure the success of GHRM in an organization, strategic changes and conscious awareness of every employee are required for the greater good.

KEYWORDS

- green human resource management
- pandemic
- sustainable
- post pandemic era
- green evolution
- ecological sustainability
- human resource practices

REFERENCES

Adams-Prassl, A.; Boneva, T.; Golin, M.; Rauh, C. Inequality in the Impact of the Coronavirus Shock: Evidence from Real Time Surveys. *J. Public Econ.* **2020,** *189,* 1–33. https://doi.org/10.1016/j.jpubeco.2020.104245.

Ahmad, S. Green Human Resource Management: Policies and practices. *Cogent. Busi. Manage.* **2015,** *2015.*

Ali, S.; Asaria, M.; Strange, S. COVID-19 and Inequality: Are We All in This Together? *Can. J. Public Health* Jun **2020,** *111* (3), 415–416. DOI: 10.17269/s41997-020-00351-0

Atchison, C. J.; Bowman, L.; Vrinten, C.; Redd, R.; Pristera, P.; Eaton, J. W.; Ward, H. Perceptions and Behavioural Responses of the General Public during the COVID-19 Pandemic: A Cross-sectional Survey of UK Adults. Med Rxiv. DOI: 10.1101/2020.04.01.20050039.

Bombiak, E.; Marciniuk-Kluska, A. Green Human Resource Management as a Tool for the Sustainable Development of Enterprises: Polish Young Company Experience. *Sustainability* **2018,** 10, **1739,** 1–22. DOI: 10.3390/su10061739

Butterick, M.; Charlwood, A. HRM and the COVID-19 Pandemic: How Can We Stop Making a Bad Situation Worse? *Human Resour. Manage. J.* **2021**. https://doi.org/10.1111/1748-8583.12344

Deka, R.; R. *Green HRM: Meaning, Advantages, Policies, and Practices.* Vantage Circle, June 5, 2021. https://blog.vantagecircle.com/green-hrm/

Denton, D. K. Employee Involvement, Pollution Control and Pieces to the Puzzle. *Environ. Manage. Health* **1999**, *10*, 105–111.

Dolan, K. A. Kinder, Gentler M.B.A.s. *Forbes* **1997**, *2*, 39–40.

Florida, R.; Davison, D. Gaining from Green Management: Environmental Management Systems Inside and Outside the Factory. *Calif. Manag. Rev.* **2001**, *43*, 64–84.

Forde, C.; Mclachlan, C.; Spencer, D.; Stuart, M. *COVID-19 and the Uncertain Future of HRM: Furlough, Job Retention and Reform.* Working Paper, Centre for Employment Relations Innovation and Change, University of Leeds, 2020.

Green HRM: Definition, Advantages, Green HRM Practices, Policies. iEduNote. July 22, 2020. https://www.iedunote.com/green-hrm

Intensive Care National Audit and Research Centre. ICNARC COVID-19 Study Case Mix Programme. London, **2020**, April 10, 2020. https://www.icnarc.org/DataServices/Attachments/Download/c31dd38d-d77b-ea11-9124-00505601089b

Lallanilla, Marc. The History of the Green Movement. Treehugger. Oct 30. 2020. https://www.thoughtco.com/what-is-the-green-movement-1708810.

Lather S. A.; Garg, S.; Vikas, S. *Green HRM Practices—A Case Study of a Few Selected Indian Companies presented at National Conference on Organizational Re-engineering: New Age Tool for Competitive Advantage.* [Paper presentation]. National Conference on Organizational Re-engineering: New Age Tool for Competitive Advantage **2014**, Rohini, India, Jan 2014. https://www.researchgate.net/publication/322635703_Green_HRM_Practices_-_A_Case_Study_of_a_Few_Selected_Indian_Companies_presented_at_National_Conference_on_Organizational_Reengineering_New_Age_Tool_for_Competitive_Advantage

Mandip, G. Green HRM: People Management Commitment to Environmental Sustainability. *Res. J. Recent Sci.* **2012**, 244–252.

May, D. R.; Flannery, L.; B. Cutting Waste with Employee Involvement Teams. *Busi. Horiz.* **1995**, *38* (5), 28–38.

McGreal, C. The Inequality Virus: How the Pandemic Hit America's Poorest. *The Guardian* [Internet]. 2020 [cited Apr 26, 2020]. https://www.theguardian.com/world/2020/apr/09/america-inequality-laid-bare-coronavirus (accessed June 4, 2020).

Mishra, P. Green Human Resource Management: A Framework for Sustainable Organizational Development in an Emerging Economy. *Int. J. Organ. Analys.* **2017**, *25* (5), 762–788. DOI: 10.1108/IJOA-11-2016-1079

Mishra, R. K. et al. Green HRM: Innovative Approach in Indian Public Enterprises. *World Rev. Sci. Technol. Sustain. Dev.* **2014**, *11* (1), 26–42.

Mishra, S.; Rath, N. Green Human Resource Management Practices in Leading Indian Banks during Covid Pandemic. *J. Contemp. Iss. Busi. Govern.* Vol **2021**, *27* (1).

Muller-Carmem, M.; Jackson, S.; Jabbour, C. J. C. & Renwick, D. Green Human Resource Management. *Zeitschrift für Personal forschung* **2010**, *24* (1), 95–96.

Nijhawan, G. Green HRM- A Requirement for Sustainable Organization. *Paripex- Indian J. Res.* **2014**, 69–70.

Opatha, H. H. & Arulrajah, A. A. Green Human Resource Management: Simplified General Reflections. *Int. Busi. Res.* **2014**, *7*, 101–112.

Parida, R.; Raj, S.; Sharma, P.; Yadav, V. Green HR: Analysis of Sustainable Practices Incorporated by IT Firms in India. *J. Manage. Res.* **2015**, 1.

Peerzadah, S. A.; Mufti S.;Nazir, N. Ah.; Human Resource Management: A Review. *Int. J. Enhanced Res. Manage. Comput. App.* **2018,** *7* (3), 790–795.

Phillips, L. Go green to Gain the Edge over Rivals. *People Manage.* **2007,** *13,* 1–9.

Popli, P. A Study of Green HR Practices, Its Awareness, and Implementation in the Industries in Nashik. *Global J. Com. Manage. Persp.* **2014,** *3* (1), 114–118.

Prasad, R.S. Green HRM—Partner in Sustainable Competitive. *J. Manage. Sci. Technol.* **2013,** *1* (1), 1–4. https://apeejay.edu/aitsm/journal/docs/ajmst-010103oct13.pdf

Quagraine, T. L. Employee Involvement as an Effective Management Tool in Decision Making: A Case Study of Merchant Bank. http://ir.knust.edu.gh/bitstream/1 (accessed June 2, 2016).

Saifudin, A.; Aima, M. H.; Sutawidjaya, A. H. The Effect of Green Human Resources Management on Service Quality in the Pandemic Time of Covid-19 on Hospitals State-Owned Enterprise the Republic of Indonesia. In *2nd African International Conference on Industrial Engineering and Operations Management, IEOM* **2020,** 2020; pp 1008–1019.

Sarode, A. P.; Patil, Jayashree.; Patil, D. T. A Study of Green HRM and Its Evaluation with Existing HR Practices in Industries within Pune Region. *Int. J. Res. Eng. IT Soc. Sci.* **2016,** *6* (4), 49–67.

Schmitt-Grohé, S.; Teoh, K.; Uribe, M. Covid-19: Testing Inequality in New York City. National Bureau of Economic Research, 2020. 10.3386/w27019

Sengupta, M.; Sengupta, N, S. Green HRM: A Tool for Organizational Sustainability. In Proceedings of the Fourth International Conference on Global Business, Economics, Finance and Social Sciences, Kolkata, Paper ID: K512, 2015.

Sharma, R.; Grover, G. Green HRM: A Key to the Success of an Organization. *Biz and Bytes* **2018,** *9* (1), 184–188.

Thoreau, Henery David, 1817–1862 *In the Wildness is the Preservation of the World, from Henery David Thoreau*; Sierra Club: San Francisco, 1962.

Wehrmeyer, W. *Greening People Human Resources and Environmental Management*; Greenleaf Publishing: Sheffield, 1996.

Warhurst, C. & Knox, A. Manifesto for a new Quality of Working Life. *Human Relat.* **2020,** 1–18. DOI: 10.1177/0018726720979348

Yancy, C. W. COVID-19 and African Americans. *J. Am. Med. Assoc.* **2020,** *323* (19), 1891–1892. DOI: 10.1001/jama.2020.6548.

Zoogah, D. The dynamics of Green HRM Behaviors: A Cognitive-Social Information Processing Approach. *Zeitschriftfur Personalforschung* **2011,** *25,* 117–139.

CHAPTER 18

Post-Pandemic Vocational Compass: A Perspective on Career Navigation Dynamics

MALABIKA TRIPATHI[1], SRITAMA MITRA GHOSH[2*], and SAMRAT RAY[3]

[1]Amity University, Kolkata, India

[2]H.M. Education Centre (CBSE), Hoogly, India

[3]Peter the Great Saint Petersburg Polytechnic University, Russia

*Corresponding author. E-mail: sritama.mitra@gmail.com

ABSTRACT

The current Covid 19 pandemic has created a void in career progress of many aspiring candidates leading them to stress and anxiety globally. There have been incidences of sales going up and down apart from complete shutdown as well. But this has a far-reaching effect on young professionals who are just to enter the job market or are in their early careers. There have been direct impacts on selection of industries by candidates, or the ways in which candidates are selected by companies and there are massive changes that impact career seekers in the post-pandemic period. With this background the present chapter attempts to discuss the career compass of candidates looking for job or employees already in job, through a new lens after the pandemic. What are the post-pandemic upskilling requirements for a career seeker? How job seekers need to focus on soft skills, etc.? This chapter also suggests recommendations toward post-pandemic career move and discusses careers that are suitable during this pandemic. Finally, the chapter tries to throw light on the mental health aspects that might be related to post-pandemic career aspects. In a nutshell, this chapter tries to encompass how the future of career looks like after the pandemic.

18.1 INTRODUCTION

The COVID-19 pandemic has unleashed different arenas of human development in a more sustainable approach. This situation has taught us to think intensely about the present job scenario across the world. The extensive use of the ICT technique supporting remote working practices, unstable environment, and organizational policy changes have caused sheer dissatisfaction among workforces. Many employees lost their livelihood and many transcended into new dimension to earn money. This sustainable approach manifests that job dissatisfaction is not meant to quit in an overall manner but to think and opt for new things, to explore new opportunity, and to step forward accordingly. In a nutshell, this means some adjustments to the situation. According to the successful career planning model, an employee aspires to reach to the optimum level in his or her career path depending on the nature of the occupation. To achieve this goal, successful self-evaluation is mandatory on the part of every professional. Generally, working individuals perceive less opportunity and tend to confine their aptitude within a single array of professional field which suits their nature and temperament, but there are several fields that might be good choices. In early stage of career building, an individual has less experience and finding suitable alternatives may become stressful and very much engaging. In these kinds of situations, awareness about personal choice and attributes proves to be helpful. The COVID 19 pandemic has taken many things from our lives, but, on the other hand, it also did help many individuals to decide and identify substitute career opportunities by granting them extra period. This introspective approach, when matched with employee's unique requirements, morals, and wishes, can give excellent results even during the toughest phase of life. So, prospective employees can engage in thorough planning of their career and navigating their ways with definite guidance. Strategic thinking and planning help in restructuring human subconscious for better decision-making. With this background, the present chapter attempts to focus on the career compass of candidates looking for job or employees already in job, discusses the post-pandemic upskilling requirements for career seekers, and talks about how job seekers need to focus on soft skills and other skill requirements. The chapter also suggests recommendations toward post-pandemic career progress and converses about careers that are apposite during this pandemic.

The aim of this chapter is to focus on mental health aspects that might be related to post-pandemic career facets.

18.2 CAREER THROUGH A NEW LENS AFTER THE PANDEMIC

The pandemic that has caused a drastic change in the career of people needs the career prospects to be handled with care. The pandemic left numerous influence and negative impact on the careers of people. This is such a crisis when people's existing beliefs about their careers might appear to be wrong (Paul, 2021), so they need to think differently. Career aspirants need to see the career through a new lens after the pandemic altogether. To establish a clear set of decisions-making some new choices can help leaders steer their organizations, also youngsters find their right way, and it might mark a new beginning. With increased vaccination status, reopening of business sectors everywhere, and the massive number of people recovering from the disease, the career compass might take a different shape. For 2021, experts predict that the economy will certainly increase approximately 7%—the fastest calendar year growth since 1985 (Castrillon, 2021). A recent Robert Half survey established that as high as 38% employees report that they are not able to progress in their job, from the time of onset of the pandemic (Castrillon, 2021). Career leaders in such a scenario need to come up with their suggestions directed toward career seekers. The most important moves that today's career seekers should do are things such as understanding their present qualities. The qualities that the pandemic time needs are to be emphasized in the career guidance frameworks. This might be different from yesteryears. If that needs upskilling, career seekers should go for that. In case they are aware of their weaknesses, it is suggested to be more careful. Hard and smart working qualities of the aspirants need to be encouraged. It is very important that the candidate can sell himself to the prospective employer, that he is really qualified and able to handle the job requirements. The strengths that the candidate is confident about should be focused with utmost emphasis. It can be said that candidates would require more specific and targeted career development moves in the Post-Pandemic Workplace. The pandemic has brought to light candidates' needs for guidance in navigating their professional growth. The expectations of the companies to make targeted investments in the personal and professional growth are on the increase. Prospective candidates are required to understand the skills of negotiation, critical business decisions, communication, virtual team spirit; they need to engage in brainstorming sessions, getting sensitive feedback and strategies to handle work remotely.

18.3 POST-PANDEMIC UP GRADING PREREQUISITE

With the changes in workplace pattern, with more competition, with job losses in the market, and work-from-home requirements, it is an utter necessity that existing employees and job seekers upskill themselves. Employees must engage themselves in more enrichment programmes to upskill their aptitude and also to look for organizations that can sustain the wrath of this pandemic. When they plan some short- or long-term goals, breaking their large goals down into manageable parts is always a great plan. For example, if an individual is hoping to get a promotion or a job change in the upcoming year, it is suggested that the candidate should be present in social media sites and keep updating his or her job profile and stay in touch with someone who can help in his aspired role. The need for digital upskilling can in no way be ignored at this stage (PricewaterhouseCoopers, n.d.).

18.4 JOB SEEKERS NEED TO FOCUS ON SOFT SKILLS

Soft skills include attributes such as communication, appropriate attitude, teamwork, leadership qualities, and apt decision-making capabilities. For all kinds of managerial jobs, soft skills are the ultimate requirement in today's world. These skills are unlike the hard skills to be seen in working environment but to be manifested spontaneously by an employee when the situation demands. The most important soft skill required by managers is emotional intelligence (EI). In general, EI is explained as the quality to be able to navigate through any kind of difficult situation and connect with stakeholders in a much more successful manner. During a time like a pandemic, the role of EI becomes more applicable. Employees aspiring better career opportunities should upgrade EI, skills of empathy, flexibility, and those skills that are all about augmenting their emotional intelligence. From the onset of pandemic, we are gradually losing the human touch, face-to-face communication, and it has become tremendously complex to develop and display soft skills. But now, more than ever, the necessity and significance of soft skills are at their crest. We invariably need empathy, EI, leadership, resilience, and communication skills in every facet of personal and work life to prosper today. Most of the organizations these days try to work with employees' soft skills and highlight on it in the natural process of selection. Thus, displaying EI during the selection process becomes quite pertinent. The phase of Covid 19 has been difficult for every sector of survival and the career of individuals is also included. The digitalized move, the transition to the world of information technology has offered a new dimension where one-to-one meetings are substituted by computer-generated reality (Chakraborty et al., 2021a, 2021b). Thus, acquisition of soft skills has become obligatory so that one does not become obsolete in the workplace. There always exists a positive correlation between soft skill and professional growth (Vanzara, 2021). So, career aspirants during the post-pandemic phase should exceedingly concentrate on developing their soft skills.

18.5 RECOMMENDATIONS TOWARD POST-PANDEMIC CAREER MOVE

As discussed, after the pandemic, the job world is going to witness a major shift; it is suggested that job seekers take a completely newer approach toward their job finding. Certain traditional ways of looking at vacancies might not work at this time. The strategy of only online job search might not work; in fact, it is important that effective and powerful networking is taken. Linking with mentors, colleagues, friends, and every possible significant grid under one networking can open keys for jobseekers. It is advisable that job seekers must be aware of the job market to make the correct rational decision. Adequate reading, talking to people, and gathering knowledge about key courses are very important to select and proceed in the correct direction. It is also necessary to target a particular career move or a type of job; inappropriate choices must be ruled out with the remaining alternatives, where it can be difficult for the individual to identify and stick to the best alternative. Preparation of knowledge base is mandatory now as it will always be. So, a sufficient research and looking into company portals and getting sufficient information to prepare oneself for the job is fundamental.

18.6 CAREERS THAT ARE SUITABLE DURING THIS PANDEMIC

An employee must be well versed with all the demands that the new professional choice would ask for. Some industries might well operate during and after the pandemic better as compared with others. To discuss about a few, the design industry might not appear to be a great place to work right at this moment. The entire business of designs, advertising, and creative work started visualizing difference. This area might call for a massive upskilling nd new-skilling to be thriving. Customer support jobs might be on the higher side, as organizations are creating virtual network to facilitate WFH with supporting calls. Officials are stereotypically dealing with clients through generating continuous and appropriate offers. Those who want a career in marketing, for them it might not be a good news that marketers are already in a dilemma about the effects of lockdown and work-from-home strategies, Under remote working, new marketing skills such as digital marketing and social media marketing would be the more coveted areas. So, those who are looking for careers in marketing need to programme. Those who are in the field of writing, publishing, editing, and reviewing should not see much change. Academic contributions would always thrive, no matter whether it is work from home or workplace. One of the areas that are thriving in such a situation is that of online instruction. As online learning is thriving, so is the career for online instructors. Education has changed radically, during the pandemic, witnessing distinguishing upsurge of online education which is successfully adopted by all. Slow but steady increase in digital education was observed in pre-pandemic days as well (Cathy and Lalani, 2020). COVID-19 came with an unprecedented notion and kept the workforce totally confused about their progress and prosperity in career. According to Ardi et al. (2021) the COVID-19 questioned the whole world's sustainability quotient and also put forward many ways. Some of the psychological resources such as career, competencies, and resilience might have differential implications over time on different people. Unemployment rates during the pandemic have drastically increased. According to a report published by International Labour Organization (ILO, 2021) by the fag end of 2020, the industry across the globe will experience a diminish in 7% working hours which may leave 200 million people jobless mostly effecting individuals engaged in small business, travel and tourism, and retail marketing. In one of the studies by Stanford, it has been found that maximum an employee will be present in the office twice a week; some reported for five days a week while others reported they will never be at office (Davenport and Redman, 2021). While considering women in employment, it was found in a study by McKinsey that if childcare issues are addressed, companies will be able to retain their woman employees (Madgavkar et al., 2021). In another study by Gartner, it is been posited that workplace will become flexible and there will be more employment for contingent workers, marking a change in job models of the companies (Baker, 2020). This is important for career aspirants to understand that the nature of job in coming future is changing; they have to be more prepared for seasonal jobs, as contingent jobs, temporary assignments, and part-time jobs will be on the rise in the post-pandemic workplace.

18.7 COVID-19 AND LABOR IMMIGRANTS IN ASIA

The era of COVID-19 has witnessed a tremendous reduction in placements of the migrant workers globally, particularly in Asia. Primarily, many Asian nations have imposed barriers on migrant workers in terms of entry restriction through the borders and visa permit to curb the growth of COVID-19 in general population. Second, some of them fully restricted migrant laborers from entering workforce. Third, the sloth in economic growth rate has resulted in complete shutdown of many leading industries. Finally, the restrictions imposed on aviation industry also broke the chain of successful labor supply and deployment (ILO, 2021).

Migrant workers have felt this impact more. There have been huge effects of pandemic on employment. The changes in jobs were visible; there are limited scopes for permanent absorption by any industry subjected to sudden termination of job role requirement. In maximum ASEAN countries, migratory laborers join the workforce on contractual basis in temporary positions. Migratory workers are subjected to lay-offs in the first go, if any economic or other crises are being faced. For example, Malaysia's Ministry of Human Resources directed in April 2020 that migratory workforce should be terminated first compared to their own citizens. It is a learning experience with the pandemic, where each one learnt to adapt to a new working environment with improved technology and self-understanding of it. So, it is evident that the pandemic has hit the career plans of migratory employees to a great extent. These aspirants need to look for home country assignments or jobs where work from home is permissible for the time being. The expectations on pay and other benefits might as well need to be compromised to this effect temporarily.

18.8 PANDEMIC AND EMPLOYABILITY

The COVID-19 pandemic has created enough hindrance in the field of education and progress of students' mobility. Likewise, the recruitment will be on hold at least when the economy can reopen. The thriving young generation and older population of labor force faced the wrath of this pandemic at a worst level. Economics predicts that this trend of vulnerable job market may continue to exist still 2023 and employees would tend to maintain their existing job status quo for survival, as in society unemployment still is a matter of stigma and negative perception (Fiske et al., 2002). Working hours for employees have been lost due to the pandemic. In 2020, 8.8% employee working hours were gone as compared with the fourth quarter of the previous year, which implies 255 million full-time employments.

18.9 UNEMPLOYMENT AND MENTAL HEALTH

Mental health status of employed individuals as well as of those new graduates looking for job has been impacted during the pandemic. This current pandemic has developed some kind of fear psychosis among all population. People are afraid of physically commuting to any place that also includes workplaces. Other than a few emergency services, most employees have developed and adapted successfully to WFH concept. Physically commuting to workplace creates an additional mental pressure that many are unable to manage. There are some witnessed mental health syndromes that accompany the pandemic. For example, people have been suffering from isolation or cabin-fever syndrome resulting from limited social interaction. As it is dangerous not to have a job, equally disastrous is the fear of contaminating while going to work. Besides, not having a work appears to be a double-edged knife, no income on one side and not having social interaction with friends and colleagues on the other side. This directly affects individual subjective well-being. As a result people have started inclining immensely on social networking sites (Chakraborty et al., 2021a, 2021b). Besides people have also started sensing a loss of purpose in their lives; this appears to be one of the psychological effects of being unemployed (Murphy and Athanasou, 1999; Paul and Moser, 2009). When people do not have jobs they lose self-worth and become insecure in life (Joelson and Wahlquist, 1987). Not having a job takes their security down and they feel frustrated. Sometimes, people show up symptoms of irritability, depression, and anxiety (Mandal et al., 2011).

18.10 ARE THERE WAYS TO HANDLE THE CAREER ANXIETIES?

It is therefore imperative to suggest some recommendations that might work at addressing the mental health of career aspirants or change seekers. It is suggested that career aspirants take a very methodical look toward their career now. They need to reflect on transferable skills and strengthen new ones. It is important to research organizations that align with the person's skills, interests, and values. If such steps are not adopted it might lead to stress and career anxiety. Career seekers need to review and reassess the strengths. It is the high time that they relook their orientations and strengths. They need to review and renew professional networking. The LinkedIn team explore how to build the individual's best possible network. NABS knowledge hub is another greet place to find resources to help you at this time. There are various types of teams, such as careers team, support team, events teams, fundraising team, and strategy team, who actually support in various ways. NABS also offers free, personal supervisory training to support during the career journey. The coaches there help to make better decision-making in life by choosing the right career path. The IPA is committed to nurturing existing talent, monitoring diversity within the industry, and championing inclusively in the workplace. Creative Pioneers has helped in placements over 750 young people in the industry. When thinking about career progress one must think on multidimensional aspects. Digital networking helps to reconnect with the old contacts. So, reconnecting with former contacts that were already lost is helpful in getting entry to the job market. These agencies help in building healthy public relations and make the candidate aware of the prospective job market and its possible dynamics in every possible way. It is important to fill the gaps of knowledge with new skills and knowledge. Use social media to start building new connections, companies, share common grounds etc. with many people. Those who have not taken up postgraduate study might opt for it during this social distancing time, utilizing their stay-at-home period. Studies in postgraduation level must focus more on industry-specific skills and knowledge.

18.11 PREPARING FOR A POST-PANDEMIC TOMORROW

This is the time to realize that two life events are beside us at this moment. We are living through a pandemic and also we are planning to change our career. Yes, these are both major life events. Those who are aspiring for a career move desperately at this time should be well prepared to do it. It is understood that it is a tough situation. But careful planning and strategizing might help as discussed. In this situation the individual might work virtually with few colleagues and work force; hence, it becomes difficult to develop connections. Think about the potential financial influence on the career change a person wants to make during this economic climate. So it is very tough to adjust with the reduction in the salary and maintaining the previous lifestyles. During this time the most important suggestion is to research, observe, and decide. The one-job, one-career work–life concept has become much outdated with 12 jobs from careers work life. Employees are quiet often comfortable with older job roles and are reluctant of choosing a new one.

So, individuals should develop many possible salves. Presently, more than ever, the path to the next career will be circuitous. Hold that process with care and explore as many options as probable. The trademark of the career alteration procedure is the psychological understanding of liminality. The current crisis is likely to prolong this in between state. Although unsatisfying at times, the state has its benefits. Downtime is important for refilling the brain's stores of attention and motivation along with accommodating the cognitive processes that helps in development, the consolidation of memory, integrated learning, future planning, maintaining moral compass, and construction of the inner sense. So, this is the time to ask yourself:

a) How will identification of your purpose propel you into the new future?
b) What projects do you really feel passionate about and
c) How am I prepared for the new normal?

The virus propagates the fact that change in career path needs time if related to exclusive skills and certification.

It is unclear that how long the COVID-19 will keep on affecting the job scenario. However, the candidates aspiring job transformation must focus on their existing skills and qualities. It is sometimes evident that there exists lack of skilled workers across all professional fields, such as manufacturing, technological, healthcare, education. Many employers have come forward and extended their help to upskill and educate the people who aspire job switch. Thus, the pandemic has two sides, one might appear to be negative which reminds one of all the losses at the human, social, and economic levels and another is a positive one representing a symbol of the opportunity to reimagine the future through the lens of right planning, right guidance, research, and implementation.

18.12 CONCLUSION

This pandemic has taught us to fight strategically with unprecedented catastrophe upon our life. It helped us to be more resilient, optimistic, and sustainability focused. The transition of ICT mode for doing work has become mandatory. This is the ideal time to restructure the entire system and make it more sustainable in terms of health care and workplaces. But there are some feasible options for career choosing also. If the individual can successfully strike a balance between the mental well-being and employability status, career development becomes a smooth pathway. The virus does not change its effect on human life, but we, the human, should modify the life to proceed with it more efficiently.

KEYWORDS

- pandemic
- sustainability
- career compass
- job switch
- ICT

REFERENCES

Ardi, Z.; Mharchelya, M.; Ifdil, I. The Employee's Job Satisfaction during Pandemic Covid-19 and the Counselor's Role. *J. Counsel. Educ. Technol. 2021, 4* (1), 51–10.

Baker, M. *9 Future of Work Trends Post-COVID-19*. Smarter With Gartner, June 8, 2020. https://www.gartner.com/smarterwithgartner/9-future-of-work-trends-post-covid-19/

Castrillon, C. *Why Millions Of Employees Plan To Switch Jobs Post-Pandemic*. Forbes, May 18, 2020. https://www.forbes.com/sites/carolinecastrillon/2021/05/16/why-millions-of-employees-plan-to-switch-jobs-post-covid/?sh=1b60cfdb11e7

Cathy Li, C.; Lalani, F. *he COVID-19 Pandemic Has Changed Education Forever. This Is How*. World Economic Forum, Apr 29, 2020. https://www.weforum.org/agenda/2020/04/coronavirus-education-global-covid19-online-digital-learning/

Chakraborty, T.; Kumar, A.; Upadhyay, P.; Dwivedi, Y. K. Link between Social Distancing, Cognitive Dissonance, and Social Networking Site Usage Intensity: A Country-Level Study during the COVID-19 Outbreak. *Internet Res. 2021, 31* (2), 419–456. DOI: 10.1108/intr-05-2020-0281

Chakraborty, T.; Tripathi, M.; Saha, S. The Dynamics of Employee Relationships in a Digitalized Workplace: The Role of Media Richness on Workplace Culture. In *Critical Issues on Changing Dynamics in Employee Relations and Workforce Diversity*; IGI Global, 2021; pp 175–205.

Davenport, T. H.; Redman, T. C. *Experiments and Data for Post-COVID-19 Work Arrangements*. MIT Sloan Management Review, Mar 23, 2021. https://sloanreview.mit.edu/article/experiments-and-data-for-post-covid-19-work-arrangements/#:~:text=According%20to%20a%20Stanford%20study,%2C%20and%2020%25%20said%20never

ILO. *ILO Monitor: COVID-19 and the World of Work. Seventh Edition Updated Estimates and Analysis*, Jan 25, 2021. https://www.ilo.org/wcmsp5/groups/public/@dgreports/@dcomm/documents/briefingnote/wcms_767028.pdf

Joelson, L.; Wahlquist, L. The Psychological Meaning of Job Insecurity and Job Loss: Results of a Longitudinal Study. *Soc. Sci. Med. 1987, 25* (2), 179–182.

Joseph, A.; Mary, J. Career Counselling : Process, Issues and Techniques, 1998. https://books.google.co.in/books/about/Career_Counseling.html?id=j6dIAAAAYAAJ&redir_esc=y

Kaln, S. Astin's Model of Career Development: The working Lines of Women and Men. *Counsel. Psychol.* **1984**, *12*, 145–146.

Madgavkar, A.; White, O.; Krishnan, M.; Mahajan, D.; Azcue, X. *COVID-19 and Gender Equality: Countering the Regressive Effects*. McKinsey & Company, Apr. 10, 2021. https://www.mckinsey.com/featured-insights/future-of-work/covid-19-and-gender-equality-countering-the-regressive-effects#

Mandal, B.; Ayyagari, P.; Gallo, W. T. Job Loss and Depression: The Role of Subjective Expectations. *Soc. Sci. Med.* **2011**, *72* (4), 576–583.

Murphy, G. C.; Athanasou, J. A. The Effect of Unemployment on Mental Health. *J. Occup. Organ. Psychol.* **1999**, *72* (1), 83–99.

Pascal, A. Global Internal Displacement Database, 2020. https://www.internal-displacement.org/database/displacement-data

Paul, K. I.; Moser, K. Unemployment Impairs Mental Health: Meta-Analyses. *J. Vocational Behav.* **2009**, *74* (3), 264–282.

Paul, R. *Managing Your Career during COVID-19*. India Development Review, July 7, 2021. https://idronline.org/managing-your-career-during-covid-19/?gclid=CjwKCAjwuvmHBhAxEiwAWAYj-EQRDY5VVN6S8V5n_vW-eOuGMmfImkUqZ3GW4SliqForkONFWAZmGxoCotIQAvD_BwE

PricewaterhouseCoopers. Upskilling for the New Normal. PwC (n.d.). https://www.pwc.com/c1/en/future-of-governmentcee/covid19/Upskilling_for_the_new_normal.html

Vanzara, A. *The Importance of Soft Skills in a Post-Pandemic World*. OpenGrowth, May 18, 2021. https://www.opengrowth.com/article/the-importance-of-soft-skills-in-a-post-pandemic-world

CHAPTER 19

Post-Pandemic Business Scenario: Outlining HR Challenges in the Tourism Sector

TAHIR MUMTAZ AWAN* and MUHAMMAD AWAIS

Department of Management Sciences, Comsats University Islamabad, Park Road, Islamabad, Pakistan

*Corresponding author. E-mail: tahir_mumtaz@comsats.edu.pk

ABSTRACT

The Coronavirus disease (COVID-19), declared as a pandemic by the World Health Organization, affected almost every walk of life, and the disastrous effect was noted in the tourism sector. Huge losses due to the full and partial lockdowns globally restricted every tourism activity. Besides lockdowns and other similar strategies adopted to save the lives of people at large, there is a need to address post-pandemic recovery strategies for the tourism industry. In this chapter, a systematic review to cover the literature of 20 years (2000–2020) published on post-disaster recovery was conducted. The literature focuses on multiple disasters including, but not limited to, pandemics, floods, earthquakes, tsunami, and terrorist attacks. Due to the persistent key role of human resource management in post-disaster recoveries, the employee psychological capital was found seriously depleted from the pandemic. Four key themes, namely, communication, the role of media, marketing strategies, and tourist behavior were found that helps the recovery of the tourism sector. This chapter closes with suggestions for the tourism sector and post-pandemic strategies for effective recovery from the devastating effects of COVID-19.

Human Resource Management in a Post-Epidemic Global Environment: Roles, Strategies, and Implementations.
Tanusree Chakraborty, Nandita Mishra, Madhurima Ganguly, & Bipasha Chatterjee (Eds.)
© 2023 Apple Academic Press, Inc. Co-published with CRC Press (Taylor & Francis)

19.1 INTRODUCTION

The Coronavirus Disease (COVID-19) is among the most influential and terrible outbreaks of the modern age; the world had not faced any other disaster with such a notorious effect on the economy and society. Many tourism businesses went into default or registered huge losses due to lockdown and travel restrictions, imposed by authorities to control the disease from further spread (Yang et al., 2020). The psychological resources of employees in the tourism sector are also found seriously depleted during the pandemic (Mao et al., 2020), as it creates health and job-related threats. Besides the absolute priority of saving lives, it also needs to discuss the recovery techniques for the tourism sector, as being a post-pandemic challenge in this sector that is found slow in recovery from crises and disasters as compared with other businesses (Cassedy, 1992). But due to the persistent key role of human resource management in any event (Gauss et al., 2020) first, the tourism sector needs to recover the employee psychological capital. Shreds of evidence show that psychological capital can have a huge effect on employee's attitudes toward work, work behavior, and working performance. Newman et al. (2014) and the same is expected to happen in the tourism sector after the end of this pandemic. In the unrivaled time of battle against COVID-19, tourism companies had to concentrate on developing the psychological capital of workers by empowering self-efficacy, hope, resilience, and optimism.

Further for tourism recovery four other themes were identified: First, communication, which is necessary to deepen the understanding of varied impacts and outcomes among stakeholders during disaster recovery and reconstruction (Lin et al., 2020), as during crisis tourists were found to be more vulnerable due to lack of knowledge and so in the regard of knowledge and advice, communication with customers is also necessary (Mair et al., 2016); second, media is essential in providing the public with timely news coverage (Wen et al., 2020), acts as a medium to make public aware of latest situation, and can also help destinations to combat from any adverse publicity that damages destinations' image or reputation (Zheng et al., 2020); third, when the disaster is over, marketing plays a fundamental role in the recovery of tourist destination (Hystad and Keller, 2008), is found more productive in the post-disaster stage, is also used to rebuild customer's trust, and attracts markets back to the destination in the long run (Mair et al., 2016); and fourth, tourist behavior, which is found to be changed in disaster conditions (Sheresheva, 2020) due to dangers involved in traveling and mostly results in cancelation of traveling plans (Lew et al., 2020; Wang, 2009). However, for the tourism industry, there are no easy solutions, but these four themes are found to be very productive in a lot of cases held before.

The tourism industry is economically recognized worldwide as one of the most important industries, but it is still one of the most prone to emergencies and disasters. It is commonly recognized as the third economic sector and still keeps on growing. According to World Tourism Organization (UNWTO), international arrivals of tourists grow to 1.5 billion in 2019, showing the tenth year of successive growth (UNWTO, 2020) and it is forecasted that 1.8 billion peoples will travel internationally by 2030 (UN News, 2017). The cost, threats, and effects of global environmental risks on hospitality and tourism need to be understood much more than ever by authorities and stakeholders in the tourism sector. Two massive forces of transformation for the tourism sector in the 21st century are global warming and global health emergencies. The currently novel COVID-19 is also one example of such an emergency that affects the tourism sector very badly. The recovery of tourism is often complicated and based on the nature and scale of the disaster it will take a significant amount of time. Post-disaster recovery is the process of designing and executing plans and activities to restore the destination to a regular state. Recovery may start quickly aftermath of a disaster/crisis or can be postponed before a destination may make attempts to recover. This chapter focuses on the above-mentioned four themes and employee psychological capital and will highlight the important issues in the tourism sector and suggest guidelines for saving this industry from facing bigger losses in the coming years.

19.2 METHODOLOGY

This chapter used a systematic approach for the review of previous work on disasters and crises in the tourism sector. Denyer and Tranfield (2009) explained systematic review as a well-defined technique that identifies, collects, and reviews existing literature, analyzes and synthesizes information, and reports the result in such a way that makes it possible to draw a clear and reasonable conclusion regarding what is known and unknown. As the chapter includes literature from both quantitative and qualitative papers, a purely quantitative analysis is not acceptable. Further, a narrative technique is used due to less possibility to access all the literature written on tourism crises and recovery. The narrative approach is defined as a systematic analysis of findings from multi-studies and it generally describes findings through words and text (Popay et al., 2006). Therefore, the narrative approach is helpful to draw results when using both quantitative and qualitative data. For this chapter 40 papers in the domain of tourism crisis management are reviewed. Table 19.1 presents the covered articles in this chapter. Various terms were used to search such as post-disaster tourism recovery, post crises recovery in tourism, tourism disasters, and destination recovery. Most of the papers that are reviewed were taken from journals related to the tourism sector. Some papers are also reviewed from hospitality journals, but these papers were in the tourism domain. Different sources were used to search papers, such as journals home pages, google.com, and google scholar. Most papers were searched on google scholar because it is the biggest platform for scholars. Further, papers from only journals of repute were included and no online reports, book chapters, and conference papers were used.

19.2.1 ANALYSIS OF RECOVERY THEMES

The main purpose of this review study is to provide the best recovery strategies for the tourism sector from previous studies. As economically being one of the most important sectors, tourism is still more prone to disasters. A lot of natural and man-made disasters have already affected this sector such as 9-11 terrorist attacks, SARS, tsunami, earthquake, foot and mouth disease, and currently COVID-19, but studies show that this sector had overcome all disasters. So this review found five main themes that are found to be helpful for tourism in fast recovery after COVID-19. These five themes are employee psychological capital, communication, marketing, media, and tourist behavior.

Theme 1: Employee Psychological Capital

Psychological capital plays a core part in positive organizational behavior by developing a positive psychological state of individuals. Also, it is found to be a key factor for employees to overcome stressful events or conditions at work. Psychological capital was first introduced by Luthans et al. (2004); further, the concept of positive psychology in Human Resource Management (HRM) and organizational behavior was advanced by Luthans et al. (2007). Since then it has attracted much interest of psychologists, researchers, and managers and made them realize that employee psychological capital is extremely important for organizational competitiveness. As COVID-19 directly hits the employee psychological capital by creating a lot of stress and

TABLE 19.1 Summary of Reviewed Articles.

S. no.	Year	Country	Journal	Study type	Disasters	Broad area	Main findings	Source
1	2020	New Zealand	Tourism Management Perspectives	Quantitative	Earthquake	Tourism post-disaster recovery and reliance	Tourist reliance can be enhanced by knowledge sharing and awareness further media play an important role in it	Fountain and Cradock-Henry (2020)
2	2019	US	Current Issues in Tourism	Exploratory Research	Hurricane Irma	Role of social media during crises communication	This study proposed a framework to properly utilize social media marketing communication and crises communication	Park et al. (2019)
3	2018	Turkey	Journal of Travel & Tourism Marketing	Qualitative, in situ interviews	Not specified	Key success factors during crises	Coordination, communication, strategy formation, and collaboration are found key success factors in crises recovery	Cakar (2018)
4	2017	Asia	Journal of Travel & Tourism Marketing	Systematic Qualitative Analysis	Not specified	Destination marketing during crises to overcome the negative image	Three media strategies were found effective, focus on massage source, focus on the target audience, and focus on the message	Avraham and Ketter (2017)
5	2017	Australia	Journal of Hospitality and Tourism Management	Qualitative	Not specified	Role of stakeholders' collaboration in crises	Collaboration can improve recovery outcomes. Communication and trust were found effective in collaboration	Jiang and Ritchie (2017)

TABLE 19.1 *(Continued)*

S. no.	Year	Country	Journal	Study type	Disasters	Broad area	Main findings	Source
6	2016	Australia	Journal of Hospitality and Tourism Management	Empirical Study	Bushfire	Effect of media reporting on tourism	Media strongly affect tourist during a bushfire in Australia by spreading misperceptions	Walters et al. (2016)
7	2015	US	Journal of Travel Research	Quantitative	Sea Storm	Communicating experience of disasters	Results show that experience, gender, and residence contribute to voluntary evacuation decisions	Cahyanto and Pennington-Gray (2015)
8	2012	Australia	Journal of Travel & Tourism Marketing	Review	Bushfire	Post-disaster recovery	During crises communication with tourist is key for marketing and overcoming misperceptions spread by media	Walters and Mair (2012)
9	2012	Malaysia	Tourism Management Perspectives	Quantitative	H1N1, SARS, Avian Flu, Tsunami, Bali Bombing, 9-11 Terrorist Attacks	Crises affect island	Malaysian destination found to recover quickly but further a close cooperation between tourism stakeholders and well-developed management plans is needed to avoid future damages	Ghaderi et al. (2012)
10	2010	Australia	Journal of Travel & Tourism Marketing	Exploratory Research	Bushfire	Disasters affect tourist intention and destination image and the role of media	The main findings of the study are media sensationalism, destination image, and changes in tourist behavior found during any disaster	Walters and Clulow (2010)

TABLE 19.1 *(Continued)*

S. no.	Year	Country	Journal	Study type	Disasters	Broad area	Main findings	Source
11	2010	Taiwan	Tourism Management	Exploratory Research	Earthquake	Disaster management mechanism	This study proposed a model for crises assessment in the tourism sector	Tsai and Chen (2010)
12	2009	Taiwan	Tourism Management	Empirical Study	SARS, financial crises 1977, 9/11 Attacks	Crises events affect tourism	Tourist health and safety are important to maintain tourism demand.	Wang (2009)
13	2008	Not Specified	Journal of Travel & Tourism Marketing	Quantitative	Not Specified	Restoring traveler's intentions	The pleasure domain of tourist found effective in restoring traveler's intentions	Lehto et al. (2008)
14	2008	Maldives	Journal of Travel & Tourism Marketing	Qualitative and Quantitative	Tsunami	Tourism recovery	Marketing, media, and crises communication play a key role in tourism recovery after crises	Carlsen and Hughes (2008)
15	2008	Australia	Journal of Travel & Tourism Marketing	In-depth Interviews	Bushfire	Marketing and recovery campaigns	Open communication, message consistency, financial support, quick response are found key components in disaster recovery	Armstrong and Ritchie (2008)
16	2008	Taiwan	Journal of Travel & Tourism Marketing	Case Study	Earthquake	Tourism restore planning	A strong disaster management plan with strong strategies is required to reduce the devastating effect of crises	Huang et al. (2008)

TABLE 19.1 (Continued)

S. no.	Year	Country	Journal	Study type	Disasters	Broad area	Main findings	Source
17	2008	US	Journal of Travel & Tourism Marketing	Qualitative and Quantitative	Hurricane	Disaster and leisure tourism	Results show that destinations need to focus on marketing to improve the image and overcome the negative effect of media	Pearlman and Melnik (2008)
18	2008	Not Specified	Current Issues in Tourism	Qualitative	Not specified	Disaster planning in tourism	Results show that training for disaster management is very important for the tourism sector	Ritchie (2008)
19	2008	Not Specified	Journal of Travel & Tourism Marketing	Qualitative	Avian Flu	Destination crises communication	Destination marketing organizations Web sites and crises communication are proposed for destination recovery	Volo (2008)
20	2008	US	Journal of Travel & Tourism Marketing	Case Study	Hurricane	Destination repositioning	It is found that recovery marketing strategies and repositioning strategies were used to recover from disaster	Chacko and Marcell (2008)
21	2008	Canada	Tourism Management	Qualitative	Forest Fire	Disaster management framework	Marketing, advertisement, and disaster management plan are proposed to help during a disaster	Hystad and Keller (2008)
22	2007	Australia	Tourism Management	Qualitative	Bush Fire	Disasters affect small firms in tourism	Results find that marketing and media is effective for the recovery of small businesses in the tourism sector during crises	Cioccio and Michael (2007)

TABLE 19.1 (Continued)

S. no.	Year	Country	Journal	Study type	Disasters	Broad area	Main findings	Source
23	2007	Thailand	International Journal of Hospitality Management	Review	2004 Indian Tsunami	Disaster's effect on hotel companies	This review illustrates the importance of corporate social responsibility in tourism disaster management	Henderson (2007)
24	2006	Hong Kong China	Journal of Travel & Tourism Marketing	Computer-Assisted Survey	SARS	Effect of SARS on outbound tourism	Traveling is a cathartic experience that will support the entire recovery procedure. Further marketing efforts were found effective in recovery.	Mckercher and Pine (2006)
25	2006	Austria	Journal of Travel & Tourism Marketing	Qualitative	Snow Slides	Snow slides disaster at winter sport resort	The paper indicates that after experiencing a crisis, destinations strongly develop their instruments and processes for emergency management.	Peters and Pikkemaat (2006)
26	2006	Australia	Tourism Management	Qualitative	9/11 Terrorist Attacks	Preparedness for crises	The study found that there were little preparations for these events	Anderson (2006)
27	2006	Canada	Journal of Travel & Tourism Marketing	Secondary Data Analysis	9/11 Terrorist Attacks	Travel patterns after the 9/11 attacks	An immediate shift in travelers pattern and behavior has found	Smith and Carmichael (2006)
28	2006	Scotland	Journal of Travel & Tourism Marketing	Exploratory	9/11 Terrorist Attacks, Foot and mouth disease	Assessment of tourism-related disasters effect	Effective communication strategies are needed for both tourist and media	Eugenio-Martin et al. (2006)

TABLE 19.1 (Continued)

S. no.	Year	Country	Journal	Study type	Disasters	Broad area	Main findings	Source
29	2006	US	Journal of Travel & Tourism Marketing	Secondary Data Analysis	9/11 Terrorist Attacks	Importance of crises communication after 9/11 attacks	Communication, public relation, advertising are effective tools for crises recovery	Fall and Massey (2006)
30	2004	Australia	Journal of Vacation Marketing	Quantitative	Bush Fire	Destination recovery	Results illustrate that public relation is important for crises management, and further public relation strategies are strongly based on functions of management	Fall (2004)
31	2004	UK	Journal of Travel & Tourism Marketing	Secondary Data Analysis	Foot and Mouth Disease	Tourism recovery and crises	Lack of crises communication, recovery marketing strategies are main factors found by study during the foot and mouth disease in the UK	Ritchie et al. (2004)
32	2004	US	Journal of Travel & Tourism Marketing	Telephonic survey	9/11 Terrorist Attacks	Travelers' risk perceptions after the disaster	Travel intentions after crises were related to safety, income, risk, and experience	Floyd et al. (2004)
33	2003	US	Journal of Travel & Tourism Marketing	Quantitative	9/11 Terrorist Attacks	Terrorist attacks affect motorcoach tourism	Media base communication and price discount era key finding of the study	Ready and Dobie (2003)
34	2003	UK	Journal of Vacation Marketing	Exploratory Study	9-11, Foot and Mouth Disease	Crises communication	Media and communication play a key role in the recovery after foot and mouth disease in the UK	Frisby (2003)

TABLE 19.1 (Continued)

S. no.	Year	Country	Journal	Study type	Disasters	Broad area	Main findings	Source
35	2002	Southeast Asia	International Journal of Hospitality & Tourism Administration	Secondary Data Analysis	Environmental crises, economic and political issues	Tourism crises	Communication and media are found very effective in many crises situations	Henderson (2002)
36	2002	Middle East	Journal of Vacation Marketing	Review	WAR	Destination marketing during crises	Distribution channels, media, and government are found to be a key factor	Beirman (2002)
37	2002	USA	Tourism Management	Secondary Data Analysis	9/11 Terrorist Attacks	9/11 attacks immediate impact on tourism	Total infrastructure and psychology of tourism are found changed just after attacks.	Goodrich (2002)
38	2002	Taiwan	Tourism Management	Qualitative	Earthquake	Tourism recovery after the earthquake	Media was found to mislead many potential tourists	Huang and Min (2002)
39	2001	Australia	Tourism Management	Qualitative	Flood	Flood effect on tourism	This study highlights the role of communication and media	Faulkner and Vikulov (2001)
40	2000	Not Specified	Journal of Risk Research	Review	Not Specified	Influence of media in risk perception	Media just found to influence general risks, instead of personal risks	Wahlberg and Sjoberg (2000)

threats related to health and job losses, in this critical situation for employees, it is hard to recover their psychological capital on their own. During crisis events employee psychological capital is found to play a key role to support at work (Mao et al., 2020), as evidence shows that it can increase performance by influencing employee attitude toward work. A study by Jung and Yoon (2015) revealed that employee psychological capital was significantly related to key factors that lead to enhanced organizational outcomes and built better individuals. Literature shows different studies concerning the factors that lead to an elevated level of employee psychological capital, such as tourism corporate social responsibility (Mao et al., 2020), person group fit and person supervisor fit (Safavi and Bouzari, 2020), diversity climate (Newman et al., 2018), high-performance working system (Agarwal and Farndale, 2017), and work engagement (Karatepe and Avci, 2017).

Being one of the core principles of effective organizational behavior, psychological capital consists of four elements named optimism, hope, resilience, and confidence. Optimism is defined as positive thinking and looking at the more favorable side of an event and expecting the most favorable outcomes. It is the descriptive form in which favorable outcomes are linked to internal, perpetual, and universal causes, and negative events to external, transient, and situation-specific causes. Hope is defined as having the willpower to accomplish one's goals. It is a positive state of mind that is based on the anticipation of good consequences in regards to events and situations. Resilience is defined as the potential to bounce back when coming across challenges and problems. Training on resilience is a productive way to improve workers' abilities to handle stress effectively and to get over problems. Confidence is the trust of individuals in their abilities to activate their motivation, cognitive capabilities, and perform under the circumstances required to effectively achieve a specific task (Luthans et al., 2007). Further, the importance and effect of employee psychological capital in the tourism and hospitality sector is revealed by considerable researchers in the context of life satisfaction, customer value creation and creativity, work engagement, service sale ambidexterity, employee morale, and service-oriented organizational citizenship behavior (Bouzari and Karatepe, 2017; Karatepe and Karadas, 2015; Lee et al., 2017; Paek et al., 2015; Wu and Chen, 2018).

In the contemporary world, where uncertainty is the new normal and science has still not been able to invent a cure, positive psychological capital is the key to coming out of the crisis stronger, smarter, and healthier. High-performance employees are known to be important assets for the organizations during crises and contribute to the post-crisis recovery. Tourism businesses should also strive to hold workers during the pandemic. It is a need to ensure physical well-being, psychological well-being, position, and income for front-line workers. Luthans et al. (2006) stated that the organization can help their employees to overcome stress-related issues by strengthening their psychological capital. For this, a strong relationship is required between employees and organizations and this can be gained with more frequent interaction between both (Walumbwa et al., 2011). So today in this pandemic condition organizations and leaders in tourism need to build hope, confidence, resilience, and optimism to increase both employee and organizational performance.

Theme 2: Communication

Communication with consumers is also essential at the time of the disaster, not only in the context of marketing but also in the form of information and instruction for tourists at a destination. Crisis communication is primarily about offering the public accurate and appropriate knowledge and improving the organization's image experiencing a crisis. During an emergency that may potentially create an irreparable loss, a focus on communication and public relations is required to reduce harm to an organization. In tourism crisis management, effective communication has been described as a key factor (Ghaderi et al., 2012). Cooper (2006) argues in his study on Japan SARS Epidemic of 2003 that frequent communication between public health authorities and health care professionals and timely transmission of information are important to control outbreaks. Because of not having proper access to local knowledge visitors are often found more insecure in periods of crisis (Ritchie, 2008). Hystad and Keller (2008), Smith and Carmichael (2006) emphasize the importance of receiving accurate and complete information from emergency managers, both within and outside organizations, also stressing that to facilitate crisis communications there is a need for productive partnerships. Whatever the situation, the best solution is to communicate reliable, accurate, and clear facts on time; this will enable stakeholders to act on it and tourists to make appropriate travel arrangements.

Further, the consequences of sensationalist reporting can also be minimized if there is a proper crisis communications plan, which can easily transform a small event into a big disaster. Marra (1998) stated that weak communication strategies will also intensify the incident. Communication with tourists is also essential in the form of information and instructions with those present at the time of the disaster, especially if their lack of local knowledge and potential displacement is considered. Further, many tourists who have already scheduled holidays to the destination will also require updated information about the accessibility and condition of the destination (Henderson, 2007). Writing on Bali bombings, Henderson (2007) proposed that hotel and restaurant managers should provide accurate information regarding status and condition at destination. Anderson (2006) also stated that managers and employees need support during disaster condition and the timely and reliable information is one form of support that organizations can offer. One main issue of a mismanaged incident is the lack of information from the officials, and a carefully planned communication strategy will help to prevent that. There are some key domains that need to communicate during crises, emergency managers to stakeholders, from destination to market, and tourism stakeholders.

Marketing and advertisement are also noted as a key part of crisis communication, particularly when there is a long-term recovery period after crises. As Heath (1998) noted, to manage a crisis is to deal with people's perception about the crisis as much as physically fix the crisis. This suggests that in managing crises and disasters, communication is a key part and it will also be an important factor to consider for the tourism sector. Destinations should prepare crisis marketing and communication strategy for marketers, as this will cost much less than the costs associated with tourism decline due to a poor response. Sönmez et al. (1999) proposed several approaches to enhance crisis communication for disaster management in tourism, including the creation of a private and public sector task force, with a public relation team, recovery marketing team, information coordination team, and a finance and fund-generating team. Further, industry experts focus on communication to overcome crises (Ghaderi et al., 2012). However, studies also found a lack of crisis communication techniques at the local level (Ritchie et al., 2004).

Theme 3: Media

The role of media is as a medium for delivering accurate and relevant information, but for both sensationalism and negativity, there was also much media criticism. It was also a perception that when an event occurs media provide proper information, but over time to create suspense and get the attention of people media create different stories. Just after the outbreak of COVID-19 a broad range of misinformation spread through traditional media and social media which made it difficult for the public to find a reliable source of information. As Tedros Adhanom Ghebreyesus, Director-General of the World Health Organization, says that "We are not just fighting an epidemic, we are fighting an infodemic" (Pennycook et al., 2020). Social media play a major role in the spread of misinformation and rumors. People generally do not want to share misinformation, but the excessive amount of misinformation makes it difficult to identify the authentic source so people ignorantly share misinformation (Garrett, 2020). Further, in the tourism field, it has been observed that the effect of disaster events on the industry is mostly out of proportion as compared with its real effects due to media overstatements. Media reports can put a devastating effect on destinations affected by the disaster. Further, as pleasure travel is a discretionary item, and in the consumer's mind, "the pursuit for paradise will instantly become a dangerous journey that most visitors will prefer to avoid" (Cassedy, 1991).

Also, because of the media's influence and the propensity to linger with negative images, destination recovery typically takes longer than the time required to restore services to normalcy. It has been reported in a variety of case studies including the Fiji Coup in 1987, the San Francisco Earthquake in 1989, the Tiananmen Square incident in 1989, and the 2003 SARS outbreak. In Canada, tour operators on Prince Edward Island (1600 km from Toronto) noticed that SARS deterred many Japanese from coming to Canada primarily because of media reports. Some case was found in 2005 Hurricane Katrina in which media sensationalism had a significant negative impact on the tourism and travel industries (Pearlman and Melnik, 2008). Walters and Mair (2012) have acknowledged that in Victoria's Black Saturday bushfires media coverage provided the increased intensity of event than actual. In Malaysia Ghaderi et al. (2012) carried out a study in which participants claimed that the media overstated the frequency of crisis damage. And the same study also states that the media ignored the post-crisis phase because of trying to restore and maintain confidence in the affected area. Peters and Pikkemaat (2006) presented clear evidence of media blunder which indicate that a significant fault from media side was to criticize the locals for the event.

This type of media coverage not only creates a problem for the community but also damages the destination image for many years after the event. The growing controversy regarding the role of the media in the SARS pandemic can be seen as a result of their role as "creators" of the crisis (Japan Times, 2003, Oct 30). When the data were examined for actual possible cases during the so-called crisis, it became clear contrary to media reporting. Although in a variety of studies, several findings have noted that media had a significant positive impact in crisis and post-disaster stages. For example, media reporting helped to speed up the supply of state and local funds to restore and strengthen tourist destination image in North East Victoria Australia during destructive bushfires (Cioccio and Michael, 2007). Chacko and Marcell (2008) also claimed that the transmission of positive media reports may be very successful in neutralizing any adverse effect by media. Tsai and Chen

(2010) believed that to build destinations' confidence media reports need to be capitalized and reported through good management. One assumption can be made that in the recovery process media can also play a key role (Huang et al., 2008). Nowadays, the conducting patterns of businesses and consumer behavior are both changed. Organization's ways of dealing with crises are shaping their business in the future. On the other side, consumers show more interest in trusted brands that act responsibly. In this pandemic situation organizations need to engage with their customers through two-way communication and timely sharing of accurate information regarding destinations. This can win customers' mind and could be a competitive edge in the post-pandemic recovery process. Media play an important role in changing people's behavior by shaping their thoughts. So media have an undeniable role in human societies most importantly in crisis events where it can help organizations to overcome; besides it can increase their problems and make them suffer.

Theme 4: Marketing Strategies

In the recovery of a crisis or disaster marketing and advertising play a fundamental role, and it has been found that specific marketing strategies are more productive in the post-disaster stage (Peters and Pikkemaat, 2006). Post-disaster recovery is crucial to the tourism sector and media campaigns are commonly viewed as an integral part of any recovery plan. In the tourism sector the recovery depends upon the nature of crises like just after four weeks of the 9/11 attacks, potent advertising was given credit for inspiring Americans to continue traveling in large numbers (Floyd et al., 2004). But for those crises, where there are health-related risks, more comprehensive strategies are required, including media management to control the image displayed during the crises. And after the crisis is over more aggressive marketing is needed to show the business as usual, instead of reminding about crises. The same thing is found in the case of the SARS epidemic; initially, there was a rapid reduction in tourism but the sector recovered quickly just after the epidemic end (Zeng et al., 2005). In the tourism sector, the key focus of marketing strategies should be on the recovery phase. This has also been found that for destinations it is very difficult to hold people on track and keep up a satisfying image. Key aims regarding post-disaster marketing are to regain trust in the destinations, recover a positive destination image, fix a negative image, and in some situations build a new image by clarifying misunderstandings about the event. In post-disaster and crisis marketing, public relations also have been described as a core component.

Further, based on the nature of the incident, the marketing message can be designed to address specific objectives. It should be aimed at minimizing disaster scale, removing misperceptions to prove the business is operating. Messages should accessible, clear, and straightforward to tackle misperceptions regarding disaster. Repeating marketing messages is often seen as productive to convince the target audience and underpin the perception that the destination is attractive and protected. To make the campaign successful all stakeholders must be on message. Further, capitalizing on emotions by using marketing messages, solidarity-type messages, and celebrities was also found beneficial. Walters and Mair (2012) pointed out nine types of messages that are frequently used and proved productive. These nine message types are open business as usual message, community readiness message, solidarity/empathy message, celebrities endorsement message, restoring confidence message, change misperception message, short-term discounts/price reduction, visitor testimonial, festivals, and events and curiosity enhancement. Although most of these messages would be successful in various contexts, Walters and Mair (2012) illustrated that using celebrity has been reported as the most likely to convince tourists to return. They also observed that a marketing message promoted by a well-known and well-associated celebrity would generally be more successful in attracting visitors to return or to visit a destination hit by a disaster. The usage of short-term discounts would possibly have been the least successful because tourists would not trade off their health safety for discount. For COVID-19 airlines, restaurants, and spas could be the first to offer various discounts and packages to visitors. A study by Rittichainuwat (2008) has identified stimulating interest to motivate tourists back to destination. Open business as usual interestingly found less productive messages that seem counter to research in other post-disaster contexts. However, each disaster and crisis is different and every marketing recovery strategy should need to understand what kind of disaster is. It is clear that recovery is a complicated process for tourism, which takes significant time and effort, but the role of marketing is undeniable in recovering tourists toward the destination.

Theme 5: Tourist Behavior

Infectious diseases have a strong effect on tourism and on the preference of a tourist destination in particular by increasing the tourists' concern about health risks. The main issue for a destination is related to changes in the traveler's behavior due to the risks involved. Like the 2003 SARS outbreak in Hong Kong resulted in serious inbound tourism fluctuations, which negatively affected the behavior of tourist arrivals, and also neighboring regions (Henderson, 2004). Nearly 3000 people have died in Hong Kong from 2003 SARS. Tourist flow toward reign was disrupted by the epidemic, severely damaging the economy. It also affected other sectors including labor, airlines, and hotel. Wang (2009) found that if tourists feel that traveling to a destination involves too much danger, obviously they would cancel their trip arrangements. Nonetheless, after the acute problem is over there is always little danger. Interestingly, at this point, the risk is less of a concern than health and safety, social risk, and the risk of undermining the quality of travel experience (Floyd et al., 2004). More cancelations, more bookings at the last minute, more self-drive traveling, more domestic trips, and more family and friends trips all are possible behavioral changes regarding a tragic incident.

It is possible that some people who have positive potential to assist in disasters will return, but most tourists remain anxious to visit. Further, it is possible that people do not actually cancel their trips but somewhat will change their plans. Family and friends travel is perceived as a more secure and safer type of holiday and could also increase during disaster era. Peoples from various regions often respond differently to disasters. So it is recommended that identifying and approaching the most risk-averse countries will help to limit the target audience to relief efforts following a disaster. Studies also show that crises event has fewer effects on individuals who have a sense of loyalty for a destination. Walters and Mair (2012) noticed that visitors who had previously visited a disaster-affected region were more probably to return as compared to infrequent visitors. Two segments of tourists show more interest to return to destinations. First are loyal visitors, and the second segment is of repeat visitors. The key to motivating such loyal visitors is through relationship marketing. Nevertheless, as Walters and Clulow (2010) figured out, it is easy to encourage visitors who show loyalty to the destination; further this segment of tourists can contribute to the recsovery process by being the first to come back toward the destination.

Tourism has long been known to be prone to disasters and crises that pose risk to people's life, health, and security. The recovery process following any disaster also needs to analyze the changing attitude and expectations of customers to determine shifts in market demand. As such, customer expectations, priorities, and travel behaviors changed due to the pandemic. Therefore, after the pandemic, tourism organizations should also change their strategies following the changes in tourists' demand and behavior. Typically, tourism demand has been severely reduced and changed in response to disasters. COVID-19 has called attention to the hygiene problem for the general public. Hygiene and safety are considered an important factor when people make decisions for travel and tourism. Improved hygiene would be a big factor in enhancing the image of the destination and the business. It is therefore proposed that national standards should be developed for tourist attractions; transport means, hotels, and compulsory steps should be taken by tourism organizations to ensure the safety and hygiene requirements of visitors.

19.3 DISCUSSION

We focused on problems to find suitable recovery strategies for the tourism sector. The COVID-19 pandemic is found one of the most influential diseases and has a direct effect on the tourism sector due to travel restrictions. So we took a review of past studies and found five key themes that could help the tourism sector to recover from this pandemic. First, we focus on employee psychological capital because it was found seriously depleting during a pandemic by creating health and job-related threats. Employee psychological capital is found as a key factor to overcome stressful events at work so tourist organization needs to build employee psychological capital by strengthening self-efficacy, hope, resilience, and optimism. Then secondly we discuss the communication factor. During any disaster condition communication with tourists is very important to share information and the current status of the destination. Communication could also help to improve destination's image by providing accurate and proper knowledge. As communication is a two-way process, it will also help to understand the tourist's problems. Next, we explain the important role of media as it acts as a medium to deliver information. On the other hand, media also act to spread sensationalism and negativity among the public. This type of negative news can affect the overall image of a destination, which then takes a long time to recover. In many cases, it is found that due to media the effect of a disaster event on any industry is observed mostly out of proportion as compared with its real effect. So the tourism sector needs to manage media properly. In the case of COVID-19 as it is a global pandemic the other higher authorities such as governments need to focus on media activities. After the media, the next factor that we focus on is marketing strategies. In recovery from any disaster or crisis, marketing plays an important role. Through marketing tourism sector can recover the destination image and can also clarify the misunderstanding about any event. In post-disaster recovery, marketing is defined as a core component. The last factor that we discuss is the tourist's behavior that mostly changes during a crisis, especially when there is a risk related to health, as COVID-19 had created attention toward a hygiene problem for the public. So improving hygiene and safety would be a key factor in the fast recovery of the sector. Further, we hope that this suggested guideline could help to save this industry from facing bigger losses in the coming year.

19.4 CONCLUSION

This chapter has highlighted the post-pandemic challenges in the tourism industry and several recovery strategies to keep it under observation that currently, the whole world is facing the deadly outbreak of COVID-19. World Health Organization proclaimed it to be an ongoing global pandemic (WHO, 2020). Because human mobility is an influential factor in the emergence and spreading of the disease the authorities impose travel restrictions (Yang et al., 2020), and peoples are instructed to stay at their homes with the narration "Stay home, stay safe." Government alerts further fueled public fear and travel bans limited outdoor activities all of which compounded negative effects for the tourism industry (McLaughlin, 2020). Health and job-related threats deeply affect employee psychological capital, which has a significant influence on working behavior and performance. Further, four key themes are discussed in this chapter for post-pandemic recovery: (1) Communication, as providing accurate and appropriate knowledge to the public will help to improve the destination's image facing the crisis. (2) The role of the media, as it acts as a medium to make public aware of latest situation, it can also help destinations to combat from any adverse publicity that damages the destination's image and reputation. (3) Marketing, as it plays a fundamental role in the destination's recovery of a crisis or disaster, also in the post-disaster stage it seems more productive. (4) Tourist behavior changes due to dangers involved in visiting a destination and it could result in the cancelation of travel plans. However, for the tourism industry, there are no easy solutions, but these four strategies are found to be very productive in many cases held before.

Further destinations should focus on the key needs of stakeholders, suitable communication strategies, and marketing channels according to the range of stakeholders, a suitable time to start recovery campaigns, and should focus more on loyal customers. Correspondingly, it is significant to note that all pandemics are different in scale, circumstances, intensity, and may involve various destinations and actors. All the planning should be made keeping this in mind. Recovery from COVID-19 may take longer time than expected, but the proper planning can make it fast to recover. Also, it requires further research to explore more solutions to handle bad situations such as COVID-19.

KEYWORDS

- COVID-19
- tourism
- employee psychological capital
- post-pandemic recovery

REFERENCES

Agarwal, P.; Farndale, E. High-Performance Work Systems and Creativity Implementation: The Role of Psychological Capital and Psychological Safety. *Human Resour. Manage. J.* **2017,** *27* (3), 440–458.

Anderson, B. A. Crisis Management in the Australian Tourism Industry: Preparedness, Personnel and Postscript. *Tour. Manage.* **2006,** *27* (6), 1290–1297.

Armstrong, E. K.; Ritchie, B. W. The Heart Recovery Marketing Campaign: Destination Recovery after a Major Bushfire in Australia's National Capital. *J. Travel Tour. Market.* **2008,** *23* (2–4), 175–189.

Avraham, E.; Ketter, E. Destination Marketing During and Following Crises: Combating Negative Images in Asia. *J. Travel Tour. Market.* **2017,** *34* (6), 709–718.

Beirman, D. Marketing of Tourism Destinations during a Prolonged Crisis: Israel and the Middle East. *J. Vacation Market.* **2002,** *8* (2), 167–176.

Bouzari, M.; Karatepe, O. M. Test of a Mediation Model of Psychological Capital among Hotel Salespeople. *Int. J. Contemp. Hosp. Manage.* **2017.**

Cahyanto, I.; Pennington-Gray, L. Communicating Hurricane Evacuation to Tourists: Gender, Past Experience with Hurricanes, and Place of Residence. *J. Travel Res.* **2015,** *54* (3), 329–343.

Cakar, K. Critical Success Factors for Tourist Destination Governance in Times of Crisis: A Case Study of Antalya, Turkey. *J. Travel Tour. Market.* **2018,** *35* (6), 786–802.

Carlsen, J. C.; Hughes, M. Tourism Market Recovery in the Maldives after the 2004 Indian Ocean Tsunami. *J. Travel Tour. Market.* **2008,** *23* (2–4), 139–149.

Cassedy, K. *Crisis Management Planning in the Travel and Tourism Industry: A Study of Three Destination Cases and a Crisis Management Planning Manual*; Pacific Asia Travel Association, 1991.

Cassedy, K. Preparedness in the Face of Crisis: An Examination of Crisis Management Planning in the Travel and Tourism Industry. *World Travel Tour. Rev.* **1992,** *2,* 169–174.

Chacko, H. E.; Marcell, M. H. Repositioning a Tourism Destination: The Case of New Orleans after Hurricane Katrina. *J. Travel Tour. Market.* **2008,** *23* (2–4), 223–235.

Cioccio, L.; Michael, E. J. Hazard or disaster: Tourism Management for the Inevitable in Northeast Victoria. *Tour. Manage.* **2007,** *28* (1), 1–11.

Cooper, M. Japanese Tourism and the SARS Epidemic of 2003. *J. Travel Tour. Market.* **2006,** *19* (2–3), 117–131.

Denyer, D.; Tranfield, D. Producing a Systematic Review, 2009.

Eugenio-Martin, J. L.; Sinclair, M. T.; Yeoman, I. Quantifying the Effects of Tourism Crises: An Application to Scotland. *J. Travel Tour. Market.* **2006,** *19* (2–3), 21–34.

Fall, L. T. The Increasing Role of Public Relations as a Crisis Management Function: An Empirical Examination of Communication Restrategising Efforts among Destination Organisation Managers in the Wake of 11th September, 2001. *J. Vacation Market.* **2004,** *10* (3), 238–252.

Fall, L. T.; Massey, J. E. The Significance of Crisis Communication in the Aftermath of 9/11: A National Investigation of How Tourism Managers Have Re-Tooled Their Promotional Campaigns. *J. Travel Tour. Market.* **2006,** *19* (2–3), 77–90.

Faulkner, B.; Vikulov, S. Katherine, Washed Out One Day, Back on Track the Next: A Post-Mortem of a Tourism Disaster. *Tour. Manage.* **2001,** *22* (4), 331–344.

Floyd, M. F.; Gibson, H.; Pennington-Gray, L.; Thapa, B. The Effect of Risk Perceptions on Intentions to Travel in the Aftermath of September 11, 2001. *J. Travel Tour. Market.* **2004,** *15* (2–3), 19–38.

Fountain, J.; Cradock-Henry, N. Recovery, Risk and Resilience: Post-Disaster Tourism Experiences in Kaikōura, New Zealand. *Tour. Manage. Persp.* **2020,** *35*, 100695.

Frisby, E. Communicating in a Crisis: The British Tourist Authority's Responses to the Foot-and-Mouth Outbreak and 11th September, 2001. *J. Vacation Market.* **2003,** *9* (1), 89–100.

Garrett, L. COVID-19: The Medium is the Message. *Lancet* **2020,** *395* (10228), 942–943.

Gauss, T.; Pasquier, P.; Joannes-Boyau, O.; Constantin, J.-M.; Langeron, O.; Bouzat, P.; Pottecher, J. Preliminary Pragmatic Lessons from the SARS-CoV-2 Pandemic from France. *Anaesthesia Crit. Care Pain Med.* **2020**.

Ghaderi, Z.; Som, A. P. M.; Henderson, J. C. Tourism Crises and Island Destinations: Experiences in Penang, Malaysia. *Tour. Manage. Persp.* **2012,** *2*, 79–84.

Goodrich, J. N. September 11, 2001 Attack on America: A Record of the Immediate Impacts and Reactions in the USA Travel and Tourism Industry. *Tour. Manage.* **2002,** *23* (6), 573–580.

Heath, R. L. *Crisis Management for Managers and Executives: Business Crises, the Definitive Handbook to Reduction, Readiness, Response, and Recovery*; Financial Times/Pitman Pub, 1998.

Henderson, J. Managing a Tourism Crisis in Southeast Asia: The Role of National Tourism Organisations. *Int. J. Hosp. Tour. Admin.* **2002,** *3* (1), 85–105.

Henderson, J. C. Managing a Health-Related Crisis: SARS in Singapore. *J. Vacation Market.* **2004,** *10* (1), 67–77.

Henderson, J. C. Corporate social Responsibility and Tourism: Hotel Companies in Phuket, Thailand, after the Indian Ocean Tsunami. *Int. J. Hosp. Manage.* **2007,** *26* (1), 228–239.

Huang, J.-H.; Min, J. C. Earthquake Devastation and Recovery in Tourism: The Taiwan Case. *Tour. Manage.* **2002,** *23* (2), 145–154.

Huang, Y.-C.; Tseng, Y.-P.; Petrick, J. F. Crisis Management Planning to Restore Tourism after Disasters: A Case Study from Taiwan. *J. Travel Tour. Market.* **2008,** *23* (2–4), 203–221.

Hystad, P. W.; Keller, P. C. Towards a Destination Tourism Disaster Management Framework: Long-Term Lessons from a Forest Fire Disaster. *Tour. Manage.* **2008**, *29* (1), 151–162.

Japan.Times (Producer). World Eye Reports, Oct 30, 2003.

Jiang, Y.; Ritchie, B. W. Disaster Collaboration in Tourism: Motives, Impediments and Success Factors. *J. Hosp. Tour. Manage.* **2017**, *31*, 70–82.

Jung, H. S.; Yoon, H. H. The Impact of Employees' Positive Psychological Capital on Job Satisfaction and Organizational Citizenship Behaviors in the Hotel. *Int. J. Contemp. Hosp. Manage* **2015**.

Karatepe, O. M.; Avci, T. The Effects of Psychological Capital and Work Engagement on Nurses' Lateness Attitude and Turnover Intentions. *J. Manage. Dev.* **2017**.

Karatepe, O. M.; Karadas, G. Do Psychological Capital and Work Engagement Foster Frontline Employees' Satisfaction? *Int. J. Contemp. Hosp. Manage.* **2015**.

Lee, Y.-H.; Hsiao, C.; Chen, Y.-C. Linking positive psychological capital with Customer Value Co-Creation. *Int. J. Contemp. Hosp. Manage.* **2017**.

Lehto, X.; Douglas, A. C.; Park, J. Mediating the Effects of Natural Disasters on Travel Intention. *J. Travel Tour. Market.* **2008**, *23* (2–4), 29–43.

Lew, A. A.; Cheer, J. M.; Haywood, M.; Brouder, P.; Salazar, N. B. Visions of Travel and Tourism after the Global COVID-19 Transformation of 2020. *Tour. Geog.* **2020**, 1–12.

Lin, K. H. E.; Khan, S.; Acosta, L.; Alaniz, R.; Olanya, D. The Dynamism of Post Disaster Risk Communication: A Cross-Country Synthesis. *Int. J. Disaster Risk Reduction* **2020**, 101556.

Luthans, F.; Avey, J. B.; Avolio, B. J.; Norman, S. M.; Combs, G. M. Psychological Capital Development: Toward a Micro-intervention. *J. Organ. Behav.* **2006**, *27* (3), 387–393.

Luthans, F.; Luthans, K. W.; Luthans, B. C. Positive Psychological Capital: Beyond Human and Social Capital, 2004.

Luthans, F.; Youssef, C. M.; Avolio, B. J. Psychological Capital: Developing the Human Competitive Edge, 2007.

Mair, J.; Ritchie, B. W.; Walters, G. Towards a Research Agenda for Post-disaster and Post-crisis Recovery Strategies for Tourist Destinations: A Narrative Review. *Curr. Iss. Tour.* **2016**, *19* (1), 1–26.

Mao, Y.; He, J.; Morrison, A. M.; Andres Coca-Stefaniak, J. Effects of Tourism CSR on Employee Psychological Capital in the COVID-19 Crisis: From the Perspective of Conservation of Resources Theory. *Curr. Iss. Tour.* **2020**, 1–19.

Marra, F. J. Crisis Communication Plans: Poor Predictors of Excellent Crisis Public Relations. *Public Relat. Rev.* **1998**, *24* (4), 461–474.

Mckercher, B.; Pine, R. Privation as a Stimulus to Travel Demand? *J. Travel Tour. Market.* **2006**, *19* (2–3), 107–116.

McLaughlin, T. Coronavirus Is Devastating Chinese Tourism, 2020.

Newman, A.; Nielsen, I.; Smyth, R.; Hirst, G.; Kennedy, S. The Effects of Diversity Climate on the Work Attitudes of Refugee Employees: The Mediating Role of Psychological Capital and Moderating Role of Ethnic Identity. *J. Vocational Behav.* **2018**, *105*, 147–158.

Newman, A.; Ucbasaran, D.; Zhu, F.; Hirst, G. Psychological capital: A review and synthesis. *Journal of Organizational Behavior, 35* (S1), S120–S138.

Paek, S.; Schuckert, M.; Kim, T. T.; Lee, G. Why Is Hospitality Employees' Psychological Capital Important? The Effects of Psychological Capital on Work Engagement and Employee Morale. *Int. J. Hosp. Manage.* **2015**, *50*, 9–26.

Park, D.; Kim, W. G.; Choi, S. Application of Social Media Analytics in Tourism Crisis Communication. *Curr. Iss. Tour.* **2019**, *22* (15), 1810–1824.

Pearlman, D.; Melnik, O. Hurricane Katrina's Effect on the Perception of New Orleans Leisure Tourists. *J. Travel Tour. Market.* **2008**, *25* (1), 58–67.

Pennycook, G.; McPhetres, J.; Zhang, Y.; Lu, J. G.; Rand, D. G. Fighting COVID-19 Misinformation on Social Media: Experimental Evidence for a Scalable Accuracy-Nudge Intervention. *Psychol. Sci.* **2020**, *31* (7), 770–780.

Peters, M.; Pikkemaat, B. Crisis Management in Alpine Winter Sports Resorts—the 1999 Avalanche Disaster in Tyrol. *J. Travel Tour. Market.* **2006**, *19* (2–3), 9–20.

Popay, J.; Roberts, H.; Sowden, A.; Petticrew, M.; Arai, L.; Rodgers, M.; Duffy, S. Guidance on the Conduct of Narrative Synthesis in Systematic Reviews. *A Product from the ESRC Methods Programme Version* **2006**, *1*, b92.

Ready, K. J.; Dobie, K. Real and Perceived Terrorist Threats: Effects of September 11, 2001 Events on the US Motorcoach-Based Tourism Industry. *J. Travel Tour. Market.* **2003**, *15* (1), 59–76.

Ritchie, B. Tourism Disaster Planning and Management: From Response and Recovery to Reduction and Readiness. *Cur. Iss. Tour.* **2008**, *11* (4), 315–348.

Ritchie, B. W.; Dorrell, H.; Miller, D.; Miller, G. A. Crisis Communication and Recovery for the Tourism Industry: Lessons from the 2001 Foot and Mouth Disease Outbreak in the United Kingdom. *J. Travel Tour. Market.* **2004**, *15* (2–3), 199–216.

Rittichainuwat, N. Responding to Disaster: Thai and Scandinavian Tourists' Motivation to Visit Phuket, Thailand. *J. Travel Res.* **2008**, *46* (4), 422–432.

Safavi, H. P.; Bouzari, M. How Can Leaders Enhance Employees' Psychological Capital? Mediation Effect of Person-Group and Person-Supervisor Fit. *Tour. Manage. Persp.* **2020**, *33*, 100626.

Sheresheva, M. Y. Coronavirus and Tourism. *Population Econ.* **2020**, *4*, 72.

Smith, W. W.; Carmichael, B. A. Canadian Seasonality and Domestic Travel Patterns: Regularities and Dislocations as a Result of the Events of 9/11. *J. Travel Tour. Market.* **2006**, *19* (2–3), 61–76.

Sönmez, S. F.; Apostolopoulos, Y.; Tarlow, P. Tourism in Crisis: Managing the Effects of Terrorism. *J. Travel Res.* **1999**, *38* (1), 13–18.

Tsai, C.-H.; Chen, C.-W. An Earthquake Disaster Management Mechanism Based on Risk Assessment Information for the Tourism Industry-a Case Study from the Island of Taiwan. *Tour. Manage.* **2010**, *31* (4), 470–481.

UN News (Producer). World Could See 1.8 Billion Tourists by 2030 – UN Agency, 2017. https://news.un.org/en/story/2017/12/640512-world-could-see-18-billion-tourists-2030-un-agency

UNWTO. International Tourism Highlights International Tourism Continues to Outpace the Global Economy, 2020. https://www.unwto.org/international-tourism-growth-continues-to-outpace-the-economy

Volo, S. Communicating Tourism Crises through Destination Websites. *J. Travel Tour. Market.* **2008**, *23* (2–4), 83–93.

Wahlberg, A. A.; Sjoberg, L. Risk Perception and the Media. *J. Risk Res.* **2000**, *3* (1), 31–50.

Walters, G.; Clulow, V. The Tourism Market's Response to the 2009 Black Saturday Bushfires: The Case of Gippsland. *J. Travel Tour. Market.* **2010**, *27* (8), 844–857.

Walters, G.; Mair, J. The Effectiveness of Post-Disaster Recovery Marketing Messages—The Case of the 2009 Australian Bushfires. *J. Travel Tour. Market.* **2012**, *29* (1), 87–103.

Walters, G.; Mair, J.; Lim, J. Sensationalist Media Reporting of Disastrous Events: Implications for Tourism. *J. Hosp. Tour. Manage.* **2016**, *28*, 3–10.

Walumbwa, F. O.; Mayer, D. M.; Wang, P.; Wang, H.; Workman, K.; Christensen, A. L. Linking Ethical Leadership to Employee Performance: The Roles of Leader–Member Exchange, Self-Efficacy, and Organizational Identification. *Organ. Behav. Human Decision Processes* **2011,** *115* (2), 204–213.

Wang, Y.-S. The Impact of Crisis Events and Macroeconomic Activity on Taiwan's International Inbound Tourism Demand. *Tour. Manage.* **2009,** *30* (1), 75–82.

Wen, J.; Aston, J.; Liu, X.; Ying, T. Effects of Misleading Media Coverage on Public Health Crisis: A Case of the 2019 Novel Coronavirus Outbreak in China. *Anatolia* **2020,** *31* (2), 331–336.

WHO. WHO Coronavirus Disease (COVID-19) Dashboard. *World Health Organization, Geneva, Switzerland.* https://covid19.who.int/.

Wu, C.-M.; Chen, T.-J. Collective Psychological Capital: Linking Shared Leadership, Organizational Commitment, and Creativity. *Int. J. Hosp. Manage.* **2018,** *74*, 75–84.

Yang, Y.; Zhang, H.; Chen, X. Coronavirus Pandemic and Tourism: Dynamic Stochastic General Equilibrium Modeling of Infectious Disease Outbreak. *Ann. Tour. Res.* **2020.**

Zeng, B.; Carter, R. W.; De Lacy, T. Short-Term Perturbations and Tourism Effects: The Case of SARS in China. *Curr. Iss. Tour.* **2005,** *8* (4), 306–322.

Zheng, Y.; Goh, E.; Wen, J. The Effects of Misleading Media Reports about COVID-19 on Chinese Tourists' Mental Health: A Perspective Article. *Anatolia* **2020,** *31* (2), 337–340.

Index

A

Ability and willingness to work, 205–206
Acquiring new technological skills
   future prospect, perception of, 242–243
   prior exposure and learning, 241–242
   support, availability, 242
Adopting proactive approaches, 273
Agreeableness measures, 144
Alcohol consumption, 260
Anticipate crises, 48
App-based stress management, 225–226
Applying innovative practices, 273
Art of negating, 68–69
Arthritis management, 159–160
Audit communication channels, 48
Austerity—an inequity amplifier, 289–290

B

Business process outsourcing (BPO)
   cope with shifting back, 107
   methodology
      data analysis and interpretation, 102–103
      findings, 104–105
      inclusion criteria, 101
      participants, 101
      studies, 101
      tools, 102
   work from home (WFH), 100
Business scenario
   methodology, 333
      communication with consumers, 343–344
      employee psychological capital, 334, 342–343
      marketing strategies, 346–347
      media, 344–346
      tourist behavior, 347–349
   reviewed articles, 335–341

C

Communication strategies, post-pandemic
   changes in, 37
      employee well-being, 39–40
      internal communication, digital transformation, 38
      timely and factual information, 39
      traditional communication methods, 38–39
   employee communications plan, 46
      management model, 47
   employee relations, 36–37
   HR toolkit
      consistent communication, 45
      establishing sustainable leadership, 46
      organizational culture, 45–46
   online communication
      channels, availability of, 40
      internal communication, 40–41
      remote working groups, 41
   practices in maintaining
      anticipate crises, 48
      audit communication channels, 48
      internal audience, 48
      safety and emergency protocols, 49
      team and assign responsibilities, 48
      two-way crisis alert system, 49
   team communication
      compassionate leadership, 44–45
      crisis, demonstration of, 42–43
      decisions amid uncertainty, 43–44
      dynamic and collaborative team structure, 42
Conservation of resources (COR), 72–73
Coronavirus Disease (COVID-19), 332
Covert casualty
   gender equity
      austerity—an inequity amplifier, 289–290
      diversity resistance to learning, 287–289
      women in leadership roles, 290–293

post-pandemic HRM discourse
  fostering authentic inclusion, 295
  organizational resilience, 295–296
road to gender parity till 2020, 283
  empirical evidence, 285
  gender role stereotypes, 286
  glass ceiling, 284–285
  illusory claims, 284
social distancing of women, 293–294
Critical HRM (CHRM), 179

D

Data analysis and interpretation, 102–103
Decisions amid uncertainty, 43–44
Demographic statistics, 203
Demonstration of disease
  learned behaviors, 165, 173
Demystifying wellness, 155
Developing learning environment, 272
Diabetes mellitus (DM) management, 157–158
Digital forms, 77
Disturbances in online workplace, 70–71
Diversity resistance to learning, 287–289
Dynamic and collaborative team structure, 42

E

Effective employee retention
  ASSOCHAM, 134
  defined, 135
  individual-level factors of
    agreeableness measures, 144
    extraversion, 143–144
    neuroticism, 143
    openness to experience, 144
    perceived job satisfaction, 144–145
    personality, 142–143
    work life balance, 145–146
  organizational level factors
    coaching, 137
    communication, 138–139
    leadership, 140–141
    mentoring, 137–138
    opportunity, 136–137
    salary and perks, 135–136
    security, 141
    support from management, 139–140
    training, 137
    work environment, 140
  strategies in
    bridging communication gaps, 148–149
    employee assistance program (EAP), 147
    mental health wellness services, 147–148
    safety measures, 149
Embedding disease
  arthritis management, 159–160
  cardiovascular diseases management, 159
  diabetes mellitus (DM) management, 157–158
  hypertension or high blood pressure, 158–159
  kidney diseases management, 160–161
  respiratory diseases management, 161
Embrace culture of well-being (EWC), 157
Employee wellness focus
  employee's well-being and organizations
    COVID-19, 200–203
    employee perspectives, 200–203
    workplace wellness programs, 200
  methodology
    ability and willingness to work, 205–206
    analysis, 204
    demographic statistics, 203
    health & safety concerns, 206–207
    personal protection equipment (PPE), 204
    staff fear, catching the virus, 207–209
    willingness to work, 206–207
  studies, 199
Employees well-being
  demonstration of disease
    learned behaviors, 165, 173
  demystifying wellness and, 155
  embedding disease
    arthritis management, 159–160
    cardiovascular diseases management, 159
    diabetes mellitus (DM) management, 157–158
    hypertension or high blood pressure, 158–159
    kidney diseases management, 160–161
    respiratory diseases management, 161
  existing wellness initiatives
    evaluation of, 155

Index

A

Ability and willingness to work, 205–206
Acquiring new technological skills
  future prospect, perception of, 242–243
  prior exposure and learning, 241–242
  support, availability, 242
Adopting proactive approaches, 273
Agreeableness measures, 144
Alcohol consumption, 260
Anticipate crises, 48
App-based stress management, 225–226
Applying innovative practices, 273
Art of negating, 68–69
Arthritis management, 159–160
Audit communication channels, 48
Austerity—an inequity amplifier, 289–290

B

Business process outsourcing (BPO)
  cope with shifting back, 107
  methodology
    data analysis and interpretation, 102–103
    findings, 104–105
    inclusion criteria, 101
    participants, 101
    studies, 101
    tools, 102
  work from home (WFH), 100
Business scenario
  methodology, 333
    communication with consumers, 343–344
    employee psychological capital, 334, 342–343
    marketing strategies, 346–347
    media, 344–346
    tourist behavior, 347–349
  reviewed articles, 335–341

C

Communication strategies, post-pandemic
  changes in, 37
    employee well-being, 39–40
    internal communication, digital transformation, 38
    timely and factual information, 39
    traditional communication methods, 38–39
  employee communications plan, 46
    management model, 47
  employee relations, 36–37
  HR toolkit
    consistent communication, 45
    establishing sustainable leadership, 46
    organizational culture, 45–46
  online communication
    channels, availability of, 40
    internal communication, 40–41
    remote working groups, 41
  practices in maintaining
    anticipate crises, 48
    audit communication channels, 48
    internal audience, 48
    safety and emergency protocols, 49
    team and assign responsibilities, 48
    two-way crisis alert system, 49
  team communication
    compassionate leadership, 44–45
    crisis, demonstration of, 42–43
    decisions amid uncertainty, 43–44
    dynamic and collaborative team structure, 42
Conservation of resources (COR), 72–73
Coronavirus Disease (COVID-19), 332
Covert casualty
  gender equity
    austerity—an inequity amplifier, 289–290
    diversity resistance to learning, 287–289
    women in leadership roles, 290–293

post-pandemic HRM discourse
  fostering authentic inclusion, 295
  organizational resilience, 295–296
road to gender parity till 2020, 283
  empirical evidence, 285
  gender role stereotypes, 286
  glass ceiling, 284–285
  illusory claims, 284
  social distancing of women, 293–294
Critical HRM (CHRM), 179

D

Data analysis and interpretation, 102–103
Decisions amid uncertainty, 43–44
Demographic statistics, 203
Demonstration of disease
  learned behaviors, 165, 173
Demystifying wellness, 155
Developing learning environment, 272
Diabetes mellitus (DM) management, 157–158
Digital forms, 77
Disturbances in online workplace, 70–71
Diversity resistance to learning, 287–289
Dynamic and collaborative team structure, 42

E

Effective employee retention
  ASSOCHAM, 134
  defined, 135
  individual-level factors of
    agreeableness measures, 144
    extraversion, 143–144
    neuroticism, 143
    openness to experience, 144
    perceived job satisfaction, 144–145
    personality, 142–143
    work life balance, 145–146
  organizational level factors
    coaching, 137
    communication, 138–139
    leadership, 140–141
    mentoring, 137–138
    opportunity, 136–137
    salary and perks, 135–136
    security, 141
    support from management, 139–140
    training, 137
    work environment, 140
  strategies in
    bridging communication gaps, 148–149
    employee assistance program (EAP), 147
    mental health wellness services, 147–148
    safety measures, 149
Embedding disease
  arthritis management, 159–160
  cardiovascular diseases management, 159
  diabetes mellitus (DM) management, 157–158
  hypertension or high blood pressure, 158–159
  kidney diseases management, 160–161
  respiratory diseases management, 161
Embrace culture of well-being (EWC), 157
Employee wellness focus
  employee's well-being and organizations
    COVID-19, 200–203
    employee perspectives, 200–203
    workplace wellness programs, 200
  methodology
    ability and willingness to work, 205–206
    analysis, 204
    demographic statistics, 203
    health & safety concerns, 206–207
    personal protection equipment (PPE), 204
    staff fear, catching the virus, 207–209
    willingness to work, 206–207
  studies, 199
Employees well-being
  demonstration of disease
    learned behaviors, 165, 173
  demystifying wellness and, 155
  embedding disease
    arthritis management, 159–160
    cardiovascular diseases management, 159
    diabetes mellitus (DM) management, 157–158
    hypertension or high blood pressure, 158–159
    kidney diseases management, 160–161
    respiratory diseases management, 161
  existing wellness initiatives
    evaluation of, 155

Index

A

Ability and willingness to work, 205–206
Acquiring new technological skills
  future prospect, perception of, 242–243
  prior exposure and learning, 241–242
  support, availability, 242
Adopting proactive approaches, 273
Agreeableness measures, 144
Alcohol consumption, 260
Anticipate crises, 48
App-based stress management, 225–226
Applying innovative practices, 273
Art of negating, 68–69
Arthritis management, 159–160
Audit communication channels, 48
Austerity—an inequity amplifier, 289–290

B

Business process outsourcing (BPO)
  cope with shifting back, 107
  methodology
    data analysis and interpretation, 102–103
    findings, 104–105
    inclusion criteria, 101
    participants, 101
    studies, 101
    tools, 102
  work from home (WFH), 100
Business scenario
  methodology, 333
    communication with consumers, 343–344
    employee psychological capital, 334, 342–343
    marketing strategies, 346–347
    media, 344–346
    tourist behavior, 347–349
    reviewed articles, 335–341

C

Communication strategies, post-pandemic
  changes in, 37
    employee well-being, 39–40
    internal communication, digital transformation, 38
    timely and factual information, 39
    traditional communication methods, 38–39
  employee communications plan, 46
    management model, 47
  employee relations, 36–37
  HR toolkit
    consistent communication, 45
    establishing sustainable leadership, 46
    organizational culture, 45–46
  online communication
    channels, availability of, 40
    internal communication, 40–41
    remote working groups, 41
  practices in maintaining
    anticipate crises, 48
    audit communication channels, 48
    internal audience, 48
    safety and emergency protocols, 49
    team and assign responsibilities, 48
    two-way crisis alert system, 49
  team communication
    compassionate leadership, 44–45
    crisis, demonstration of, 42–43
    decisions amid uncertainty, 43–44
    dynamic and collaborative team structure, 42
Conservation of resources (COR), 72–73
Coronavirus Disease (COVID-19), 332
Covert casualty
  gender equity
    austerity—an inequity amplifier, 289–290
    diversity resistance to learning, 287–289
    women in leadership roles, 290–293

post-pandemic HRM discourse
   fostering authentic inclusion, 295
   organizational resilience, 295–296
   road to gender parity till 2020, 283
     empirical evidence, 285
     gender role stereotypes, 286
     glass ceiling, 284–285
     illusory claims, 284
   social distancing of women, 293–294
Critical HRM (CHRM), 179

D

Data analysis and interpretation, 102–103
Decisions amid uncertainty, 43–44
Demographic statistics, 203
Demonstration of disease
   learned behaviors, 165, 173
Demystifying wellness, 155
Developing learning environment, 272
Diabetes mellitus (DM) management, 157–158
Digital forms, 77
Disturbances in online workplace, 70–71
Diversity resistance to learning, 287–289
Dynamic and collaborative team structure, 42

E

Effective employee retention
   ASSOCHAM, 134
   defined, 135
   individual-level factors of
     agreeableness measures, 144
     extraversion, 143–144
     neuroticism, 143
     openness to experience, 144
     perceived job satisfaction, 144–145
     personality, 142–143
     work life balance, 145–146
   organizational level factors
     coaching, 137
     communication, 138–139
     leadership, 140–141
     mentoring, 137–138
     opportunity, 136–137
     salary and perks, 135–136
     security, 141
     support from management, 139–140
     training, 137
     work environment, 140
   strategies in
     bridging communication gaps, 148–149
     employee assistance program (EAP), 147
     mental health wellness services, 147–148
     safety measures, 149
Embedding disease
   arthritis management, 159–160
   cardiovascular diseases management, 159
   diabetes mellitus (DM) management, 157–158
   hypertension or high blood pressure, 158–159
   kidney diseases management, 160–161
   respiratory diseases management, 161
Embrace culture of well-being (EWC), 157
Employee wellness focus
   employee's well-being and organizations
     COVID-19, 200–203
     employee perspectives, 200–203
     workplace wellness programs, 200
   methodology
     ability and willingness to work, 205–206
     analysis, 204
     demographic statistics, 203
     health & safety concerns, 206–207
     personal protection equipment (PPE), 204
     staff fear, catching the virus, 207–209
     willingness to work, 206–207
   studies, 199
Employees well-being
   demonstration of disease
     learned behaviors, 165, 173
   demystifying wellness and, 155
   embedding disease
     arthritis management, 159–160
     cardiovascular diseases management, 159
     diabetes mellitus (DM) management, 157–158
     hypertension or high blood pressure, 158–159
     kidney diseases management, 160–161
     respiratory diseases management, 161
   existing wellness initiatives
     evaluation of, 155

Index

factors contributing
  exercise, efficacy of, 162
  good sleep, 163
  health monitoring, 163
  health regulatory bodies, 162–163
integrated employee
  embrace culture of well-being (EWC), 157
  positive psychology practitioners (PPPs), 156
interventions, 155–156
knowledge
  PERMA model, 164
  positive emotion, 165
positive emotions, 166–172
recommended practices, 166–172
Employee's well-being and organizations
  employee perspectives, 200–203
  workplace wellness programs, 200
Employee's well-being and organizations
  COVID-19, 200–203
Environmental management system (EMS), 113

G

Gen-Y respondents, 26
Green human resource management (GHRM), 111
  advantages of, 118–119
  advantages and disadvantages, 309
  challenges of, 119
  definition and purpose, 307–308
  endorse advancement, 114
  environmental management system (EMS), 113
  findings, 120–123
  history and origin, 306–307
  HRM and COVID-19, 312–314
  Indian companies
    case studies, 310–311
  methodology, 120
  practices, 309–310
    in India, 311–312
  processes involved in
    green compensation and reward, 117
    green development, 116–117
    green employment relations, 117–118
    green HR operations, 114–115
    green performance management, 116
    green recruitment, 115–116
  relevance and significance, 307
  research findings, 123–125
  studies, 119–120
  sustainability, 126

H

Hamilton Anxiety Rating Scale (HAM-A), 264–265
HR toolkit
  consistent communication, 45
  establishing sustainable leadership, 46
  organizational culture, 45–46
Human resource management (HRM)
  COVID-19 impact, 1
  new roles
    counseling and collaboration, 5–6
    employee wellness, 9
    employees motivation, 12
    innovation and up skilling, 7–8
    new age policies, 9–10
    programs, 12
    reinforcement and job awareness, 7
    undisrupted workflow, 8–9
    virtual learning, 10
    work life balance, 11
    workforce analysis, 11
  pandemic and digitization, 2
    organizations, 3
    stakeholders, 4
  paradigm shift
    opportunity, 4
    remotely working employees, 5
  work from home (WFH), 2

I

Individual-level factors
  agreeableness measures, 144
  extraversion, 143–144
  neuroticism, 143
  openness to experience, 144
  perceived job satisfaction, 144–145
  personality, 142–143
  work life balance, 145–146
Interpretative Phenomenological Analysis (IPA), 239–240

K

Knowledge hoarding
  arguments, 67
    art of negating, 68–69
    conservation of resources (COR), 72–73
    digital forms, 77
    disturbances in online workplace, 70–71
    political skill, 71–72
    practicing managers', 73–75

M

Mental health and economic downturn
  adopting proactive approaches, 273
  alcohol consumption, 260
  applying innovative practices, 273
  clinical comorbidities, 261
  COVID-19 rapid spread, 257–258
  deteriorating economic condition, 262
  developing learning environment, 272
  employee up-skilling, 272
  ensuring employee wellness, 272
  equipping and training workforce, 271–272
  findings and interpretation
    groups 1 to 3, 266
    groups 4 to 7, 266
    groups 8 to 9, 266–269
  fostering culture of openness, 273
  framing new normal policies, 273–275
  general health protocols, 255
  Hamilton Anxiety Rating Scale (HAM-A), 264–265
  India, lockdown phases, 254, 255
  OECD economic outlook projections, 256
  recognizing employee efforts, 272
  recruitment methods, 271
  research problem
    FGD technique, 263–264
    sampling design, 264
  Severe Acute Respiratory Syndrome (SARS), 259
  social distancing protocol and isolation, 261
  substance user disorders (SUD), 260
  top five infected countries, 255
Ministry of Human Resource Development (MHRD), 235

O

Online communication
  channels, availability of, 40
  internal communication, 40–41
  remote working groups, 41
Organizational level factors
  coaching, 137
  communication, 138–139
  leadership, 140–141
  mentoring, 137–138
  opportunity, 136–137
  salary and perks, 135–136
  security, 141
  support from management, 139–140
  training, 137
  work environment, 140

P

PERMA model, 164
Personal protection equipment (PPE), 204
Positive psychology practitioners (PPPs), 156
Post-pandemic HR roles
  challenges, 19
  COVID-19, 19
  Generation-Y in India, 20
  impact
    COVID-19, 20
    Generation-Y, 21–22
    HR practices, 22, 24
    labor force participation, 22
    organizations, 21
    work from home (WFH), 21
  methodology, 24
    Gen-Y respondents, 26
    multitasking, 26
    perspective HR activities, 26
    post-COVID, 25
    qualitative data analysis, 28
    qualitative details, 27
    response analysis, 25
  right HR policies
    mind-set shift, 29
    outstanding effort, 28
  technological and cultural changes, 18
  workplace, 18
Post-pandemic work strategies
  American Government, 83

Index

Australian Government, 83
Canada Government, 83
Chinese authorities, 83
game changer, use
   Google Meet, 90
   Microsoft Team, 91
   Skype, 89
   WebEx, 89–90
   Zoom, 90
literature, review
   WFH with computers, 87
new normal
   adaptation, 93–96
New Zealand Government, 83–84
research and findings, 91
   messaging platforms, 93
   Work-Life Balance, 92
UK Government, 83
work from home (WFH), 84
   collaboration, 88
   communication, 88
   conflict resolution, 88–89
   diffusion of innovations, 86
   opportunities with, 89
   persuasion, 86
   Technology Acceptance Model (TAM), 85
   technology adoption, 87
   Theory of Planned Behavior (TPB), 85
work life, reckoner of
   constraints and challenges, 96
   vaccination drive, 96

S

Self-development
   acquiring new technological skills
      future prospect, perception of, 242–243
      prior exposure and learning, 241–242
      support, availability, 242
   enhancing knowledge base
      broadening one's perspective, 244
      research activities, 244
      web-based programs, 243–244
   findings, 241
   innovative application
      evaluation process, 247
      online enterprise, 246
      online whiteboard, 246–247
      study materials, 246
   literature review, 237–239
   methodology
      Interpretative Phenomenological Analysis (IPA), 239–240
      procedure, 240–241
      research question, 239
      sample, 240
   preferred activities, 244
      familial responsibilities, 246
      old hobby or discovering new ones, 245
      recreational activities, 245
   teaching–learning system, 236
Severe Acute Respiratory Syndrome (SARS), 259
Substance user disorders (SUD), 260

T

Team communication
   compassionate leadership, 44–45
   crisis, demonstration of, 42–43
   decisions amid uncertainty, 43–44
   dynamic and collaborative team structure, 42
Tech detox
   digital detox, 54
      necessity, 55–56
      programs, 61–62
   digitalization and HR functions, 56
      benefits of, 56–57
      better employee experiences, 58
      connection/experience, 57
      data and analytics, 58
      digital recruitment, 58
      effectiveness, 57
      efficiency, 57
      employee self-service, 59
      information, 57
   excessive digitalization
      post pandemic situations, 59
   pandemic COVID-19, 60–61
   positive impacts, 55
   social-interpersonal skills
      digitalization and impact, 60
Technology Acceptance Model (TAM), 85
Theory of Planned Behavior (TPB), 85

V

Vocational compass
  career move, 323–324
  career seekers, 326–327
  career through new lens, 321
  COVID-19 and labor immigrants, 325
  pandemic and employability, 325–326
  planning and strategizing, 327–328
  post-pandemic up grading prerequisite, 322
  soft skills, 322–323
  unemployment and mental health, 326

W

Work from home (WFH), 2, 21, 84, 100
  collaboration, 88
  communication, 88
  conflict resolution, 88–89
  diffusion of innovations, 86
  opportunities with, 89
  persuasion, 86
  Technology Acceptance Model (TAM), 85
  technology adoption, 87
  Theory of Planned Behavior (TPB), 85
Work from Home Culture (WFHC), 178–179
  EWB
    and contemporary HRM, 181–183
    social factory, 183–186
    socialized workers and employees, 187–189
  methodology, 180
Work-life issues and stress
  e-stress management
    app-based stress management, 225–226
    challenges of, 226
    online stress management, 225
  new normal in work environment, 227–228
  post-COVID stress management
    challenges, 228
  pre-COVID stress management, 216
    stress management techniques, 218–219
    work-life-balance, 217–218
  remote working environment, 222
    e-stress management, 223–224
    modern stress management techniques, 223
  stress management in pandemic situation, 219
    adaptation, 221
    alarm (fight-or-flight), 220
    burnout, 221–222
    coping (recovery), 221
    resistance, 221
  work-life balance, 224